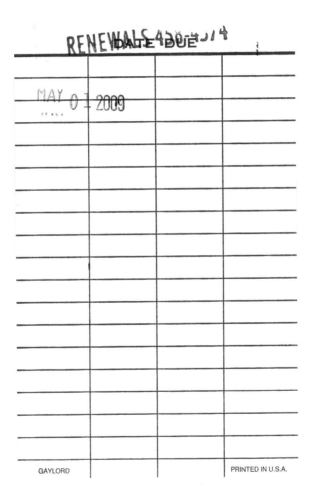

Algorithm Design for Networked Information Technology Systems

Springer

New York
Berlin
Heidelberg
Hong Kong
London
Milan
Paris
Tokyo

Sumit Ghosh

Algorithm Design for Networked Information Technology Systems

With a Foreword by Dr. C.V. Ramamoorthy, Professor Emeritus

With 161 Figures

Springer

Sumit Ghosh
Stevens Institute of Technology
Department of Electrical and
    Computer Engineering
Castle Point on Hudson
Burchard Building, Room 211
Hoboken, NJ 07030
USA

Cover illustration: ADDM algorithms encapsulate a fundamental microcosmic design principle that governs the organization of complex, real-world phenomena: astronomical systems, world civilization, computer electronics, and biological systems.

Library of Congress Cataloging-in-Publication Data
Ghosh, Sumit, 1958–
    Algorithm design for networked information technology systems / Sumit Ghosh
        p. cm.
    Includes bibliographical references and index.
    ISBN 0-387-95544-5 (hc: alk. paper)
    1. Computer algorithms. 2. Data structures (Computer science) 3. Information networks.
I. Title
QA76.9.A43G46   2003
005.1—dc21

                                                                    200344588

ISBN 0-387-95544-5   Printed on acid-free paper.

Printed in the United States of America.

9 8 7 6 5 4 3 2 1   SPIN 10886377

www.springer-ny.com

Springer-Verlag   New York Berlin Heidelberg
A member of BertelsmannSpringer Science+Business Media GmbH

In Memory of My Loving Parents

Foreword

I felt deeply honored when Professor Sumit Ghosh asked me to write the foreword to his book with an extraordinary perspective. I have long admired him, first as a student leader at Stanford, where he initiated the first IEEE Computer Society's student chapter, and later as an esteemed and inspiring friend whose transdisciplinary research broadened and enhanced the horizons of practitioners of computer science and engineering, including my own. His ideas, which are derived from his profound vision, deep critical thinking, and personal intuition, reach from information technology to bioscience, as exhibited in this excellent book. To me, an ordinary engineer, it opens up a panoramic view of the Universe of Knowledge that keeps expanding and inspiring, like the good Indian proverb, which says, "a good book informs you, an excellent book teaches you, and a great book changes you." I sincerely believe that Professor Ghosh's book will help us change and advance the methods of systems engineering and technology.

Vision

Inspired vision sees ahead of others what will or may come to be, a vivid, imagined concept or anticipation. An inspired vision personifies what is good and what like-minded individuals hope for. Our vision is one of creating an Internet of minds, where minds are Web sites or knowledge centers, which create, store, and radiate knowledge through interaction with other minds connected by a universal shared network.

This vision will not just hasten the death of distance, but will also incarcerate ignorance. We note that the rapid growth of many disciplines in the sciences, humanities, technology, and business, has been promoted by the convergence of ideas through knowledge transfer across traditional boundaries. This is what a distinguished business leader and entrepreneur, Professor George Kozmetsky, calls the transdisciplinary movement in education. Professor Ghosh is a great mentor, who teaches by this principle. In some sense, knowledge transfer across traditional disciplinary boundaries is the first phase in the Internet of the Mind paradigm.

Preliminary Issue

A critical and difficult to resolve issue is how to fine tune educational processes and maximize the flow of educational information from the source—the transmitter (knowledge bases, mentors, books, teachers, etc.)—to the needy individual, the student at the receiving end. These processes must ensure that the recipient obtains the needed education in the most effective way at the most appropriate time and place. Two issues are paramount here: The first is how to make knowledge "fluid" ; the second is how to personalize educational processes to fit the intellectual infrastructure of the recipient. The concept of fluidity is similar to the Keynesian concept of liquidity of capital, which makes knowledge easily storable, transferable, and transportable across heterogeneous intellectual boundaries. The second issue will be addressed later.

Knowledge and Technology: Their Growth and Implications

We shall now tread on the unknown and unexplored area of knowledge and technology growth. We are fully aware of their exponential growth rates, but unfortunately, there are no precise methods or rigorous approaches to measure them. A Harvard Business School study many years ago found that "knowledge doubles every seven years." More recently, former U.S. President Bill Clinton and Vice President Al Gore have indicated in their speeches that knowledge doubles every three years, and they refer to U.S. Department of Education studies.

The technology growth rate can be surmised from the progress of the high-tech semiconductor and communication industries. The famous Moore's law states that semiconductor chip performance doubles every eighteen months; while the price stays the same. Thus, we shall assume that the knowledge growth rate based on "expert" evaluation is about 30% per year; likewise, the technology growth rate based on Moore's law is about 66% per year. In a later section, we shall try to answer an apparent anomaly: Why is the growth rate of technology (which is derived from knowledge) much higher than the growth rate of knowledge itself?

Knowledge Obsolescence Rates

Bill Joy, the chief scientist of Sun Microsystems, has surmised in his featured interviews and articles that professional obsolescence creeps at the rate of 20% per year. In other words, after five years, we will be strangers in our professional disciplines, no better than college freshmen. One may quibble about the magnitude of the rate, but the trend appears to have some validity. This obsolescence figure may be more applicable to mature professionals beyond the age of 40 who have not actively kept up with technological advances than to younger ones.

Technology Growth, Knowledge Growth, and Moore's Law

Technology is derived from scientific knowledge, but Moore's law tells us that technology grows much faster than knowledge. We shall offer a subtle explanation. Knowledge is a result of rational and physical discoveries. These processes can be slow and incremental, but they rarely leapfrog. Knowledge and its discoveries are like dots on the radar screen in an air traffic control center: New dots appearing, old dots always moving and changing. Technology is derived from connecting and linking the dots and creating useful patterns that can be made from them. It is like knitting a beautiful mosaic that connects and provides meaning (satisfies human needs) to the patterns. Given N dots (e.g., knowledge discoveries or inventions), the number of patterns they create is an exponential power of N. This heuristically explains Moore's law and the more rapid growth of high-tech industry. The dots and patterns are always moving and changing, and this also is a prominent characteristic of technology. Technology always advances faster than knowledge. The former subsidizes its own growth and that of science through the creation of automated tools and computer-aided adjuncts. This, in turn, fuels the accelerated growth of technology, à la Otto Hahn's chain reactions and the Livermore loops.

The Challenge

Our real challenge: how to develop a feasible and realizable approach to reducing the nonlinearly growing chasm between the advancement of technology and the increase in the knowledge content of any individual. In theory, the chasm cannot be completely and conclusively bridged. Although this raises many unanswered—and perhaps unanswerable—questions, several approaches that can slow down the overtake and obsolescence are conceivable. A key approach is compression of learning time by innovative teaching methods, which underscores the need to personalize educational processes to fit the intellectual infrastructure of the recipient. In this book, Professor Ghosh proposes interdisciplinary approach as the fundamental source of new teaching techniques. This transdisciplinary approach is fluid-like and flexible, allowing one to easily penetrate a number of different disciplines at once. The objective of a proper match between the knowledge generators and knowledge recipients is analogous to the issue of impedance matching in electrical engineering, which ensures an efficient transfer of electric power from the power-generating stations to the power-consuming towns. The objective is also critical because it holds the key to opening a path for every willing individual to continue to be an active and valuable participant in society, despite the march of time. We are now living longer and healthier lives and working for many more years, and the idea of mandatory retirement has clearly fallen from grace. This then propels us to envision an environment and an educational framework in which a new knowledge infrastructure may be established in each individual to help him or her remain matched with the advancing technology. It then becomes the purpose of the environment and educational framework to provide caring and personalized mentors to help in the assimilation of new technologies; casting them in the molds of individuals' infrastructures for ultrafast absorption. Even as each of us ages with time, the promise that we can continue to keep pace with exciting new technologies and remain valuable and contributing members of society as long as we wish is a shining beacon of hope.

The Three Visions and Their Manifestations in This Book

Through many decades of my association with academic research and teaching, I have come to a firm belief that the interplay of three types of vision is critical for progress. These include (1) eagle vision, (2) frog vision, and (3) fish vision. The eagle soars high, has a commanding view of the entire ground in every direction, and, when necessary, is able to bring its eyes to a pinpoint focus on a scurrying rat, miles below. In this book, the eagle-eye vision constitutes the overview, a survey, a perception about the integrated whole, from the past, the present, and the future. Frog vision refers to microscopic vision, or an up-close view of an object that reveals an extraordinary level of detail. Here, the frog-eye vision is manifested in the details of the algorithms, methods, and concepts that the book articulates so well. The fish views the entire world outside the water, all 180 degrees, compressed through a narrow cone of 98 degrees. However, its vision can detect fast changes because its eyes' fields of vision do not overlap; and the fish cannot afford to shut its eyes even for a moment. The fish-eye vision assumes the form of an emphasis on the dynamics of change and movement and the inevitable progress and advances that the book will produce.

This book is not just for specialized scientists and engineers; its essence is easily accessible to the nonspecialists who will find their curiosity aroused, their need to learn stimulated, and their minds changed.

Dr. C.V. Ramamoorthy, Professor Emeritus
EECS Department, University of California, Berkeley
April 3, 2003

Preface

Overview

Networked information technology (NIT) systems, also referred to as network-centric or net-centric systems, are already pervasive and promise to become even more encompassing, powerful, highly capable, and greatly useful in the future, touching nearly every element of human endeavor and society. Already, today, NIT systems underlie much of e-commerce, banking and financial transactions, online airline reservation systems, worldwide communications, distance learning, and remote data acquisition and control, to name a few. In the near future, NIT systems will encompass patient medical records, remote surgery, intelligent transportation systems (ITS), communications and control in deep space, and innumerable innovative services and products, limited only by our imagination. Under the Future Combat Systems (FCS) program, the U.S. military, especially the U.S. Army, is committed to a total transformation to bring itself in line with the new network-centric warfare idea. Under the emerging Homeland Defense program, the objective is to preempt threats and attacks on the nation through processing a tremendous volume of intelligence data from a large number of diverse sources, without becoming overwhelmed from information overload, and coordinating the activities of geographically dispersed public safety agencies in a precise, accurate, and timely manner. Fundamentally, in an NIT system, first, the relevant data are identified and acquired from geographically dispersed points; second, the raw data are transformed into usable information through computational intelligence techniques; and third, the information is disseminated to other geographically dispersed regions, as needed. The traditional, uniprocessor-based, centralized algorithms cannot represent NIT systems faithfully and are, clearly, inadequate and unnatural. Synchronous distributed algorithms are equally inappropriate because they represent a simple extension of the centralized approach. Asynchronous, distributed decision-making (ADDM) algorithms constitute the most logical approach to serve as the underlying control of NIT systems and is the subject of this monograph.

NIT systems are complex, as opposed to toy academic problems, and are intended to operate in the real-world environment. If the incredible potential of the information age is to be brought to fruition, NIT systems must be designed precisely and operated correctly. This, in turn, requires the development of a new scientific and pragmatic approach. When designed correctly and effectively, NIT systems may last a very long time, perhaps 50 to 150 years. The consequences of failure may be serious, ranging from unnecessary loss of lives to a collapse of the public's confidence. As an example, consider VHDL, a very high-speed integrated circuit hardware description language, that was intended to be a state-of-the-art tool to describe and validate any electronic design accurately and efficiently. Initiated in 1985, a billion dollars has already been invested in the VHDL effort by the government and industry. However, its most basic objectives—accuracy and efficiency—that were mandated in its specifications back in 1985, are far from being realized. More important, its limitations have done little to facilitate the growth of innovative and complex design capability. The principal cause underlying the inadequacies of VHDL may be traced to the incorrect application of the notion of timing to hardware systems that are intrinsically asynchronous and distributed.

As a second example, consider the following occurrence in New Jersey involving the E-ZPass system [1], a cashless toll collection system for interstate highways. Motorists are required to purchase magnetic toll cards of specific dollar values and place them on their visor. When passing through the toll booth at a maximum speed of 15 mph, the toll is magnetically deducted from the card and the driver passes through the toll booth. For a period of time following the installation of E-ZPass, motorists received in the mail citations from the New Jersey Department of Motor Vehicles for speeding along the toll highways in excess of 80 to 150 mph. Apparently the E-ZPass system was being used to record the times a vehicle passed through the toll booths, from which the elapsed time between two successive toll booths was calculated and the car's speed computed. The only problem was that many of the cited drivers were driving older vehicles that were not even capable of running faster than 65 mph. Protests by the cited drivers were initially met by stiff official resistance, but when an investigation was eventually launched, it was revealed that the clocks in the different toll booths in the E-ZPass system were never synchronized. The architects responsible for computing the vehicle speeds had overlooked the basic notions of timing and clock drifts in distributed systems.

For a third example, consider the worldwide Internet whose spectacular growth and success are rapidly being dwarfed by its lack of security, underscored by its fundamental inability to track IP packets and prevent denial-of-service attacks. Triggered by the events of September 11, 2001, fueled by the belief that the Internet may have been used by the terrorists for money laundering, and threatened by the fear that dramatic cyberattacks are not preventable, increasingly, courts and corporations are attempting to wall off portions of cyberspace. In so doing, according to Lessig [2], they are destroying the Internet's potential to foster democracy and economic growth worldwide and ending the Internet revolution just as surprisingly as it began.

Relative to the Internet and in the light of the growing attacks on the Internet from computer viruses worldwide, even reputed scientists and corporate executives of leading NIT companies have acknowledged, publicly and privately, that the Internet is far too complex to secure. At the NSF-sponsored workshop on the Modeling and Simulation of Ultra-Large Networks: Challenges and New Research Directions, held at the Sheraton in Tucson on November 19-20, 2001, the consensus among thirty top-flight researchers from the areas of network design, simulation modeling and analysis of networks, and modeling and simulation methodology was that the key principles underlying the successful scaling of the Internet are neither known nor understood. For the sake of science and our progress towards the future, respectfully, this is not acceptable. We conceived and designed the Internet and we must understand it. Lawson [3] traces the origin of the complexity in the computer industry to the deployment of compromised hardware design for all types of computing, leading to the demand for unprecedentedly complex system software that, despite involving thousands of code developers, was never completely understood. Leading researchers from the top telecommunications companies [4] have expressed their serious concern over the occurrence of inconsistencies and failures in the context of feature interactions and the current inability to understand and reason about these events. For example, while private telephone numbers are successfully blocked from appearing on destination caller ID screens under normal operation, as they should be, these private numbers are often unwittingly revealed during toll-free calls [5]. As a second example, despite the telephone subscriber paying a monthly fee for the caller ID service, incoming phone calls from the outside, including those initiated by the local telephone service provider, often show up as out of area on the consumer's caller ID display. Under such difficult circumstances, the scientific tradition recommends that we not be overwhelmed, but rather search for the fundamental principles that are usually few in number, easy to comprehend, and on which all systems, regardless of their complexity, are based. The goal of this book is to uncover these fundamental principles, where possible, in the form of ADDM algorithms. The vision underlying this book finds support from four recent discoveries.

The first is our proven ability to successfully design and operate digital computers consisting of millions of logic gates. Despite the bewildering number of gates, the key principles underlying the success are (i) there are only a handful of different types of gates, (ii) each gate is a self-contained entity [6] whose behavior and interactions with other gates are simple and well understood, and (iii) the gates are organized hierarchically to successively build bigger and more complex building blocks. The second is the discovery that underlying the perplexingly complex behavior of an ant colony, consisting of hundreds of thousands to millions of ants, are only a few types of ants—queens, foragers, guards, etc.—and that every ant within any given type is guided by a few simple rules. The third is the discovery by geneticists that, despite the overwhelming number of genetic combinations that are conceivable in the millions of lifeforms, Nature employs only a limited number of genes, repeatedly using them over and over to create a seamless ocean of different lifeforms. The fourth is the growing acceptance among geologists that behind all the complex and bewildering physical changes we see at the earth's surface, is an underlying simple set of principles, the key being the mantle's massive heat engine that drives the tectonic plates. The inspiration from these discoveries is that underlying the highly complex yet successful systems may be a set of constituent elements that are well defined and interact through simple, provably correct rules.

The motivation for precision in NIT system design comes from another most unusual and unexpected source, namely, law enforcement. The rapid proliferation of NIT systems in society and the growing concern over how to prosecute increasingly sophisticated NIT-related crimes, coupled with the socially accepted, strict, legal threshold implied in beyond reasonable doubt, virtually necessitates precision in every phase of NIT systems design. Conceivably, spurred by law enforcement, legislation may enact laws mandating precision in NIT systems.

Careful analysis of the VHDL and E-ZPass examples and other difficulties in the distributed systems literature points to deeper problems. In the article titled, "Parallel Processors were the Future ... and May Yet Be," in IEEE Computer (December 1996), Michael Flynn of Electrical Engineering at Stanford University observes candidly that the promise of parallel processing has not been fulfilled. He notes two primary reasons. First, for most science, the mathematical representations were developed largely in the nineteenth century, and they represent a simplified idealization of reality. Second, and more important, the mathematical modeling reflects the human reasoning process as sequential. Flynn's observation is true, as evidenced by the fact that although most real-world, large-scale, computing-based systems today are driven by centralized algorithms, the literature in electrical and computer engineering, computer science, and operations research is dominated by centralized algorithms and synchronous distributed algorithms. As stated earlier, the latter constitutes a logical extension of the centralized approach and inherits the same fundamental limitations. Examples of the use of centralized and synchronous distributed algorithms may be found in payment processing, airline reservation systems, inventory management, traffic control, etc. Flynn's two reasons may be complemented by a third reason, namely, our desire to find a simple parallel approach that applies to all problems, quickly and uniformly.

The real world, however, is complex and much like fractals. The deeper we dive and the greater our desire to understand the fundamentals in depth, the more complex it gets. It is, therefore, no surprise that the desire to uncover a simple parallel approach that applies to all problems has not yet been realized. In truth, if such a simplistic approach did exist, life for us scientists would be boring, uneventful, and uninteresting. There would be no room left for challenges or creativity.

Anil Nerode of the Mathematics Department at Cornell University observes that among traditional engineering and computing research personnel, given a real-world problem, there is a strong tendency toward quickly establishing a mathematical model. Because the model is subject to the available analytical manipulation tools, a belief develops that the real-world problem has been successfully rendered amenable to rigorous mathematics. Nerode points out that this belief may be misplaced in that the very process of deriving a quick mathematical model strips the real-world problem of its essential characteristics. Thus, the mathematical model is grossly approximate. In contrast, an effort to develop a physical model of the problem may be far more challenging, but it is likely to yield highly accurate and realistic results.

Aim and Scope

This book presents a radically different paradigm, one where the basic premise is to precisely understand and accurately model real-world NIT systems, in their true form, to the best of our current ability. The paradigm begins with the recognition that many of the classical mathematical representations and models that we have grown up with since the nineteenth century may not apply meaningfully to the complex NIT systems of today. Practical examples include computer networks such as the Internet, banking infrastructure, credit card transaction processing networks, and inventory management systems. Second, the lens of the sequential human reasoning process through which we learned to view reality may not always provide the correct view of the world.

The author's pursuit of key problems from a number of disciplines ranging from hardware description languages, networking, inventory management, military command and control, and banking to intelligent transportation systems, and the synthesis of innovative control algorithms has serendipitously revealed this unique insight: that there is a fundamental micro-cosmic design principle of this universe, an archetype that extends from the astronomical-sized galaxies down to the minutest atom in the universe. At any level of abstraction, the subsystems of a system inherently possess independence, autonomy, and their own sense of timing; where they interact with each other, the interaction is asynchronous. The independence of each subsystem with respect to all others poses no paradox. It refers to the fact that the existence of a subsystem is independent of all others. Thus, even when a star undergoes a supernova, the rest of the universe continues to exist, although it may be subject to the flying debris and radiation from the dying star. Furthermore, at any level of abstraction, while the behavior of the subsystems and the interactions between them may be encapsulated through relatively simple rules, the repeated application of these rules to increasing numbers of constituent elements gives rise to systems of increasing complexity. In the discipline of biology, according to Franklin Harold [7], every cell constitutes a unitary whole, a unit of life, and a tremendous diversity of complex lifeforms results from the interaction of a number, say N, of cells that come together, where N may range from two to millions, or more. Although there may be data and information dependency between two or more subsystems of a system, each subsystem possesses its own processing or decision-making engine. The interactions enable the subsystems to learn, grow, and evolve.

This book develops and presents ADDM algorithms as an encapsulation of the universal micro-cosmic design principle, serving in the role of the underlying control and coordination of NIT systems. It develops ADDM algorithms as a systematic, scientific, and canonical approach to the design and analysis of NIT systems. In essence, however, ADDM algorithms may constitute the scientific core of any real-world system. An ADDM algorithm that is successfully designed for a given NIT system reflects the higher meta-level purpose or intent of the system while underlying the behavior of every constituent subsystem. Metaphorically, the ADDM algorithm represents the big picture, the bird's-eye view of the total NIT system behavior. Prof. C.V. Ramamoorthy of the University of California, Berkeley, refers to this as eagle vision. In the classic Public Broadcasting Service (PBS) television interview with Bill Moyers titled, "Joseph Campbell and the Power of Myth," Joseph Campbell rephrases the philosopher Schopenhauer: In this universe, everything [including every human life] influences everything else as if all lives are the dream of a single dreamer in which all the characters are also dreaming. Campbell describes the idea of the net of gems, also known as the net of Indra, the king of gods, as one where every life is represented as a gem, every gem reflects all others, and all gems are rising, spontaneously, simultaneously, and in harmony, as if there is an intention of cosmic proportion behind it. Fundamentally, the goal of ADDM algorithms is to encapsulate the intent underlying any complex real-world system in a systematic scientific manner. ADDM algorithm design represents an integrated exercise in both top-down design, where one starts with an intended overall behavior and attempts to synthesize the behaviors of the constituent lower-level entities, and a closely knit bottom-up phase, where the focus is on the design of the traits of the individual entities, such that together they yield the intended high-level behavior. The ADDM algorithm design effort is generally accompanied by a validation effort—a testing of the theory under realistic conditions before developing and deploying the actual system—through modeling and asynchronous distributed simulation of the underlying NIT system under ADDM algorithm control.

The content of this book is based on actual research and the experience of the author and his research group over the past twenty-two years, acquired through conceiving, building, testing, and analyzing real-world systems across a number of diverse disciplines. This book stands apart from virtually all of the books currently available on distributed algorithms in that it views asynchronous distributed algorithms in their true natural form. No constituent entity is presumed to possess any kind of global knowledge. In contrast, most of the currently available books cast distributed algorithms in the light of centralized thinking and frequently refer to concepts such as shared variables, global snapshots, knowledge of every state of a system at every time instant, awareness of deadlock in the entire system, asynchronously connected processors maintaining communication with a central facility, and certainty of distributed termination, all of which fundamentally contradict the essence of asynchronous, distributed, real-world systems. A likely reason may be that the authors of these books analyze the problems, understandably, through sequential reasoning and then inadvertently presume that the constituent entities have access to the authors' global knowledge of the problems. The authors of several books reveal a keen underlying desire to bring inherently asynchronous real-world processes under synchronous control, arguing that synchronous algorithms are simple to design. In one book in particular (*Parallel and Distributed Computation: Numerical Methods*, by Dimitri P. Bertsekas and John N. Tsitsikilis, ISBN 0-13-648700-9, 1989), the authors write, "it is quite hard to synchronize a data communication network and, even if this were feasible, it is questionable if the associated overhead can be justified." Clearly, the fundamental truth that geographically dispersed, inherently asynchronous systems may never be accurately encapsulated by synchronous algorithms and global synchronization is lacking.

Organization and Features

Chapter 1 defines NIT systems and ADDM algorithms and explains their relationship following a review of the current distributed systems literature and a critical analysis of the current computing paradigms. Chapter 2 presents the nature and fundamental characteristics of ADDM algorithms in light of how they influence and relate to each other and together solve the challenges underlying the NIT system. These principles are neither esoteric nor meant for toy academic problems. They are simple yet canonical and apply to actual problems in the real world. The U.S. Defense Advanced Research Projects Agency (DARPA) [8] observes that today's complex systems pose a formidable challenge in the form of scalability of the underlying control algorithm. A solid understanding of the principles, presented in Chapter 2, is the only known scientific approach today; by applying them, one may synthesize precise ADDM algorithms for NIT problems that will function correctly if the number of constituent entities were to increase from 10 to 50 or 5,000 or even 100,000, subject to other design limitations.

Chapter 3 presents a series of actual case studies in which ADDM algorithms have been successfully synthesized for a number of NIT systems, implemented through large-scale distributed simulations, and subject to performance analysis. The scope of the problems ranges from distributed discrete-event simulation of hardware description models in VHDL, railway networks, international payment processing, military command and control, fault simulation of digital systems, domestic payment processing in a partially connected network of banks, and a hierarchical distributed dynamic approach to inventory management. As evidence of the real-world nature of the problems studied, consider the following anecdote. The U.S. Department of Transportation (DoT) had recently commissioned [9] the Institute for Simulation at the University of Central Florida to review all of the commercial simulators manufactured in the United States and abroad and the MIT-developed simulator for the Boston Tunnel project, to examine their suitability for autonomous simulation of a large number of drivers and vehicles. The Institute evaluated a total of 51 simulators and provided a short list of 11 simulators that they felt met the DoT's criteria. After closer examination, the DoT concluded that neither of the commercial simulators in the short list nor the MIT-developed simulator satisfied its needs. In contrast, the DICAF algorithm [10] [11] developed by the author's research group has been successfully validated through an asynchronous distributed simulator executing on a network of more than 65 Sun spare 10 workstations, for a total of 45,000 autonomous vehicles representing a highly congested traffic scenario in Rhode Island.

Chapter 4 details key issues in debugging complex NIT systems. Chapter 5 argues the crucial importance of proofs of correctness for ADDM algorithms and presents techniques to develop such proofs. Chapter 6 presents a mathematical framework for synthesizing ADDM algorithms, starting with a centralized algorithm, and illustrates it for a specific military command and control problem. Chapter 7 reviews the conventional approach to performance analysis of distributed systems and presents a radically different paradigm for ADDM algorithms. Chapter 8 argues the need to perform perturbation analysis. It presents key principles and reasoning and describes results obtained from the stability analysis of representative ADDM algorithms. Chapter 9 recognizes the need for creativity and imagination in the synthesis of ADDM algorithms, argues from logical principles the role that high-quality interdisciplinary thinking may play in realizing this goal, and presents new techniques to instill such thinking in future NIT engineers and scientists. Finally, Chapter 10 summarizes the book and presents some reflections on the benefit and impact of ADDM algorithms in the future.

Audience

This book has been developed with three types of audiences in mind and has been written to facilitate straight-to-the-point, intense, and in-depth self-study. The only prerequisites are knowledge of the basic principles of physics and mathematics, logic, common sense, and a serious desire to learn. First, this monograph is a reference book intended to serve as a reader for a graduate- or senior-level undergraduate course titled, "Algorithm Design for NIT Systems" within the traditional computer engineering program or a new program such as the one in Networked Information Systems Engineering currently being developed at Stevens Institute of Technology. The monograph's intent is to constitute a key starting point for developing a theoretical and practical understanding of NIT systems in doctoral, graduate, and advanced undergraduate students who plan to pursue a career in NIT system design. It presents a scientific and pragmatic approach, developed in a canonical fashion, focusing on the underlying physical meaning and the fundamental mathematical reasoning, unlike the tradition of a purely mathematical treatment that is often devoid of pragmatics. The author hopes that the book will not only help students learn how to design, operate, maintain, and evolve NIT systems precisely but also inspire them to take on the role of leading thinkers and guide the evolution of the information age. In addition, the newly created interdisciplinary programs in NIT and business management, such as the Howe School of Technology Management at Stevens Institute of Technology (Hoboken, NJ), the Indian Institute of Information Technology and Management (Gwalior, India), and the Jerome Fisher Program in Management and Technology at the University of Pennsylvania (Philadelphia, PA), may also use this reference book to teach the technology of ADDM algorithms within the context of a high-level overarching course in future technologies. Second, the book targets policy makers in NIT within the industry, military, and government and aims to educate them from a fundamental perspective, in an intensive short-course style, on the nature, scope, potential, and limits of NIT systems. Third, the monograph offers to managers, consultants, and other professionals of the NIT industry successful examples of NIT system design, analysis of their performance, and the design of unique measures of performance. To practitioners, the book presents an integrated approach to the issues of algorithm design, distributed systems, and concurrent processing.

Acknowledgments

The author gratefully acknowledges the insights, encouragement, thoughts, and support of many individuals, including Dr. Erik DeBenedictis formerly of Bell Labs.; Prof. C.V. Ramamoorthy of the University of California, Berkeley; Prof. Anil Nerode of Cornell University; Prof. Larry Ho of Harvard University; Prof. Kinchi Mori of the Tokyo Institute of Technology; Dr. Jagdish Chandra formerly of the U.S. Army Research Office; Louis Lome of BMDO; Dr. David Hislop of the U.S. Army Research Office; Dr. Gottfried Luderer, emeritus professor at Arizona State University; Dr. Seong-Soon Joo, visiting research scientist in the Networking and Distributed Algorithms Laboratory at Arizona State University, 1996-1997 and 1999-2000, and currently department head at ETRI, Korea; Dr. Al Aho, vice president of Bell Labs (Lucent Technologies); Bernie Gallois, former dean of the School of Engineering at Stevens Institute of Technology; Dr. Frank Fernandez, former director of DARPA and currently director of institute initiatives at Stevens Institute of Technology; Prof. Stu Tewksbury of the ECE Department at Stevens Institute of Technology; Prof. Domenico Ferrari formerly of the University of California, Berkeley; Prof. Bernie Zeigler of the University of Arizona; Dr. Norm Sorensen, principal director of the Space Technology Directorate at the Aerospace Corporation; Colin Gillis, Eugene Kim, Arthur Chai, Raj Iyer, M.D., Mariano

Fernandez, Pierre Sorel, Peter Lee, Dr. Joanne Law, Tom Morrow, Noppanunt Utamaphethai, Kwun Han, Raymond Kuo, and Anish Bhimani, all former undergraduate researchers at Brown University; Drs. Tony Lee, Ling-Rong Chen, and Peter Walker, former doctoral and postdoctoral researchers at Brown University; Drs. Qutaiba Razouqi, Jerry Schumacher, P. Seshasayi, and Ricardo Citro, former doctoral researchers at Arizona State University; Peter Heck, former Ph.D. advisee at Arizona State University; and Subhendu Ghosh, currently Ph.D. advisee at Stevens. The author thanks all of the anonymous referees of the archival papers on which this book stands for their thoughtful comments and constructive criticism. The author is indebted to the U.S. Army Research Office and the BMDO Office for encouraging and supporting the research that underlies this book. For help with transforming a mental image of the book cover into an actual cover page, my sincere thanks to my son, Abhinav Ghosh. For their continued encouragement and support, Wayne Yuhasz and Wayne Wheeler of Springer Verlag deserve my utmost gratitude. Last, my sincere thanks to the entire production staff at Springer, especially Lesley Poliner.

Contents

List of Tables

List of Figures

1

Introduction

1.1 What Are Networked Information Technology Systems?

Fundamentally, in any networked information technology (NIT) system, also referred to as networked or network-centric systems, first, the relevant data are identified and acquired from geographically dispersed points; second, the raw data are transformed into usable information through computational intelligence techniques; and third, the information is disseminated to other geographically dispersed regions as needed. The functions are carried out by the individual constituent subsystems, which are executing concurrently and independently. Thus, the decision for the entire underlying NIT system comprises the local decisions at all of the subsystems and the local decisions are, in turn, derived using appropriate information obtained from a wide geographical area. In essence, NIT systems stand on three pillars—computing engines, networking infrastructure, and the underlying control. NIT systems are complex, involving hundreds or possibly thousands of geographically dispersed nodes executing autonomously and interacting asynchronously under real-world conditions to achieve the objectives of the NIT system. NIT systems are rapidly proliferating and promise to become even more encompassing, powerful, capable, and beneficial in the future. NIT systems are likely to encompass patient medical records, remote surgery, intelligent transportation systems (ITS), communications and control in deep space, and innumerable innovative services and products, limited only by our imagination.

1.2 What Are Asynchronous, Distributed Decision-Making Algorithms?

In the current literature on computer decision-making algorithms, a reference to a distributed algorithm invariably alludes to a synchronous, distributed algorithm. Asynchronous, distributed, decision-making (ADDM) algorithms are rarely referenced in the literature, primarily because they are very difficult to understand, more difficult to implement and test on parallel processors, and even more difficult to conceive and synthesize. They require a total and comprehensive grasp of the entire system, with all of its finite yet large number of possibilities, at once. Ironically, these difficulties eclipse the fact that ADDM algorithms are naturally suited to provide control and coordination to real-world NIT systems and that they are capable of delivering the maximal parallelism inherent in the system and, therefore, the highest efficiency. ADDM algorithms are ideally suited to describe most natural, i.e., occurring in nature, and physical processes, including man-made ones, that constitute distributed and asynchronous systems.

Although ADDM algorithms exhibit a number of unique characteristics, which will be examined later, a simple yet powerful distinguishing feature is that it underlies the control of all of the subsystems that interact with each other and with the external world, asynchronously. That is, each subsystem maintains its own sense of timing control, perhaps manifested through a clock, that is unique and independent of all others and of the external world. A simple, everyday example is the man-made smart traffic light controller[1] and the automobiles passing through it. The controller sits at an intersection, driven by its own clock, and has absolutely no a priori knowledge of when an automobile will land on one of its magnetic loop sensors on the pavement and cause it to be activated. On the other hand, the driver of the automobile has no a priori knowledge of the phase of the controller's clock, at any given instant of time. Each unit is independent, autonomous, concurrent, and interacts with the other unit asynchronously, i.e., at irregular intervals of time that may not be exactly predicted ahead of time.

Consider radioactive decay, a natural process, and assume that we have a system consisting of two separate lumps, L1 and L2, of an identical radioactive material. Radioactivity is spontaneous, which the *American Heritage Dictionary* [12] defines as unpremeditated, triggered without any apparent external cause, and self-generated. Thus, the occurrences of the α particle emission from L1 and L2 will be asynchronous, i.e., they occur irregularly in time. What is even more fascinating is that if L1 is further subdivided into two separate lumps, L11 and L12, the emission of particles from L11 and L12 will be asynchronous with respect to each other. Other examples of asynchronous natural processes include the ice ages that occur irregularly in time; the earth's rotation that is not exactly periodic [13]; the reversal of the earth's magnetic polarity that has occurred irregularly in time; and the unpredictable, sudden, and apparently unprovoked attack of a living body by a virus that has otherwise been dormant within it for a very long time. Consider the following asynchronous system consisting of the buildings and houses being developed

---

[1] We are not referring to the simplistic traffic light controllers that merely change the lights at a predetermined interval regardless of the traffic.

by Californians, a physical process, and the earth's plate tectonics, a natural process. We are aware that the fault line between the Pacific and North American plates is severely strained. Although this clearly implies a major earthquake will occur in the next 50 years, the exact date of the occurrence is unknown. Regardless, Californians have continued with their business of erecting buildings and houses. It is accurate to state that the plate tectonics process is unaware of the intentions of the Californians relative to the buildings. Thus, both subsystems are proceeding at their own unique timing and each is unaware of the other's timing, but they are clearly headed toward an inevitable interaction. Examples of man-made physical processes that are asynchronous and distributed include the field of digital systems design, today's battlefield, computer networks, banking systems, retail industry, etc.

For an excellent example of asynchronous entities interacting with one another across vast geographical distances and over immense time scales, consider the following. According to geologists, prior to 20 million years ago, the North and South American continents were separated from each other, the Pacific and Atlantic Oceans were connected, and the warm waters from the present-day Gulf of Mexico traveled into the Pacific Ocean. Europe was a very cold place, and the present-day Sahara desert was covered by a lush forest. Starting 20 million years ago, eruptions from a series of volcanos started to close the gap between the continents, eventually completing the land bridge approximately 18 million years ago. Cut off from the Pacific Ocean, the Gulf stream was diverted into the Atlantic Ocean, reaching as far north as Europe and then circling back toward the coast of Africa. Gradually, Europe became warm, providing homes for animal and plant species, and the lush forest in Africa withered away, paving the road for the arid Sahara desert. Thus, the profound change in the earth's climate resulted from the interactions of three asynchronous processes: the volcanic activity in present-day Central America, the Gulf stream, and the atmospheric temperature over Europe and Africa, separated by thousands of miles and millions of years.

The philosophy of ADDM algorithms may be understood from a different perspective, by contrasting it with a line of thinking in the literature, termed emergent behavior. When the individual elements of a colony are characterized by specific behaviors, the resulting aggregate behavior of the colony is interesting, often unexpected, and labeled as emergent. Examples are cited from Nature, including the foraging activity of ants and nest-building activity of termites. The implications of the literature in emergent behavior are twofold. First, emergent behaviors constitute a resulting effect with the choice of the individual behaviors representing the cause. Second, Nature, the champion of emergent behavior, tries out different possible characteristics at the level of the individual entities, at random, and the one that corresponds to a successful or surviving emergent behavior, is allowed to continue. The thinking in emergent behavior reflects a bottom-up approach in that the goal is to decipher the underlying meta-level intent from the observed behaviors. However, there is no certainty that the sample set of behaviors under consideration is either complete or representative. More important, the critical element missing from the emergent behavior thinking is the recognition that the purpose or intent is of paramount importance. This book respectfully opposes both of these implications and presents a diametrically opposite view. Nature's approach is methodical, well considered, and deliberate, not based on trial and error. She starts with a specific goal, purpose, or intent; looks at how the current processes function and fail, if applicable; and generates a solution in the form of an (1) overall meta-level control and coordinating algorithm and (2) specific traits for the individual, lower-level, constituent entities. Nature validates her meta-level algorithm in the crucible of the real world, and the testing often spans very long durations and assumes a gigantic scope, extending well beyond our ability to comprehend. Thus, in this view, the intended colony behavior serves as the cause and the determination of the coordinating algorithm and the specific individual traits constitute the effect. The ADDM algorithm design philosophy parallels this view of Nature.

ADDM algorithm design represents an integrated exercise in both top-down design, where one starts with an intended overall behavior, and a closely knit bottom-up phase, where the focus is on the design of the traits of the individual entities. The ADDM algorithm design effort is generally accompanied by a validation effort—a testing of the theory under realistic conditions before developing and deploying the actual system—through modeling and asynchronous distributed simulation [14] of the underlying NIT system under ADDM algorithm control.

Clearly, the scope of application of asynchronous distributed algorithms is vast. However, the literature is sparse. To understand this dichotomy, consider three key questions:

1. What are synchronous systems and why have they been the sole focus of the computing community until now?
2. Why are natural and physical processes asynchronous?
3. Are ADDM algorithm–controlled NIT systems going to be important to our future?

1.3 The Current Focus of the Distributed Computing Community on Synchronous, Distributed Algorithms, and Why

In synchronous distributed systems, the timing of all of the subsystems is carefully designed such that all of the activities occur at fixed predetermined intervals. Thus, every event in every subsystem plus any stimulus from the external world must, by definition, occur at the fixed intervals. Should an event from the external world occur at a different time instant, it may not be intercepted by the system immediately on its arrival and it must wait until the subsequent interval. Because the notion of timing among all of the subsystems must be exact, they must all share the same clock signal. Thus, at any given instant of time, the phases of the different copies of the clock signal in the respective subsystems must be identical and exact. Every subsystem knows precisely when inputs are expected at its input ports from either other subsystems or the external world and when the outputs will be generated by all subsystems.

The use of synchronous distributed algorithms to model complex real-world systems runs into several important limitations. First, as we noted earlier, most natural and physical processes are asynchronous, which clearly cannot be modeled by synchronous distributed algorithms without sacrificing accuracy. The loss of accuracy of an asynchronous system when modeled under the synchronous paradigm may be explained as follows. Consider an input stimulus asserted by the external world along a wire to a device. The arrival of the input does not coincide with the timing of the synchronous clock, so the stimulus is not registered by the device. It must wait until the arrival of the synchronous clock. Conceivably, before the clock edge arrives, the external world may assert a new stimulus along the wire, which overwrites the previous stimulus and is intercepted by the device. Thus, the device fails to receive the previous stimulus and may generate erroneous results. Second, synchronous systems are generally limited to small geographical distances. For the clock to be consistent in every subsystem, it must first be generated by a single unit and then propagated to all subsystems. Given that the propagation of any signal is fundamentally limited by the speed of electromagnetic waves, the propagation of the clock signal to the different subsystems will incur skews or unequal delays, leading to difficulties in the fundamental assumption of synchronous design. Third, although long geographical distances are aggravating, even where the distances are relatively short, as the clock signal is transmitted to the subsystems, other disturbances and electromagnetic interferences may also cause unequal phase shifts. Last, when a signal arrives later than expected, even by a marginal quantity, the synchronous design is unforgiving, and erroneous results are generated. Consider the following argument posed by a number of highly experienced researchers. An individual in Arizona may easily set his or her watch to match that of a person in Washington, D.C., by using satellites, so where is the problem with synchronization? The flaw in this argument stems from overlooking the nature of the tolerance of error and its resulting impact. At the human level, our speed of comprehension, rated approximately at the speed of sound, permits us to forgive errors in the range of seconds. However, given two computers—A and B, one located in Arizona, and the other in Washington, D.C., both executing 10^9 instructions per second—an error of even 1 μs between their respective timings implies that A and B are off by 1000 instructions, enough to seriously jeopardize any precise synchronization.

Despite their limitations, synchronous distributed algorithms have been the focus of the computing community. Virtually all synchronous designs found today are made by humans. Examples include many microprocessors such as the Motorola M6809, most integrated circuits, the traffic light controller by itself, etc. Other examples include the convention of conducting business meetings between 8 A.M. and 5 P.M., classes in educational institutions at a predetermined fixed schedule, and the election of the U.S. president on the first Tuesday in November. The control of a synchronous system is simple to design and relatively easy to implement, debug, and test. Unlike the uncertainty, chaos, and unpredictability in asynchronous systems, synchronous systems are regular, easy to comprehend, and predictable; they are therefore preferred by human beings. Our ability to understand order, coupled with our helplessness in the face of uncertain asynchronous events, has caused us to impose discipline and order in most of our activities. We have even projected the idea, in our own image, that regularity and periodicity are signs of intelligence, forgetting that the paradigm may not be universal. Thus, the regular and periodic radio pulses from what we now know as pulsars were originally interpreted as being sent by extraterrestrial intelligence.

It must be remembered that the notions of chaos and order are subjective. What appears to be chaos to a population of ants, displaced by a tree being felled in a forest, is order and discipline to us in our quest for a new city. Thus, to an agent endowed with the superior power to grasp and comprehend at a higher level, a process may appear perfectly coherent while the same process may appear totally incomprehensible to others. Thus, there is the danger that an excessive obsession with order, coupled with the fear of the uncertain, lack of vision, and the absence of the adventurous spirit may lead to too much discipline and complacency and may stifle growth and progress.

1.4 Why Are Most Natural and Physical Processes Asynchronous?

Careful analysis of physical and natural processes reveal that for every given system, the constituent subsystems possess independence, autonomy, and their own sense of timing, and where they interact with each other, the interaction is asynchronous. The case of a system with no subsystems is conceivable but uninteresting. This phenomenon appears to be manifest among the galaxies of the universe, the star systems (solar systems) of each galaxy, and the planets of every star system, down to the individual molecules of a gas enclosed in a given container. One possible reason may lie in the idea that, at any given level of abstraction, every subsystem embodies an entity, where an entity reflects a self-contained unit that is independent, autonomous, and concurrent relative to other units at that level of abstraction. Although energy, in some form, must be associated with every entity, an entity must possess intelligence and a deliberate decision-making ability, which implies the presence of some form of a computing engine. Conceivably, the notion of entity constitutes the most fundamental, microcosmic design principle of this universe.

It is known independently from physics that this universe is character- ized by two key properties: the intervening space (or distance) and the finite propagation of electromagnetic radiation. Thus, the propagation of any in- formation between any two points in space requires a finite interval. We will examine how these properties relate to asynchronicity and the significance of asynchronicity in the universe through an understanding of its profound impact on one of the fundamental conservation laws of physics.

The law of conservation of charge, due to Michael Faraday, originally stated that the net charge in the universe is conserved. Let us devise a nonlocal sys- tem, one where the distances between two extreme points may be nontrivial. For Faraday's law of conservation of charge to hold true in this system, if a charge at point A disappears, an identical charge must appear at another point B. Feynman [15] argued that we cannot know precisely whether a charge appears at B at the very instant it disappears from A. Simultaneity of events at two spatial points, according to relativistic physics, is subjective. Therefore, we are compelled to modify the law of conservation of charge to be applica- ble, only locally. Thus, the two properties of the universe, described earlier, preclude the occurrences at A and B from being synchronous. Furthermore, the asynchronous nature of our reality, i.e., this universe, is so powerful and all encompassing that it even disproved the law of conservation of charge, as originally stated by Michael Faraday.

Thus, in implying asynchronous interactions as a general mechanism, the universal properties of spatial distance and finite propagation of electromag- netic radiation are consistent with the entity design principle that intrinsically implies asynchronous interactions between the constituent entities of a system.

1.5 The Importance of ADDM Algorithm-Controlled NIT Systems in Our Future

The continued improvement in technology, coupled with the current climate of worldwide economic cooperation, has launched an unprecedented opportu- nity for progress. The opportunity has assumed the form of NIT systems. The enormous processing capabilities of today's computers, their affordability and portability, the software sophistication, and the increasing ability of communi- cations networks to deliver messages over large geographical distances reliably and affordably are providing the vehicle for individuals and corporations all over the world to share information and interact in a timely and profitable manner. The world has already started to witness the value and potential of large-scale systems such as the Internet. Furthermore, the current climate is encouraging the ordinary human being to assume a more active role in to- day's society by gathering relevant information, creatively processing it, and disseminating it for others' benefit. Even major corporations are eager to ride the wave, and we see the power grid of the entire United States connected through an integrated network to facilitate more efficient sharing of electric power and the use of the World Wide Web (WWW) for commerce, airline reservation etc.

This trend is genuine and will only increase with time because it is based on a fundamental human character—sharing knowledge, helping and serving others, whether it is sharing be it sharing medical information, a solution to an engineering problem, or at which restaurant to eat during a visit to a foreign city. Although the nature and content of the information shared will surely evolve with society, the underlying philosophy will remain.

Careful examination reveals that all large systems currently in operation are being migrated toward network-centric systems through patchwork; a representative example is the nationwide automated teller machine network. Even systems currently under design betray the ad hoc nature of the development, where many of the basic issues are yet unresolved. The rapid movement of commerce over the Internet, for example, is in spite of the fact that the privacy issue is not yet resolved. Our experience over the past 300 years has taught us that for sustained growth, the solid grounding of ideas and concepts on well-established scientific and mathematical principles is critically important.

ADDM algorithms encapsulate the science of describing, characterizing, and reasoning about large-scale, asynchronous, distributed systems that are inevitable in our future. Given that asynchronous, distributed systems constitute a manifestation of the natural and physical processes in this universe, as argued earlier, at the conceptual level, ADDM algorithms represent the highest-level architecture and the meta intelligence that underlies the system. Although the current view of the asynchronous, distributed processes of nature is chaotic compared to more order in synchronous systems, as noted earlier, both chaos and order are subjective. To one who has the ability to grasp the total situation and extract the most important parameters to infer conclusions, a chaotic process is easily "transformed" into an ordered process. ADDM algorithms promise to foster this unique ability. Furthermore, the study of such algorithm development and use will also serve as a training tool to foster "parallel thinking" in future engineers and scientists.

Under certain conditions, the use of ADDM algorithms over traditional centralized algorithms can make a difference between survival and death, as illustrated through the following example [16] [17]. During World War II, the spectacular success of German U boats up to March 1943 was due, in part, to two key techniques: (1) the assignment of a specific territory, usually in hundreds of square miles of the Atlantic Ocean, to a U boat when it left port on an autonomous 60 to 90 day mission, and (2) the use of sophisticated cryptographic codes and enigma machines for radio communication of new orders, if any, from the German naval headquarters to specific U boat commanders. Given that the communication was asynchronous, i.e., irregular in time, sparse, and of limited duration, the allied submarine hunters failed to find the exact locations of the U boats using directional range finders (DRFs). As the war progressed, the German high command, in an effort to micro-manage the fleet, wanted to know the exact position of every U boat at all times. As a result, the U boats were ordered to periodically report their positions through radio. This migration from an asynchronous to a synchronous strategy constituted a fatal flaw in the system. The allied warships were able to quickly tune in to the synchronous radio communications between a U boat and the German high command and through triangulation obtain its exact location within seconds through the radio DRFs that had been perfected by that time. In addition, the allies had already broken the enigma code, which the German military did not know and their military scientists considered too good to be broken, and were able to verify the computed locations by deciphering German radio communication. The consequence was that the U boats suffered devastating losses, as many as 44 in May 1943, and their threat was permanently eliminated. In the twenty-first century, in the U.S. Navy the only people who know the precise whereabouts of a Trident nuclear submarine, when it is on a mission are those on-board [18]. Although the navy commander who originally assigned the few-hundred-square-mile territory of the Atlantic Ocean to the submarine may have some idea, even he or she does not know the submarine's exact location at any time.

As a second example of ADDM algorithms' capacity to tilt the balance in life-and-death situations, consider an episode, "Suspicions," from *Star Trek: The Next Generation.* In this episode, an alien being appears to die and then, while being transported on a shuttle, comes to life and attacks the pilot, the ship's doctor. The physician fires her weapon at the heart of the alien. Despite a hole being punched right through the body, the alien is not incapacitated because the blood purification and pumping system is distributed throughout his body. The alien starts to close in on the doctor, who is forced to alter the weapon's settings and incinerate the enemy.

In summary, an ADDM algorithm intelligently distributes the decision-making task among its constituent entities to maximize local computations, minimize communications, exploit maximal parallelism inherent in the system, yield the highest conceivable throughput performance, enhance resistance to intrusion, and achieve robustness, efficient employment of resources, scalability, stability, and significantly reduced vulnerability to catastrophic failures. Furthermore, the decentralized architecture of an ADDM algorithm offers the advantages of simplicity, flexibility, and resilience to rapid dynamic changes.

The future will see increasingly large-scale systems, spanning greater and greater geographical distances. They will be driven by increasingly creative and imaginative human beings, motivated by the primary goal of capturing every unique quality and talent of every human being on earth. In such systems, data will be gathered from a wide range of sources and geographical locations, processed, and disseminated throughout the network. With an increase in the geographical boundaries and as the number of participating agents swells, the system will inevitably be asynchronous in every aspect—data gathering, data processing to generate information, and information dissemination. Even where the lower-level components or subsystems are synchronous, for the big-picture view, the higher-level architects must understand the asynchronous nature of the system. Conceivably, the future will see an increasing number of specialized consultants (and small consulting groups) rather than large corporations. In these smaller firms, the unique and creative talents of the individual (or group) will be efficiently used and more appreciated. The revolution is already crystallizing in one sector, the military. As opposed to the classic Greek and Roman military paradigm, where a soldier was viewed as no more than a spear-carrying object, the U.S. military's view of the future C^4I warrior [19] is an intelligent individual who, endowed with information-gathering gear and sophisticated decision aids and other relevant resources, is capable of synthesizing intelligent decisions and executing them to beat the enemy.

1.6 Review of the Distributed Systems Literature

According to the literature, the earliest underlying algorithms used to model and control physical systems were centralized in nature. In this paradigm, data from one or more sources are collected at a central site and a single processor uses it to compute the systemwide decisions through sequential execution. Centralized decision-making algorithms have been used to model battlefields [20], schedule trains in a railway network [21], perform inventory management [22], realize highway management [23], and for distributed federated database management [24]. While the use of the sequential centralized scheduler, inherent in centralized algorithms, to model the asynchronous, distributed physical system is unnatural, there are additional difficulties. With increasing system complexity, the computational burden on the central processor continues to increase, eventually leading to lower throughput and poor efficiency. For many systems, such as real-time international payment processing, a centralized algorithm may not be realizable. Centralized algorithms are also highly vulnerable to catastrophic failures.

According to the literature, distributed algorithms generally promise higher throughput and efficiency through sharing the overall computational task among multiple concurrent processors. Markas, Royals, and Kanopoulos [25] report a distributed implementation of fault simulation of digital systems and note throughput improvements over the traditional centralized approach. While distributed and parallel algorithms are generally viewed as synonyms, Tel [26] revealed a subtle and accurate distinction between them. Parallel algorithms are used to perform a computational task, and the parallelism contributes to a faster completion time, especially where the computational task is prohibitively large for a sequential processor. Parallel algorithms do not capture the basic definition of parallelism, i.e., events occurring simultaneously. In contrast, distributed algorithms are designed for tasks wherein the processes and the data are physically dispersed and meaningless within the context of a single sequential process. The distributed nature is an inherent and intrinsic property of a distributed algorithm.

Of the two major forms of distributed algorithms, the synchronous style has been most widely used in practice and reported in the literature. The synchronous distributed approach [27] is characterized by the presence of a single control processor that schedules the executions of all of the remaining processors. The presence of the sequential control node theoretically limits the performance advantage of the synchronous approach. As the number of processors is increased, the synchronization requirement imposed by the control node will effectively counteract the potential advantages of the multiple concurrent processors. Where the number of subsystems is large and the problem does not intrinsically require all subsystems to synchronize periodically, the use of the synchronous algorithm is neither natural nor logical. The single scheduler node will require significant time to complete its communication, corresponding to a specific iteration, with every subsystem, one at a time, before it can proceed to the next iteration cycle. As a result, the subsystems would be forced to slow down unnecessarily. Fundamentally, however, the use of the synchronous paradigm to model a physical or natural process that is inherently asynchronous implies inaccuracy in modeling. The efforts reported in [28] [29] [30] [31] [32] [33] [34] [35] [36] [37] [38] [39] [40] [41] [42] [43] [44] [45] [46] [47] [48] [49] [50] are generally applicable to data-parallel, i.e., SIMD, and synchronous-iterative distributed programs [31], both of which have a limited range of practical application in the real world. In addition, all of these efforts were either based on pure theoretical assumptions or limited to small-scale implementations, and they fail to address the unique characteristics of large-scale, asynchronous, distributed systems.

As noted earlier, the literature on synthesizing distributed decision-making algorithms and evaluating the quality of distributed decision making is sparse. Asynchronous, distributed systems feature dispersed processes and data, where the processes operate concurrently and thus ADDM algorithms are both distributed and parallel. Rotithor [51] proposes to distribute the overall tasks—system state estimation and decision making—of a distributed decision-making system among independent decision-making processing elements and attempt to improve the overall performance of the system by optimizing the performance of the individual decision makers. Rotithor modeled the problem of load balancing in distributed computing and noted substantial performance improvements. Capon [48] accurately notes that understanding the behavior of asynchronous parallel programs is extremely difficult and is chiefly responsible for the limited parallelism reported in the literature.

In 1984, Tsitsiklis and Athans [52] considered the distributed team decision problem, wherein different agents obtain different stochastic measures related to an uncertain random vector from the environment and attempt to converge asymptotically on a common decision, and they derive the conditions for convergence. In 1985, Tsitsiklis and Athans [53] studied the complexity of basic decentralized decision problems, which are variations of "team decision problems," and concluded that optimality may be an elusive goal. In 1988, Bertsekas and Tsitsiklis [54] defined distributed asynchronous algorithms and used them to execute iterative problems of the type $x = f(x)$. In their definition, the iterative problem is decomposed and assigned to a number of processors and, during execution, each processor performs the computations asynchronously, using the outdated values in the event that not all messages have been received from the previous iteration. Although it is unclear that such iterative problems are naturally asynchronous, distributed systems, a difficulty with the proposed definition is that it aims to compensate for the lack of accurate input data through asynchronicity. The existence of asynchronicity between two or more units imparts to them the characteristics of independence and concurrency, but it cannot intrinsically compensate for erroneous input data. Thus, the occurrence of the convergence problem is not surprising. In 1995, Tsitsiklis and Stamoulis [55], proposed another definition of asynchronous, distributed algorithms. The simplest form for an asynchronous, distributed algorithm, according to them, is one where each processor stores in memory a local variable, while estimates of the value of the local variable are maintained by each of its neighboring processors. The local variable is updated occasionally, based on some function of its previous value and other estimates, and this new value is sent to the neighbors that, in turn, update their estimates. This characterization is also limited because in any distributed system no processor can ever know immediately the exact state of a different processor, due to latency. Furthermore, this definition of asynchronous, distributed algorithms is difficult to generalize because there is more than one example of an asynchronous, distributed system where a processor is not concerned with estimating the variable values of its neighbors. In summary, the problems studied in [52] [53] [54] [55] reflect limited applications, and the proposed definitions are unable to capture the general behavior of asynchronous, distributed systems. A general asynchronous, distributed system is one in which each entity derives its own unique decisions, asynchronously and independent of the decisions of other entities, with the goal of obtaining a solution to the overall problem.

Ihara and Mori [56] were the first to introduce the notion of autonomous, decentralized computer control systems (ADS) in 1984; they described an implementation for train control in Japan. A key characteristic of their approach is the absence of hierarchy, integrated control, and a centralized controller. Instead, all subsystems are homogeneous, uniform, intelligent, equivalent in capacity and performance, and free from any master-slave interactions. A subsystem does not function under instructions from any other subsystem and does not issue any such instructions. All information is transmitted by the generating point to all adjoining subsystems, and each subsystem, in turn, detects and picks up messages targeted for it. The basic approach applied to both control systems, such as traffic and plant control, and information systems, such as telephone and banking applications. Partial loss of data is permitted in control applications but no data loss can be tolerated in information systems. Key differences between Ihara and Mori's approach and ADDM algorithms are that subsystems are heterogeneous, information is exchanged between specific subsystems as warranted by the original problem, control is integral though distributed, and unless specific exceptions are incorporated, loss of data is generally not tolerated. Ishida [57] stated two key characteristics of ADS. First, ADS consists of autonomous agents on which most of the decisions of the ADS ride. Second, the structure of ADS is dynamic, so it may not be either designed or specified a priori. The difficulty with these characterizations is that they leave the behavior of the agents unspecified, unknown, and potentially arbitrary, which raises concerns of safety and reliability. Kremien, Kramer, and Magee [58] proposed to use scalable, decentralized state-feedback algorithms for distributed systems resource management. They note that while formal analysis of correctness of such algorithms is difficult, a distributed simulation supported trial-and-error approach is a superior alternative to prototype implementation. In addition to yielding scalability and performance, the execution of a decentralized algorithm on a distributed system allows a user to employ the same algorithm that will be used by an implementation with all the primitives required for expressing distributed algorithms.

None of the following books on distributed systems [59] [60] [61] addresses the topic of asynchronous distributed algorithms. A relatively recent book [62] allocates a single paragraph to the topic of asynchronous distributed algorithms. Respectfully, while it details asynchronous systems, the description occurs in the light of centralized thinking. The reference to global snapshots, awareness of the entire system being deadlocked, and distributed termination, reflects centralized reasoning and access to global knowledge of the problem, both of which are logically incompatible with the characteristics of the constituent entities of the asynchronous distributed system. In defining timed asynchronous systems as a model for current distributed systems, such as a network of workstations, Christian and Fetzer [63] require all services to be timed. That is, any message sent by a correct process to a correct destination is received at the destination within a known amount of time. They also argue that measurements on actual message and processing delays and hardware clock drifts confirm their theory. There are two difficulties with this definition. First, the key requirement that a message propagation be completed within a known time interval poses a fundamental contradiction with the definition of any asynchronous system [64] [65]. The only guarantee in any asynchronous system is that no constituent entity can a priori state with certainty the exact time interval necessary for the completion of any message communication between any two entities. Of course, successful message communications may be ensured by using special mechanisms such as handshaking [64]. Second, today's measurements of message and processing delays and clock drifts, which may lie in the range of milliseconds or microseconds, are likely to be grossly superseded by future systems, which may exhibit a range of nanoseconds or femtoseconds. Thus, Christian and Fetzer's timed asynchronous distributed model that relies on such fleeting parameters raises serious concerns from the scientific perspective.

The Nature, Fundamental Characteristics, and Philosophical Implications of ADDM Algorithms

2.1 Nature of ADDM Algorithms

Most physical and natural systems may be classified as asynchronous, distributed decision-making systems, wherein, despite significant and unique diversity in the system details, the geographically dispersed subsystems acquire local data, receive information from other subsystems asynchronously, where necessary, and compute and execute decisions independently and concurrently. Following execution, the subsystem transmits information to other remote subsystems, where necessary. Thus, the decision for the entire system is reflected by the local decisions at all of the subsystems, and the local decisions, in turn, are derived using appropriate information obtained from a wide geographical area. For many real-world problems from different disciplines, the formulation as an asynchronous, distributed decision-making system is natural.

Asynchronous, distributed decision-making algorithms constitute the highest-level architecture and the meta intelligence underlying the design of asynchronous, distributed, decision-making systems. ADDM algorithms are a natural choice and may find use in either modeling systems in the computer for simulation, debugging, and performance estimation or actual system implementations. ADDM algorithms offer innovative solutions and hold the potential of exploiting the maximal parallelism inherent in the problem. Furthermore, local computations are maximized and communications between the entities are minimized, implying high throughput, robustness, and scalability. Unlike the data-parallel and synchronous-iterative algorithms, there is no forced synchronization in asynchronous algorithms.

The traditional approach to asynchronous, distributed decision-making systems has been centralized decision making, which is documented as slow, inefficient, vulnerable to catastrophic failures, and prone to failure. Often, the centralized decision-making paradigm fails to provide a solution to a real-world problem.

The synthesis of an ADDM algorithm for a given real-world problem is difficult and will be addressed later. However, the key elements of an ADDM algorithm are the entities of the system, the exact behavior of the entities, the complete set of asynchronous though precise interactions between the entities, and the overall task of intelligently distributing the computational task among the entities. This chapter presents the nature and fundamental characteristics of ADDM algorithms, in light of how they influence and relate to each other and together solve the challenges underlying the NIT system. These principles are neither esoteric nor meant for toy academic problems. They are simple yet canonical and apply to actual problems in the real world. As correctly observed by the U.S. Defense Advanced Research Projects Agency (DARPA) [8], the formidable challenge posed by today's complex systems is the "scalability" of the control algorithm. A solid understanding of the definition of "scalability" and the principles outlined in this chapter is the only known scientific approach today; applying it, one may synthesize precise ADDM algorithms for NIT problems that will function correctly if the number of constituent entities were to increase from 10 to 50 to 5,000 or even 100,000, subject to other design limitations.

ADDM algorithms hold enormous potential and, thus far, they have been successfully used to model problems from the disciplines of broadband ISDN or ATM networks, computer-aided design of digital systems, railway scheduling, intelligent transportation systems, banking, military command and control, etc. A total of 45,000 asynchronous, intelligent, independent, concurrent processes have been executed successfully and synergistically on a total of 65 workstations configured as a loosely coupled parallel processor to solve a single problem correctly and accurately, under algorithmic control.

2.2 Fundamental Characteristics of ADDM Algorithms

The character of ADDM algorithms is reflected through the eight fundamental characteristics: the definition of entities; the asynchronous behavior of the entities; concurrent execution; asynchronous interactions between the entities; and proof of correctness of the algorithm including consistency, robustness, performance, and stability.

2.2.1 Entities in ADDM Algorithms

Entities constitute the basic decision-making units of the ADDM algorithm and define the resolution of the decision behavior of the asynchronous, distributed system. Entities must be natural, i.e., they must correspond to the actual elements of the system. Entities are self-contained, independent, and asynchronous. The choice of the granularity of the entities is a function of the desired resolution of the decision making, the degree of concurrency, and the complexity of the communication between the entities. In principle, a natural or physical system may possess a natural hierarchical organization, although, for simplicity, many complex, real-world systems may be expressed as a collection of entities at a single level. Examples of systems organized hierarchically include digital systems, computer communication and control networks, and international payment processing.

The concept of entity is fundamental in this universe and to our understanding of the universe. Although the universe and all knowledge about it may be one continuous thread to the creator, our understanding is that the universe, at any level of abstraction, consists of entities. The *American Heritage Dictionary* [12] defines the word entity: "the fact of existence, being. Something that exists independently, not relative to other things." Thus, an entity exists and its existence is guaranteed independent of all other entities. Because it exists, an entity must be self-contained, i.e., its behavior, under every possible scenario, is completely defined within itself. Because the entity exists independent of all other things, its behavior is known only to itself. Unless the entity shares its behavior with a different entity, no one has knowledge of its unique behavior. Conceivably, an entity may interact with other entities. Under such conditions, its behavior must include the scope and nature of the interactions between itself and other entities. The notion of entity is deeply rooted in our philosophy and culture. The Yoga Vasistha [66] wrote, "In the infinite consciousness, there are countless universes which do not know of one another's existence." The idea finds support in the present-day findings of modern cosmology. The principle of individualism, on which the U.S. Constitution is founded believes in each individual human being as an important person in society with an independent will; this is synonymous with the concept of entity. Individuality reflects a separate and distinct existence—a sense of I—a continuous current that is atomic at a given level of representation.

For example, in the discipline of digital systems, hardware is organized through entities, at any level of abstraction. Examples include an AND gate at the gate level, an ALU at the register-transfer level, and the instruction decode unit at the architecture level. The behavior of each entity must include all that is relevant at that level of abstraction, such as the logic, timing, control, and exceptions. Because every entity is independent of all others and no entity has explicit knowledge of another entity's behavior, each entity may conceivably possess its own notion of timing including clocks, timing constraints, and delays. Philosophically, asynchrony appears to be a manifestation of the concept of entity. However, one may argue that asynchrony is the more basic of the two and the point is therefore debatable.

Although we may desire the behavior of every entity to be self-consistent, it does not necessarily follow from the concept of entity. However, one may argue that the issue of existence, independent of time, provides the motivation for self-consistent behavior of the entities. We will assume that in every system each entity is characterized by a self-consistent behavior.

2.2.2 Asynchronous Nature of the Entities

In most complex real-world systems, the nature of the subsystems are asynchronous. Thus, the behavior of one entity is independent of others and unless an entity, A, propagates its state explicitly to other entities, no one has knowledge of the exact state of A. Even where two or more entities relate to the same generic unit, i.e., they share a common description, during execution, each entity would assume its own unique state, reflected by the data value of the variables. In the event that a complex real-world system is designed to operate synchronously, the asynchronous interaction model is a general principle and is ideally suited to represent both synchronous and asynchronous interactions in systems.

Consider that a system is organized hierarchically, with E1 and E2 as entities at a given level with {E11, E12, ... } and {E21, E22, ... } constituting the lower-level entities of E1 and E2, respectively. Under these circumstances, entities E11, E12, ... and E21, E22, ... all interact asynchronously.

Time constitutes an important component in the behavior of the entities and their interactions. Although every entity, by virtue of its independent nature, may possess its own unique notion of time, when a number of entities E_1, E_2,... choose to interact with each other, they must share a common notion of time, called universal time, that enables meaningful interaction. Universal time is derived from the lowest common denominator of the different notions of time and reflects the finest resolution of time among all of the interacting entities. However, the asynchronicity manifests as follows. Between the successive interactions of entities A and B, each of A and B proceeds independently and asynchronously. That is, for A, the rate of progress is irregular and uncoordinated and reflects lack of precise knowledge of the rate of progress of B and vice versa. At the points of synchronization, however, the time values of A and B must be identical. Where entities X and Y never interact, their progress with time is absolutely independent and uncoordinated with one another, and the concept of universal time is irrelevant.

At a given level of abstraction, although each entity may have its own notion of time, both entities A and B must understand the universal time; otherwise, A and B will fail to interact. Entertain the following scenario. GG1 and GG2 are two great gods of time. The length of the interval of GG1's opening and closing of the eye is 1 million years of our time, and that for GG2 is 1 nanosecond. Thus, the resolutions of the messages emanating from GG1 and GG2 are 1 million years and 1 ns, respectively. Clearly, during the million years that GG1 has the eye closed, all messages from GG2 to GG1, sent at intervals as short as one nanosecond, will be ignored by GG1. In contrast, assuming that GG2 has a finite life span, when GG1 opens its eyes and sends a message to GG2, GG2 has long been dead. Even if GG2 is not dead, there is no known way for GG1 to be certain that this is the same GG2 to which GG1 had sent an earlier message, prior to opening the eye. There is also the strong possibility that GG2 will view the message from GG1, which is unchanging for billions of its time steps, as inert and devoid of any interesting information. In the *Star Trek* episode titled "Wink of an Eye," the beings from the planet Scalos below the *Enterprise* are somehow transformed into an accelerated state. While the crew of the *Enterprise* appear to be in slow motion to the beings, the Scalosians are invisible to the crew of the *Enterprise*. As expected, there is no meaningful interaction between the two life forms until the captain and the science officer of the *Enterprise* are also transformed into the accelerated state.

Thus, at any given level of abstraction, the entities must understand events in terms of universal time, and this time unit sets the resolution of time in the ADDM algorithm. Consider a module A with a unique clock that generates pulses every second connected to another module B whose unique clock rate is a millisecond. Figure 2.1 shows a timing diagram corresponding to the interval of length 1 s between 1 s and 2 s. Figure 2.1 superimposes the 1000 intervals, each of length 1 ms, corresponding to the clock of B. Clearly, A and B are asynchronous. Module A is slow and can read any signal placed on the link every second. If B asserts a signal value v1 at 100 ms and then another value v2 at 105 ms, both within the interval of duration 1 second, A can read either v1 or v2 but not both. The resolution of A, namely, 1 second, does not permit it to view v1 and v2 distinctly. Thus, the interaction between A and B is inconsistent. If A and B were designed to be synchronous, i.e., if they shared the same basic clock, A would be capable of reading every millisecond, and there would be no difficulty.

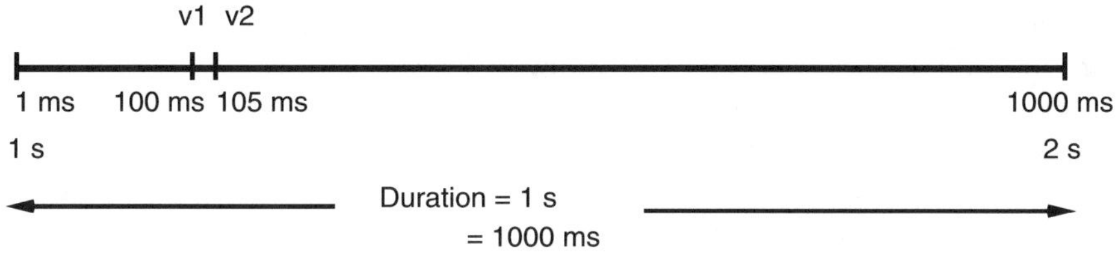

Fig. 2.1. The Concept of Universal Time

2.2.3 Concurrency in the Entities

Except for the necessary interaction with other entities, every entity is concurrent. That is, the progress and rate of its execution are independent of those of other entities and, at any given instant during execution, the states of the entities are unique. In an implementation of an ADDM algorithm, every entity may be mapped to a concurrent process of a processor.

From the first principles, because every entity exists independent of others, entities must be concurrent. The *American Heritage Dictionary* [12] defines concurrency as simultaneous occurrence. As an example, consider the digital hardware process. If a hardware system consists of N entities at a given level of abstraction, the potential concurrency is N. The nature of concurrency, however, is complex and requires a careful analysis of the fundamentals.

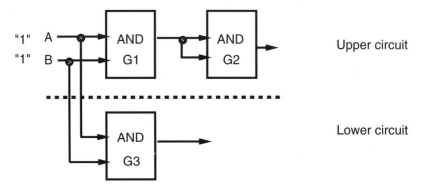

Fig. 2.2. Understanding Concurrency in Hardware

Consider a simple digital circuit consisting of three interconnected AND gates G1 through G3, organized through upper and lower circuits, as shown in Figure 2.2. Consider first the upper circuit and that a logical 1 value is asserted at both inputs A and B of G1. At first sight, to one familiar with hardware design languages (HDLs), it may appear that gate G1 will execute first for the given external input stimulus, possibly generate an output, and then G2 will execute. In reality, however, as soon as power is turned on, both gates G1 and G2 start to function simultaneously, and this is a key basis for the claim that hardware is concurrent. Electrically, the gates operate continuously. It is not true that the gates are inactive when no signal is asserted at their inputs and that they "wake up" when a new signal is asserted at their input port(s). In Figure 2.2, G2 is not even aware that it is connected to G1 and G1 does not know that its input ports are primary, i.e., external signals may be asserted on them. For our convenience, we may view hardware through its activity, but that view is not reality.

The recognition that entities are concurrent is important for two reasons. First, it reflects the correct view of reality and, as a result, ADDM algorithms represent reality closely. Second, when the ADDM algorithm is executed on a host computer system that contains adequate computing resources, the concurrent entities may be executed simultaneously by dedicated computing engines to achieve faster overall execution. Faster execution will enable, realistically, the execution of an ADDM algorithm many times, for different parameters, yielding insight into the system design issues.

$$\vec{O}_{t2} = f(\vec{I}_{t1}, \vec{S}_{t1}) \tag{2.1}$$

To understand concurrency, consider equation (2.1) in the context of digital hardware. The $\vec{O}$ represents the output vector at time $t2$ of a sequential hardware entity and is expressed as a function of the input vector, $\vec{I}$, and state vector, $\vec{S}$, at time $t1$. Where $t1 = t2$, the output is considered to be generated instantaneously, as is the manner in which the gravitation law of action at a distance is expressed. However, according to relativistic physics, any action or output is limited by the speed of light and the output of an entity requires a finite time, termed propagation delay, to be realized at the output port. Thus, for all real systems including digital designs, $t1 \neq t2$.

In equation (2.1), consider that a new input signal, $\vec{I_1}$, is asserted at the input port of the entity. Assume that an output $\vec{O_1}$ is generated. Where the output is identical to its previous value, the underlying execution mechanism— event-driven simulation—considers the case to be insignificant because there is no change at the output of the entity. In the case that $\vec{O_1}$ is different from its previous value, the event-driven simulation considers the case significant and the new value is propagated to other entities that are connected to the entity in question. Thus, in the execution mechanism, only changes in the logical value of input and output ports of the entities are important.

In Figure 2.2, assume that the circuit is powered and stable and that the starting point of the circuit operation is considered as time 0. Clearly, new signals are asserted at the input ports of gate G1 and it must be executed. In contrast, gate G2 does not have a new signal asserted at its input at time 0, so it need not be executed. Thus, at time 0, only gate G1 needs to be executed and the potential concurrency is 1. Consider that gate G1 generates a new signal value at time 10, which then is asserted at the input of gate G2. Also assume that a new signal value is asserted at the primary input ports of gate G1 at time 10. There is no activity between time 0 and time 10, so neither of the gates need to be executed and concurrency is 0. At time 10, however, both G1 and G2 must be executed, implying a potential concurrency of 2. This describes the first source of concurrency. That is, if the host computer system had two separate processors available, they could simultaneously execute G1 and G2 and accelerate the overall execution task. It is pointed out that despite G2's dependence on G1 for signal values, both G1 and G2 may be executed simultaneously at time 10. An automobile assembly line manufacturing scenario may serve as an excellent analogy. Consider that worker W1 attaches a car body onto a chassis, and upon completion, the conveyor belt moves it forward to the next station, where worker W2 inserts the headlamps onto the body and chassis. While W2 is working on the headlamps, W1 is working to attach another body onto the subsequent chassis. Clearly, both workers W1 and W2 are working simultaneously despite W2's dependence on W1 for a body attached to a chassis, and as a result, the overall rate of auto production is high.

In Figure 2.2, now consider both the upper and lower circuits. At time 0, gates G1 and G3 both receive new signals at their input ports. They do not depend on one another for signal values. Therefore, they may be executed simultaneously, yielding a potential concurrency of 2 at time 0. Thus, if a host computer makes two distinct processors available, G1 and G3 may be executed simultaneously, thereby speeding up the execution. This describes the second source of concurrency. This scenario is analogous to two automobiles traveling simultaneously from point A to point B along two parallel lanes of a highway.

2.2.4 Communication between the Entities

Although, in theory, entities may choose to interact with others or remain completely aloof, in reality, most complex, real-world systems are character-ized by some interaction between the entities. Conceivably, an entity may not possess total and accurate knowledge of everything it may need for its con-tinued functioning, at every instant of time, due to the universal properties of intervening space and the finite speed of propagation of electromagnetic radiation. Therefore, the sharing of data and knowledge through interaction with other entities may constitute an important and integral character of the system. We argue that the case where the entities are completely aloof is uninteresting.

In ADDM algorithms, entities are assumed to interact with one another. The nature of the interaction may assume different forms. First, each set of entities that interact among themselves is identified; they exactly reflect the corresponding complex real-world system. In an extreme case, any entity may interact with any other entity. Second, the necessary data and informa-tion must be shared between the interacting entities and appropriate message structures must be developed. Third, the information may be shared on a need-to-know basis to ensure privacy and precision. Fourth, all message com-munication is assumed to be guaranteed. That is, once a sender propagates a message, it is guaranteed to be received by the receiver(s). In principle, when an entity possesses an input port, it expects to receive input stimulus through it. The input stimulus arrives from the external world or another en-tity, although the entity may not possess exact knowledge. Upon receiving the stimulus, the entity uses it to compute its own response. A missing stimulus is viewed as a system failure, unless the ADDM algorithm is specially designed for such exceptions. For an output port of an entity, failure to successfully propagate an output response also corresponds to system failure.

Clearly, the sharing of data and information among entities implies a com-munication network that interconnects the entities and is an integral compo-nent of the ADDM algorithm. The topology of the network is determined by the nature of the interactions.

In developing the communication between the entities, precision in tim-ing is of paramount importance, especially for high-performance real-world NIT systems of the future. To appreciate the problem better, consider the objection raised by a leading academician. Using satellites, GPS, and today's technology, an individual in Arizona can easily synchronize his or her watch with that of another individual in Washington, D.C. Why, then, is there any need to focus on the subject of timing precision? Any synchronization must necessarily be qualified by the resolution of time. To human beings, synchronizing our watches accurately to the second, is often more than adequate. Our biological response characteristics, i.e., reaction time, are such that we can easily tolerate errors of a few seconds, or even minutes. However, when we consider the two individuals replaced by two computers, each of which is executing instructions at the rate of 10^9/sec, an unanticipated error of even 1 second may throw the computers far out of sync. Although human beings are not computers, we constitute the force behind the architecture and design of computers and systems and therefore it is imperative that architects of NIT systems understand very well the importance of precision in timing.

Within the discipline of timing, the importance of relative timing far outstrips that of absolute timing, as illustrated as follows. Consider a vehicle, A, proceeding along the right lane of a freeway. A second vehicle, B, is riding along the entrance ramp on the right, attempting to merge onto the freeway. Both A and B increase their speeds, asynchronously, i.e., without explicitly coordinating with each other, to get ahead of the other without running into a collision. Consider two scenarios. Under scenario 1, assume that their speeds reach 50 mph and 51 mph respectively, and that B barely fails to clear the front of A, causing an accident. Under scenario 2, assume that their speeds are at 200 mph and 204 mph respectively, and that B fails to clear the front of A by a few inches, causing an accident. Upon reflection, it is clear that while the absolute speeds of A and B are important, of far greater importance, as far as the cause of the accident is concerned, are their relative speeds. Had B accelerated faster and A slowed down sharply, or viceversa, the accident could have been averted. The importance of relative timing is a key characteristic of Nature, including hardware and software systems. It originates in the fact that while events are fundamentally governed by the universal law of cause and effect and manifest themselves in the form of asynchronous activities, it is in our comprehension that they bear relative timing relationship to one another.

2.2.5 Proof of Correctness of ADDM Algorithms

In his commentary on parallel processors [67], Prof. M.J. Flynn of Stanford University correctly notes that while the mathematical representations constitute the basis for our representation of reality, they were invented to facilitate the sequential reasoning by the human mind. Thus, by their very nature, ADDM algorithms, involving hundreds of autonomous entities executing simultaneously and asynchronously with no centralized agent responsible for controlling their activities, are difficult for the normal sequential human mind to comprehend. To ensure accuracy, correctness, and safety of a complex real-world system under control of an ADDM algorithm, it is therefore crucial to develop a proof of correctness.

Fundamentally, the proof of correctness must guarantee that the system operates correctly. Where the purpose of the ADDM algorithm is to simulate a natural process, correctness is synonymous to the simulation accurately reflecting reality. Where the ADDM algorithm constitutes an implementation of a complex real-world system, correctness implies the lack of any inconsistency, i.e., there should be no violation of any basic premise. This requirement is especially important because each decision-making entity uses a subset through a relevant fraction of the systemwide information and the data from other entities is subject to latency. Furthermore, the execution of the ADDM algorithm must ensure that the system progresses toward its unique objective. For the system to operate correctly, while the execution of each entity and the interactions between the entities must be correct, the set of all individual decisions generated by the entities must be consistent and imply the progress of the system to the final solution.

System characteristics may also impose special requirements on the proof of correctness. Where a system is expected to converge to a solution following the execution of a finite number of steps, the proof of correctness must include a proof of termination of the ADDM algorithm. However, the proof of termination is irrelevant for systems that, by design, must run continuously.

Deadlock manifests in the form of two or more independent processes, each of which is waiting for the other to respond before executing its response. Analysis of the occurrence of deadlock reflects the lack of knowledge of a process of the states of other processes as the primary reason and the presence of feedback loops as the chief cause. Clearly, where the underlying execution occurs on a uniprocessor, a single centralized global scheduler is completely aware of the state of every process, and deadlock will not occur. Where the underlying execution occurs on a number of processors, utilizing asynchronous, distributed simulation techniques, first Peacock et al. [68] and later Chandy and Misra [69] proposed algorithms to avoid deadlock through the use of "probe" and "null" messages, which essentially violate the principles of event-driven simulation. Later, Chandy, Haas, and Misra [70] had developed an asynchronous, distributed simulation algorithm that did not use null messages but suffered from the problem of deadlocks. Implementations of their approach [71] are reported to be nonlinear and highly inefficient. In the course of its execution, the algorithm runs from deadlock to deadlock. Thus, it is crucial to develop mathematical proofs of freedom from deadlock for any ADDM algorithm especially if the underlying system contains feedback loops.

In a traditional centralized algorithm, the centralized decision maker has complete access to the state of every entity. One may reason that where an overall goal is to achieved, the system's decisions, synthesized by the centralized decision maker, will progress in a coordinated manner to approach that goal. If one were to argue, based on this reasoning, that these decisions are "correct," a counterargument may be made as follows. First, the data obtained from the different geographical sites are subject to latency. Second, the collection of all the data at a central unit is time-consuming, especially if there are many sites. Third, the propagation of the decisions from the central decision maker to the individual entities at different sites is again subject to latency.

2.2.6 Robustness of ADDM Algorithms

A natural outcome of using an ADDM algorithm is a robust system that is much less vulnerable to natural and artificial disaster than a centralized system. Each geographically dispersed entity is an autonomous decision-making unit and the likelihood of a disaster affecting every entity is remote. Thus, even if one or more of the asynchronous entities fail, the remaining entities are not likely to be completely affected, and the system is likely to continue to function, in a degraded mode. For an ADDM algorithm to operate under partial failures, exception handling must be incorporated into the design of the entities and their asynchronous interactions. In addition to realizing high reliability, the autonomous nature of the entities of an ADDM algorithm implies that very little human intervention may be required during system operation. While this is likely to translate into low operational cost, the absence of human intervention will permit the fast executing computational intelligence to yield high throughput. As a reference, consider that for every hour a complex F-18 fighter jet is in the air, a total of 18 hours of ground maintenance is required. Clearly, a key necessity is to expend the necessary time and energy to ensure the correctness of the design and its extensive validation through modeling and asynchronous distributed simulation [14].

2.2.7 Performance of ADDM Algorithms

The use of multiple processors, executing concurrently under any ADDM algorithm implies superior performance. The degree to which a specific ADDM algorithm is able to exploit the parallelism inherent in the underlying real-world problem is reflected in its performance metric. While every problem is likely to require its unique set of metrics, two criteria may be applied uniformly across all ADDM algorithms.

The first, "performance scalability" [72], is defined as the ability of the ADDM algorithm to continue to function, i.e., to achieve the primary performance objective, despite increasing system size, i.e., an increase in the number of entities constituting the system. The fundamental key to scalability is as follows. As the problem size increases, the design of the ADDM algorithm is such that the number of computational engines also increases naturally and proportionately. The result is that the performance of the growing system continues to increase and the degradation in any system performance metric is relatively nonappreciable. In NIT systems, the computation underlying the systemwide decision making is distributed among all entities. Thus, as the system size increases, both the demand for increased computational power and the number of computational engines increase. Assuming that the communication network experiences proportional expansion, the ratio of available computational power to the required computational power is expected to decrease only by a marginal fraction, implying that the achievement of the primary performance objective will be affected only marginally. Unless the nature of the NIT system is one where the increase in the communications network is nonlinear with an increase in the number of entities, the corresponding ADDM algorithm must exhibit performance scalability.

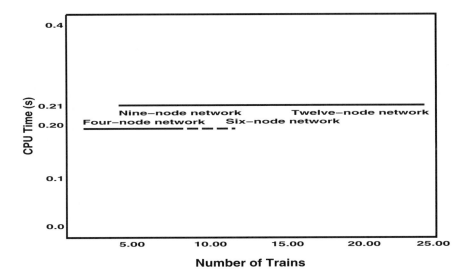

Fig. 2.3. Performance Scalability Relative to Increasing System Size

DARYN [10][72] constitutes an ADDM algorithm for railway networks wherein the notion of central dispatcher is completely eliminated and the trains communicate with the local stations as they navigate autonomously toward their ultimate destinations. Figure 2.3 displays the CPU times required by a single train to travel a fixed distance at a fixed speed under different scenarios, i.e., where the number of trains and the network size are varied. The graphs in Figure 2.3 show that, as the railway network grows in size, as would be expected over time, the performance degradation is relatively minor, reflecting DARYN's performance scalability and implying DARYN's potential for growth.

Figure 3.107 in Section 3.6 of this book attests to the performance scalability of the ADDM algorithm proposed for banking transactions. The nature of the graphs show that even when the size of the network increases fivefold, the average time to process a transaction in the network of SUN workstations increases only by 26 percent.

Intuitively, scalability is realized in an ADDM algorithm design, where possible, by focusing on the design of each constituent entity as a completely autonomous unit except for its asynchronous interactions with other units. The entities, executing together, yield the high-level behavior of the ADDM algorithm. The design of each entity, in turn, consists of its internal behavior and takes into consideration every legitimate interaction between the entity in question and all others with which it may interact during its lifetime.

Second, consider a hypothetical mechanism that is capable of determining the ideal performance of any given real-world problem that, in turn, may serve as a fundamental framework to evaluate the performance of any ADDM algorithm. Chapter 7 will introduce the notion of PGOD as a basis for determining an absolute performance metric.

2.2.8 Stability of ADDM Algorithms

Where the ADDM algorithm constitutes an implementation of a complex real-world system, it is likely to be subject to unexpected changes in the operating conditions. The property of stability refers to the behavior of the ADDM algorithm under representative perturbations to the operating environment. A thorough analysis of this issue is presented in Chapter 8.

2.3 A Meta Issue: On the Existence and Synthesis of ADDM Algorithms for Arbitrary Real-World Problems

The concern—whether an ADDM algorithm exists for a given problem and, if so, how one can synthesize it for a given asynchronous, distributed, complex, real-world system—constitutes meta-level issues. Although the literature is rich on the development of sequential algorithms and substantial research is reported on the design of synchronous, distributed algorithms, a general principle toward the synthesis of ADDM algorithms for natural and physical problems is elusive. Although ADDM algorithms have been successfully developed for a number of real-world problems, as described in subsequent chapters, the approach used has been to address each problem individually. First, the problem is analyzed carefully and then the ADDM algorithm is synthesized.

The lack of a guarantee that an ADDM algorithm does exist for any arbitrary real-world problem, characterized by the eight primary characteristics and the absence of a general mathematical theory to synthesize one, may be viewed as a limitation. However, from a different perspective, the task of ADDM algorithm development offers a unique opportunity for human imagination, creativity, and a determination to solve a problem. It also offers one the chance to confirm Jules Verne's belief, "What one person can imagine, another person can build." Chapter 6 describes a mathematical framework, MFAD, based on the Kohn-Nerode distributed hybrid control paradigm, to describe a centralized decision-making algorithm and to synthesize from it a distributed decision-making algorithm.

The pursuit of a synthetic ADDM algorithm for a given problem represents an integrated exercise in both top-down design, where one starts with an intended overall behavior and attempts to synthesize the behaviors of the constituent lower-level entities and a closely knit bottom-up phase, where the focus is on the design of the traits of the individual entities, such that together they yield the intended high-level behavior. Each of the constituent entities is viewed as a completely autonomous unit, except for its asynchronous interactions with other units. The design of each entity, in turn, consists of its internal behavior and takes into account every conceivable legitimate interaction between the entity in question and all others with which it may interact during its lifetime. In Chapter 3, for each case study, the synthesis of the corresponding ADDM algorithm is explained in detail.

In addition to the successful development of ADDM algorithms for more than a dozen real-world problems and the introduction of the mathematical framework, MFAD, a great source of confidence in the existence of ADDM algorithms for arbitrary real-world problems is one of the most important real-world problems in the universe—human civilization. In this world, each human being may be viewed as an entity—independent, concurrent, and interacting asynchronously with other human beings. The degree to which an individual may be viewed as an entity has fluctuated with time—less independence during oppressive regimes and ruthless rulers and greater freedom during the reign of philosopher-kings and governments built on democratic principles. The belief in the existence of an ADDM algorithm underlying human society finds evidence in the unmistakable observation that civilization as a whole has progressed with time. Furthermore, while greater freedom, fair assignment of responsibility of tasks, and a wide latitude of autonomy among people to determine their own destiny, subject to certain basic principles such as noninjury to others, have generally been associated with prosperity, oppression, and lack of independence have invariably contributed to misery and stifled progress. It may be conjectured that perhaps human civilization is a grand manifestation of an ADDM algorithm conceived by the Creator. However, even as complex and large a problem as human society has lent itself to a successfully architected ADDM algorithm. By its very nature, the underlying ADDM algorithm is unceasing in its drive to bring equality to all individuals, and its ultimate goal may well be a society with no hierarchy. While most nations today continue to be organized through a hierarchy, one society, the Swiss, appear to possess a radically different philosophy. Quoting from [73], "Another likeable trait of the Swiss is their disregard for heroes, generals, and political leaders. They are quite unshakeable in their claims that they never had any."

As an illustrative example, consider the following true anecdote from WWII that represents a highly successful, practical, and original ADDM algorithm design. Despite its simplicity, it contained all the important elements of an ADDM algorithm design. In Figure 2.4, assume A and B represent Britain and France, respectively, during WWII. At first, the German air force, Luftwaffe, built two towers along the coast of France, at G and E, whose function was completely beyond allied intelligence. At the same time, the allies noticed that German bombing campaigns had become increasingly precise and highly damaging. Analysis revealed that squadrons of German bombers would take off from any given location in France, say C, and virtually all of them would converge over the target, mysteriously and with great precision, regardless of weather, wind speed, visibility, day or night. The allies were completely baffled and it was only much later that the approach was fully understood. From the top of the towers E and G, two invisible electromagnetic beams, EF and GH, with frequencies f_e and f_g were directed toward A. The operators at E and G could alter the direction of the beams at will. When the bombers took off from their bases, they were not provided with the name and coordinates of the intended target as was the custom at the time. Instead, they were provided with specialized equipment and precise instructions, as follows. The navigators and pilots were instructed to continue along a specified heading, CD, at the time of takeoff, until their instruments detected a beam of frequency f_e, directed, of course, from tower E. At that time, denoted by point J, the pilot would change course and follow beam EF and the bombing crew would open the bomb bay doors and stand by to drop the payload. As soon as the instruments would subsequently encounter a beam of frequency f_g, at point K, the bomber was directly over the target and the crew were instructed to release the bombs. The algorithm was clearly distributed in that neither the operators on the tower knew the exact purpose of the beams nor the bomber crew were aware of their target as well as the source and control of the beams. There was no single operational entity that contained complete and exact knowledge of the entire system at any give time, nor were all the constituent components required to synchronize with each other periodically, thus making it very difficult for an outsider to break into the system. Except for the architect(s) of the algorithm and military authorities who were briefed, no one else possessed a total understanding of the algorithm. Even the architects would not know precisely the target that may have been selected for any given bombing run. Thus, while a downed and captured pilot could not reveal the bombing target, the German air command could easily select an alternate target at the very last minute, before the bombs were dropped, by simply adjusting the directions of the beams, without resorting to any radio communication that could invariably compromise their plan. The asynchronous nature of this activity, i.e., the absence of any explicit synchronization with the bomber squadrons in flight, left the allies in complete confusion and seriously undermined their ability to even begin to decipher the underlying Luftwaffe technology. Furthermore, the allies also could not always scramble their fighters in time to successfully intercept the enemy bombers. In retrospect, had the Luftwaffe employed mobile towers and driven them around asynchronously, i.e., irregularly in time, the degree of stealth would have been unthinkably higher. For the period 1939–1945, when today's GPS was unknown and the best navigational system of the time—a variation of dead reckoning, was susceptible to weather, wind, and poor visibility, the algorithm offered unprecedented accuracy and stealth.

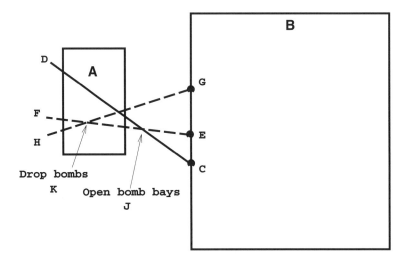

Fig. 2.4. A Practical ADDM Algorithm Design from WWII

A unique characteristic of ADDM algorithms is that from the perspective of the constituent entities, the algorithm is a meta concept. The implication is that the entities may not be consciously aware of the existence and influence of the underlying algorithm. This has led many practitioners in the systems community to voice concern over an ADDM algorithm's ability to exercise effective control over its constituent geographically dispersed entities. Under the traditional centralized control paradigm, the central control unit has access to information from every entity and is able to control them directly. In theory, therefore, the central unit is in position to draw inference about whether the overall system is under attack. In contrast, under the ADDM paradigm, while the constituent entities are not necessarily aware of the presence of each other, centralized coordination is absent. Under such circumstances, many practitioners are concerned that no constituent entity appears to be in position to draw any inference on whether the system is under attack. In reality, ADDM algorithms can detect highly sophisticated attacks many times faster than the centralized unit's ability to react. The key to a ADDM algorithm's apparent invisible control lies in the design of the algorithm itself. At the meta level, the algorithm designer takes into consideration every conceivable interaction between the system and the external environment throughout the life cycle of the system and incorporates appropriate measures into the ADDM algorithm. These, in turn, are realized through the behaviors of the constituent entities. Clearly, for a system of reasonable complexity, practical considerations may limit the range and scope of the interactions that the designer may consider in the process of algorithm design. Logically, all important interactions must be reviewed and, where possible, the designer must resort to brainstorming and other creative efforts to identify rare and unexpected scenarios. The more comprehensive the effort, the more robust and reliable the system. Despite the best efforts, however, if the system encounters an unprecedented interaction or event during its lifetime, depending on the seriousness of the reaction, there is a chance that the system may fail. Nature provides a number of illustrative examples.

Consider shoaling, the synchronized motion of a school of fish consisting of hundreds of thousands of individual fish. Nature achieves this harmonious motion by conceiving an ADDM algorithm and realizing it through two rules imparted to every constituent member. Under the first rule, every fish maintains a fixed distance from each of its six neighbors—front, back, up, down, left, and right—at all times, under normal conditions. Thus, when the lead fish for a given direction alters its course to match, for example, the temperature gradient, water current, or underwater obstacle, its immediate neighbors adjust their distances appropriately, which is followed by their neighbors adjusting, and so on, resulting in a spectacular synchronized motion. The second rule provides protection to the school from predators. When a predator swoops into the school with the intent of grabbing a meal, the one or more individual fish that sense the foreign invader immediately take evasive action and maneuver as far away from the invader as possible. Their neighbors sense the sudden maneuver and attempt to match it, in terms of distance and direction. As a result, the space immediately surrounding the point of attack quickly becomes a void, leaving the predator confused. The fish resume their normal behavior immediately after the threat disappears. Thus, the hundreds of thousands of units appear to behave as one highly coordinated unit without the presence of a centralized control. Clearly, the ADDM algorithm design reflects a meta-level effort by Nature. The individual fish and birds are not conscious of the fact that their independent behaviors help the entire school survive the predators. The algorithm fails catastrophically when a fish school encounters a much bigger and highly intelligent predator leading up to interactions and events that Nature may not have considered at the time of the algorithm design. When they spot a school of herring, a pack of humpback whales encircle it, then emit a loud high-pitched sound, 180 dB in intensity, as strong as a jet engine and churn the waters around the fish school in an attempt to gradually tighten their formation and force the frightened individual fish to huddle together more densely. Next, they force the school to the surface of the ocean by blowing air bubbles beneath the school. Finally, with their huge jaws open, the giant whales take giant gulps from the densely packed school, each gulp consisting of hundreds of fish [74].

The adaptive immune system [75] in human beings constitutes another example of a highly successful ADDM algorithm found in Nature. In protecting the complex body from simple microscopic microbes, the immune system's front line of defense consists of the skin that is virtually impenetrable by most microbes while the hairs and mucus guard the nose, mouth, and other openings, killing most of the invading microbes on contact. For microbes that slip the outer defenses and attack the body from within, the immune system maintains, as the second line of defense, a number of different types of specialized autonomous cells, T-cells, white blood corpuscles, antibodies, etc., numbering in the hundreds of thousands, that constantly patrol up and down the bloodstream, searching out, immediately attacking foreign microbes, and destroying them whenever possible. At the same time, the autonomous brain, the third line of defense, asynchronously monitors the result of the T-cell battles through two key metrics—temperature and acidity-alkalinity (pH) of the blood—systematically analyzes the outcome of the battle in light of all previous such battles, and creates long-term memory cells that circulate in the bloodstream, ready to create new T-cells should the body be attacked by an identical or similar microbe in the future. Clearly, Nature's deliberate design enables the immune system to learn from its current battles with microbes and evolve to meet future challenges. Despite its exceptional success in that it has successfully defended billions of human beings against millions of different types of microbes over the last hundreds of thousands of years, a crippling weakness has recently been observed in the ADDM algorithm design. A tiny hantavirus has learned not only how to penetrate the defense mechanism but to bring about complete self-destruction. The mechanism it employs is fascinating. The tiny hantavirus enters the human body through the skin and propagates toward the lungs, easily slipping through the thin walls of the blood vessels lining the air sacs. Before the virus can do any discernible damage, the antibodies have detected the invader and quickly give chase, forcing their way through the blood vessels in the lungs. In the process, however, their much bigger size forces the blood vessels to rupture, and plasma leaks into the air sacs, causing death within hours from respiratory failure.

3

Case Studies: Synthesis of ADDM Algorithms for Real-World Systems

3.1 Asynchronous, Distributed Event-Driven Simulation Algorithm with Inconsistent Event Preemption for Accurate Execution of VHDL Descriptions on Parallel Processors

This section presents a new approach, P^2EDAS, that is capable of asynchronous and concurrent simulation of VHDL models on parallel processors, including the detection and preemption of inconsistent events. This section is organized as follows. Section 3.1.1 introduces the concept of simulation of digital computer systems and the key challenges to ensure accuracy in today's complex systems. Section 3.1.2 details the P^2EDAS algorithm, and Section 3.1.3 presents an example to illustrate the approach. Section 3.1.4 reports on the implementation of P^2EDAS on both a multithreaded shared memory multiprocessor and a network of workstations configured as a loosely coupled parallel processor and presents performance data for representative designs. The mathematical proof of correctness of P^2EDAS is presented, with the proofs of other algorithms, in Chapter 5.

3.1.1 Introduction: Review of the Literature

The principal objective [76] of the DoD VHDL [77] hardware description language has been to allow digital hardware designs to be described, simulated, and validated accurately and efficiently in the computer, prior to building a prototype. In addition, an important objective of VHDL [76] has been to allow the execution of VHDL processes in parallel on multicomputers and multiprocessors. To date, the execution of VHDL models continues to be limited to uniprocessors and is excruciatingly slow. The literature relative to deadlock-free, null-message-free, and conservative algorithms for execution of VHDL models is nil. To achieve concurrent and efficient simulation of VHDL descriptions requires an efficient algorithm for distributed, discrete-event simulation.

The literature reports three principal techniques for distributed discrete-event simulation, namely, synchronous, rollback, and asynchronous. The "time first evaluation algorithm," proposed by Ishiura, Yasuura, and Yajima [78] is potentially inappropriate for distributed execution on parallel processors. In this approach, communication between the gates, located on different processors, is reduced. However, only a very few gates may execute at any time instant while others await their input waveforms. Consequently, much of the execution will be sequential, yielding very low concurrency on parallel processors. The most significant drawback of this approach is with feedback loops [78], where the input signal waveform to a gate at a time instant is dependent on the waveform at a previous time instant as well as the behavior of other gates. This, in turn, severely limits the concurrency on a parallel processor.

Fujimoto [79] reports a state-of-the-art survey on the execution of simulation models on parallel processors. In the synchronous approach [80], a processor is designated as a centralized controller (master processor), and it is responsible for allocating all other entities to the processors (slaves) of the parallel processing system and for initiating their executions. In addition, the controller resynchronizes all processors at the end of every activity and maintains the simulation clock, i.e., global simulation time. Chamberlain and Franklin [81] describe a variation of the synchronous approach wherein a distributed algorithm is used to execute the tasks associated with the master processor. While this approach permits the concurrent execution of entities corresponding to two or more events at the simulation time given by $t = t_1$, its limitations include the following. The processors must resynchronize at the end of every activity even in the absence of data dependency, and an uncertainty is associated with the completion of message communication at the end of an activity. Consequently, the synchronous approach cannot exploit the maximal inherent parallelism. Soule and Blank [82] present an implementation of the synchronous algorithm. Although they eliminate the problem of the centralized queue by placing a queue on every processor for round-robin event insertions they report limited parallelism. In another variation of the synchronous approach, two events with different timestamps may be executed concurrently as long as they are within a small delta of each other.

In the rollback mechanism [83], also known as virtual-time algorithm or optimistic asynchronous algorithm, the states of individual models need to be saved from time to time as events occur, and a list of messages received must be saved [84] such that the simulation system may be permitted to roll back to its previous state in the event of an error caused by processing messages out of order. In the absence of information regarding a signal at an input port, a model assumes that the signal value at that input port has remained unchanged and the results of execution based on the assumption are propagated to subsequent models. If a subsequent message is received by the component that contradicts the previous assumption, new results in the form of antimessages are propagated to subsequent models. The theoretical limitations of the rollback mechanism include the significant storage requirement [85] and the uncertainty constituted by a combination of messages and antimessages propagating throughout the simulation system.

In general, the actual performance of the virtual-time algorithm is unpredictable and will depend on the example circuit being simulated, the partitioning and allocation of the components of the circuit to processors, and relative speeds of the processors and message communication. In extreme cases, domino rollbacks may occur [85], devastating the progress of simulation, and processes may spend more time on rollbacks than useful computation [84]. Sissler [86] notes that a concurrent simulator using the virtual-time algorithm may impose one to two orders of magnitude of processing overhead. Chawla, Carter, Barker, and Bilik [87] propose the design of a 256-node parallel computer that employs the virtual-time algorithm to synchronize execution of the concurrent processes. Although their approach requires computation of the global simulation time, which in turn requires all processes to synchronize, they acknowledge that the effects of rollback on the total simulation execution time is difficult to predict. A number of improvements to the virtual-time algorithm and implementations have been reported in the literature [85] [88] [89] [90] [91] [92] [93] [94]. Steinman [93] defines an event horizon as the time stamp of the earliest new event generated within a cycle and uses it to process events. This approach combines elements of the virtual-time and synchronous algorithms and estimates speedups of 32 on the 64-processor CalTech/JPL Mark III Hypercube, relative to a uniprocessor. West [94] proposed the use of lazy reevaluation, but its implementation [79] was observed to be excessively expensive. Akyildiz et al. [89] propose a new cancelback protocol to reclaim storage when the rollback system runs out of memory and developed an analytic model. The model is validated, assuming that the timestamps of the processed uncommitted events in each processor follow a Poisson distribution and that the distribution of timestamps for messages and antimessages are independent, which may not be true in reality. Nicol and Heidelberger [90] describe the use of uniformization for the virtual-time algorithm to reduce the frequency of state saving and eliminate the global virtual-time (GVT) computation. They note good speedups of queueing network simulations. Som and Sargent [91] propose a new criterion to assign logical processes to processors for the virtual-time algorithm wherein logical processes that may experience rollbacks caused by a common logical process are assigned to the same processor. This approach is limited in that rollbacks are unpredictable, i.e., their a priori prediction is difficult. During a simulation interval of 30,000 units of simulated clock ticks for example models, a total of 13,656 messages needed to be rolled back. Wen and Yelick [92] report good speedups for transistor-level timing simulations, but their failure to include the cost of rollbacks based on the presence of an "oracle" to predict the presence of an event, is unrealistic. Furthermore, the reported parallelism for benchmark combinational circuits is unnecessary because the conservative asynchronous algorithm suffers from deadlock only for circuits with feedback loops. Briner et al. [85] report a speedup of 23 on a 32-processor system over a good sequential algorithm, through the use of lazy cancellation and the virtual-time algorithm at the transistor level. They note that while lower bounding window sizes reduces speedup, higher bounding window sizes generate speedup but suffer inefficiencies from excess event handling, rollback, and wasted model evaluations. It is noted that the simulation frequently proceeds to a large simulation time and then rolls back to an earlier time value thereby requiring large amounts of storage memory and producing limited results. Krishnaswamy and Banerjee [95] use a parallel time warp simulator for VHDL but do not discuss the issue of inconsistent event preemption. Furthermore, the global virtual time management—a key component of their parallel algorithm—uses a centralized scheme, which is a clear inconsistency.

Unlike the synchronous approach, the asynchronous algorithm has the potential of exploiting the maximum parallelism inherent in the simulation system. Bailey [96] reports that for logic-level circuit simulation, the execution time of conservative asynchronous strategy is a lower bound over the synchronous strategy for variable delay, assuming an unlimited number of processors and without taking into account the overhead. In this approach, a model may execute as soon as it receives its signal transitions at its input ports, subject to certain principles detailed later, that guarantee accuracy. In contrast to the rollback approach, the asynchronous algorithm is conservative and always generates accurate results. The term *accurate* refers to preciseness and logical correctness. However, the asynchronous algorithm has the potential of executing into a deadlock. The literature contains a number of approaches—Chandy and Misra [97]; Chandy, Haas, and Misra [70]; and Peacock, Wong, and Manning [68]—to asynchronous distributed discrete-event simulation in the context of queueing networks. The approach in [97] suggests a deadlock avoidance method through the propagation of null messages whenever a model executes but fails to produce a new output transition. Thus, this approach violates the basic premise of discrete-event simulation that a message is sent only when it implies a change from its previous value. Conceivably, this technique leads to inefficiency [98]. Furthermore, the technique fails to address the issue of deadlocks in the case of networks with feedback loops. Misra [80] presents an approach for distributed simulation of networks with feedback loops. Peacock et al. [68] propose a method of detecting deadlock through the use of probe messages that is also, conceivably, inefficient. The approach in [70] suggests a distributed technique to detect and recover from deadlocks in networks with feedback loops. However, implementations [71] of this approach have been observed to be nonlinear and highly inefficient. Soule and Gupta [99] report speedups of up to 16 on a 64-node processor without memory interconnect or operating system contention. Given that the Chandy-Misra [97] approach lacks the ability to handle asymmetric rise and fall delays, Soule and Gupta predict a 50% degradation in speed due to glitch suppression and event removal, thereby implying a speedup of only 9.4 on a 64-node processor. Chandy and Sherman [100] present a new, synchronous, conservative approach that uses the notion of conditional events. Simulation experiments of a network of switches yield speedups ranging from 2 to 8 on a 24-processor Intel iPSC/1. De Vries [98] proposes methods to reduce the number of null messages in the approach presented in [80] for a few limited networks. Furthermore, performance measurements are absent in [98]. The Chandy-Misra [97] approach incurs two fundamental limitations. First, it fails to recognize the occurrence of inconsistent events and is unable to preempt them, thereby implying incorrect results. Second, it violates the basic principle of event-driven simulation and incurs the penalty of unnecessary and repeated executions of the models even when no new input stimuli are received.

DeBenedictis, Ghosh, and Yu [101] successfully introduced a novel algorithm for asynchronous, distributed discrete-event simulation, YADDES, that is mathematically proved to be deadlock-free and accurate. In discrete-event simulation, a behavior model C^1, referred to as a component or entity, executes when stimulated by an input event or cause. Upon execution, C^1 may generate an output event, which is then propagated to subsequent components, $C^i, \ldots, C^j$, connected to the output of C^1. Subsequently, one or more of the components, $C^i, \ldots, C^j$, may be executed. The process continues until there are no outstanding events. In general, execution of the components, $C^i, \ldots, C^j$, connected to the output of C^1, may be initiated by the output event generated from the execution of C^1 corresponding to an earlier event concurrent with the execution of C^1 corresponding to the subsequent event. To increase concurrency in the simulation and thereby improve efficiency, YADDES uses a scheme, referred to as the *data-flow network*, that quickly generates the "earliest time of next event" at the output of C^1 prior to the generation of the output event of C^1 following the completion of its execution. The "earliest time of next event," also referred to as the *predicted event time*, represents a conservative estimate of the time of the subsequent event at the output of C^1. Thus, components $C^i, \ldots, C^j$ may concurrently execute, without violating any data dependency, any and all input events with times less than "earliest time of next event." The underlying assumption is that the computation cost of predicting the earliest time when an event E^j may be generated as a result of the execution of C^1, corresponding to some input event E^i, is less than the computation cost of executing C^1. For simulations with complex VHDL models, this assumption is, in general, true. An added problem when simulating digital designs with feedback loops, using the traditional distributed discrete-event simulation algorithm, is that, often an output event may not be generated following execution of a component, C^1. Thus, other components connected to its output cannot execute. If the output of one of these components is, in turn, connected to the input of C^1, then deadlock occurs, leading to an abrupt and indefinite halt of simulation. The data-flow network of YADDES successfully addresses this problem.

In YADDES [101], corresponding to every component in the actual simulation, the data-flow network consists of pseudo-primed and pseudo-unprimed components. These pseudo components are purely mathematical entities that execute specific functions to generate W (or W') values at their outputs. They are interconnected in an acyclic manner that is detailed later in this chapter. The data-flow network executes concurrently with the actual simulation. The W (or W') value asserted at the input of a pseudo component from the output of another pseudo component reflects an estimate of the earliest time when an event may be propagated along the path. For complete definitions of W (or W'), the reader is referred to [101].

Consider a behavior model C^n with inputs, $\{1, 2, \ldots, i\}$. The window of temporal independence, t_{win}^n, is defined as the minimum over all W (or W') values over all inputs $i \in \{1 \ldots I\}$ of the pseudo component(s) corresponding to the model C^n. Any and all input events with time t, on an input of C^n, may be executed accurately, without violation of data dependency, provided t is less than t_{win}^n. In YADDES, t_{win}^n is represented by K^n. Correctness is guaranteed in YADDES through accurate values for W (or W'). Formally,

$$t_{\text{win}}^n = \text{minimum}(W_i \quad \text{or} \quad W_i') \qquad \forall i. \tag{3.1}$$

Although successful as a novel, asynchronous, distributed discrete-event simulation algorithm, YADDES is inappropriate for simulating behavior models such as VHDL models, because it is limited to a single input-independent propagation delay between the input and output of a component. Unlike queueing networks, most digital components require the use of unique high-to-low (t_{phl}) and low-to-high (t_{plh}) propagation delays to accurately represent the timing behavior. Consider a component C and a signal asserted at an input port at $t = t_1$. Where a high-to-low transition is caused at the output port of C, the output is asserted at a time given by $t = t_1 + t_{phl}$. In the event that a low-to-high transition is caused at the output port of C, the output is asserted at $t = t_1 + t_{plh}$. For many digital components, the values of t_{plh} and t_{phl} may differ from one another by a factor as high as 3, leading to generation of inconsistent events. For correctness in the simulation, preemption or descheduling of inconsistent events is necessitated. The YADDES algorithm lacks any mechanism to achieve inconsistent event descheduling.

3.1.2 The P^2EDAS Approach

The fundamental advances of P^2EDAS over YADDES [101] enable it to simulate behavior descriptions concurrently, efficiently, and accurately. They include:

1. In YADDES [101], each gate is characterized with a single, propagation delay associated with all input to output paths. In contrast, P^2EDAS accommodates behavior descriptions, i.e., architectural bodies corresponding to VHDL entities, with any number of propagation delays for each input to output path of the model such as inertial, transport, t_{plh}, and t_{phl} propagation delays.

2. Unlike YADDES, the P^2EDAS algorithm acknowledges the generation of inconsistent output events arising from the use of inertial delays. It possesses inherent mechanisms to preempt or deschedule such events, as defined by Ghosh and Yu [102] and imposed in VHDL [77].
3. The data-flow network, employed by YADDES is also enhanced in P^2EDAS to address output event preemption and reduce communications. P^2EDAS refers to the enhanced network as the event prediction network.

P^2EDAS assumes that the behavior models constitute entities, similar to the VHDL entities, where the input, output, and bidirectional ports are clearly defined and the specification of the functional and timing behavior is complete and self-contained. Thus, P^2EDAS targets coarse-grain parallelism.

3.1.2.1 The Role of the Event Prediction Network in P^2EDAS

A key concept in P^2EDAS is the event prediction network that is analogous to the data-flow network in YADDES and responsible for asynchronous and concurrent yet accurate simulation of the behavior models. The software simulation of a digital component's behavior description is, in essence, a mapping of the input to output behavior of the digital component corresponding to the given input stimulus. Following execution of a component, $C_{t,e}$, triggered by an input stimulus, an output response may be generated. In discrete-event simulation, input stimuli and those output responses that are different from the previous values are termed *events*. Thus, an event corresponds to an ordered pair (t,e), that is propagated from the output of a model to the inputs of other models connected to it. The first parameter of the pair, e, refers to the logical value of the signal and t implies the assertion time of the signal.

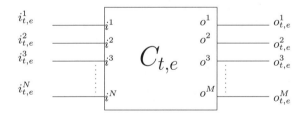

Fig. 3.1. A Behavior Model of a Digital Component

Figure 3.1 shows a behavior model $C_{t,e}$ of a component with N input ports labeled i^1 through i^N, and M output ports labeled o^1 through o^M. Input signals, expressed from $i_{t,e}^1$ through $i_{t,e}^N$ are asserted at the input ports of $C_{t,e}$. The subscript set t,e reflects events with logical value e at assertion time t that triggers the execution of the model. The principles of event-driven simulation require that where two events $i^1_{t1,e1}$ and $i^1_{t2,e2}$ are asserted in succession at the input port i^1,

$$t1 \neq t2 \quad \text{and} \quad e1 \neq e2. \tag{3.2}$$

In addition, the assertion times of events must increase monotonically, i.e., $t2$ must exceed $t1$. Following execution of $C_{t,e}$, triggered by input events, output events represented by $o^1_{t,e}$ through $o^M_{t,e}$ are asserted at the corresponding output ports. As with input events, output events must obey the conditions of equation (3.2), and the assertion times of output events at any output port must increase monotonically. The behavior of $C_{t,e}$ may be expressed through

$$o^m_{t,e} \leftarrow f^m(i^1_{t,e}, i^2_{t,e} \ldots i^N_{t,e}), \quad m \in \{1 \ldots M\}, \tag{3.3}$$

where M functions, f^1 through f^M, map the input signals to the output signal at the corresponding output port.

In uniprocessor-based discrete-event simulation, the centralized scheduler maintains a queue of all events in the system. For accuracy, the event with the smallest time is first executed. That is, the event triggers execution of the corresponding component. Then the subsequent event, i.e., the next lowest assertion time, is executed. Corresponding to every component execution, new events may be generated, and they must be appropriately sorted into the event queue. The process continues until all events are exhausted. Thus, correctness and accuracy are preserved by the strict chronological execution of the events.

To address this problem, the asynchronous distributed discrete-event simulation algorithm P^2EDAS allocates each component of a digital system under simulation to a unique process on a processor of a parallel processor. Where an adequate number of processors is available, each component may be assigned to a unique processor. Components may be executed independently and concurrently by the underlying processors as soon as events are available at their input ports. Given the absence of the global event queue, to ensure correctness of simulation, P^2EDAS requires the following. A "simulation clock value," represented through clock^N, is computed for every component N and is defined as the time up to which the model has been simulated. A model may be executed accurately for all events with assertion times up to the minimum over all event times asserted at all input ports. Thus, the simulation clock value is identical to the minimum of all input events at all input ports. A difficulty in the simulation of digital systems is that often events are not generated at an output port of a component following its execution. In such a case, events are not propagated over to the inputs of subsequent components connected to the output and the simulation clock value stagnates periodically.

A more serious problem occurs with sequential subcircuits, i.e., with feedback loops. Assume a simple circuit with two components C^1 and C^2, where the single output of C^1 is connected to the only input of C^2 and the output of C^2 is connected to the second input of C^1. The first input of C^1 is a primary input. Assume that C^1 and C^2 are allocated to two distinct processors. During the course of execution, assume that C^1 executes but generates no new output signal. Assume that there are no outstanding events at C^2; thus, no event is propagated over to C^2. The simulation clock value does not advance and C^2 does not execute. Consequently, the second input of C^1 does not receive a new event and assume that this leads to no advance in C^1's simulation clock value. Clearly, neither C^1 nor C^2 executes because each expects events from the other. In reality, many events may be asserted at the first input of C^1 but they are not executed because C^1 is unaware that the output of C^2 has remained unchanged and it can safely execute the new events without causing any loss in simulation accuracy.

P^2EDAS addresses both problems through the use of the event prediction network. The network is synthesized for a given digital system under simulation and executes concurrently with the simulation of the behavior descriptions. It consists of mathematical entities, termed *pseudo components*, that generate predicted event times. A *predicted event time*, defined at an output port of a pseudo component and associated with the corresponding output of the component, is the time at which an event is expected to be generated at that output, and it is guaranteed that no events with assertion times less than the predicted event time will be generated. The predicted event time is computed separately from, but concurrently with the actual simulation of the behavior descriptions. The simulation uses the predicted event times, generated by the event prediction network, to efficiently and correctly schedule executions of the models for appropriate events.

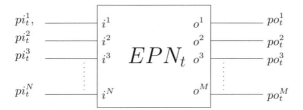

Fig. 3.2. Event Prediction Network

Figure 3.2 presents a simple event prediction network for the behavior description in Figure 3.1. Although it is constituted by pseudo component(s), the network is conceptually represented through a single black box, EPN_t with inputs $i^1, \ldots, i^N$ and outputs $o^1, \ldots, o^M$ that correspond to the inputs and outputs of the simulation model. The black box EPN_t receives predicted event times, represented by $pi_t^1, \ldots, pi_t^N$, at its input ports from the corresponding output ports of the preceding EPN_ts. Where an input port of the EPN_t is primary, the maximum predicted event time is defined by T_i. $T_{\max}$ is the maximum simulation time of interest and every primary input port is defined up to $T_{\max}$. EPN_t generates two quantities: (1) the predicted event times at its outputs that are, in turn, propagated to the inputs of subsequent EPN_ts, and (2) t_{win} that defines which input events may trigger the execution of the corresponding behavior model. EPN_t does not require detailed knowledge of the behavior expressed in the model $C_{t,e}$. The behavior of EPN_t is complex and is detailed later in this section.

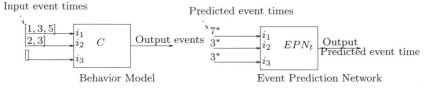

Fig. 3.3. An Example Circuit to Illustrate the Role of the Event Prediction Network

As an example, consider Figure 3.3, which shows a simple behavior model, C, with three inputs, i_1, i_2, and i_3. Assume that there are three events with assertion times of 1, 3, and 5 ns associated with i_1; two events with assertion times of 2 and 3 ns associated with i_2; and no events associated with input i_3. Clearly, the behavior model C may not be executed in the absence of input events at input i_3. Assume also that the event prediction network, EPN_t, receives the predicted event times—7, 3, and 3 ns—at input ports i_1, i_2, and i_3, respectively, prior to receiving the events at i_1, i_2, and i_3. In Figure 3.3, the predicted event times are associated with $*$ to distinguish them from regular event times. The EPN_t propagates the window of temporal independence to the model C, and the latter safely executes all events at the input ports of C with assertion times less than t_{win} as per equation (3.1). The value of t_{win} is computed as the minimum over the predicted event times at all input ports, i.e., minimum$(7*, 3*, 3*) = 3$ ns. Thus, C is executed for the event with assertion time 1 at i_1 and the event with assertion time 2 at i_2 even before any event is asserted at input i_3 of C. Therefore, the role of the event prediction network is to provide larger values for t_{win} and to facilitate quick and accurate simulation of the behavior models.

3.1.2.2 Synthesis of the Event Prediction Network

In constructing the event prediction network for a digital system under simulation, first the feedback loops and the models included in the loops are identified.

Next, for a subcircuit containing feedback loops, a feedback arc set [103] S given by $S = \{E_1, E_2, \ldots, E_n\}$ of a directed graph corresponding to the subcircuit is identified such that the graph may be rendered acyclic following the removal of all of the edges E_1 through E_n. The correctness of P^2EDAS is not affected by the identification of the minimal feedback arc set [103], which is difficult and time-consuming. For each E_i $\forall i \in \{1, 2, \ldots, n\}$, in the original directed graph, a new acyclic directed graph is constructed by replacing E_i with two unconnected edges E_i^{in} and E_i^{out} as shown in Figure 3.4. In Figure 3.4 a cyclic circuit consisting of a two-input AND gate **A** whose output is connected through edge E_2 to the input of the inverter **B** is depicted. The output of the inverter **B** is connected through edge E_1 to an input of **A**. The other input port of **A** is edge E_3.

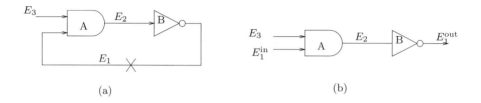

(a)   (b)

Fig. 3.4. Reducing a Cyclic Directed Graph to an Acyclic Directed Graph

Assume that the feedback arc set for the circuit is given by $S = \{E_1\}$. The graph is rendered acyclic in Figure 3.4(b) through the removal of E_1 and replacing it by E_1^{in} and E_1^{out} associated with the input of **A** and the output of **B**, respectively.

The event prediction network for the circuit is synthesized from connecting two identical copies of the acyclic circuit through a "crossbar switch." The crossbar switch represents a static connection of the output of a gate to the inputs of other gates that are affected. The two acyclic circuits to the left and right of the crossbar switch are referred to as the "tail network" and "head network," respectively. The entities in the event prediction network are termed pseudo components and identified individually as X_t and X_h, respectively, where X refers to the corresponding simulation model. Pseudo components in the tail network are identified through X_t, and those in the head network are expressed through X_h. Every input port of a pseudo component X_t that has a label of the form E_i^{in} is permanently held at an infinitely large number represented by the symbol ∞. Because inputs to pseudo components are times of events, the symbol ∞ represents the fact that no finite time values will be propagated through such inputs. An output port of every X_t that has a label of the form E_j^{out} is linked to the input port of any pseudo component Y_h in the head network that has a label of the form E_j^{in}. A link connecting the output port E_i^{out} of a pseudo component X_t in the tail network to an input port E_j^{in} of a component Y in the head network merely functions to propagate the predicted event times from the tail network to the head network. For the cyclic graph in Figure 3.4(a), the corresponding event prediction network is shown in Figure 3.5.

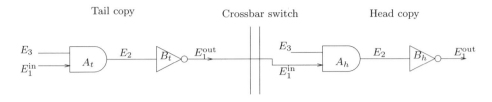

Fig. 3.5. Event Prediction Network for the Cyclic Circuit in Figure 3.4(a)

In Figure 3.5, the pseudo components A_t and B_t constitute the tail network where the input port E_1^{in} of A_t is permanently connected to ∞. A_t and B_t correspond to the AND and inverter gates in the simulation system. Pseudo components A_h and B_h constitute the head network. The output port E_1^{out} of B_t is connected via the crossbar switch to the input port of E_1^{in} of A_h because the activities of the behavior models A and B may affect each other. The first input ports of both A_t and A_h are connected to the external path E_3.

Where an external input of a cyclic subcircuit X is, in turn, the output of another cyclic subcircuit Y, the two individual event prediction networks are linked together by connecting the output of the head pseudo component of Y to the corresponding external input port of the pseudo network for X. The final event prediction network corresponding to a digital design with three cyclic subcircuits, shown in Figure 3.6, is presented in Figure 3.7.

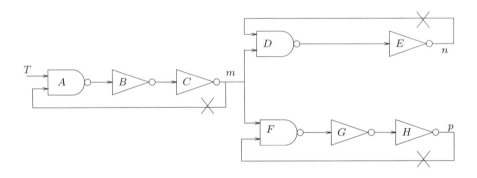

Fig. 3.6. Digital Circuit with Cyclic Subcircuits

Corresponding to a combinational subcircuit, i.e., no feedback loops, the event prediction network consists only of the head network. Thus, for the digital system consisting of a combinational and two sequential subcircuits, as shown in Figure 3.8, the event prediction network is shown in Figure 3.9.

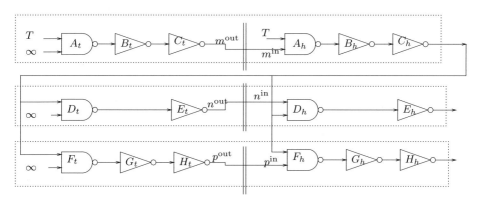

Fig. 3.7. Event Prediction Network for Figure 3.6

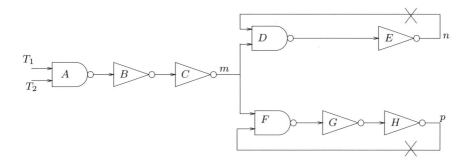

Fig. 3.8. Digital Circuit with Cyclic and Acyclic Subcircuits

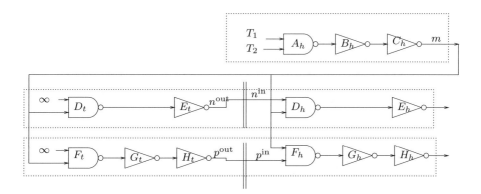

Fig. 3.9. Event Prediction Network for Figure 3.8

Within the event prediction network, the pseudo components compute the predicted event times and communicate them to other appropriate pseudo components through the interconnection links. For combinational subcircuits, the propagation of predicted event times terminates with the last head pseudo component. For sequential subcircuits, the process is more complex and is explained later.

3.1.2.3 The P^2EDAS Algorithm

In P^2EDAS, the behavior models, corresponding to the architectural bodies of the VHDL entities, and event prediction network execute asynchronously and concurrently. The dependence between them is explained as follows. When external events are asserted at the primary input ports of the models, the event times are made available to the corresponding inputs of the pseudo components. In general, a model is permitted to execute appropriate events, limited by the value of the t_{win}. The event prediction network is responsible for computing updated values of t_{win}. It uses the T_i values at its primary inputs, the predicted event times at all other inputs, the event times associated with the input ports of the behavior models, and the propagation delay values to generate two quantities. The predicted event times at the outputs are computed by every pseudo component and propagated to the inputs of subsequent pseudo components. The head pseudo components also generate t_{win} values for the corresponding behavior models which are used by the simulation system to initiate execution of appropriate events. After execution of a behavior model, events may be generated at the output port(s). However, the events are not immediately asserted at the output ports. Only those output events are asserted at the respective outputs at appropriate times that are not preempted based on the rules established in [77] [102] [104] [105].

To preserve causality and thereby guarantee correct simulation of the digital system, events must be executed in their causal order. This implies that, at every head pseudo component, the t_{win} value must increase monotonically.

Corresponding to every behavior model C^n is the simulation clock value, clock^n. C^n has access to the t_{win}^n value associated with the corresponding head pseudo component. Assume that S_o^n represents the logical value of the most recent event asserted at the output o of C^n. Given that P^2EDAS employs preemption of inconsistent events, events generated as a consequence of execution of C^n are stored in an output queue and not immediately asserted at the output port of the behavior model. Assume that $t_{e_o}^n$ represents the time of the earliest event in the output event queue corresponding to the output o of C^n. Where the output event queue is empty, $t_{e_o}^n$ is set to ∞. If one or more input ports of C^n are primary, T_i defines the assertion time of their latest input event. Assume also that t_{e_i} represents the time of the earliest event at input i of C^n. P^2EDAS is explained for cyclic subcircuits, i.e., with feedback loops, because their simulation is most complex. Thus, assuming that C^n is included in a feedback loop, the event prediction network will consist of C_t^n and C_h^n, representing the tail and head pseudo components, respectively.

Corresponding to every head and tail pseudo component of C^n, the quantities W_i^n and W_o^n are associated with every input port i and output port o respectively. While W_i^n signifies the predicted event time at the input, W_o^n represents the predicted event time at the output.

Initialization consists of the following steps:

1. Corresponding to each behavior model C^n, clock^n within the model and t_{win}^n in the head pseudo component within the event prediction network are set to 0.
2. For every pseudo component C_t^n and C_h^n, the predicted event times at all output ports are set to 0. Thus,

$$W_o^n = 0 \qquad \forall n, \quad \forall o. \tag{3.4}$$

3. Corresponding to those input ports of the tail pseudo components associated with the feedback arc set, the W_i^n values are set to ∞. The W_i^n values at all other input ports of pseudo components are initialized to 0.
4. The S_o^n values at every output of every head and tail pseudo component are initialized by the user.

The *simulation process* ensures correct execution of the models triggered by appropriate events, the generation of output events, accurate determination of inconsistent events and their preemption, and propagation of correct output events to the subsequent behavior models:

- *Model execution:* For a given component C^n, identify any and all events, t_{e_i}, at the input ports such that $t_{e_i} < t_{\text{win}}^n$. The behavior model is executed for all such events, starting with the earliest event. For every event executed, the clock^n value is advanced, where possible. The value of clock^n will always be less than t_{win}^n. The newly generated output events, if any, are included in the output event queue. They are not immediately asserted at the output. Inconsistent events, if any, are identified and deleted.
- *Identification of inconsistent output events:* Due to the nature of the timing semantics of event-driven simulation, one or more output events generated as a result of model execution may turn out to be inconsistent. Such inconsistent events are first identified and then preempted, using the following principle that is based on the principle of causality.

  Consider two output assignments—e_1, which carries a logical value v_1 at $t = t_3$, and e_2, which carries a logical value v_2 at $t = t_4$—that are generated by input events i_1 at $t = t_1$ and i_2 at $t = t_2(t_2 > t_1)$, respectively. If v_1 does not equal v_2 and $t_4 < t_3$, then e_1 and e_2 are inconsistent. In this case, e_2, the more recent effect of a later cause (input event) must take precedence over e_1, the less recent effect of an earlier cause. Therefore, e_1 is discarded, ensuring accuracy of the results.

- *Propagation of correct output events:* For each output o of C^n, mark the earliest event, $t^n_{e_o}$, in the event queue, if the following relationship is true:

$$t^n_{e_o} \leq \text{clock}^n \tag{3.5}$$

  If true, the marked event is noted as correct and asserted at the output port of C^n; S^n_o is immediately updated. Any other events in the output event queue that satisfy equation (3.5) are no longer subject to preemption and are also asserted at the output port o. In P^2EDAS, whenever an input or output event queue is observed to become empty, a dummy event with assertion time ∞ is inserted in the queue. For better communication efficiency, one could examine the output event queue with equation (3.5) after clock^n advances to the maximum allowed value short of t^n_{win} and propagate all correct events at once.
- *Updating the event prediction network:* Whenever a new event is asserted at an input port of C^n, causing a new earliest event, the assertion time is propagated to the pseudo components. In addition, whenever the output event queue for an output of C^n is updated, the assertion time of the earliest event is propagated to the head and tail pseudo components. Following the assertion of a correct output event at the output port, the new logical value at the output of the behavior model is propagated to the pseudo components.
- These three steps are continually executed until either all outstanding events are processed or clock^n exceeds the maximum simulation time of interest.

Upon *execution of the event prediction network*, a pseudo component generates a predicted event time, W^n_o, at the outputs. Where the output differs from its previous value, it is propagated right to trigger the execution of subsequent pseudo components in a chain reaction. Should the output be identical to its previous value, it is not propagated. Whenever any of the arguments of a pseudo component's W^n_o value changes, the pseudo component is executed. The underlying principle of execution of the event prediction network in P^2EDAS differs significantly from the data-flow network of YADDES. Also, unlike YADDES, P^2EDAS permits any number of propagation delays between every input and output path and ensures that inconsistent events are detected and preempted to guarantee correctness.

Corresponding to every head or tail pseudo component, a lookup table, represented through L^n, is constructed. The dimensions of the table are determined by the total number of input ports, output ports, and logical values at the outputs. For a given input port i, output port o, and current logical value s, the entry in the table is the minimum of all possible transition times to other logical values at o. P^2EDAS defines a function, minimum_inertial_delay (), which accepts three arguments—input port number, output port number, and current logical value at the output—and generates the earliest transition time to any other legitimate logical value at the output. Although VHDL

[77] proposes the use of inertial and transport delays in hardware descriptions, the semantics and implementation of transport delay are straightforward. The presentation of P^2EDAS in this section focuses on the more complex inertial delays.

Execution of the head and tail pseudo components follows these steps:

1. A pseudo component accesses the predicted event times, W_i^n, at every input port from the preceding pseudo components and assertion times of earliest events $t_{e_i}^n$ at every input port of the corresponding behavior model. It also receives the logical values S_o^n at every output port of the behavior model corresponding to the most recently asserted output events and the assertion times $t_{e_o}^n$ of the earliest events in every output event queue.

2. The pseudo component uses the accessed values to compute the predicted event time W_o^n at every output o using the following equation.

$$W_o = \text{minimum}(t_{e_o}, (\text{minimum}(W_i, t_{e_i})$$
$$+\text{minimum\_inertial\_delay}(i, o, S_o))) \quad \forall i. \tag{3.6}$$

It may be noted that where there are no events at an input port of the behavior model, t_{e_i} is set at ∞. Also, where there are no events in the output event queue of a specific output, t_{e_o} is set to ∞.

The head pseudo component also computes updated t_{win}^n values using the accessed values and the following equation

$$t_{\text{win}}^n = \text{minimum}(W_i) \quad \forall i. \tag{3.7}$$

Where a given input port, i, is primary, W_i is replaced by T_i in the computation of t_{win}^n. T_i represents the maximum simulation time of interest, and its default value is ∞.

3. The newly computed W_o and t_{win}^n values are propagated to the subsequent pseudo components and behavior model, respectively, when the values differ from their previous values.

4. Steps 1 to 3 are repeated until the simulation process terminates.

Figures 3.10 and 3.11 present the algorithms for the simulation model and pseudo components, in pseudo code.

In Figure 3.11, the statement at label L1 and the two subsequent statements are executed only by the head pseudo component, X_h.

3.1.3 An Example to Illustrate P^2EDAS

To illustrate the working of P^2EDAS, consider a cyclic subcircuit, i.e., with feedback, whose execution is more complex than a combinational subcircuit. In Figure 3.12, each of the two NAND gates, A and B, have two inertial delay values given by $T_{pLH} = 10$ ns and $T_{pHL} = 5$ ns that correspond to low-to-high and high-to-low switching at the output. The function

```
while (maximum simulation time is not exhausted)
do{
 check for messages;
   receive events at input ports from other components or external
      world;
   update event queue and order events according to assertion times;
 check for messages;
   receive updated window of temporal independence value from
      pseudo component;
 if (input event queue is modified){
      send time of earliest event in input event queue to pseudo
         components;
      }
 while (executable events at every input port or
         an executable event exists with time
          less than window of temporal independence)
     {
          advance simulation clock;
          assert events in output event queue that may not be
            preempted at output ports;
          execute simulation model;
          for each output port {
            if (new event is generated){
               include it in the output event queue;
               detect inconsistent events and preempt them;
            }
          }
          remove executed event(s) from input event queue(s).
     }
 for each output{
   if (output event queue is modified){
        propagate assertion time of earliest event in output event
            queue to the pseudo components;
        propagate logical value of most recently asserted output
            event to the pseudo components;
      }
    }
}
```

Fig. 3.10. Operations of a Simulation Model X

```
while(simulation model is executing){
        check for messages;
        receive assertion times of new earliest events at input ports
            of behavior model;
        receive logical value of most recently asserted output events
            of behavior model;
        receive assertion times of earliest events at output event
            queues;
        receive new W values at input ports from preceding pseudo
            component(s);

        for each output port {
            use the values received and delay values for every input
                output path to compute predicted event time, W, at output;
            if (W value for output is different) {
                propagate new W value to subsequent pseudo components;
            }
        }
        if (new W values received at input ports) {
            compute new window of temporal independence = minimum over
                all input W values;
        }
L1: if (window of temporal independence differs from its previous
            value) {
            propagate the new value to behavior model;
        }
}
```

Fig. 3.11. Operations of a Head (X_h) or Tail (X_t) Pseudo Component

minimum_inertial_delay(i, o, S_0) therefore returns the value for T_{pLH} corresponding to $s_0 = 0$ and the value of T_{pHL} corresponding to $s_0 = 1$. To ease representation, minimum_inertial_delay(i, o, S_0) is referred to as delay(i, o, s_0) in the rest of this section. Assume that external inputs are asserted at the primary inputs, E_1 and E_2, as shown in Figure 3.12, and that the initial values at the output ports of A and B are 0 and 1, respectively. Initially, the window of temporal independence and the local clock of the models are set: $t_{\text{win}}^A = t_{\text{win}}^B = \text{clock}_A = \text{clock}_B = 0$. In addition, the event queues associated with the output ports of models A and B are empty, i.e., $t_o^A = t_o^B = \infty$.

For the circuit in Figure 3.12, the corresponding event prediction network is shown in Figure 3.13. For the pseudo components, the predicted event time values are set to 0, i.e., $W_{t_o}^A = W_{t_o}^B = W_{h_o}^A = W_{h_o}^B = 0$. Corresponding to a change in a predicted event time value in Figure 3.13, the value is propagated toward other pseudo components to the right, and a chain reaction is initiated, as described earlier. In this section, the symbol $\rightarrow$ represents the propagation of a predicted event time value. That is, $X \rightarrow Y$ indicates the propagation

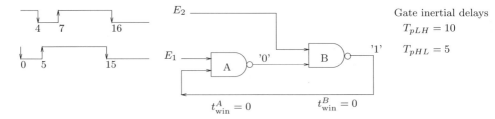

Fig. 3.12. An Example Sequential Subcircuit

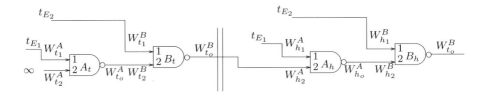

Fig. 3.13. Event Prediction Network Corresponding to Figure 3.12

of a predicted event time value from output X to input Y. Also, at any time instant, the event with the earliest assertion time at an input i of a model C is represented through t_i^C. Thus, for the event prediction network in Figure 3.13,

$$\infty \to W_{t_2}^A \qquad t_1^A \to W_{t_1}^A \qquad W_{t_o}^A \to W_{t_2}^B \qquad t_1^B \to W_{t_1}^B$$
$$W_{t_o}^B \to W_{h_2}^A \qquad t_1^A \to W_{h_1}^A \qquad W_{h_o}^A \to W_{h_2}^B \qquad t_1^B \to W_{h_1}^B$$

The execution of P^2EDAS is organized through the following steps:

1. Following the assertion of the external transitions at the primary inputs E_1 and E_2, the pseudo components in the event prediction network are initiated. New predicted event times (W values) are computed, using equation (3.6) and are shown in Figure 3.14. Corresponding to the newly generated predicted event time values, the window of temporal independence values for models A and B are computed using equation (3.7) and shown in Figure 3.14.

2. Input transitions to models A and B with assertion times less than 9 and 10 ns, respectively, may be executed. A and B may execute concurrently. Figure 3.15 describes the state of the subcircuit. First, the high-to-low transition at time 0 ns at the input of model A is executed. The execution of A generates an output event: $A_o = (0 \quad NAND \quad 1) \Longrightarrow 10 \uparrow$. Because the current logical value at A is 0, the output event queue of A will

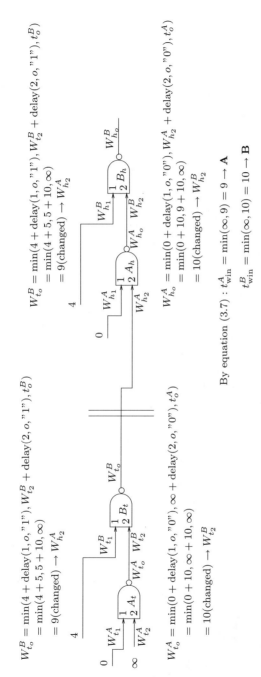

Fig. 3.14. Step 1. Execution of Pseudo Components

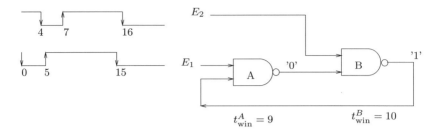

Fig. 3.15. Step 2. Execution of Models A and B Using New Window of Temporal Independence Values

contain a low-to-high transition for time $t_o^A = 10$. Simultaneous with the execution of A, the high-to-low transition at the input of B is executed. The execution of B generates an output event: $B_o = (0 \quad NAND \quad 0) \Longrightarrow 14 \uparrow$. Thus, the newly generated event is a low-to-high transition at $t_o^B = 14$. Because the current logical value at the output of model B is already high, the generated event is deleted. The output event queue of B is empty and t_o^B is reset to ∞.

The processed input transitions are deleted. For the input event queue of A, $E_1 = 5 \uparrow$ defines the subsequent transition. For the input event queue of B, $E_2 = 7 \uparrow$ defines the subsequent transition. Both of these transitions may be executed concurrently, because their times are defined within and less than the respective t_{win} values. The execution of A generates an output event: $A_o = (1 \quad NAND \quad 1) \Longrightarrow 10 \downarrow$. The previously generated event, stored in the output event queue of A, is thus rendered inconsistent. It is preempted using the principles elaborated earlier. The newly generated output event of A is also discarded because its logical value is indistinguishable from the current logical value at the output of A. Therefore, the output event queue of A is empty and t_o^A is set to ∞. The execution of B generates an output event: $B_o = (1 \quad NAND \quad 0) \Longrightarrow 17 \uparrow$ which is also indistinguishable from the current logical value at the output of B. This event is deleted and t_o^B remains at ∞.

3. The processed input transitions are deleted. For the input event queue of A, $E_1 = 15 \downarrow$ defines the subsequent transition. For the input event queue of B, $E_2 = 16 \downarrow$ defines the subsequent transition. Neither of these transitions may be executed because they exceed the respective t_{win} values. For further execution of the models, the event prediction network must execute and update the t_{win} values. The state of the subcircuit is shown in Figure 3.16.

4. The event prediction network is initiated, which uses the fact that the transitions $E_1 = 15 \downarrow$ and $E_2 = 16 \downarrow$ are asserted at the respective input ports of the models, i.e., $t_1^A = 15 \to W_{t_1}^A, W_{h_1}^A$ and $t_1^B = 16 \to W_{t_1}^B, W_{h_1}^B$. The execution of the event prediction network is shown in Figure 3.17.

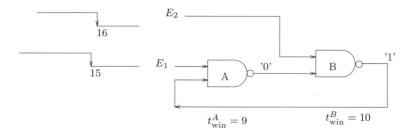

$$t^A_{\text{win}} = 9 \qquad\qquad t^B_{\text{win}} = 10$$

Fig. 3.16. Step 3. State of Subcircuit Following Execution of Models A and B

In the event prediction network, the predicted event times, $W^A_{t_o}$, $W^B_{t_o}$, $W^A_{h_o}$, and $W^B_{h_o}$, are recomputed, as shown in Figure 3.17. As a result, the window of temporal independence values for models A and B are computed using equation (3.7) and are shown in Figure 3.17. Thus, $t^A_{\text{win}} = 21 \rightarrow \mathbf{A}$ and $t^B_{\text{win}} = 25 \rightarrow \mathbf{B}$. The state of the subcircuit is shown in Figure 3.18.

5. Input transitions to models A and B with assertion times less than 21 and 25 ns, respectively, may be executed. First, the high-to-low transition at 15 ns at the input of model A is executed. The execution of A generates an output event: $A_o = (0 \quad NAND \quad 1) \Longrightarrow 25 \uparrow$. Because the current logical value at A is 0, the output event queue of A will contain a low-to-high transition for time $t^A_o = 25$ ns. Simultaneous with the execution of A, the high-to-low transition at the input of B is executed. The execution of B generates an output event: $B_o = (1 \quad NAND \quad 0) \Longrightarrow 26 \uparrow$. Thus, the newly generated event is a low-to-high transition at $t^B_o = 14$. Because the current logical value at the output of model B is already high, the generated event is deleted. The output event queue of B is empty and t^B_o is reset to ∞.

    The processed input transitions are deleted. For the now empty input event queue of A, $t_{E_1} = \infty \rightarrow W^A_{t_1}$ and $t_{E_2} = \infty \rightarrow W^B_{t_1}$. The state of the subcircuit is shown in Figure 3.19.

6. The event prediction network is initiated; it utilizes the fact that the transitions $E_1 = \infty$ and $E_2 = \infty$ are asserted at the respective input ports of the models. In the event prediction network, the predicted event times, $W^A_{t_o}$, $W^B_{t_o}$, $W^A_{h_o}$, and $W^B_{h_o}$, are recomputed, as shown in Figure 3.20. As a result, the window of temporal independence values for models A and B are computed using equation (3.7) and are shown in Figure 3.20. Thus, $t^A_{\text{win}} = 30 \rightarrow \mathbf{A}$ and t^B_{win} remains at 25.

7. Because $25 < 30$, the inequality $t^A_o < t^A_{\text{win}}$ is satisfied. That is, it is guaranteed that no new transitions will be asserted at any input port of A to preempt the previously generated output event, $t^A_o = 25$, at the output event queue of A. The output event is safely propagated to model

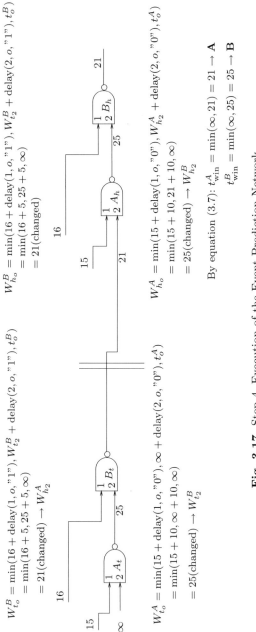

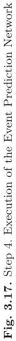

$W_{t_o}^B = \min(16 + \text{delay}(1, o, "1"), W_{t_2}^B + \text{delay}(2, o, "1"), t_o^B)$

$W_{h_o}^B = \min(16 + \text{delay}(1, o, "1"), W_{t_2}^B + \text{delay}(2, o, "1"), t_o^B)$
$\quad\;\; = \min(16 + 5, 25 + 5, \infty)$
$\quad\;\; = 21(\text{changed})$

$W_{t_o}^B = \min(16 + \text{delay}(1, o, "1"), W_{t_2}^B + \text{delay}(2, o, "1"), t_o^B)$
$\quad\;\; = \min(16 + 5, 25 + 5, \infty)$
$\quad\;\; = 21(\text{changed}) \rightarrow W_{h_2}^A$

$W_{t_o}^A = \min(15 + \text{delay}(1, o, "0"), \infty + \text{delay}(2, o, "0"), t_o^A)$
$\quad\;\; = \min(15 + 10, \infty + 10, \infty)$
$\quad\;\; = 25(\text{changed}) \rightarrow W_{t_2}^B$

$W_{h_o}^A = \min(15 + \text{delay}(1, o, "0"), W_{h_2}^A + \text{delay}(2, o, "0"), t_o^A)$
$\quad\;\; = \min(15 + 10, 21 + 10, \infty)$
$\quad\;\; = 25(\text{changed}) \rightarrow W_{h_2}^B$

By equation (3.7): $t_{\text{win}}^A = \min(\infty, 21) = 21 \rightarrow \mathbf{A}$
$\qquad\qquad\qquad\; t_{\text{win}}^B = \min(\infty, 25) = 25 \rightarrow \mathbf{B}$

Fig. 3.17. Step 4. Execution of the Event Prediction Network

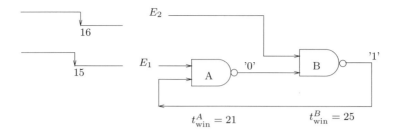

$t^A_{\text{win}} = 21$ $t^B_{\text{win}} = 25$

Fig. 3.18. State of Subcircuit with New Window of Temporal Independence Values

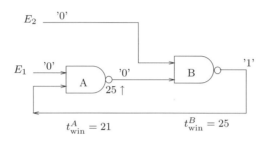

$t^A_{\text{win}} = 21$ $t^B_{\text{win}} = 25$

Fig. 3.19. Step 5. State of Subcircuit Following Execution of Models A and B

B and t^A_o is reset to ∞. The state of the subcircuit is shown in Figure 3.21.

8. Because $25 \not< 25$, the new transition at the input of model B cannot be executed with the current t_{win} value. The event prediction network is initiated, and the pseudo components are executed. In the event prediction network, the predicted event times, $W^A_{t_o}$, $W^B_{t_o}$, $W^A_{h_o}$, and $W^B_{h_o}$, are recomputed, as shown in Figure 3.22. As a result, the window of temporal independence values for models A and B are computed using equation (3.7) and are shown in Figure 3.22. Thus, $t^B_{\text{win}} = 35 \rightarrow \mathbf{B}$ and t^A_{win} remains at 30.

9. Because $25 < 35$, the low-to-high input transition at the input of model B with assertion time of 25 ns is executed. The execution of B generates an output event: $B_o = (0 \quad NAND \quad 1) \Longrightarrow 35 \uparrow$. Since the current logical value at the output of model B is already high, the generated event is deleted. The output event queue of B is empty and t^B_o is reset to ∞. Also, the processed input transitions are deleted. The state of the subcircuit is shown in Figure 3.23.

10. Corresponding to the update of the output event queue of B, namely, t^B_o is reset to ∞, the event prediction network is initiated and the pseudo components are executed. In the event prediction network, the predicted event times, $W^B_{t_o}$, $W^A_{h_o}$, and $W^B_{h_o}$, are recomputed, as shown in Figure

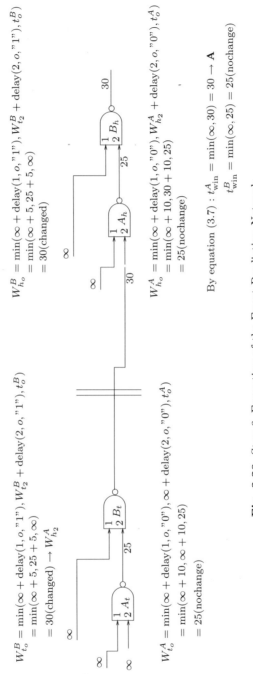

$$W_{t_o}^B = \min(\infty + \text{delay}(1, o, \text{"1"}), W_{t_2}^B + \text{delay}(2, o, \text{"1"}), t_o^B)$$
$$= \min(\infty + 5, 25 + 5, \infty)$$
$$= 30(\text{changed}) \rightarrow W_{h_2}^A$$

$$W_{t_o}^A = \min(\infty + \text{delay}(1, o, \text{"0"}), \infty + \text{delay}(2, o, \text{"0"}), t_o^A)$$
$$= \min(\infty + 10, \infty + 10, 25)$$
$$= 25(\text{nochange})$$

$$W_{h_o}^B = \min(\infty + \text{delay}(1, o, \text{"1"}), W_{t_2}^B + \text{delay}(2, o, \text{"1"}), t_o^B)$$
$$= \min(\infty + 5, 25 + 5, \infty)$$
$$= 30(\text{changed})$$

$$W_{h_o}^A = \min(\infty + \text{delay}(1, o, \text{"0"}), W_{h_2}^A + \text{delay}(2, o, \text{"0"}), t_o^A)$$
$$= \min(\infty + 10, 30 + 10, 25)$$
$$= 25(\text{nochange})$$

By equation (3.7) : $t_{\text{win}}^A = \min(\infty, 30) = 30 = 30 \rightarrow \mathbf{A}$
$$t_{\text{win}}^B = \min(\infty, 25) = 25(\text{nochange})$$

Fig. 3.20. Step 6. Execution of the Event Prediction Network

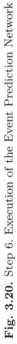

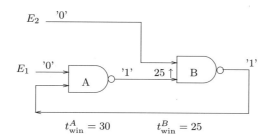

Fig. 3.21. Step 7. State of the Subcircuit Following Execution of Models A and B

3.24. The window of temporal independence values for models A and B is also computed utilizing equation (3.7) and shown in Figure 3.24. Thus, $t_{win}^B = \infty$ and $t_{win}^A = \infty$, indicating the termination of simulation.

11. In the final step, the input and output event queues are empty and the number of outstanding transitions is zero. The final output waveform produced as a result of the execution of the subcircuit is shown in Figure 3.25.

3.1.4 Implementation and Performance Analysis of P^2EDAS

P^2EDAS has been implemented in C for two parallel processing environments —(1) A four-node Sun Sparc 10 shared memory multiprocessor with 56 Mbytes of RAM and 200 Mbytes of virtual memory space supporting threads under the Sun OS 5.5 operating system and (2) a network of twenty-five 90 Mhz-Pentium workstations with 16 Mbytes of RAM and 100 Mbytes of swap, under the Linux operating system and connected through a 100-Mhz fast Ethernet and configured as a loosely coupled parallel processor. The total length of the P^2EDAS implementation is 50,000 lines of C; it builds on top of the extensively modified Pittsburgh VHDL compiler [106].

3.1.4.1 Performance Results for Shared Memory Multiprocessor Implementation

For the shared memory multiprocessor supported by multiple threads, a total of eleven representative digital designs are simulated. They include BAR (a barrel shifter with 75 components), MULT1 (a multiplier with latches consisting of 442 components), MULT41 (a four-bit multiplier with latches comprising 1768 components), MULT2 (a multiplier with multiplexors consisting of 182 components), MULT42 (a four-bit multiplier with multiplexors comprising 728 components), RCNT8 (an eight-bit ripple counter with 118 components), RCNT32 (a thirty-two-bit ripple counter with 454 components), RCNT432 (a set of four independent thirty-two-bit ripple counters with 1816 components),

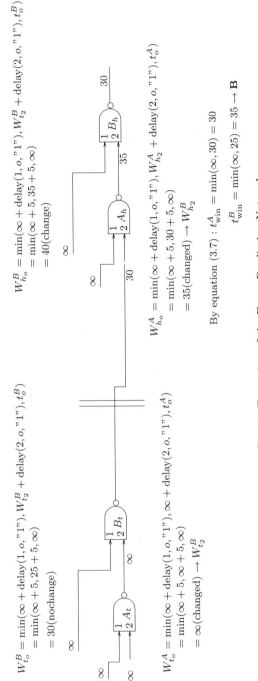

$W_{t_o}^B = \min(\infty + \text{delay}(1, o, "1"), W_{t_2}^B + \text{delay}(2, o, "1"), t_o^B)$
$= \min(\infty + 5, 25 + 5, \infty)$
$= 30(\text{nochange})$

$W_{t_o}^A = \min(\infty + \text{delay}(1, o, "1"), \infty + \text{delay}(2, o, "1"), t_o^A)$
$= \min(\infty + 5, \infty + 5, \infty)$
$= \infty(\text{changed}) \rightarrow W_{t_2}^B$

$W_{h_o}^B = \min(\infty + \text{delay}(1, o, "1"), W_{t_2}^B + \text{delay}(2, o, "1"), t_o^B)$
$= \min(\infty + 5, 35 + 5, \infty)$
$= 40(\text{change})$

$W_{h_o}^A = \min(\infty + \text{delay}(1, o, "1"), W_{h_2}^A + \text{delay}(2, o, "1"), t_o^A)$
$= \min(\infty + 5, 30 + 5, \infty)$
$= 35(\text{changed}) \rightarrow W_{h_2}^B$

By equation (3.7): $t_{\text{win}}^A = \min(\infty, 30) = 30$
$t_{\text{win}}^B = \min(\infty, 25) = 35 \rightarrow \mathbf{B}$

Fig. 3.22. Step 8. Execution of the Event Prediction Network

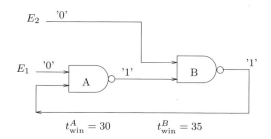

Fig. 3.23. Step 9. State of the Subcircuit Following Execution of Model B

RAM1 (a thirty-two-bit RAM with 519 components), RAM2 (a sixty-four-bit RAM with 3258 components), and SADD (a registered serial adder with 392 components). All other circuits except BAR are cyclic.

Ghosh and Yu [27] have observed that the performance benefit of distributed simulation is best realized when the computation loads of the behavior entities are appreciable compared to the communications costs. This section also observes that the performance benefit of P^2EDAS is best realized when the computational loads of the models exceed the cost of executing the event prediction network. By design, P^2EDAS focuses on coarse-grain parallelism and targets large-scale system designs. The use of synthetic loads with the eleven representative digital designs serves to emulate a suite of large-scale designs with the topologies of the representative designs that after simulation, yield P^2EDAS's performance. Thus, similar to the performance data presented in [27], the performance results reported here assume the presence of synthetic loads, i.e., within each component, the behavior model is designed to count to a large number, Max_Count. The value of Max_Count is assumed uniform across all models because the principal goal here is to study the nature of the algorithm's performance for different circuit topologies, not to focus on load balancing issues. While the value of Max_Count is set to 200,000 for smaller circuits, it is reduced to 50,000 for large circuits to limit the total simulation execution time. Figures 3.26, 3.27, 3.28, and 3.29 present the speedup graphs for the digital circuits enumerated earlier. The x-axis represents the number of threads used for the simulations, and the y-axis represents the speedup values. To obtain the speedup graphs, each design is executed on a single processor, using the Pittsburgh VHDL compiler and environment [106] to yield the corresponding uniprocessor execution time. In Figures 3.26 and 3.27, for each of the circuits, MULT41, MULT42, and RCNT432, two speedup graphs are reported corresponding to minor variations in the implementations that are not detailed here.

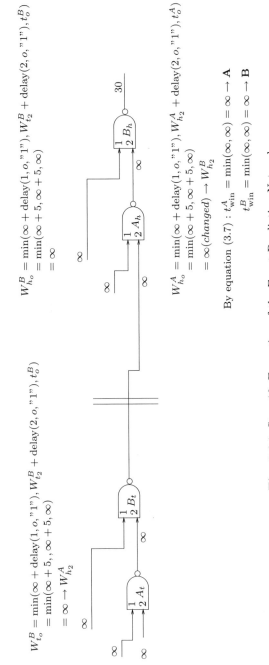

$$W_{t_o}^B = \min(\infty + \text{delay}(1, o, "1"), W_{t_2}^B + \text{delay}(2, o, "1"), t_o^B)$$
$$= \min(\infty + 5, , \infty + 5, \infty)$$
$$= \infty \rightarrow W_{h_2}^A$$

$$W_{h_o}^B = \min(\infty + \text{delay}(1, o, "1"), W_{t_2}^B + \text{delay}(2, o, "1"), t_o^B)$$
$$= \min(\infty + 5, \infty + 5, \infty)$$
$$= \infty$$

$$W_{h_o}^A = \min(\infty + \text{delay}(1, o, "1"), W_{h_2}^A + \text{delay}(2, o, "1"), t_o^A)$$
$$= \min(\infty + 5, \infty + 5, \infty)$$
$$= \infty(changed) \rightarrow W_{h_2}^B$$

By equation (3.7) : $t_{win}^A = \min(\infty, \infty) = \infty \rightarrow \mathbf{A}$
$$t_{win}^B = \min(\infty, \infty) = \infty \rightarrow \mathbf{B}$$

Fig. 3.24. Step 10. Execution of the Event Prediction Network

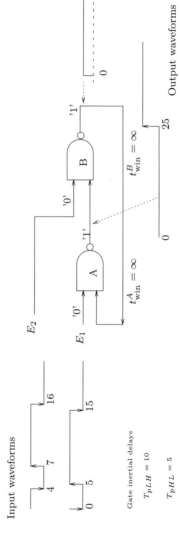

Input waveforms

Gate inertial delays

$T_{pLH} = 10$

$T_{pHL} = 5$

Output waveforms

Fig. 3.25. Step 11. Output Waveform Generated by Subcircuit Execution

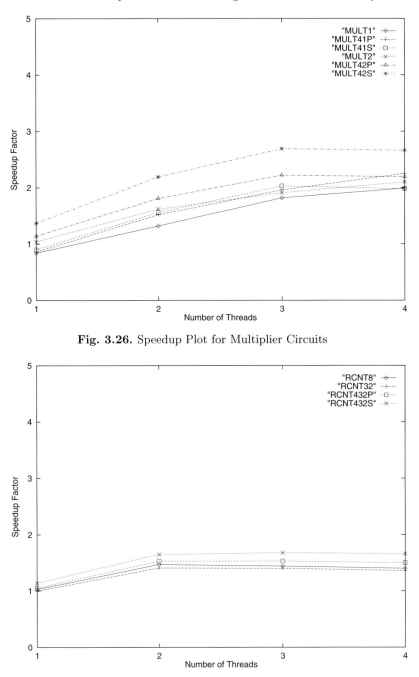

Fig. 3.26. Speedup Plot for Multiplier Circuits

Fig. 3.27. Speedup Plot for Ripple Counters

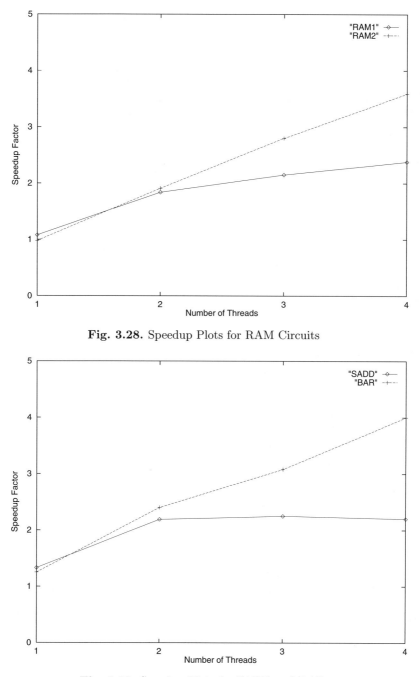

Fig. 3.28. Speedup Plots for RAM Circuits

Fig. 3.29. Speedup Plots for SADD and BAR

3.1.4.2 Performance Results for Loosely Coupled Parallel Processor Implementation

In general, messages in a loosely coupled parallel processor communicate slower than data sharing in a shared memory multiprocessor. Thus, a set of two significantly larger circuits than the eleven designs used earlier are chosen for performance analysis of P^2EDAS. As stated earlier, P^2EDAS is designed for coarse-grain parallelism and targets VHDL entities to constitute the models, especially those with significant computational complexities. The partitioning of a given system into models for P^2EDAS and their allocation to the available processors of a loosely coupled parallel processor system are both determined by the user.

3.1.4.2.1 DLX Computer Architecture

Figure 3.30 presents the DLX computer system, a hypothetical architecture described by Hennessy and Patterson [107], that is described in VHDL and simulated in P^2EDAS. Table 3.1 presents a list of the eight major functional blocks of the system along with the constituent components and signals. These blocks also constitute the eight partitions used in the simulation.

Code Name	Circuit Name	Components	Signals
CPU	DLX processor	19,092	23,749
TIMER	Timer	1,063	1,612
UROM	User ROM	852	984
SROM	System ROM	1,502	1,634
URAM	User RAM	12,480	12,581
SRAM	System RAM	12,480	12,581
Decoder	Address decoder	168	266
Resolver	Distributed resolver	32	259

Table 3.1. Major Blocks in the DLX Architecture

Table 3.2 presents the simulation execution time, in seconds, corresponding to the use of three, five, and eight processors. The simulation time is identical to the longest of the execution times of all of the processors. The reduction in simulation time from one to three processors is significant. It underscores the fact that the single processor with 16 Mbytes of RAM experiences significant swapping given that the circuit requires more than 37 Mbytes of memory for representation. While the reduction in simulation time from three to five processors clearly highlights the advantage of P^2EDAS, the slight increase in the simulation time from five to eight processors simply reflects the dominance of communication for the increased number of processors. Observations from the execution of the simulation runs indicate that the distribution of

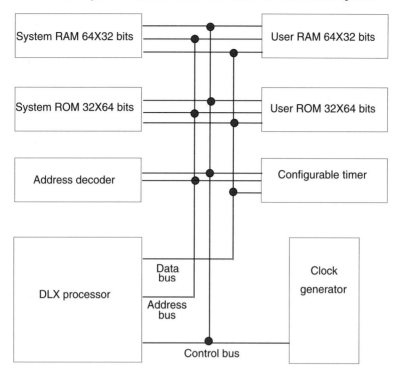

Fig. 3.30. DLX Computer Architecture

the computational load is uneven among the processors. For example, the processor that executes the DLX processor module performs the most computation and executes for the longest time. Conceivably, better performance may be achieved through further partitioning of the computationally intensive modules.

No. of Processors	1	3	5	8
Time (sec)	$\gg 43,200$	4,920	1,800	2,160

Table 3.2. Performance Results for DLX Architecture in P^2EDAS

3.1.4.2.2 Random State Generator

The second circuit for the performance analysis study consists of a pseudo random state generator that is selected because of the presence of the large number of feedback loops. To gain a better understanding of the benefits of P^2EDAS despite the presence of multiple feedback loops, substantial synthetic loads are assigned to each individual component of the generator. Table

3.3 presents the simulation execution time in seconds corresponding to the different numbers of processors being used. The simulation time decreases with increasing number of processors implying the advantages of P^2EDAS. However, when ten processors are employed, the increased cost of interprocessor communication outweighs the benefits from distributing the computational load among multiple processing engines.

No. of Processors	1	2	4	6	8	10
Time (sec)		659	411	306	302	320	424

Table 3.3. Performance Results for a Synthetically Loaded Random State Generator

The overall performance results indicate that when the digital designs under simulation are compute-intensive, P^2EDAS offers significant speedup benefits. In addition, for large circuits requiring significant memory for representation, partitioning them into multiple processors under P^2EDAS reduces the resource requirement on each processor, thereby implying better efficiency and higher performance. However, the continued increase in the number of processors allocated does not provide increasing speedup. Instead, beyond a certain number of processors, the interprocessor communication time starts to dominate and eclipses the potential advantages from sharing the computational load among multiple processing engines.

3.1.4.3 Performance Analysis

P^2EDAS is an asynchronous distributed algorithm, and it is very difficult, if not impossible, to develop an accurate analytic model of the asynchronous, concurrent execution of the behavior models on a parallel processor. That is, any effort to develop a complexity analysis to accurately predict the CPU time usage is impractical. Furthermore, an approach to classify digital designs into a finite number of classes, based on an accepted scientific definition, is still elusive. That is why considerable effort has been expended to realize a practical implementation of P^2EDAS and test it against practical designs. However, to facilitate an understanding of the general nature of P^2EDAS's performance, an approximate analysis of the total computational requirement of P^2EDAS, termed *cumulative computational burden* (CCB), is developed and presented here. It is nontrivial, unlike the traditional sequential algorithms for which the computational complexities were successfully developed, to accurately convert the CCB into the CPU time requirement for asynchronous, distributed systems.

While the null message [27] and the virtual time [83] schemes are competitors of P^2EDAS, the virtual time technique suffers from a fundamental unpredictability and is not considered in this comparative analysis. The analysis assumes a digital system with a single feedback loop, and although it may be easily extended to multiple yet independent loops, the issue of analyzing system designs with multiple interdependent loops is very complex.

In the event prediction network in P^2EDAS, the pseudo-primed and pseudo-unprimed components correspond to the models in the original system design but are merely mathematical units. Unlike the models that require, in general, significant computation, the mathematical units require only a minimum computation function. The propagation of the W and W' values and the execution of the primed and unprimed pseudo components, are both event-driven, i.e., triggered by receipt of a new transition by a behavior model:

$$CCB = (N.\alpha)(m + c). \tag{3.8}$$

Assume N behavior models rated by an average computational complexity, m. The average computational complexity of a pseudo component is p, where $p \ll m$. The communication cost per message is given by c. For a given input vector and assuming that, on an average, a fraction, α, of the total number of models is activated as a result of the input vector, the ideal or minimum CCB is given by equation (3.8):

$$CCB = (N.\alpha)(m + c) + (N\alpha)f(N)(p + c). \tag{3.9}$$

For P^2EDAS, the CCB is given in equation (3.9), where $f(N)$ implies a function with argument N whose exact nature is defined by the nature of the digital system, the nature of the input stimuli, and the asynchronous overlapping of the concurrent computations. Currently, techniques to determine $f(N)$ accurately are elusive:

$$CCB = (N.\alpha)(m + c) + (N\alpha)(k + c)\frac{T}{\sum \delta}. \tag{3.10}$$

For the null message technique, where the average time interval between two successive input vectors is T and the cumulative delay of all of the behavior models in the loop is given by $\sum \delta$, the CCB is given in equation (3.10). When a model receives a null message, it first checks to determine whether any of the other inputs have received a new value (nonnull message). If no new values have been received, it updates its output tuple and, under these circumstances, the computational complexity is assumed to be k. When a new value has been received, the model incurs an execution at a cost of m, as described earlier.

From equations (3.9) and (3.10), the difference between P^2EDAS and the null message scheme reduces to a comparison between $(p + c)f(N)$ and $(k + c)T/\sum \delta$. Clearly, c plays a fundamental role in limiting the performance of all asynchronous distributed algorithms, but its adverse impact is exerted on both P^2EDAS and the null message scheme. Where the system design is an oscillator or the value of the fraction $T/\sum \delta$ is small, close to unity, which implies either a very-high-frequency input stimulus or a small to modest size system, the null message scheme may be preferred because of its simplicity. However, where the value of the fraction $T/\sum \delta$ is large, the null message scheme may be highly inefficient and P^2EDAS would be preferred. It is expected that future parallel processors will benefit from improved communication technology and network protocol design and witness a reduction in the communication time that, in turn, will boost the advantages of both P^2EDAS and the null message scheme.

3.2 A Novel, Decentralized Algorithm for Railway Networks with Soft Reservation

3.2.1 Introduction

Railway networks are ubiquitous in today's world; they have played a dominant role in transporting freight and people since 1825 when the first common-carrier railroad was introduced. While larger countries such as the United States, Russia, China, India, and the EU benefit most from extensive and cost-effective railway networks, in many smaller but densely populated countries with large financial resources, such as Japan, railway networks contribute significantly to the well-being of the national economy by efficiently moving workers and goods. As of 1987, the U.S. [108] has maintained a total of 249,412 miles of railway tracks. It supports a total of 1,249,075,534 locomotive unit miles in one year to carry freight using 5,989,522 loaded cars. For passenger service, the total unit miles stands at 3,782,470 while carrying gross ton-miles of 1,357,097. In Japan, the East Japan Railway Company [109] carries a total of 16 million passengers each day on 12,000 scheduled trains and 7,500 km of railway track. For efficiency, modularity, and safety, in general, the tracks are divided into individual units, each of which may be controlled exclusively by the system. Thus, a train, in propagating from a location A to another location B may travel over several tracks. Given that two or more trains may compete at some time instant, for the same track and that only one train may occupy a track at any time, the principal goal of the railway network management system is to allocate tracks to trains such that collisions are avoided and the resources are used optimally.

A detailed analysis of the existing literature in centralized scheduling for railway networks is provided in [72]. In addition, the ASTREE [110] railway traffic management system maintains a distributed database of up-to-date, accurate, and comprehensive representations of route layout and train progress; it uses the information in the database to either automatically make decisions or assist human operators with decisions relative to route settings and train control. The settings are then downloaded to the wayside equipment and locomotives. Hill, Yu, and Dunn [111] report their effort in modeling electromagnetic interference in railway networks. Ayers [112] presents the use of error-correcting codes to achieve reliable radio-link communication in the Advanced Train Control System. Sheikh, Coll, Ayers, and Bailey [113] present the issue of signal fading in mobile communications. While Hill [114] presents coding issues to facilitate the communication of train positions efficiently, Shayan, Tho, and Bhargava [115] report of the use of Reed-Solomon Codec to improve the Advanced Train Control System. The Association of American Railroads [116] notes that distributed algorithms can enhance the efficacy of train scheduling and that several socioeconomic factors including ownership, track capacity, speed capability, grades, curvatures, clearances, crew districts, and operating agreements, may influence the choice of alternate paths. The DARYN approach [72] presented in the literature constitutes a novel, distributed algorithm but is limited in that it employs unit lookahead. That is, at any time instant, it reserves only one track beyond its current position. Consequently, it is unable to use congestion information, beyond its current position, to plan its future route, and this may lead to inefficiency.

This chapter presents RYNSORD, which addresses key limitations of the traditional approaches, described earlier, and marks a significant advancement. RYNSORD studies the concept of lookahead, i.e., reserving N tracks ahead of the current position to improve the utilization of the resources—tracks—and mitigate congestion. It also introduces a new concept, soft reservation, that is characterized by greater flexibility, as opposed to the conventional, hard, reservation technique wherein a reservation request for a specific time instant is either approved or disapproved.

The remainder of this section is organized as follows. Section 3.2.2 presents a detailed description of the RYNSORD approach while Section 3.2.3 describes the modeling of RYNSORD on an accurate and realistic testbed constituted by a network of 70 Sun Sparc 10 workstations, configured as a loosely coupled parallel processor. Section 3.2.4 presents key implementation issues; Section 3.2.5 first reports the performance data from executing a simulation of RYNSORD for realistic railway networks and under stochastic input traffic stimulus and then presents a detailed performance analysis.

3.2.2 The RYNSORD Approach

The RYNSORD approach for railway networks is novel and defined by the following characteristics. First, it is decentralized in that the overall task of routing all trains through the network is shared by all entities in the system—trains and station nodes. The routing is dynamic, i.e., the choice of the successive tracks as a train proceeds toward its final destination, takes into account the actual demand of the tracks by other trains in the system. What makes RYNSORD unique among all disciplines including modern communication networks is that every mobile agent—the train—possesses intelligence, information-gathering facilities, and autonomy to solely and completely determine its own routing. Trains ride on tracks and safety concerns demand that a train first gains an exclusive reservation guarantee from the owner node of a track prior to propagating on it. Conceivably, a train can insist on reserving every track from origin to destination along its chosen route before starting its journey. Such an approach may lock the train to faraway tracks too soon based on old information, and thereby fail to take advantage of better route choices that may become available as time progresses. On the contrary, the RYNSORD approach uses a lookahead N wherein every train requests reservations at intervals of N tracks and a specific reservation entails the acquisition of approvals of N subsequent tracks along its route toward its destination, before it resumes its travel. Within the reservation process for N subsequent tracks, RYNSORD proposes a novel concept—*soft reservation*. In the traditional, hard reservation, a train issues N consecutive requests for N tracks at specific time instances. The owner stations for the corresponding tracks will either approve or disapprove the reservation, depending on whether the respective tracks are free at the requested time instances. Thus, when a train requests a track from time t_1 to t_2, even if the station notes that the track is occupied up to time $t_1 + 1$ but free thereafter, it will refuse approval. Then the train will have to try an alternate track. Assume that the alternate track is a worse solution than if the train had waited idly for 1 time unit and used the original track. If the train had been aware of the knowledge possessed by the station, it could have idled 1 time unit and opted for the better solution. Thus, with regard to reservation, the nodes' behaviors are binary and rigid. In contrast, RYNSORD proposes soft reservation, wherein a train specifies monotonically increasing time instants to the successive station nodes corresponding to the N subsequent tracks. In turn, a node grants approval at either the requested time instant or the earliest time instant beyond the requested time instants when the track is available. These characteristics are expected to endow RYNSORD with efficiency, robustness, and reduced vulnerability to catastrophic systemwide failures.

In RYNSORD, a railway network is assumed to consist of a set of railroad stations, also termed nodes, that are connected by lengths of railroad track. Every station is equipped with a computing engine and communication facilities. For every pair of stations that are connected by a track, there exists a bidirectional communication link between the stations. Every track is bidirectional. Furthermore, every train is equipped with an on-board computing engine and facilities to initiate communication with the computing engine of the corresponding node when it is located at a station. RYNSORD does not require train-to-train communication or train-to-station communication while the train is moving. Each track segment is characterized by its length and the station node that owns it exclusively. A track between nodes X and Y is owned either by X or Y, and the owner is solely responsible for negotiating the use of the track with the competing trains. This characteristic is crucial to guaranteeing safety and collision avoidance in RYNSORD. Consider Figure 3.31, which presents a simple railway network with station nodes A through F that are connected through a partially connected network of track segments. The owners and lengths of the respective tracks are shown in Figure 3.31.

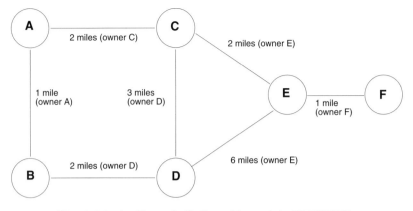

Fig. 3.31. An Example Railway Network in RYNSORD

Trains can be asserted into RYNSORD asynchronously, i.e., at any arbitrary time, and at any station. Each train is characterized by its originating station, destination station, and maximum speed. In general, the exact route, i.e., the sequence of tracks from origin to final destination, and the consequent arrival time are determined dynamically by RYNSORD. However, where specific intermediate stops are mandated, the overall path is organized into multiple sets of smaller paths, and RYNSORD is applied to each set successively. Thus, if the desired path is $A \rightarrow C \rightarrow E$, it is equivalent to first traveling from $A \rightarrow C$, under RYNSORD, and then from $C \rightarrow E$, also under RYNSORD. Excessive use of intermediate stops can lead to poor performance because RYNSORD's strength lies in the dynamic routing of trains to maximize efficiency, resources allocation, and congestion avoidance.

As indicated earlier, a key concept in RYNSORD is the notion of lookahead, which is defined as the number of track segments that a train negotiates for future use at reservation time. Lookahead reflects how far into the future a train attempts to reserve resources, and these include the subsequent track segments that the train may need to reach its destination, starting with the immediate next track segment.

After entering the RYNSORD system, every train computer first determines the shortest path between its origin and its destination. This is termed the *primary path* and is based on the mileage between the stations. The determination of the primary path does not take congestion into account. A *secondary path* is then determined whose component tracks are mutually exclusive from those of the primary path, with one exception. In a relatively few scenarios, the primary and secondary paths may share one (or more) common track segments if it is the only segment that connects one part to another part of the network. For example, in Figure 3.31, the $E \rightarrow F$ link is a necessary component of any path originating or ending at station F and will therefore occur in both the primary and secondary paths.

Next, a train extracts the stations corresponding to the first N tracks (lookahead $= N$) from both the primary and secondary paths, synthesizes reservation request packets, and initiates them. A reservation request packet consists of a list of successive stations and the expected arrival times at each one. The arrival times are calculated based on the current time, the speed of the train, the lengths of the track segments joining the stations, and the assumption that trains do not wait at the intermediate stations. That is, the departure time from station X is identical to the arrival time at station X. Of course, a train may be subject to waiting at the originating station and other stations where it initiates reservation requests for the subsequent N tracks. The arrival and departure times determine the time interval for which a track reservation is desired. Thus, for a track segment $X \rightarrow Y$, the train must reserve the track for the interval (departure time from X, arrival time at Y).

The train propagates the reservation packet to the first station in the list. If this station is the owner of the first track segment, it will negotiate for reservation for this track. Assume that the train requests reservation for the interval (t_1, t_2). If the station determines that the track is not occupied for this interval, reservation is granted. If, on the contrary, the requested interval is already occupied by another train, clearly reservation cannot be granted for the requested interval. The station then computes the earliest time interval beyond t_2 and reserves the track for this new interval, say (t_3, t_4). The length of the interval is computed using the length of the track and the train speed. It overwrites the first interval entry in the reservation packet and the subsequent intervals for the corresponding tracks are also modified. If the first station is not the owner of the first track segment, the reservation packet is forwarded to the second station which must be the owner of the first track. Following completion of reservation for the first track segment, the reservation packet is sent to the station that owns the subsequent track segment. A reservation process similar to the one described earlier is initiated, culminating in a reservation time interval for the second track segment. This process continues until reservation intervals are obtained for all N track segments. The modified reservation packet is then returned to the train, located at the station node where it had initiated the reservation process. This process is executed simultaneously for both the primary and secondary paths.

When a train receives responses to both of its reservation requests along the primary and secondary paths, it may not select as its best choice the route (say $R1$) that yields the smallest value of time to reach the station at the end of N subsequent tracks. The reason is that although the primary and secondary paths both lead to the ultimate destination, reaching the end of the N tracks along route $R1$ earlier does not automatically guarantee that the train will reach its final destination faster. Therefore, for each primary and secondary path, the train adds the arrival time at the end of the N tracks to the time of travel from the end of the N tracks to the final destination along the shortest path. Assume that these times are represented through TT_1 and

TT_2 along the primary and secondary paths. The train selects the route that yields the smaller of the TT_1 and TT_2 values. Where $TT_1 = TT_2$, the train arbitrarily selects the primary path. Then the train generates a reservation removal request and propagates it to the stations along the route not selected to free the corresponding track reservations.

As a train proceeds from one station to the next along the N tracks, it is guaranteed use of the corresponding tracks in accordance with the reservation times, approved earlier. However, should a train arrive at a station earlier than its expected arrival time and the track is available for a sufficiently long time interval, the station may permit the train to proceed immediately. The train, in turn, withdraws the original reservation time interval for the corresponding track segment and modifies its time interval of use of the track. The reason a train, upon arrival at a station node, may find a track available sooner than its requested time interval is because tracks are often freed through reservation removal requests when a train that originally requested reservation decides to select an alternate route. Thus, the previously approved reservation time interval for a track is an upper bound on the travel time for the train. In the event that there are multiple trains competing for a track freed by a train, the train that has been waiting the longest at the station is given the highest preference.

To understand the operation of RYNSORD, consider the railway network in Figures 3.32(a) and 3.32(b) that is identical to that in Figure 3.31, except that node F is missing. Assume that two trains, Ta and Tb, are asserted into the system at the same time, $t = 0$, at nodes A and B, respectively. Both Ta and Tb are destined for station E. Figure 3.32(a) describes the computations of the primary and secondary paths for Ta from the origin A to the destination E. Figure 3.32(b) describes the computations for the primary and secondary paths for Tb, from origin B to destination E. In both Figures 3.32(a) and 3.32(b), the solid and dotted lines represent the primary and secondary paths, respectively. Assume that the lookahead $N = 2$.

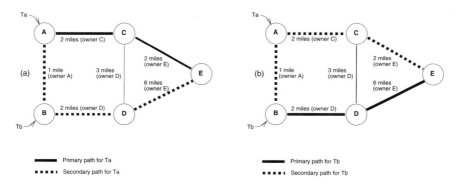

Fig. 3.32. Computation of Primary and Secondary Paths in RYNSORD (a) for Train Ta and (b) for Train Tb

Assuming the value of lookahead $N = 2$, trains Ta and Tb extract the stations relative to $N = 2$ tracks from both primary and secondary paths. For this example, assume that the primary path for Tb is selected based on the number of tracks, not the mileage from the source to the destination. The stations for the primary and secondary paths are:

```
Train Ta:
    Primary path station list:  A->C->E
    Secondary path station list: A->B->D

Train Tb:
    Primary path station list: B->D->E
    Secondary path station list: B->A->C
```

Assuming the speeds of the trains at 1 mile per minute, the reservation request packets generated and initiated by Ta and Tb are:

```
Train Ta:
    Primary path:
        arrival at A at time      0
        departure from A at time  0
        arrival at C at time      2
        departure from C at time  2
        arrival at E at time      4
        [no departure since E is the final destination]

    Secondary path:
        arrival at A at time      0
        departure from A at time  0
        arrival at B at time      1
        departure from B at time  1
        arrival at D at time      3
        [no departure since D is the last station in the
            station list]

Train Tb:
    Primary path:
        arrival at B at time      0
        departure from B at time  0
        arrival at D at time      2
        departure from D at time  2
        arrival at E at time      8
        [no departure since E is the final destination]

    Secondary path:
        arrival at B at time      0
```

```
departure from B at time    0
arrival at A at time        1
departure from A at time    1
arrival at C at time        3
[no departure since D is the last station in the
    station list]
```

Figures 3.33(a) through 3.33(d) describe the operation of RYNSORD relative to the reservation packet propagation by the trains and their processing by the respective stations. In Figure 3.33(a), $Ra1$ and $Ra2$ express the reservation packets propagated by Ta along the primary and secondary paths. $Rb1$ and $Rb2$ represent the corresponding packets for Tb. In Figure 3.33(a), $Ra2$ requests station A to reserve the track $A \rightarrow B$ for time $(0, 1)$. The request is approved successfully because the track $A \rightarrow B$ is free for the time interval $(0, 1)$. Since station A does not own track $A \rightarrow C$, $Ra1$ cannot use station A to accomplish its goal. Neither $Rb1$ nor $Rb2$ are able to use station B because the latter owns neither track $B \rightarrow D$ nor $B \rightarrow A$.

Figure 3.33(b) represents the propagation of the reservation packets to the subsequent stations. Here, $Ra1$ and $Rb1$ successfully reserve the tracks $A \rightarrow C$ and $B \rightarrow D$ for time intervals $(0, 1)$ and $(0, 1)$, respectively. $Ra2$ fails to accomplish anything because B is not the owner of track $B \rightarrow D$. When $Rb2$ attempts to reserve track $B \rightarrow A$ for the time interval $(0, 1)$, it fails since train Ta has already reserved that interval. Therefore, station A reserves the next available time interval $(1, 2)$ for train Tb. Train Tb updates its reservation packet for the secondary path as shown through the compact representation [B@0/1][A@2/X][C@X/X], which implies that train Tb waits at station B from time 0 to 1, then proceeds to station A at time 2, and then departs from A at time 2 to arrive at station C at time 4. Train Tb is restricted from reserving tracks beyond station C by the lookahead value of 2, and this is reflected by the subfield [C@4/X] where X implies unknown. Each subfield of the compact reservation packet represents [station name@arrival time/departure time (X implies unknown)]).

Figure 3.33(c) represents the subsequent propagation of the reservation packets. $Ra1$ and $Rb1$ successfully reserve tracks $C \rightarrow E$ and $D \rightarrow E$ for time intervals $(2, 4)$ and $(2, 8)$, respectively. $Ra2$ fails to reserve the time interval $(1, 3)$ on track $B \rightarrow D$, as train Tb has already reserved the interval $(0, 2)$. Train Tb is allowed reservation for the time interval $(2, 4)$; its compact reservation representation is [A@0/0][B@1/2][D@4/X]. $Rb2$ succeeds in reserving track $A \rightarrow C$ for the time interval $(2,4)$.

All of the reservation packets $Ra1$ through $Rb2$ have successfully reserved the last track under lookahead $= 2$ and are returned to the respective trains Ta and Tb at stations A and B, respectively. At node A, train Ta notes that the total time to reach destination E through the primary path is 4. The secondary path requires 4 time units to reach D, and the extra travel time to destination E will demand at least 6 time units, implying a total travel time of $4 + 6 = 10$

time units. Clearly, train Ta selects the primary path, i.e., $A \rightarrow C \rightarrow E$, as the best choice and then propagates a reservation removal request to the stations contained in $Ra2$. For train Tb, the primary path requires 8 time units to reach destination E. The secondary path requires 4 time units to reach C, and the extra travel time to destination E will demand at least 2 time units, implying a total travel time of $4 + 2 = 6$ time units. Therefore, train Tb selects the secondary path, i.e., $B \rightarrow A \rightarrow C$, and propagates a reservation removal request to free reservations that it had earlier acquired along the primary path.

Figure 3.33(d) represents RYNSORD when the trains Ta and Tb have started to travel and the reservation removal requests have been processed. It may be noted that following removal of the reservation for train Ta on track $A \rightarrow B$, conceivably train Tb may be permitted to travel earlier than its reserved time interval of (1,2).

3.2.3 Modeling RYNSORD on an Accurate, Realistic, Parallel Processing Testbed

The key contribution of RYNSORD is in distributing the overall task of routing all trains through the network among all the entities in the system—trains and station nodes. Thus, in reality, for a given railway network with N trains and S stations, the total number of coordinating computing engines is $(N+S)$. To understand its performance and its dependence on different factors, RYNSORD is first modeled and then simulated on a parallel processing testbed that is constituted by a network of workstations configured as a loosely coupled parallel processor. The simulation coupled with the testbed virtually resembles a real implementation with one exception. To facilitate the simulation of a realistic system, i.e., with a reasonable number of trains, while every station node is represented by a workstation, the trains are modeled as tasks and executed by the workstations underlying the stations. When a train is located at a host station, its computations are performed by the underlying workstation, and its communication with other stations is carried out through this station. When a train travels from the current station (say, A) to another station (say, B), the corresponding train task in the underlying workstation for A is encapsulated through a message, propagated to B, and remanifested as a train task in the underlying workstation at B. Thus, trains move in the simulation at electronic speeds instead of their physical speeds, and a train's computation and communication subtasks are executed on the host station's underlying workstation.

While trains propagate at approximately 120 miles/hour, the underlying, fast, computing engines of the testbed enable the simulation to execute many times faster than reality. This, in turn, facilitates the rapid performance evaluation of RYNSORD for different values of the parameters. The basic unit of time in the simulation is termed a *timestep*, and it defines the finest resolution of train movements. Thus, while the smallest distance traveled by any train is limited to that within the interval of one timestep, a train must wait at

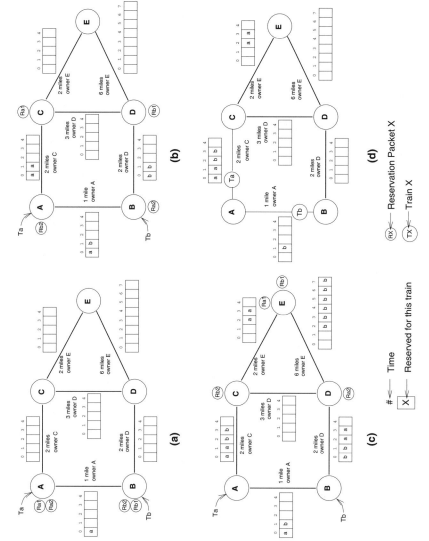

Fig. 3.33. Initiation and Progress of Reservation Processing

a station for at least 1 timestep if it has not received the necessary reservations to commence travel. In the current implementation of RYNSORD, the timestep value is set to 1 minute of actual operation. The principal reasons for this choice are, (1) the distance traveled by the fastest train, namely 2 miles, is significantly smaller than the shortest track length of 50 miles and (2) relative to processing a reservation for N tracks, all necessary computing and electronic communication between stations and trains may be accomplished within 1 minute. While a train requires on the order of minutes to travel a single track, a message propagation and computing function only requires on the order of 10 milliseconds. RYNSORD permits trains to be introduced into the system asynchronously, i.e., at irregular intervals of time. In addition, the trains themselves are autonomous and, therefore, their decisions are executed asynchronous with respect to each other. Furthermore, the testbed consists of heterogeneous workstations that may have differing clock speeds. Therefore, for consistency and accuracy of the propagation of the trains in the system, RYNSORD requires that the timestep values of every station node and train be synchronized. This guarantees that if two trains, Ta and Tb, reach their destination, station E, at actual times 12:01 P.M. and 12:05 P.M. (say), in the corresponding RYNSORD model, Ta must arrive at E prior to Tb, despite differing processor and communications link speeds. Synchronization is achieved in RYNSORD through an asynchronous, distributed, discrete-event simulation technique using null messages [27] [80] and is not detailed here.

The previously stated assumption that all message communications and decision processes relative to a reservation request must be completed within a timestep, implies the following. If a train Ta at station A initiates a reservation packet at timestep t_1 and propagates it to other appropriate stations $(X, Y, Z, \ldots)$, the reservation packet must be processed at the appropriate stations and returned to Ta at A prior to advancing the timestep value at A and every workstation underlying the stations $(X, Y, Z, \ldots)$ to timestep value $t_1 + 1$. To achieve this objective, RYNSORD employs a special, synchronizing node that is connected to all station nodes. It monitors whether all necessary communications and responses corresponding to all reservations that are launched out of the stations, if any, are completed before permitting the station nodes to increment their timestep values. The special synchronizing node in RYNSORD is an artifact of the parallel simulation on the testbed and has no counterpart in reality. In an actual railway network, electronic communication and computations will require approximately 10 to 100 milliseconds within which the fastest train will have traveled a mere 18 feet of track. Thus, for all practical purposes, communications and computations are instantaneous.

The basic functionalities of every station node and the special synchronizing node are encapsulated in pseudocode as shown in Figures 3.34 and 3.35, respectively.

RYNSORD requires four types of communication messages:

```
while simulation is not finished {
  send out reservation requests
  while not done {
     process incoming trains
     process incoming reservation requests
     process incoming reservation responses
     if received responses to all reservation requests
         send done to synchronization node
     if received update from synchronization node
         set done to true
  }
  update internal time
}
```

Fig. 3.34. Functionality of a Station Node in Pseudocode

```
while simulation is not finished {
   while not done {
      if received done from station node
          increment count
      if count is equal to number of stations
          set done to true
   }
   send update to all stations
   update internal time
}
```

Fig. 3.35. Functionality of the Special Synchronizing Node

1. to represent reservation packets that are initiated and launched by trains;
2. to model the encapsulation and propagation of trains from one station to the subsequent station;
3. to allow a train to negotiate with the owner station for earlier than the scheduled travel on the subsequent track if it arrives early at a station at the head of the track; and
4. to allow a station to grant permission to a train to travel on a track immediately.

Reservation packets are assumed to propagate without any delay, i.e., within the same timestep. Once received at a station, they are processed immediately and within the same timestep. The final approved reservation packets are returned to the originating trains within the same timestep. At the originating station, initially a train lacks a reservation packet. It creates and then launches the reservation packet. Upon receiving the approved reservation packets, the train selects one of them as its best choice, which thereafter becomes its reservation packet. The reservation packet, however, is only good for N subsequent tracks and the train will need to repeat the process until it reaches its final destination. A reservation packet is characterized by five fields, which are enumerated and explained as follows:

1. **Station list:** The complete station list, including the station ID, arrival time, and departure time, for each station.
2. **Status:** The status of the reservation (i) RESERVING if the reservation packet is traveling forward through its station list attempting to make reservations; (ii) REMOVING if the reservation removal packet is propagating forward while releasing the previously granted reservations; or (iii) ACCEPTED if the reservation packet is returning to the originating train.
3. **Train ID:** The unique identification number for the train. The ID = (originating station ∗ 100,000) + time at which the train is introduced into the system.
4. **Train speed:** The speed information is necessary when the station must modify the reservation time for the train because the original request cannot be satisfied. The speed information is used to compute the travel time over the track.
5. **Reservation ID:** The unique identification number for the reservation.

Because a train may require a substantial amount of travel time from one station to the next, the train packet is not assumed to propagate instantaneously. In fact, every train packet is labeled with a timestamp value, which represents the timestep at which it is expected to arrive at the destination station. Upon receiving a train packet, a station node stores it in a buffer until the timestamp value of the packet equals the station's own timestep value. Then the train is assumed to have arrived at the station node, and further processing is initiated. A train packet consists of six fields that are enumerated and detailed here:

1. **Timestamp:** The expected arrival time of the train at the receiving station.
2. **Train ID:** The unique identification number for the train. The ID = (originating station ∗ 100,000) + time at which the train is introduced into the system.
3. **Origin:** The originating station of the train.
4. **Destination:** The final destination station of the train.
5. **Path:** A sequential list of the tracks traveled by the train for the purposes of data collection and analysis.
6. **Reservation:** The reservation packet associated with this train.

Because a train may request cancellation of previously approved reservations for tracks along a path when it decides to select an alternate path, conceivably, a train arriving at a station may find its subsequent track unoccupied. For efficient use of tracks, the train must be allowed to travel along the track, if possible. To achieve this objective, when a train arrives at a station before its scheduled departure time from that node, it generates and propagates a waiting packet to the station that owns the track. After receiving the waiting packet, the corresponding owner station queues the train. At every timestep, the station examines whether the track is free and notes the number of timesteps (say Q) for which the track is unreserved. The station then selects from the queue a train that may successfully complete the travel within Q timesteps and that has been waiting the longest. The station sends a permission packet to the train, allowing it to use the track immediately and removes the corresponding entry from the queue. The waiting packet consists of four fields, as shown here:

1. **Train ID:** The unique identification number for the train. The ID = (originating station ∗ 100,000) + time at which the train is introduced into the system.
2. **Train speed:** The train's speed, which is needed to calculate the travel time over the subsequent track.
3. **Wait start time:** The timestep at which the train arrives at the station, earlier than its scheduled departure time, and is queued.
4. **Location:** The station, at the head or tail of a track, where a train is waiting. This information is used by the station that owns the track to direct the permission packet, if and when necessary.

The permission packet contains a single field:

1. **Train ID:** The unique identification number for the train. The ID = (originating station ∗ 100,000) + time at which the train is introduced into the system.

To facilitate understanding the distributed, dynamic routing of trains in RYN-SORD and the impact of different parameters on the performance of RYN-SORD, a visual display of the operation of RYNSORD is achieved through its use of a graphical front end. The graphics supports the following characteristics.

- Developing and editing a railway network.
- Viewing a replay of a simulation run.
- Monitoring and interacting with the simulation at run time.
- Viewing statistical information related to the input traffic, results, and run-time performance of a simulation run.

The run-time display also shows the following parameters.

- The location of the train.
- The cumulative number of reservations processed at each station.
- The number of trains waiting at each station.
- The cumulative number of reservations propagated along every segment, categorized by type—Reserving, Removing, or Accepted.
- The cumulative number of trains that have propagated over each track.

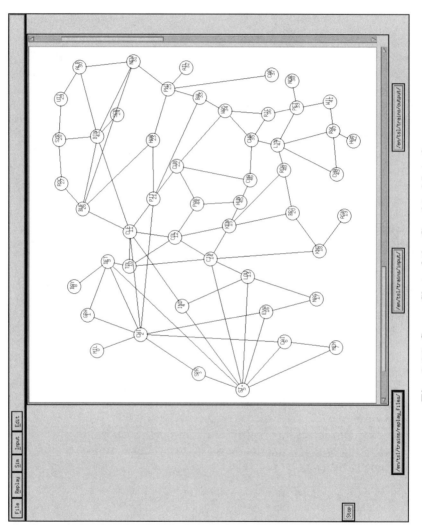

Fig. 3.36. Screen Shot of the Graphical Interface

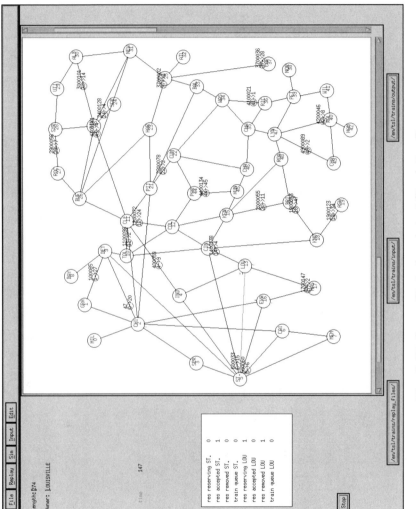

Fig. 3.37. Screen Shot of an Actual Simulation Run

Figure 3.36 presents a screen shot of the graphical interface that displays the 50-station railway network detailed in Figure 3.38. In Figure 3.36, each station is labeled by the first three characters of its name and its unique identification number. Stations and links are easily added or deleted directly through this interface and the graphical program will reconfigure RYNSORD, automatically and correctly, to execute the simulation accurately. Figure 3.37 presents a screen shot of an actual simulation run. The trains are described through circles and are located on top of the tracks on which they are traveling. They are identified by their respective identifiers, origins and destinations. During an actual simulation run, a user may interactively communicate with any of the stations, retrieve any desired data structure and information, and generate and introduce trains into the system at any timestep and at any station.

3.2.4 Implementation Issues

The RYNSORD model and simulator are written in C and are designed to execute on a heterogeneous network of Unix-based workstations connected through a 10-Mbit/sec Ethernet and configured as a loosely coupled parallel processor. The workstation mix includes Sun Sparc 1, Sparc 2, and Sparc 10 under Sun OS 4.1.2 and Sun Solaris 5.3 operating systems and Intel 486DX2/66 and Pentium under the freely available and copyrighted Linux operating system. Station nodes and trains are modeled through processes and communicate through TCP/IP. The code segment for every station, including the trains located at it, is approximately 1700 lines of C code, and the networking code is approximately 1000 lines of C code. The simulator is complied by the public domain GNU C compiler, gcc, and executed at a low priority in the background, using the "nice" utility. It may be noted that the workstations may be executing primary jobs for the users at the consoles. With 50 Sun Sparc 10 workstations executing concurrently, the average execution time of a single simulation experiment is approximately 2 hours of wall clock time.

RYNSORD is an application program built on top of the transport layer, TCP/IP. By definition, the layers in the ISO-OSI model starting with the session and beyond are responsible for any required data conversion while communicating between two or more machines. Because Intel 80X86 machines use Little Endian model and Sun Sparc machines utilize the Big Endian model [107], the necessary conversion of data in the heterogeneous network of workstations is achieved through the use of n-to-h l (network-to-host long integer), n-to-h s (network-to-host short integer), h-to-n l (host-to-network long integer), and h-to-n s (host-to-network short integer) utilities [117].

In this section, a subset of the eastern United States railroad network is selected, based on the existing primary railroads in the eastern United States, as shown in the 1994 *Rand McNally Commercial Atlas*. A few additional tracks are added to represent a few secondary railroad segments. Figure 3.38 presents the representative railway network, which consists of 50 major stations, 84 track segments, and a total length of 14,469 miles of track. A model of the network in Figure 3.38 is developed in RYNSORD, and the simulation is executed on a network of 50 workstations with one station being executed on a workstation.

To obtain representative performance results, a number of experiments are executed with input trains generated stochastically and asserted into RYN-SORD. Guidance relative to the choice of density of train traffic, i.e., the number of trains introduced into the system per unit timestep, is obtained from the actual number of freight trains per 365 day-year that utilize the tracks of the eastern United States railroad. For the experiments in this section, three train traffic densities are selected—low, medium, and high. For low, medium, and high traffic densities, the probabilities that a train is generated within a timestep, i.e., 1 minute of real time, are set at 0.075, 0.15, and 0.30, respectively. For every train originating at a station, train speeds are generated stochastically; they range from 60 to 100 mph. The final destination is also generated stochastically by assigning equal weight to every station, except the originating station, and selecting a station at random. Geographic proximity plays no part in the selection process. Because major stations, corresponding to major urban cities, are more likely to encounter high traffic densities, a set of nine high-traffic stations are selected from Figure 3.38. They include Chicago, Detroit, St. Louis, Philadelphia, New York, Washington, Pittsburgh, Columbus, and Cincinnati. For the stations corresponding to these cities, the input train traffic densities are assumed to be doubled. Also, during the process of selecting final destinations of trains, these cities are assigned twice the weight of other stations.

The representative railway network is simulated more than 150 times under different scenarios and for different parameters. Every simulation is executed for 10,080 timesteps, which corresponds to one week of real-time operation. As indicated earlier, while a typical simulation experiment executes for approximately 2 hours of wall clock time, the longest running of the 50 workstations often executes for 7 hours. Input trains are introduced throughout every simulation run at a constant and uniform rate that is set at the start of the simulation. Table 3.4 presents the cumulative number of trains introduced into the system and the estimated cumulative miles traveled by the trains, for each of the low, medium, and high input train densities. The estimate is based on the assumption that every train actually travels along the shortest path from the origin to destination, which may not be true in every case.

3.2.5 Simulation Data and Performance Analysis

To understand the performance of RYNSORD, first the independent parameters and key performance measures are identified and a number of simulation experiments are executed on the realistic railway network presented in Figure 3.38. The independent parameters include (1) the number of trains asserted

88

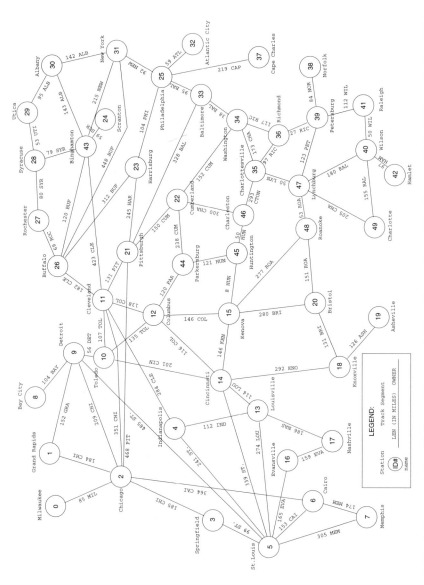

Fig. 3.38. A Representative Railway Network: A 50-station subset of the Eastern United States Railroad Network

Input Traffic Density	Cumulative Trains Introduced in RYNSORD	Estimated Cumulative Distance Traveled by All Trains (miles)
Low	484	288,860
Medium	869	497,658
High	1,772	1,033,123

Table 3.4. Input Train Traffic Parameters

into the system; (2) the density of trains, i.e., the frequency with which the trains are input into the system; and (3) the lookahead employed. To evaluate the role of soft reservations objectively, this section also implements a competing distributed routing algorithm, referred to as approach B. Approach B is similar to RYNSORD in all respects except that it employs the traditional hard reservations policy. A train first sends out a hard reservation request for the primary path. The stations, in sequential order, will try to reserve the requested track at the desired timesteps. If successful, the train uses the approved tracks of the primary path. Otherwise, if any of the tracks are busy, the reservation request is denied and immediately returned to the train at the originating station. Under these circumstances, the train then sends out hard reservation request on the secondary path. If this also fails, the train must wait a minimum of one timestep before initiating another request to the primary path. This process continues until the train is able to acquire reservation and move forward. Conceivably, a train may have to wait at a station prior to acquiring reservation approval. If the reservation request is successfully approved, the train moves along the N consecutive tracks.

The key performance measures include (1) the travel time of trains, averaged over all trains arriving at their destinations; (2) the percentage of trains reaching their destinations; (3) the distribution of the number of hops (tracks) used by the trains; (4) the average number of hops traveled by the trains as a function of the lookahead; (5) the travel time of individual trains as functions of the times of their assertion into the simulation; and (6) the track utilization. Furthermore, to understand the importance of distributing the overall computation and communication tasks among all entities, three additional performance measures are defined. They include the distribution of computations performed by the trains, the distribution of the numbers of reservations processed by the stations, and the maximum communication rate of the interstation links.

Figure 3.39(a) presents a plot of the (actual travel time of a train minus its ideal travel time), averaged over all trains, as a function of the lookahead size. The ideal travel time of every train is used as a reference and it refers to the travel time that a train would require if it was the only one in the entire system and could proceed to its destination along the shortest path unhindered by other trains. Clearly, with other trains in the system, a specific train may not succeed in acquiring reservation for and traveling on the tracks along its short-

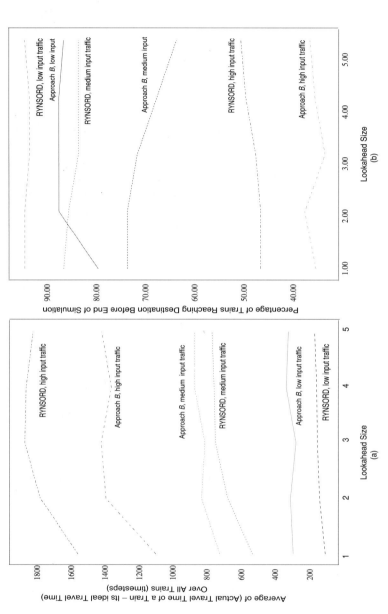

Fig. 3.39. (a) Average over All Trains of (Actual Travel Time of a Train Minus Its Ideal Travel Time), as a Function of the Lookahead, and (b) Percentage of Trains Reaching Their Destinations within the Maximum Simulation Time

est path. Figure 3.39(a) shows six graphs, corresponding to RYNSORD and approach B for each of the three densities. For low and medium input traffic densities, RYNSORD's performance consistently exceeds that of approach B. Figure 3.39(a) reveals that the average travel time of trains increases modestly with increasing lookahead size. For high traffic density, the relatively poor performance of RYNSORD compared to approach B is an aberration that may be explained by the graphs in Figure 3.39(b). Figure 3.39(b) plots the percentage of trains reaching their destinations prior to the termination of simulation, for both RYNSORD and approach B and for all three densities. As the density increases, the consequent greater congestion is responsible for lowering the percentage of trains that are able to finish their journeys. Also, in every case, a greater percentage of trains reach their destinations under RYNSORD than approach B, implying the superiority of soft reservations. Furthermore, because significantly fewer trains reach their destinations in approach B under high traffic density than with RYNSORD, the corresponding travel time graph for approach B in Figure 3.39(a) fails to include trains that run to farther destinations and is therefore skewed.

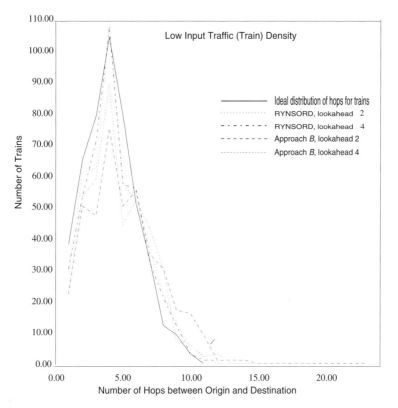

Fig. 3.40. Distribution of Actual Number of Hops for Trains in RYNSORD vs. Approach B vs. Ideal Distribution

Figure 3.40 shows a plot of the hop (track) distribution of trains, i.e., the number of tracks, ranging from 1 to 20, that are used by the trains to reach their destinations, corresponding to low input traffic density. Figure 3.40 shows five graphs, one corresponding to the ideal scenario, two relative to RYNSORD for lookahead values of 2 and 4, and two corresponding to approach B for lookahead values of 2 and 4. The ideal scenario, described earlier, refers to the computation of the ideal paths that trains would take if every train was assumed to be the only one in the system. Under actual conditions simulated on the testbed, it is highly probable that most trains will fail to acquire reservations for every track of their ideal paths because there will be demand for them from competing trains. In sharp contrast, the graphs obtained from the simulation show that the hop distribution closely follows the ideal scenario. That is, despite 484 trains competing for tracks, RYNSORD's distributed, dynamic routing with soft reservation yields results that are close to ideal. The graphs are especially revealing for the following reason. There is a belief in the technical community that while distributed algorithms may yield faster results, in general, the quality of the distributed solution cannot approach that obtained from centralized algorithms. This belief is fueled by the fact that in distributed algorithms, local agents execute the decision making but are allowed access to only a fraction of the systemwide data. The results from the rigorous RYNSORD simulation unquestionably refute the generality of the belief. RYNSORD shows that under certain circumstances, distributed algorithms may yield very high-quality solutions quickly. The author's research group is currently engaged in studying a new mathematical framework to extract distributed algorithms from centralized descriptions of problems. The graphs also reveal the superiority of RYNSORD's soft reservation over approach B's hard reservations.

The graphs in Figures 3.41(a) through 3.41(c) contrast the hop distribution of RYNSORD under different lookahead values relative to the ideal scenario for low, medium, and high traffic densities. The RYNSORD graphs in each of the figures differ slightly from one another, implying that the impact of lookahead on the hop distribution is modest. Furthermore, with increasing traffic densities, the hop distributions increasingly deviate from the ideal scenario, implying that the increased competition for the tracks causes individual trains to select tracks other than those along the shortest paths from the origin to the destinations. In each of the figures, the graphs corresponding to lookahead 2 reveal that a small but nontrivial number of trains require excessive number of hops. This is due to double-backs, i.e., where a train oscillates back and forth between two or more stations, attempting to negotiate a suitable route to its destination. Despite the fact that this normally implies inefficiency of track usage, results from Figure 3.41(a) show that trains under lookahead 2 generally reach their destinations faster. The occurrence of double-backs decreases substantially with higher lookahead values.

Figure 3.42 reports on the effort to study the impact of lookahead size on the average number of hops (tracks) for RYNSORD and approach B, for

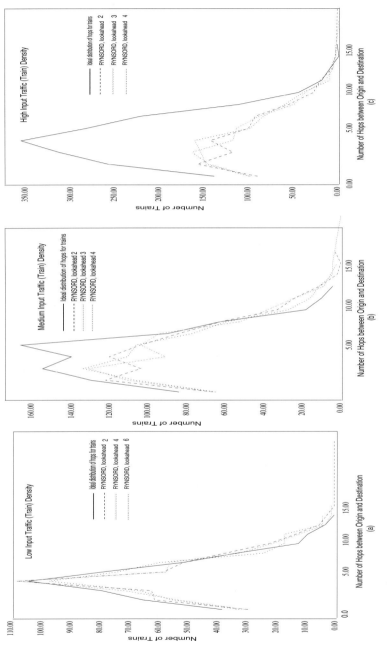

Fig. 3.41. Distribution of Actual Number of Hops for Trains in RYNSORD vs. Ideal Distribution under (a) Low Input Train Density, (b) Medium Input Train Density, and (c) High Input Train Density

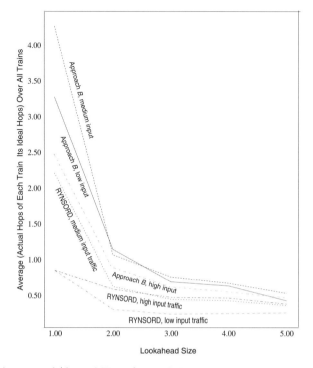

Fig. 3.42. Average of (Actual Hops for Each Train Minus Its Ideal Hops) Over All Trains, as a Function of Lookahead

each of the three input traffic density values. Once again, for every train, the ideal number of hops is computed and utilized as the standard against which the actual number of hops used by the train is contrasted. The graphs for all three density values in RYNSORD appear to converge to a small value that is slightly lower than the corresponding value for approach B, once again demonstrating the superiority of soft reservations. Furthermore, for lower lookahead values in every case in Figure 3.42, the average number of hops relative to the ideal hop count is significantly higher. This corroborates the earlier finding that lower lookahead encourages frequent switching of tracks in the course of routing, and trains traverse more tracks in the process.

Figures 3.43(a) through 3.43(c) present the tuples ((actual travel time of a train minus its ideal travel time), (time of assertion of the train into the system)) for all trains that reach their destinations. Figures 3.43(a) through 3.43(c) correspond to low, medium, and high input traffic densities, respectively. In general, as more trains compete for tracks, trains will require longer to reach their destinations. This is reflected by the increasing timestep scales along the y-axes from Figure 3.43(a) to Figure 3.43(c). For low input traffic density, most trains reach their destinations regardless of their time of assertion into the system, and this is reflected by the relatively uniform distribution

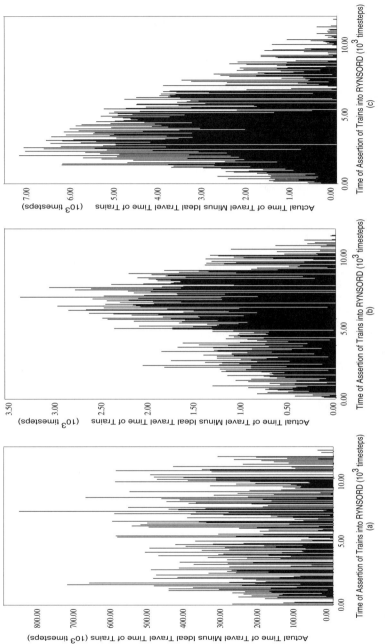

Fig. 3.43. Actual Travel Time of a Train in RYNSORD Minus Ideal Travel Time for Lookahead 4 as a Function of Assertion Time of the Train in, (a) Low Input Traffic Density, (b) Medium Input Traffic Density, and (c) High Input Traffic Density

in Figure 3.43(a). While the plot in Figure 3.43(b) exhibits modest cutoff at high values of assertion time, i.e., 10,000 timesteps, that for Figure 3.43(c) is quite severe. This reflects the fact that under higher input traffic densities, a train, Ta, that is asserted later into the system relative to another train, Tb, may require more time for travel than Ta and, under certain circumstances, it may not succeed in completing its journey within the maximum allowed simulation time. Clearly, to achieve a stable, continuously running system with minimal cutoff, one must select an appropriate input traffic density.

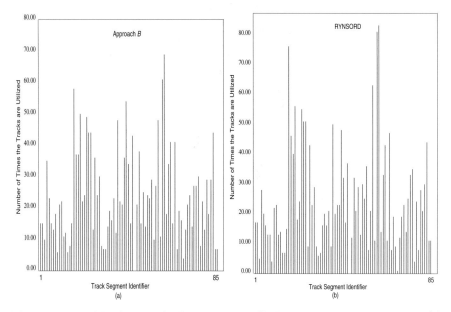

Fig. 3.44. Track Utilization for Low Input Traffic Density and Lookahead 6 in, (a) Approach B, and (b) RYNSORD

Figures 3.44(a) and 3.44(b) present track utilization results, i.e., the cumulative number of times every track is utilized by trains, for approach B and RYNSORD. Track segments are identified by unique identifiers 1 through 84. While most of the tracks are utilized reasonably, reflecting efficient resource utilization, a few tracks exhibit high utilization which merely reflects the stochastic destinations of trains and the choice of the high traffic stations. The track utilization plot in Figure 3.44(b) is observed to be, in general, higher than that in Figure 3.44(a), implying the superiority of RYNSORD's soft reservation system over the hard reservation system in approach B.

Figures 3.45(a) and 3.45(b) present the track utilization for high input traffic density and, clearly, it is significantly higher than that for low input traffic density in Figure 3.44(b). However, the track utilization in RYNSORD is not significantly affected by the choice of lookahead value.

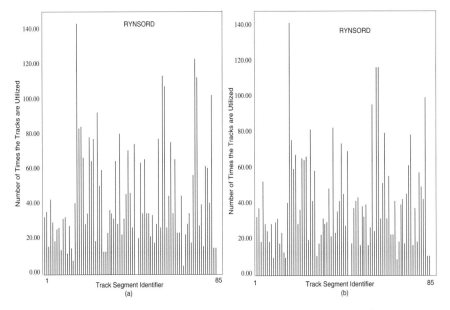

Fig. 3.45. Track Utilization in RYNSORD for Medium Input Traffic Density in (a) Lookahead 2, and (b) Lookahead 4

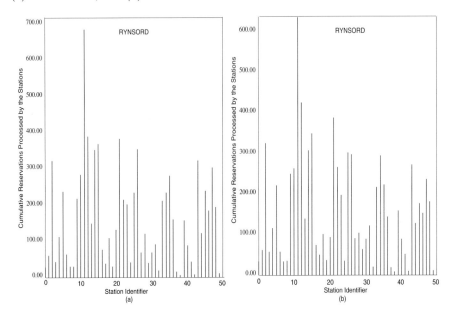

Fig. 3.46. Distribution of Reservations Processed by Stations in RYNSORD for Medium Input Traffic Density as a Function of Stations in (a) Lookahead 2, and (b) Lookahead 4

Figure 3.46 presents the distribution of a part of the overall computation task of routing the trains among the stations. A principal component of the overall computation task is reservations processing. While Figure 3.46(a) corresponds to lookahead 2, Figure 3.46(b) relates to lookahead 4. The computational load distribution among the stations is slightly higher for lookahead 2 than for lookahead 4. Although the individual trains, under low lookahead, execute Dijkstra's shortest-path computations more frequently, they reserve fewer stations at any given time. Both Figures 3.46(a) and 3.46(b) underscore the achievement of the original goal of efficiently distributing the overall task among the station nodes. The nonuniform distribution of the reservations processing is due to the stochastic destinations of trains that, in turn, affects their routing.

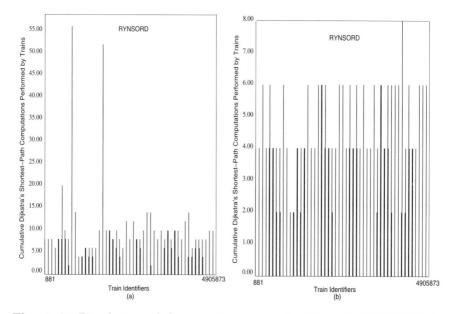

Fig. 3.47. Distribution of Computation among the Trains in RYNSORD for Medium Input Traffic Density for (a) Lookahead 2 and (b) Lookahead 4

Figure 3.47 presents the distribution of the remainder of the overall computation task, among the trains. A principal component of the overall task is the Dijkstra shortest-path algorithm execution by the trains for computing the primary and secondary paths. While Figure 3.47(a) corresponds to lookahead 2, Figure 3.47(b) relates to lookahead 4. Both Figures 3.47(a) and 3.47(b) underscore RYNSORD's original goal of efficiently distributing the overall task among the trains. In both Figures 3.47(a) and 3.47(b), with the exception of a few trains, the computational burden is uniform among most trains which underscores the achievement of equitable distribution of the overall task among all trains. The computational load in Figure 3.47(a) is significantly higher than that in Figure 3.47(b) since, under low lookahead, trains perform shortest-path computations more frequently.

Lookahead Value	Link Usage (%)	Total No. of Hops	Total No. of Double-backs	Average No. of Hops per Train	Average Time	Average Miles per Train	Average Waiting Time (timesteps)
1	27	2,313	321	5.039	122.11	620	113
2	27	2,053	17	4.483	151.91	627	119
3	27	2,026	5	4.443	164.24	619	137
4	27	2,029	3	4.450	170.56	627	136
5	27	2,046	2	4.458	182.01	620	151

Table 3.5. Comparative Impact of Lookahead on Performance Parameters in RYN-SORD under Low Input Traffic Density

Lookahead Value	Link Usage (%)	Total No. of Hops	Total No. of Double-backs	Average No. of Hops per Train	Average Time	Average Miles per Train	Average Waiting Time (timesteps)
1	52	4,656	1274	6.151	545.94	647	615
2	48	3,428	144	4.565	688.95	619	647
3	46	3,194	12	4.357	759.77	610	711
4	45	3,186	9	4.341	769.62	604	728
5	45	3,137	3	4.274	780.01	603	737

Table 3.6. Comparative Impact of Lookahead on Performance Parameters in RYN-SORD under Medium Input Traffic Density

Tables 3.5 and 3.6 present data collected from the simulations to assist in the understanding of the impact of lookahead on key performance measures. The *average time* refers to the travel time of trains relative to the ideal travel times and is computed as equal to ((sum over all trains of (actual travel time of a train minus its ideal travel time)) ÷ by the total number of trains). While Table 3.5 presents data for low input traffic density, Table 3.6 corresponds to medium input traffic density. In Table 3.5, for high lookahead values, the average travel time of trains increases and correlates to the commensurate increase in the average waiting time. The latter, in turn, is due to the fact that to reserve more tracks for increasing N, trains must wait longer at the host stations where they initiate reservations while communicating with more stations. However, the average number of hops decreases with increasing lookahead while the decrease in the number of double-backs is even more dramatic.

The contrast between low and high lookaheads is more pronounced in Table 3.6.

For low lookahead, the average travel time of trains and average waiting time are significantly lower. However, the average miles traveled by trains, the average number of hops, and the link usage are higher. In addition, the number of double-backs is particularly high. Trains under low lookahead have a restricted view of the systemwide congestion and are more likely to make poor long-term choices. However, they make routing decisions more frequently, and although this increases their computational burden, their decisions are up to date and superior as reconfirmed by the shorter average travel times. In contrast, trains under high lookahead are locked into tracks for longer periods of time and fail to take advantage of rapid dynamic changes in the systemwide track usage, as reflected by their longer average travel times. Nevertheless, their routing is more organized, requires fewer hops and less distance traveled, and virtually eliminates double-backs. Thus, where shorter travel times are of paramount importance and the cost of track usage is negligible, low lookahead values are logical. Where the cost of using tracks is appreciable relative to the idle waiting of trains at stations, a high lookahead value is recommended.

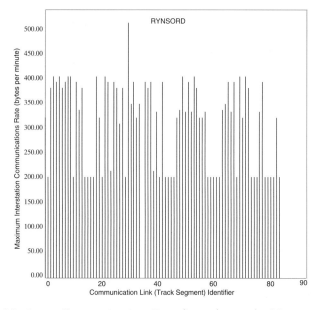

Fig. 3.48. Maximum Communications Rate (bytes/minute) of Interstation Links

A principal objective of RYNSORD is to minimize the intranetwork communications through distributing the overall computational task to the local entities. Figure 3.48 presents a plot of the maximum communications rate for every interstation communication link. Given that the resolution of the simulation is 1 timestep or 1 minute of real operation, the resolution of the data presented here is also limited to 1 minute. A maximum of 500 bytes/minute of data propagation is observed in Figure 3.48, which is easily realizable through commercial wireless modems rated at 9,600 or 19,200 baud. Thus, one of the principal objectives of RYNSORD is achieved. In contrast, a centralized algorithm would theoretically require a much higher communication rate implying expensive interfaces.

One limitation of the current RYNSORD implementation is that it does not model abrupt track failures. Conceivably, track failures may cause severe local congestions, which may spread to other parts of the network. While RYNSORD allows trains to use congestion information to replan their routes, its performance in the event of track failures warrants further study.

3.3 A Novel Architecture for Asynchronous, Hierarchical, International, Distributed, Real-Time Payment Processing

A key difficulty in international banking is that, despite the existence of the U.S. Federal Reserve System and equivalent central (or reserve) banks in other countries such as Canada, France, Germany, India, Japan, Switzerland, and the United Kingdom, an equivalent central (or reserve) bank system for the world has never been established by the United Nations (UN). Banks around the world use a variety of techniques to settle payments, using strategic alliances, local arrangements, limited credits, loss-sharing arrangements, and collaterals in the form of U.S. Treasury notes. This invariably results in arbitrary delays of months and lost interest suffered by users engaged in international business. Furthermore, as the number of international transactions is multiplied, the weakness of the current method of batch-mode transaction processing, employed by the central banks of the world's nations, begins to magnify. Such weaknesses include the (1) increased vulnerability, i.e., stress on the payment system leading to financial crisis, of a single central bank; (2) arbitrary delays, associated with each transaction processing; and (3) the lack of efficient scalability of the current banking system. For the benefit of the world economy, in which every country is a bona fide participant, this research argues that it is imperative to create an international federal reserve banking system.

This section introduces the NOVAHID approach to achieve real-time banking at the international level. NOVAHID is organized as a hierarchical approach. It is assumed, for economic, cultural, and geopolitical reasons, that the world's nations may be organized into unique and autonomous entities, termed *groups*. The lower level of the hierarchy consists of discrete "group-networks" where each group-network is synthesized from the equivalent Federal Reserve banking nodes of the nations served by the group-network. At the highest level of the hierarchy, representative entities of the groups are interconnected through a top-level network. The speed of local transaction processing, i.e., within a group-network, is likely to be much faster than the processing of international transactions that involve two group-networks and the top-level network. The hierarchy reflects the underlying assumption that a significant fraction of all transactions are local to the group-networks, and a relatively smaller fraction of all transactions transcends group boundaries. At its core, NOVAHID utilizes the principles of YADDES [118], which embodies the principle of an asynchronous, discrete-event simulation algorithm for cyclic circuits and mathematically guarantees the accuracy of the execution of events. Each banking transaction may be modeled as an event in a discrete-event simulation. NOVAHID guarantees the accuracy of every transaction and, hence, the accurate balance of every account at all times. That is, at any node, a transaction at time t_1, relative to a given account, is executed only when no other outstanding transactions in the system may affect the state of the given account prior to time t_1. This guarantee takes into account the assertion time of transactions and processing delays at the banking nodes and requires that nodes within a group be connected through a logical ring. As a result, banks will no longer be exposed to the risk of fraudulent or bad credits, and users are not denied complete access to their most recent balances. Unlike batch-mode processing, where no new transactions may be introduced after the normal operation hours so that accuracy in bookkeeping may be maintained, NOVAHID offers to any user, perhaps, for the first time, the banking privileges of withdrawal, deposit, and transfer anywhere and at any time in the world. This chapter also describes a model and implementation of NOVAHID on a loosely coupled parallel processor.

3.3.1 Introduction

The payment processing mechanism in most industrial nations resembles that used by the U.S. Federal Reserve system, with minor differences regarding the role of the central bank. As mandated by the U.S. Congress, the U.S. Federal Reserve system maintains the dual roles of (1) operation and competition and (2) regulating the payment system [119]. In France, the central bank plays a major operational role in the payment system on behalf of the banking system. It provides the payment infrastructure. In Canada and the United Kingdom, payment processing is largely carried out by private enterprises and the central bank simply coordinates the governing body constituted from the members of the financial sector and provides its books for settlement [120]. In addition, each nation adheres to its own notion of of daylight overdrafts, which refers to an intraday extension of credit by the central bank to a participating institution such that payment instructions of an account holder are honored even though there is an insufficient balance available in the account to fund the transaction when it is made. In the United States, daylight overdrafts are permitted generously to the tune of $70 billion, at no charge, although measures to charge a fee for use are being considered by the Federal Reserve

Board of Governors [119]. In Switzerland, the SIC [121] system eliminated the daylight overdraft system completely. In Japan [119], the central bank provides no daily overdrafts while private markets are permitted to provide for intraday liquidity.

Given such differences in the payment systems of different nations, it is logical to expect the lack of a uniform international payment processing system, as noted by Summers [119]. Thus, despite an average daily foreign exchange turnover of at least $650 billion, neither a uniform scheme nor a currency has been standardized for intercountry payments.

In general, international payments under open account terms in the banking system can take place in one of the two following categories: fund transfers and negotiable instruments. In addition, fund transfers include the submodes of cable transfer and mail payment order, while negotiable instruments may assume the form of bank drafts and business checks. The basic mechanics of the international payment procedures are identical for all four payment methods. Contrary to uninformed expectation, the currency involved in the payments do not actually move across the international borders. Rather, the payments are made via bookkeeping entries to the demand deposit accounts that the corresponding banks in different nations maintain with each other.

In general, in any given country, only the largest banks, i.e., those with substantial international presence, maintain foreign currency accounts with foreign banks. For example, Citibank of New York maintains a British sterling account with Barclays of London, while Barclays of London, in turn, maintains a U.S. dollar account with Citibank of New York. Foreign currency accounts held by U.S. banks in foreign banks are called *nostros accounts* ("our" account with other banks), while dollar accounts maintained by foreign banks in U.S. banks are termed *vostro accounts* ("your" account with the U.S.) [122]. International banking privileges, however, are not limited to the large international banks. Smaller regional banks may also access international banking privilege, at the cost of further intermediation, through the following mechanism. Consider, for example, that user A maintains an account (say, 1) at Last National Bank in Anytown, USA, and wishes to make a deposit of $1M to his/her daughter's account (say, 2) at Barclays Bank in London.

Under the current batch-mode transaction-processing scheme, such a transaction is queued for settlement first at the national level, i.e., through the U.S. Federal Reserve system, and then at the international level [122]. At the end of the current business day and prior to the following business day, when all the U.S. banks are off-line, the transaction amount—$1M—is subtracted from the reserve account that Last National Bank in Anytown, USA, maintains with its local federal reserve bank. This transaction is then relayed to the Federal Reserve Bank of New York where a credit is placed for Citibank. Then Citibank settles the transaction, issuing a credit to its nostros account with Barclays Bank. Upon receipt of the credit from Citibank, Barclays issues a credit to the destination account corresponding to the transaction. Barclays

Bank, a foreign bank, is not permitted to maintain a reserve account with the United States Federal Reserve system.

With the batch-mode scheme, the multistage processing for international transactions is not initiated until the end of the business day. In addition, the exact time required for completion of all of the steps depends (1) largely on the location of the originating and destination accounts and (2) on whether the banks are members of a private clearing network. In New York, for example, there is a private clearing house, CHIPS (Clearing House Interbank Payments systems), which is a network of major international banks. CHIPS is operated by the New York Clearing House Association, and it maintains an account with the Federal Reserve Bank of New York. Members of CHIPS settle transactions among themselves at the end of the day, and those banks with a net debit request the Federal Reserve to shift a part of the funds from their reserve holdings to the CHIPS account. Foreign banks that are not served by the Federal Reserve system normally acquire lines of credit from other members of CHIPS that are served by the Federal Reserve. Where both the payer, i.e., depositor of a transaction, and the payee, i.e., creditor of the transaction, hold accounts with banks that are part of the CHIPS network, settlement of a payment may take place within a day. Otherwise, settlement of international payments may vary from several days to weeks or months, depending on the payment clearance facilities available to the individual banks involved.

As the volume of transactions multiplies, the credit extended by the Federal Reserve system often exceeds billions of dollars, and occasional glitches such as power failures or computer errors compound to create extreme financial risks. This was exemplified by the Bank of New York (BONY) incident [120] that led to the largest overnight loan from the discount window at a value of $22.6 billion. In this case, the culprit was a computer program that somehow failed to accommodate an unusually large volume of transactions. BONY lost several million dollars in the form of interest payments from the overnight loan.

It has been estimated [123] that the size of the foreign exchange market may be approximated by an average daily turnover of $650 billion. The traditional settlement practices for foreign exchange contracts present special risks [124] because the payments and counterpayments are settled at different times in different countries.

Thus, the drawbacks of batch-mode processing include risk reliance on daylight overdraft, risk borne even by the payee from daylight overdrafts, and denial of immediate access to the funds from transactions. In addition, the current scheme relies heavily on (1) the assumption of trust that often translates into specified limits placed on withdrawal, (2) the deposit of collateral in the form of U.S. Treasury bills and others, and (3) explicit loss-sharing arrangements between the participating banks as in the case of Chase Manhattan Bank in Tokyo, which serves the Japanese and Asian interbank markets. As a specific example, consider the Chase Manhattan Bank in Tokyo [124] that operates a dollar-clearing arrangement to serve the Asian and Japanese interbank markets. Operating during the Tokyo business day ahead of the U.S. markets, Chase will enact debits and credits to its customers, at levels set by predetermined limits, throughout the day. Evidently, only those users who are Chase customers benefit from this arrangement, and this underscores the need for a more open international payment processing scheme, one that is easily accessible by any citizen of the world.

The inherent risk borne by the payer bank may be understood as follows. Consider that Bank A has transferred a billion dollars to Bank B. While the Federal Reserve issues a daylight overdraft on behalf of Bank A as a credit to Bank B, the billion dollars is not available to Bank B until the end of the day. Meanwhile, the billion dollars remains an asset to Bank A, which may use it for short-term lending purposes. The risk associated with this business decision is now borne not only by Bank A but by Bank B as well as by the Federal Reserve system.

A new approach to real-time domestic payments processing, NOVADIB, has been presented in the literature [125]. Under NOVADIB, the United States Federal Reserve system has been modeled and studied. The banking process is mathematically mapped to a discrete-event simulation system with feedback loops wherein deposits, withdrawals, and transfers are modeled as events that are introduced into the system asynchronously, i.e., at irregular intervals of time. The initiation of a transaction is analogous to the creation of an event. While NOVADIB achieves its aim of an integrated, real-time payment processing scheme for the United States Federal Reserve, it is limited. In NOVADIB, the Federal Reserve banks are connected through a single ring architecture, which although adequate for the United States, is inappropriate for an international payment processing system. First, merely expanding the ring to include the equivalent Federal Reserve banks of other nations may ultimately fail to deliver real-time performance. Second, from genuine concerns to protect privacy and other geopolitical reasons, the world's nations may want to exercise some form of localized control. Third, it is generally agreed that a significant number of transactions within a nation are local and only a relatively small fraction of transactions cross a nation's boundaries. Therefore, the underlying single ring architecture of NOVADIB may not be the logical choice.

This section presents a new architecture for international banking, NOVAHID. The remainder of this chapter is organized as follows. Section 3.3.2 presents the details on the NOVAHID approach, and Section 3.3.3 describes a model of a representative international banking model consisting of three group-networks and its operation. Section 3.3.4 describes the implementation details of NOVAHID and reports the performance results.

3.3.2 The NOVAHID Approach

The design of the NOVAHID architecture takes into account the following premises:

serve banking nodes of the group-network or a completely separate entity. It maintains the aggregate financial holdings of all banks that are served by the group-network. This entity is connected directly to every node of the group-network. At the top level of the NOVAHID hierarchy, the designated entities of the different groups are connected through a ring network and subject to the NOVADIB algorithm. Although international transactions originate in the group-networks, they are eventually asserted at the top-level network by the group-network where the transaction originates. The NOVADIB algorithm at the top-level network executes these transactions in an independent, asynchronous, and concurrent manner.

Thus, given an organization of, say, 15 groups, the NOVAHID approach consists of a total of 16 instances of the NOVADIB algorithm executing the 15 group-networks and the top-level network independently and asynchronously. For a group-network, external transactions are asserted at the equivalent Federal Reserve banking nodes by either local customers or the top-level network. Local transactions are processed by NOVADIB within the group-network such that causality, i.e., the time order, of the transaction-events is preserved. International transactions that are asserted by the group-networks to the top-level network are viewed by the NOVADIB algorithm at the top level as input transactions and are executed based on their times of assertion at the top-level network.

Consider the following example. Figure 3.49 illustrates a simple representative model based on the NOVAHID approach. The model consists of three groups, and for simplicity, the United States, the United Kingdom, and Japan, each of which is served by only two equivalent Federal Reserve banks, termed as group-nodes in this chapter. Assume, for simplicity, that the group-networks for the United States, the United Kingdom, and Japan consist of the group-nodes {New York, Philadelphia}, {London, Glasgow}, and {Tokyo, Kyoto}, respectively. Thus, the lower level of the hierarchy consists of three unique group-networks, one for each group. The top-level network consists of three entities, termed Int-Nodes, each of which is connected to the nodes of the corresponding group-network.

While each of the group-nodes within a group-network maintains reserve account balances of all of the banks serviced by the group-network, every Int-Node maintains the aggregate account balances for all of the groups.

In this section, a transaction asserted either at a group-node or Int-Node is synonymously termed an *event*. One such event may be asserted at a group-node of a group either by one of the regional banks, served by the group-network, from another group-node within the group-network, or by its Int-Node corresponding to an international transaction asserted at a different group-network. The event received, say E_{Ai}^{Aj}, where Ai and Aj denote the payee and payer banks, respectively, may not always be executed immediately. This may be necessary to ensure that all events are executed chronologically. Consider two events, E_{Ai}^{Aj} and E_{Ak}^{Aj}, introduced into the system at two distinct nodes N_1 and N_2 of a group-network at time instants given by $t = t_1$ and

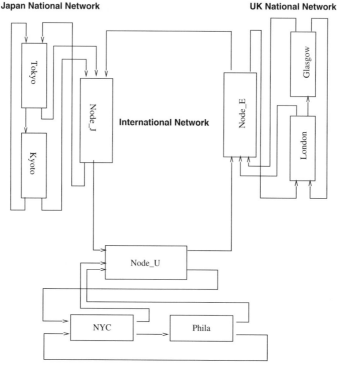

Fig. 3.49. A Representative NOVAHID Model Consisting of Three Groups, Each with Two Group-Nodes

$t = t_2$, respectively. While both transactions affect the same payer bank, A_j, it is necessary to preserve the logical order of the transactions. Because events are generated asynchronously, i.e., irregularly in time, and as the propagation of messages may experience arbitrary delays, the lack of enforcing the correct logical order of execution may result in serious accounting errors. The logical order of events may be determined as follows. Where $t_1 < t_2$, and the subsequent execution of E_{Ai}^{Aj} at N_1 results in the propagation of an event to N_2 at time $t = t_3$, where $t_3 < t_2$, then execution of E_{Ak}^{Aj} at N_2 must be deferred until the event propagated from N_1 is received and executed at N_2. In the case where $t_1 = t_2$, however, both transactions may be executed simultaneously. Furthermore, where the subsequent event caused by execution of E_{Ai}^{Aj} at N_1 is at $t = t_4$, and $t_4 > t_2$, then the execution of E_{Ak}^{Aj} at N_2 is deferred only until E_{Ai}^{Aj} has been executed and the subsequent event is propagated and received at a different group-node in the group-network. NOVAHID inherits the general philosophy of YADDES [118] in that events are executed consistent with the increasing order of their assertion times and an event E_i at $t = t_6$

is executed at a node, N_r, only when the execution of no other transaction in the NOVAHID network may cause a new event at N_r at time $t = t_7$ such that $t_7 < t_6$. In the absence of global knowledge of all transactions introduced into the NOVAHID network, and where each group-node receives a distinct set of external transactions, the conservative nature of the NOVADIB algorithm guarantees that all transactions are executed in the same logical order in which they are asserted at either a group-network or the top-level network. It is reasonable to expect that due to the extremely high volume of transactions in the system and the uniformity of the number of transactions at all group-nodes of all groups, at any instant of time, at least one transaction will be available for execution at every group-node. Thus, every group-node will continuously process payments, implying efficiency through concurrent processing.

It is noted that, in the present banking culture, often a transaction may be deliberately executed out of logical order in an attempt to maximize the number of transactions processed. That is, a bank may bump a big check to clear a number of smaller checks. Conceivably, transactions in NOVAHID may be additionally characterized by priorities, to address such cultural issues.

3.3.2.1 The NOVAHID Algorithm

In the NOVAHID architecture, each of the group-networks and the top-level network are executed by a unique instance of the NOVADIB algorithm. Although the executable behaviors of the different instances of the NOVADIB algorithm are identical, the results of their executions are different due to their unique input stimulus, position of the network within the hierarchy, i.e., whether it is a group-network or top-level network and the topology of the network. In addition, the instances are asynchronous and concurrent, and they interact through messages that encapsulate international transactions.

A brief motivation and description of the essential components of NOVADIB are presented to facilitate the operational understanding of NOVAHID. In payment processing, a transaction is asserted asynchronously by a customer. The transaction requires finite processing time at a banking node and may require to be forwarded to other banking nodes for further processing. NOVADIB models the transaction processing as a distributed discrete-event simulation wherein every transaction constitutes an event. In general, a distributed discrete-event simulation algorithm may execute into a deadlock when, in a system consisting of feedback loops, the execution of an event may not generate a subsequent event. This is a likely scenario in payment processing when the execution of a transaction does not affect a bank's net asset. For instance, when a check drawn on bank A and pertaining to the account of a different person is deposited by an individual into his or her account, also with bank A, the reserve account balance of bank A with the equivalent Federal Reserve banking node would remain unaffected. Under such circumstances, a subsequent event may not be generated following execution of this payment.

By design, NOVADIB avoids deadlock and achieves the successful distributed execution of the transactions.

The NOVADIB algorithm is organized into three distinct subsections—s-function, puc-function, and ppc-function. The primary goal of the s-function is to execute the payment-processing operations such as credit, debit, and updating balances. The s-function is incapable of accurately determining when an event may be executed. The puc- and ppc-functions determine when the actual execution of the s-function may be permitted in a deadlock-free manner and ensure the correctness of the event corresponding to the s-function. The puc- and ppc-functions, collectively, constitute the data-flow network and are referred to as pc-functions. Figure 3.50(a) presents a network of two nodes, A and B. The s-function represents the executable simulation models. Figure 3.50(b) shows the corresponding data-flow network in NOVADIB. A and B are either both Int-Nodes or both group-nodes of a group. In Figure 3.50(a), the solid lines indicate the flows of events, while the dotted lines represent the flow of acknowledgments.

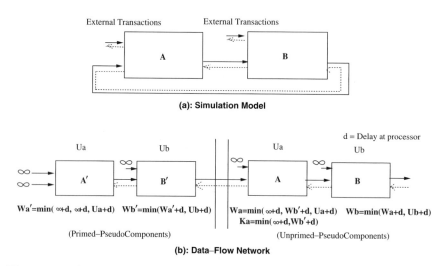

Fig. 3.50. NOVADIB Algorithm for a Group Network (or Top-Level Network) with Two Group-Nodes (or Int-Nodes)

The data-flow network in Figure 3.50(b) is synthesized as follows. First, the feedback arc set for the network is identified. For the network in Figure 3.50(a), the feedback arc set is, say, the solid line from the output of B to the input of A. Then an acyclic circuit, i.e., without any loops, is obtained by severing the solid line. Two copies of the acyclic circuit are then connected through a crossbar switch. The acyclic circuits on the left and right of the crossbar switch are termed pc- and puc-functions, respectively, and their components (mathematical entities) are marked $\{A', B'\}$ and $\{A, B\}$. For the network in

Figure 3.50(a), the crossbar switch reduces to a single connection from B' to A. An event at a banking node may either refer to an externally asserted transaction or an event asserted from a subsequent node. The solid line input to a node from another node represents the flow of events from a subsequent node. The unconnected solid line represents external inputs while the dotted input line refers to the flow of acknowledgments. The head of the event queue at a node, say A, is represented through the symbol U_A and is referred to as the U value. It signifies the time of assertion of the transaction that must be processed next.

Each component of the pc-function is required to compute a quantity time of next event (W') at its output line by applying the minimum operator over the W' values at its input lines and adding the propagation delay of the node. The quantity, W', reflects a measure of the time at which the next event is expected at that path. Similarly, every component of the puc-function must compute the time of next event (W) at its output line by applying the minimum operator over the W values at its input lines plus the propagation delay of the node. While the W' values of the pc-function are imprecise, the W values of the puc-function accurately take into account all appropriate events in either the group-network or the top-level network. The unconnected input lines of the components of pc- and puc-functions have their W' and W values set to infinity so that they may not influence other W' and W computations. A quantity, K, is computed using the accurate W values of the puc-function. When the K value for a node exceeds the U value at the node, the event at the head of the event queue for that node is executed. This condition implies that there is no transaction whose influence at the node can precede execution of the event at the head of the event queue. When a component of either the pc- or puc-function computes the W' or W value at its output line, any change from its previous value will trigger the W' or W computation of the subsequent component(s).

Consider the international payment processing network in Figure 3.49. It consists of three groups, each in turn, consisting of two group-nodes. The top-level network consists of the three Int-Nodes; Node-U, Node-E, and Node-J. While Figure 3.51 presents the s-function and data-flow network for the execution of the top-level network in NOVADIB, Figure 3.52 describes that for the United States group-network.

When a local transaction is asserted at a group-node or an international transaction is asserted at an Int-Node, the s-function for the node executes. It initiates the executions of the corresponding puc- and ppc-functions and then disengages itself. The ppc- and puc-functions execute asynchronously and concurrently with respect to each other and update their W' or W values. Any changes in the W' or W values relative to their previous values will cause other components to be initiated, and this process continues as long as the subsequent W' or W values change. Then the pc- and puc-functions propagate an acknowledgment to the s-function, following which the s-function determines whether the K value at the node exceeds the U value. If the result

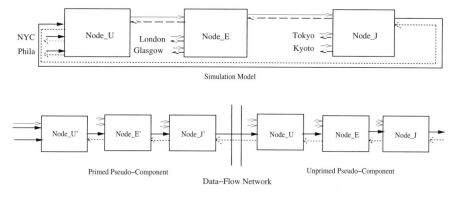

Fig. 3.51. Representation of the Top-Level Network in NOVADIB

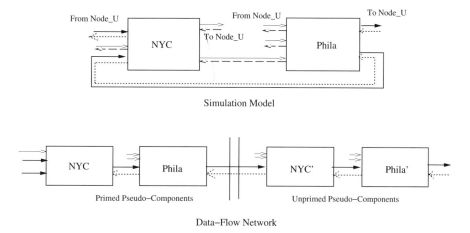

Fig. 3.52. Representation of the United States Group-Network in NOVADIB

of the comparison is affirmative, the transaction is executed. When a new event is generated, it is asserted at the subsequent node. Upon receipt of the new event, the subsequent node propagates back an acknowledgment. The original node receives the acknowledgment, removes the executed transaction from the event queue, and updates the U value. The updating is associated with another round of execution of the pc- and puc-functions, and the W' and W values are updated. The process continues until all externally asserted events at the nodes are exhausted. While new events and changes in W' and W are propagated from left to right, acknowledgments propagate in the reverse direction.

3.3.2.1.1 Execution of International Transactions

A local transaction, i.e., one whose influence is limited to the group, is processed by the corresponding NOVADIB algorithm. In contrast, international

transactions require execution of the NOVADIB algorithm corresponding to the group-network where the transaction originates, the NOVADIB algorithm in the top-level network, and the NOVADIB algorithm corresponding to the group-network where the transaction terminates. In addition, transaction and account information are transferred between the group-nodes and Int-Nodes. Within each group-network, each of the group-nodes maintains the most recent balances of all banks served by the group-network. Each of the Int-Nodes maintains the most recent aggregate balances for all of the participating groups. Thus, in Figure 3.49, Node_U, Node_J, and Node_E each carries the aggregate balances for Japan, the United States, and the United Kingdom. While a local transaction may affect the account balances of one or more banks served by the group-network and, therefore, the balances of the group-nodes, an international transaction may affect the account balances of individual banks, group-nodes, and Int-Nodes.

For simplicity and without any loss in generality, this section assumes that the international transactions are simple credits; that is, a credit is issued by a bank within a group-network for a destination account in a different group-network. The originating bank's balance is assumed to be automatically debited for the amount of the transaction. Upon successful completion, an international transaction in this section adds to the balance of the destination account. Simple debit transactions may be implemented as follows. Within a group-network, a debit transaction is processed identical to a credit transaction except that a test is conducted to verify that there is a sufficient balance in the account and, if so, the balance is reduced by the dollar amount. If the balance is insufficient, the transaction fails. International debit transactions are executed identical to international credit transactions with one exception. The transaction is first processed within the group-network, say A, where it originates and is propagated to the Int-Node for A. Within the top-level network, the transaction is processed. If the aggregate balance of the group-network, say B, that serves the payer bank is inadequate, the transaction fails immediately. If the balance of B is adequate, a subsequent event, e, of the transaction propagates to the Int-Node of B. This event causes an event to be propagated to B to ensure that the payer account balance is adequate. If the result is positive, the payer account balance is debited and e is executed. If, however, the payer account balance is insufficient, a subsequent event is generated to undo the effect of e at the top-level network. Other more complex transactions may be synthesized from a combination of simple credit and debit transactions. When a transaction, I_i, is asserted at a group-node by a bank, first the corresponding NOVADIB algorithm determines that I_i is an international transaction. Then it ensures that I_i is processed in the correct order, i.e., with respect to the time of assertion, with respect to other international transactions within the group-network. Next, I_i is propagated from the group-node to the corresponding Int-Node, say Node_U, of the top-level network. At the top-level network, the NOVADIB algorithm guarantees the execution of I_i in the correct order with respect to all other transactions within

the top-level network. When the execution of I_i at the top-level network is complete, the aggregate balance for the group with Int-Node Node_J say, is updated in each of the Int-Nodes—Node_J, Node_U, etc. Next, the transaction is propagated to the Japan group-network to update the appropriate destination account. Thus, the execution of I_i involves the asynchronous, concurrent, and cooperative executions of the NOVADIB algorithms corresponding to two group-networks and the top-level network.

3.3.2.2 Modeling NOVAHID on a Loosely Coupled Parallel Processor System

To study the performance issues through simulation, NOVAHID is modeled on a testbed, namely, a network of workstations, configured as a loosely coupled parallel processor system. The testbed closely resembles reality in that an international banking network will constitute a geographically distributed network of asynchronous, concurrent, and cooperative computing units. Every processor in the loosely coupled parallel processor is independent, asynchronous, concurrent, and maintains privacy of its own data except when it communicates information to other processors through messages. An additional benefit of the testbed is that, unlike a uniprocessor, the loosely coupled parallel processor is expected to deliver simulation results quickly.

The modeling of NOVAHID on the testbed, however, poses the following problem. Within every group-network, the external transactions asserted by the local customer and the transactions asserted by the top-level network (corresponding to international transactions generated in other group-networks) constitute the input stimulus. The corresponding NOVADIB algorithm guarantees that every external transaction as well as events generated subsequently as a result of execution of the transaction, are executed correctly. Because every NOVADIB algorithm instance is asynchronous, i.e., it executes as fast as possible, and the rate of its progress is a function of the speed of the underlying processors, the necessary and sufficient conditions for the guarantee are as follows:

1. The list of transactions must be logically consistent at every time instant.
2. The list of events at a group-node must never be empty except when all events that should have been executed at the group-node have, in fact, been executed.

If it happens that an event with assertion time t_1 is on its way from the top-level network to be executed at a group-node when the event queue at the group-node becomes empty, the NOVADIB algorithm will erroneously interpret that the group-node has completed execution. Also, if the event arrives too late, i.e., after the group-network has already executed other transactions with assertion times greater than t_1, NOVADIB will yield errors. In the distributed simulation, while all external transactions from local banks to

a group-network may be made available to the appropriate group nodes, the corresponding NOVADIB has no a priori knowledge of the international transactions that originate in other group-networks and arrive subsequently as new events. The same problem plagues the NOVADIB algorithm for the top-level network, i.e., it has no a priori knowledge of the international transactions that originate in the different group-networks. Without the knowledge, it is difficult for the NOVADIB algorithm at the top-level network to guarantee the accuracy of every transaction. Thus, if two international transactions, I_1 and I_2, originating at two different group-networks should be asserted to the top-level network at simulation times t_1 and t_2 $(> t_1)$, respectively, based on their assertion times, the delays due to the processing nodes, and the propagation delays of the links, I_2 may arrive earlier than I_1 in the simulation, causing a discrepancy.

It is pointed out that this problem is an artifact of the distributed implementation of NOVAHID on a loosely coupled parallel processor. First, different processors may execute and communicate at different speeds. Second, the clocks in the different parallel processors are not synchronized. Third, in the current implementation, all external transactions to a group-node are stored in its event queue. In reality, however, the clocks at all banking nodes will be synchronized to the Coordinated Universal Time (UTC) [126], so that each one will refer to the same Universal Time at the same instant. Every transaction will be ordered in time, i.e., time-stamped, by the absolute (UTC) value of its arrival time at a node. In addition, in an actual international banking network, the assertion of external transactions to the group-nodes must be implemented through independent processes that will continue to execute indefinitely along with the NOVADIB algorithms. These processes will receive the external transactions from the customers asynchronously. Thus, none of the NOVADIB algorithms executing either the group-network or the top-level network will either erroneously receive out-of-order transactions or misinterpret the termination of a group-node. Consequently, transactions will be executed in the correct order, on all of the networks.

For a better appreciation of the problem stated earlier, consider the following scenario. Ideally, a transaction received at $t = t_1$ at a node must be considered to have arrived earlier than a transaction received at the same node at $t = t_2$ $(> t_1)$. That is, the arrival time of a transaction at a node must determine its assertion time. In the simulation on the loosely coupled parallel processor, however, given the lack of a one-to-one correspondence between the actual arrival times of the messages at the destination nodes and the simulation times at which they are launched by the sending nodes, the notion of simulation time is encapsulated in a field associated with each transaction. Therefore, when a message arrives at a node, its assertion time is given by the contents of the field in the message. Now, when a network A receives a transaction T with an assertion time of t_1 from a different network B the assertion time, t_1, that was valid in B is no longer applicable within A. The reason is as follows. Assume that the nodes within A execute much faster

than those within B. Thus, within B transactions at times greater than t_1 may have already been executed. The arrival of T at A may cause it to be executed out of order with respect to other transactions within A leading to erroneous results.

This section proposes a mechanism to resolve this discrepancy by enforcing a common and uniform notion of simulation time across all group-networks and the top-level network. This will guarantee that all externally applied local and international transactions and the events, generated subsequently, are executed in the correct order, regardless of their origin. First, every group-network must be artificially forced to await the arrival of a subsequent international transaction, if any, before removing the previously executed international transaction and initiating the execution of other transactions. Otherwise, as stated earlier, the event queue for the appropriate group-node may either become empty or contain out-of-order events, thereby causing the NOVADIB algorithm to generate errors. This scheme of enforcing waiting is termed first *enforced wait*. Second, every group-network that may receive subsequent events due to international transactions originating in other group-networks must be aware a priori, i.e., supplied by the user statically, of the number of such transactions. Note that these requirements are simply artifacts of the distributed simulation and are absolutely unnecessary in an actual distributed international payment processing system.

For the top-level network, the exact number of international transactions expected from each group-network must also be known a priori. This information is statically stored in a file by the user and is read prior to initiating simulation. Furthermore, at the top-level network, a second enforced wait prevents initiation of the NOVADIB algorithm until at least one international transaction has been asserted at every Int-Node that expects one or more international transactions based on the a priori information. At every Int-Node, if the event queue is empty following completion of execution of an international transaction but more international transactions are expected, a third enforced wait prevents the NOVADIB algorithm from erroneously concluding termination of the Int-Node.

3.3.3 Modeling in NOVAHID

The representative international banking network in Figure 3.49 is modeled in NOVAHID, and its operational details are explained for a given set of transactions, tabulated in Figure 3.53. Assume that each group-network has a maximum of nine accounts. A total of four transactions are considered, originating at the group-nodes, NYC (New York City), Phila (Philadelphia), London, and Tokyo. The final account destinations for these transactions are coded as follows. Where a destination account value lies in the range 0 through 9, the transaction is referred to as *local*, i.e., it is restricted to the group-network where it originates. The first digit of a two-digit destination code refers to the group-network, where 1, 2, and 3 refer, respectively, to USA, UK, and

Japan. The second digit of the destination code refers to the actual account number within the appropriate group-network. Thus, transactions 1 and 2 originate from the USA group-network and are destined for accounts #0 and #5 within the UK group-network. Transaction 3, a local type, is destined for account #0. Transaction 4, originated in the Tokyo group-node of the Japan group-network, is destined for account #2 of the UK group-network. Furthermore, a propagation delay is associated with every pair of group-nodes, and it encapsulates the physical time required for a transaction to be processed by the computing entity at the sending node plus the time to propagate to the receiving node. Evidently, the propagation time within a group-network, assumed to be 20 time units in this research, is, in general, smaller than the corresponding time, i.e., 50 time units, for the top-level network. In this section, a transaction is represented by a triple {Origin, Time, Account Destination}. The Time field, as with all assertion times, is specified in simulation time units.

Transaction No.	Origin	Dollar Amount	Assertion Time	Acct. Destination
1	NYC	20	70	20
2	Phila	10	40	25
3	London	5	50	0
4	Tokyo	30	40	20

Fig. 3.53. Transactions Asserted at the NOVAHID Model

To facilitate understanding, each of the group-networks is examined and then the processes within the top-level network are analyzed.

U.S. Group-Network. There are two transactions to consider, namely, {NYC,70, 20} and {Phila,40,25}. As evident from their destination accounts, they are both international. Recall that given a transaction pending for execution with assertion time, $t = t_d$, at any given node in a group-network, its execution is permitted as long as there is not a transaction at another node with an assertion time less than $(t_d - 20)$. Thus, {NYC,70,20} may be executed provided that there is not a pending transaction at Phila with an assertion time less than $70 - 20 = 50$ time units. This, however, is false, and {NYC,70,20} may not be executed immediately. The execution of the transaction {Phila,40,25} on the other hand, may proceed because there is no NYC transaction with assertion time less than $40 - 20 = 20$. Note that the U.S. group-network does not expect any international transactions to be asserted at it. Therefore, execution of {Phila,40,25} results in the subsequent propagation of an event {Phila,60,25} to N_U, the corresponding Int-Node of the U.S. group-network.

Then, {NYC,70,20}, the only remaining transaction, is executed and the event {NYC,90,20} is propagated to N_U.

UK Group-Network. Although there is a single transaction, it is not executed because the group-network, upon accessing and reading the external file, realizes that it expects two international transactions to be asserted at its input. Therefore, this group-network is forced by the first enforced wait to remain idle until at least one of the two international transactions has been received.

Japan Group-Network. Because there is only one international transaction in this network, {Tokyo,40,20} is permitted to execute and propagate a subsequent event, i.e., {Tokyo,60,20} to N_J, the Int-Node corresponding to the Japan group-network.

Operation of the Overall NOVAHID Model

Each of the ten steps, Step 0 through Step 9, is illustrated in Figures 3.54 through 3.63.

0. At the start of the simulation, transaction packet 1 is asserted at the NYC group-node of the U.S. group-network, while transaction packet 2 is asserted at the Phila group-node. Transaction packet 3 is asserted at the London group-node of the UK group-network and 4 is asserted at the Tokyo node of the Japan group-network.

1. With the exception of 3, which is forced to wait until the arrival of at least one of the two expected international transactions at the UK group-network, all transactions are executed and the subsequent events are propagated to the top-level network. The subsequent events from 1, 2, and 4 are referred to as event packets 1, 2, and 4 respectively. A subsequent event, following execution of a transaction, refers to a change in the account balance. While this is true for the simple credit-type transactions, in general, for complex debit-credit transactions, a subsequent event may not always be generated.

2. As events with the lowest assertion times, 2 and 4 are executed at N_U and N_J, respectively. Their assertion times are increased by the propagation delay, 50 time units, and then propagated to the subsequent Int-Node in the top-level network. Event packet 2 is propagated to N_E and 4 to N_U.

3. Transaction packet 1, with the lowest assertion time, is executed in the top-level network. The subsequent event's assertion time is increased by 50 time units and then propagated to N_E.

4. Event packets 2 and 4 are executed at N_E and N_U respectively. Packet 2 is subsequently propagated to the London group-node and Int-Node, N_J. Event packet 4 is propagated to N_E following its execution at N_U.

5. The packet 1 is executed at N_E and is propagated to the London group-node and Int-Node N_J. Similar to packet 2 in Step 4, event packet 1 has finally reached its destination within the UK group-network. Event packet 2 is executed at London and the balance of account #5 of London group-node is 10.

6. With the arrival of event packet 1 for account #0, transaction 3 within the UK group-network is finally allowed to execute. The new balance for account #0 is 5.

7. Event packet 2 is executed at N_J and propagated to N_U. Next, event packet 1 is executed at account #0 within the UK group-network, bringing the balance of account #0 in the UK up to 25. Then, event packet 4 is executed at N_E, and the subsequent event packet is sent to the UK group-network as well as Int-Node N_J.

8. Event packet 1 is executed at the UK group-network and N_J. The execution of 1 at N_J is followed by its subsequent propagation back to N_U.

9. At this point, event packets {1}, {2} and {4} have been returned to the originating nodes and are removed. Event packet 3 was removed earlier following its execution and the subsequent update of account #0 within the UK group-network.

Within the UK group-network, account #5 is updated to a new balance of 10 when it receives {N_U,160,5}, the subsequent event generated from transaction {Phila,40,25}. Account #0 is updated, following the enforced wait only when event {N_U,190,0} is asserted. First, the transaction {London,50,0}, with the lowest assertion time, is executed. Then the events {N_U,190,0} and {N_J,210,0} are executed given the lack of transactions asserted at the Glasgow group-node. At the end of the simulation, the final balance of account #0 at both London and Glasgow group-nodes will be 55. As indicated earlier, corresponding to a change in the balance of account #0, due to execution of an event at the London group-node, a subsequent event is propagated to the Glasgow group-node.

3.3.4 Implementation and Performance of NOVAHID

The NOVAHID approach is implemented in C through two separate but similar software programs, each approximately 3000 lines long. Both programs are executed on a network of 20 Sun Sparc workstations, configured as a loosely coupled parallel processor. The first program, labeled national-bank.c models the group-network, and an instance of national-bank.c is created corresponding to each group-network in the international banking network. The second program, labeled int-bank.c models the top-level network, and only one instance of this program is required.

For the representative 2_3 model in Figure 3.49, a total of nine processors of the parallel processor are used to model the six group-nodes of the three group-networks and and three Int-nodes of the top-level network. The name 2_3 refers to an international network with three groups and two group-nodes associated with each group. Two additional representative international banking networks, namely, 3_3 and 2_4, are also modeled in NOVAHID and implemented on the parallel processor.

To analyze NOVAHID's performance, the desired measures include (1) the CPU time required for all transactions and (2) the total time required by the

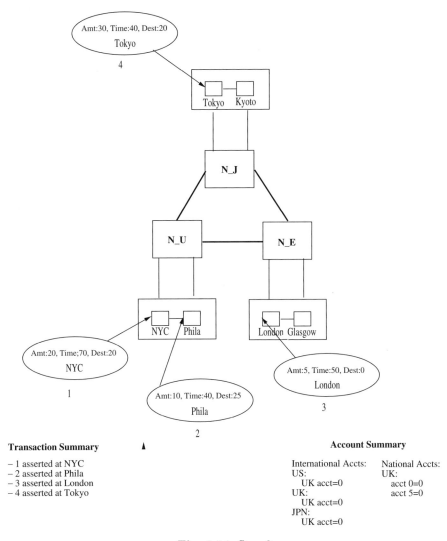

Fig. 3.54. Step 0

international transactions. The total time includes the CPU time required for processing as well as the propagation delays through the communication network of the parallel processor. These measures are obtained for a number of distinct values for the variables:

1. the three representative networks, 2_3, 3_3, and 2_4,
2. the volume, i.e., total number, of transactions, and
3. the composition of transactions, i.e., the relative percentages of international and local transactions. The externally asserted transactions are generated stochastically.

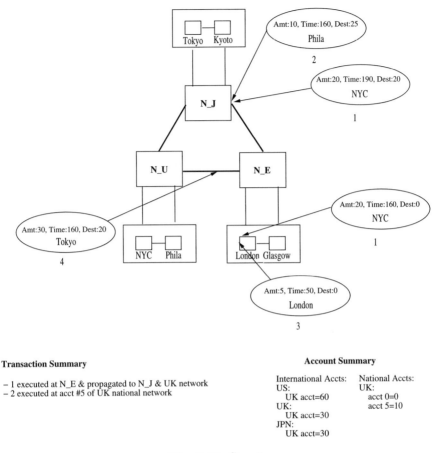

Fig. 3.59. Step 5

Transaction Summary

– 1 executed at N_E & propagated to N_J & UK network
– 2 executed at acct #5 of UK national network

Account Summary

International Accts:	National Accts:
US:	UK:
UK acct=60	acct 0=0
UK:	acct 5=10
UK acct=30	
JPN:	
UK acct=30	

It implies an unstable scenario in that transactions, asserted to the network later in simulation time, may fail to execute. This effect is again an artifact of the distributed simulation and is principally due to the slow communication speed between the processors, relative to the frequent assertion of international transactions. It is pointed out that the workstations are connected through Ethernet hardware. Every international transaction involves multiple events, many of which transcend the boundaries of the group-networks.

Given the slow communication, their processing is slow and time-consuming. When the frequency of assertion of international transactions is high, relative to the communication, the overall effect is that new assertions are asserted before the previous ones are completed. In an actual international processing system, conceivably, the ratio of local to international transactions will, in general, be high. Therefore, every node will execute many national transactions, which are substantially faster, between two consecutive international

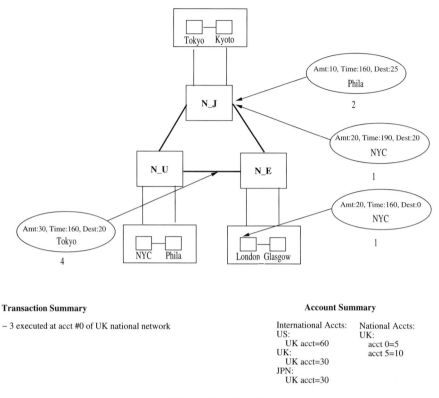

Transaction Summary

– 3 executed at acct #0 of UK national network

Account Summary

International Accts:	National Accts:
US:	UK:
UK acct=60	acct 0=5
UK:	acct 5=10
UK acct=30	
JPN:	
UK acct=30	

Fig. 3.60. Step 6

transactions. Furthermore, high-capacity fiber optics and specialized communication hardware promise faster message passing mechanisms in the future.
In any event, the real-time performance of an actual implementation, i.e., the
volume of transactions processed per unit time, will be limited by the speed
of message communication.

To resolve this limitation, the rate of assertion of the international transactions to NOVAHID is slowed down through the use of the Unix sleep function. Following the execution of every transaction, marked and unmarked,
each node is forced to sleep, i.e., remain idle, for a specific number of time
units. The correspondence between the values of the sleep factor, utilized in
the simulation, and those that are likely to be realistic for an actual implementation, is not known at this time. In this experiment, the values chosen
for the sleep factor vary from 0 to 15 seconds. In the graphs in Figure 3.65,
the transactions are asserted as fast as possible and, therefore, they pertain
to the value of sleep factor equal to 0.

The performance of the 3_3 NOVAHID model with sleep factor values of
5, 11, and 15 seconds are shown in Figures 3.66(a) through 3.66(c). Figure
3.66(a) shows that the marked transactions require roughly the same total

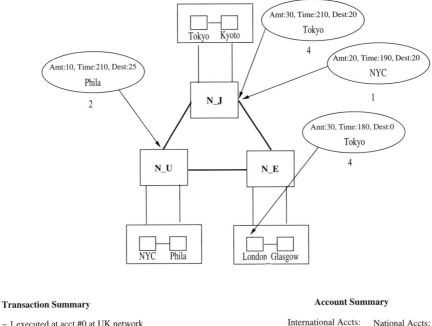

Fig. 3.61. Step 7

Transaction Summary

– 1 executed at acct #0 at UK network
– 2 executed at N_J & propagated to N_U
– 4 executed at N_E & propagated to N_J & UK network

Account Summary

International Accts:	National Accts:
US:	UK:
UK acct=60	acct 0=25
UK:	acct 5=10
UK acct=60	
JPN:	
UK acct=40	

time, regardless of their identifiers, i.e., the time of assertion. This behavior holds true for load_var values ranging from 1 to 20. While the slight gradual increase in the total times for the marked transactions from Figure 3.66(a) through 3.66(c) is expected, given the delays from the sleep function, the behavior of the corresponding graphs for each of the load_var values of 1, 5, 10, and 20 in Figures 3.66(a) through 3.66(c) are similar. This implies that 5 sec is an adequate value for the sleep factor to suppress the dominant effect of the slow communication that plagued the graphs in Figure 3.64.

Figures 3.67(a) through 3.67(c) present the data from simulation of the models 2_3, 3_3, and 2_4 for a sleep factor value of 5 sec. While the corresponding graphs for load_var values of 1 and 5 in Figures 3.67(a) through 3.67(c) resemble each other closely, the graph for the 2_4 network, for load_var value of 20, increases sharply, implying instability. Thus, for international banking networks with more group-networks, stability, i.e., uniform total times for marked transactions, regardless of their time of assertion, is achievable at lower load_var values.

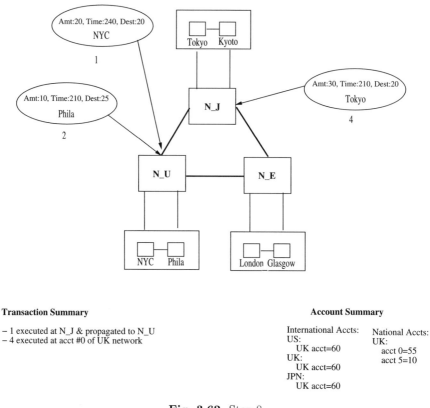

Fig. 3.62. Step 8

3.3.5 Limitations of NOVAHID

An underlying assumption in this research is that the banking network is secure and transactions are not lost due to congestion and link failures.

3.4 A Novel Approach to Asynchronous, Decentralized Decision-Making in Military Command and Control

The current "airland battle" military doctrine is characterized by four key ingredients—depth, initiative, agility, and synchronization. The term *synchronization* implies bringing to bear, at one time and place, the combined power of maneuver, artillery, air, deception, and other systems to strike the enemy repeatedly with an impact that exceeds the sum of all the parts. Throughout military history, in general, synchronization has been achieved through centralized command, control, and communication (C^3), i.e., one where all intelligence is collected and decisions generated at a centralized, sequentially

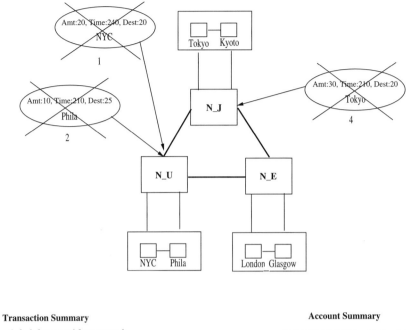

Fig. 3.63. Step 9

executing entity. While the military synchronization is laid down by a higher command and must be obeyed, the lower-level units are granted military initiative as to how to achieve the requirements of synchronization. However, at any given level in the military hierarchy, the synchronization requirement is logically inconsistent with the three other directives, particularly initiative. Evidence from World War II and Operations Just Cause and Desert Storm indicate that excessive synchronization, realized through centralized C^3, may have caused (1) unnecessary mission failure, (2) fratricide, and (3) failure to take advantage of the maximal distributed and concurrent intelligence from the different combat units.

This section presents a novel asynchronous, decentralized decision-making algorithm for military command and control. Unlike centralized command and control, in the proposed approach, all entities—infantry, tanks, and aircraft—of the system are granted significant autonomy, subject to strict guidelines and directives, and are provided with the necessary computing power, intelligence-gathering facilities, communication gear, and decision-making aids. The overall decision task is distributed among these entities. As a result, every entity's

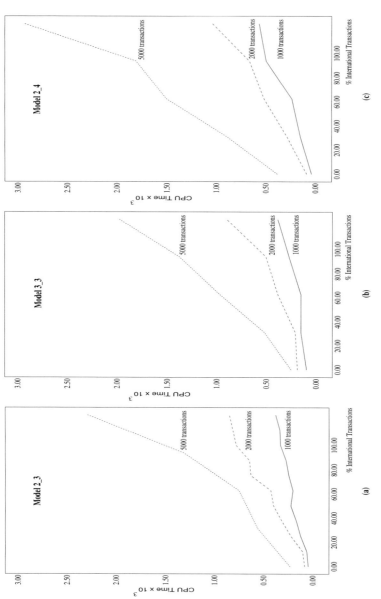

Fig. 3.64. CPU Time (millisec) required by All Transactions as a Function of the Number and composition of Transactions: (a) Model 2_3, (b) Model 3_3, and (c) Model 2_4

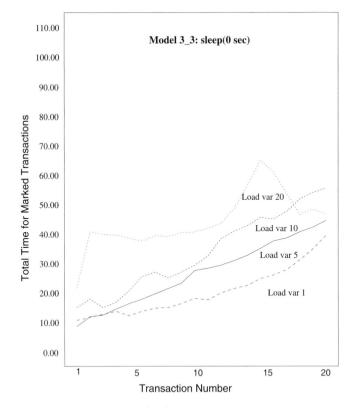

Fig. 3.65. Total Simulation Time (sec) Required for Processing the Marked International Transactions in the 3_3 Model (sleep factor 0)

execution is asynchronous, concurrent, and autonomous, leading to efficient and fast decision making. Asynchronous, distributed, discrete-event simulation techniques are used to model the problem of military command and control. This ability to model is made possible by the fact that the transfer of discrete data, geographically dispersed decision-making entities, asynchronously generated stimuli, and the presence of feedback in the data transfer process are the properties of an asynchronous, distributed discrete-event simulation algorithm. This approach has been implemented on a testbed of 40+ Sun Sparc workstations, configured as a loosely coupled parallel processor. A key goal is to evaluate the performance of the decentralized C^3 algorithm through simulation, under representative battlefield scenarios, and contrast it with the traditional, centralized C^3. Another goal is to determine which scenarios, if any, where decentralized C^3 is effective. A number of experiments are designed to model different engagement scenarios, executed on the simulation testbed, and performance results are reported. This research is the first attempt to scientifically model decentralized C^3 and assess its performance through ex-

132

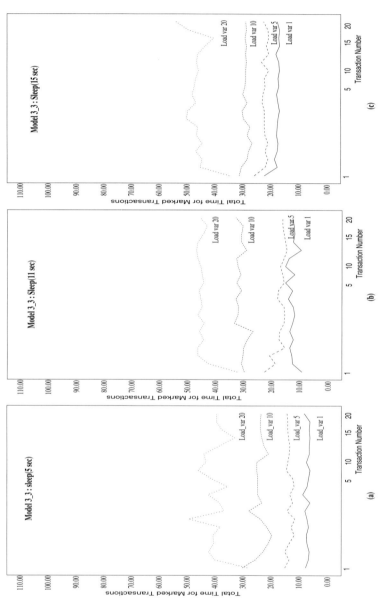

Fig. 3.66. Total Simulation Time (sec) Required for Processing the Marked International Transactions as a Function of the Volume of Transactions, and Sleep Factor Values in (a) Model 2_3, (b) Model 3_3, and (c) Model 2_4

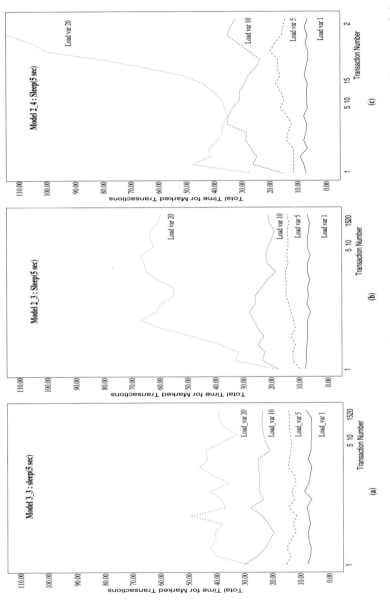

Fig. 3.67. Total Simulation time (sec) Required for Processing the Marked International Transactions as a Function of the Volume of Transactions and for a Sleep Factor Value of 5 sec in (a) Model 2-3, (b) Model 3-3, and (c) Model 2-4.

tensive parallel simulation. The asynchronism and the resulting complexity of the battlefield and the state of current knowledge limit our ability to develop an accurate analytical model. In contrast, this approach, coupled with the parallel simulation testbed, permits a systematic modeling of decision making in warfare and provides a fast, efficient, and accurate, i.e., in terms of spatial and timing resolution, simulation environment.

3.4.1 Introduction: History and Structure of Military Command and Control

The issues of command and control are central to the science of military warfare. *Command* refers to the intelligent and, usually, human decision-making process. *Control* refers to the process of actual execution of the decisions. While the process of decision making may be achieved through centralized or distributed means, the execution process may be organized through centralized or distributed mechanisms. Thus, the principal variations are: (1) centralized command with centralized control, (2) centralized command coupled with decentralized control, and (3) decentralized command with decentralized control. Decentralized command with centralized control is logically inconsistent, and meaningless.

The historic battles of the Greeks, Macedonians, Phoenicians, Trojans, Romans, and other nations may be classified under centralized command with centralized control. Support for this approach may have stemmed from the general belief that the commander was the most intuitive, insightful [127] [128], intelligent, and able decision maker. In contrast, every soldier was expected to be weapon-bearing, loyal solely to the commander's directives, brave, courageous, skilled in combat, but not endowed with the necessary skills or facilities to determine and execute autonomous decisions. The battles were planned centrally, usually by the kings, generals, and commanders, and executed directly under centralized supervision. As a result, the commander usually needed to observe the progress of the battle on a continual basis and did so from a hilltop or simply a safe distance away from the main battlefield. In addition, messengers carried vital information from the battlefield back to the commander, who might recompute a new strategy and issue new orders, which would then be carried back to the battlefield. The battles were usually slow and the scope of destruction of the weapons limited, thereby permitting longer times for a commander to react to new information, possibly with a new decision.

As the science of warfare evolved, it became increasingly evident that entrusting every aspect of the command and control to a single entity was inefficient at times and could lead to catastrophe should the centralized decision maker be severely crippled. In addition, the speed of the newly developed military vehicles, the extensive area of coverage of new sophisticated weapons, and the widening geographical area of the theater of war relegated the centralized execution of the decisions impractical and unrealistic. The evolution of warfare also witnessed a gradual increase in the organization and formal training of the troops with the goal of using the increased intelligence and sophistication of the lower ranks. Centralized control was increasingly replaced with decentralized control, wherein minor decisions related to the execution of the centrally planned command were subject solely to the local combat units. The authority to execute or alter every minor decision did not need to come from the central decision maker. World War II witnessed the overwhelming superiority of centralized decision making and decentralized control in the German blitzkriegs [129] [130] and the spectacular drive of General George Patton and Major General Wood from Normandy into the German heartland. Patton [131] [132] [133] believed that the harder his forces attacked and the faster they advanced the fewer casualties they would suffer. Both Generals Patton and Wood believed that the actions of a combat unit should be limited only by the actions of the enemy, not by restraints from his own higher headquarters. However, the basic military entities, such as the infantry soldier, marine, or tank, still lacked sophisticated intelligence acquisition facilities and decision-making aids that were available, at best, only to the centralized commander. Consequently, the role of the basic military entities was still limited to decentralized control.

It is generally agreed that the best overall initial military strategy is probably determined by a centralized commander who possesses and uses the complete knowledge of the resources and capabilities of both sides. The strategy is a culmination of the commander's logic, experience, creativity, initiative, and, perhaps, a sixth sense. However, once the war has been initiated, it is illogical, unrealistic, and possibly dangerous to assume that the commander will continue to possess, despite confusion, smoke, and hidden enemy weapons, a complete and accurate knowledge of the resources of the enemy and the self. Even in the recent Operation Desert Storm, Col. Swain [134] claims that the difference between General Schwarzkopf's understanding of General Franks' intent and reality is principally due to the seven intervening command nodes between the theater commander-in-chief and the forward elements of the VII Corps. On the other hand, a combat unit is most likely to possess detailed and accurate information about the enemy in its immediate vicinity and, conceivably, it may have neither the resources to communicate the information to the centralized commander nor the desire to do so from fear of exposing its presence to the enemy. Furthermore, as stated earlier, a centralized commander is highly vulnerable to enemy attack and, if destroyed, may lead to the catastrophic breakdown of coordination and, ultimately, complete paralysis. Although the speed of communication has increased dramatically, today's fast-paced wars and ultraprecise weapons neither permit long reaction times [135] to enemy maneuvers nor are forgiving the slightest errors in decision making. While planning an operation cycle required two weeks during the Vietnam War, Desert Storm [136] [137] witnessed the reduction of the cycle time to two days [135]. General Powell notes that while the planning time for a major battle in Europe in the 1980s was estimated at between 2 and 3 weeks, today's new nukes, coupled with the unpredictable behavior of many nations and groups, may reduce the operational planning time to less than 24 hours. There is an increasing desire to reduce the cycle time to a few hours at the joint task level [19], i.e., involving components from the Army, Navy, Air Force, and Marines, which, given the current complexity, is very difficult to achieve without resorting to a new command and control structure. Finally, the future warrior [19] of the United States will be provided with sophisticated systems to gather intelligence and data, compute elements, and extract valuable information through intelligent decision aids. These may include GuardRail, portable radio, and access to the global grid. Therefore, it is imperative, for efficiency and survivability, to design new principles to permit effective use of the future warrior's localized decision-making ability in the overall theater of war.

Perhaps the most unique characteristic of the U.S. military doctrine is "initiative," wherein a combat entity at any rank is given wide latitude in the conduct of operations and encouraged to use his or her leadership and vision to address the immediate situation. In recent times, the quality of initiative has been stressed repeatedly through the U.S. Army Field Manuals FM 101-5 and FM 22-103 and the Air Force's ACC [138]. General George Washington [139] practiced the art of initiative, which be believed was critical to foster leadership and command at all levels, particularly the senior levels. Although history notes that the lack of centralized command from General Washington may have cost him the initial battles, it also records that confidence and trust were instilled as a result of his policy, which ultimately led to victory. Recent evidence from Operation Just Cause [140] shows that under realistic conditions of (1) a special mission, (2) poor communication, and (3) fear of being exposed while trying to communicate, neighboring teams developed a decentralized command and control network wherein they only communicated essential information with each other to rapidly exploit situations and achieved great operational success. Lt. Col. Dubik [141] notes that while the notion of decentralized command is extremely important for successful operations by individual unit commanders with the least amount of interference, it is also a great motivation to train and develop not only commanders but their subordinate leaders and units. In fact, the 1949 Army Field Manual, FM 100-5 [127] [128], Field Service Regulations, Operations, states: "The commander who inspires his subordinates to speak with frankness, who never upbraids them for faulty opinions, who never ridicules them, who encourages them their personal confidences, has a hold over them that is difficult to shake . . . ."

Military science [139] records two principal strategies for war: (1) complete destruction of the enemy through attrition, practiced by Caeser of Rome and (2) a limited, more humane, style stressing maneuver and siege warfare, suggested by Marshal de Saxe in his *Reveries*. Within the U.S. military establishment, the current airland battle military doctrine [142] is defined by four important components—depth, initiative, agility, and synchronization—that constitutes a radical shift from the previous doctrine of firepower, attrition, and destruction during the Vietnam era. The U.S. Army uses the term *synchronization* to imply bringing to bear at one time, and placing the combined power of maneuver, artillery, air, deception, and other systems, to strike the enemy again and again with massed power the impact of which exceeds the sum of all the parts. While the military synchronization is laid down by a higher command and must be obeyed, the lower-level units are granted military initiative as to how to achieve the requirements of synchronization. However, at any given level in the military hierarchy, the synchronization requirement is logically inconsistent with the other three directives, particularly initiative. General Boyd [143] comments, quite accurately, "... synchronized units can only move at the pace of the slowest unit, therefore the agility and initiative of the entire force will suffer ...." Recent analysis of data from Operation Desert Storm [143] reveals that repeated synchronizations and refueling of the M1A1 tanks, under General Franks, undermined the superior capability of the U.S.-led coalition forces and caused much of the Iraqi Republican Guard to escape north into safety. Furthermore, due to overcautiousness and strict adherence to the synchronous processes, agreed upon a priori, General Franks' units suffered the heaviest losses from fratricide. It is only logical to expect that, at any given level, synchronous processes, agreed to prior to the start of war, will be severely compromised as the war unfolds due to the smoke, confusion, deception, and other factors. Even General Schwarzkopf reports pulling back General McCaffrey, who was poised to attack the Republican Guard from the south, from fear of exposing a flank and lack of synchronization.

Military history records that in the battle for Anzio in World War II, when General Leslie secured the beachhead and his subordinates wanted permission to march into Rome, only a few hours away, General Leslie denied their request, citing caution and the lack of adequate intelligence report. General Leslie continued to adhere to his decision even when an official American reporter drove a jeep to and from Rome and reported that the city had been abandoned by the German army. When General Leslie finally did issue the command to attack, the Germans had already built strong fortifications and decimated the first and second battalions of the U.S. Ranger Division. General Leslie's decision reflects the strong desire to adhere to the traditional military principle of synchronization at every level. In contrast, Shapiro [144] notes,

> ... Patton's ability to shift, at a moment's notice, three entire divisions from one front to another, during the Battle of the Bulge, was considered one of the most brilliant maneuvers of the war. But it was not a miracle. It was the way Patton did things, aided by a group of loyal, hard-working staff officers. It was often said of Patton that he had flashes of intuition, hunches that paid off. ... His intelligence chief (G-2) kept him up to date on everything that was happening not only in Third Army's sector, but everywhere else along the Western Front. Patton himself often flew over the battlefield, dodging enemy fighter planes. His combat commanders did the same. His fast moving patrol

reconnaissance reported everything they observed, bypassing normal Army communications channels. They fed Patton far better information than he could get from Eisenhower's Intelligence section. Often, it was the information gleaned from these patrols that prompted Patton's seemingly risky maneuvers.

General Sullivan [145] stresses the need to modernize synchronization, particularly because the modern battlefield has changed in a number of variables—speed, space and time, and combat operations taking place in larger areas (greater depth, breadth, and altitude) and more rapidly and continuously. The traditional philosophy of centralized planning and decision making is not only confined to command and control but it has also contributed to limitations in weapons design. Both Lt. Col. Hartel [19] and Lt. Gen. Nelson [146] note that the fundamental problems of AWACS and JTAG stem from the propagation of extremely time-consuming repetitive information, a consequence of synchronous design philosophy. For success in the future— decentralized battle space in a time-sensitive manner—the design philosophy must be changed to propagate only "change" information. The tragic incident on April 14, 1994, probably underscores the need for intelligent data processing and decision making in today's fast-paced battles. Following extensive investigation, the Defense Department issued the following findings:

1. Two U.S. F-15 fighters shot down two U.S. helicopters over Northern Iraq at the cost of 26 lives.
2. The AWACS crew that tracked both the helicopters and fighter aircraft was incompetent.
3. The helicopters used the wrong IFF identifying code.
4. The F-15 pilots were poorly trained in recognizing helicopters.
5. The AWACS lost the helicopters for a while but when communications were reestablished, the AWACS failed to inform and update the F-15s.

Conceivably, the AWACS crew experienced information overload and the lack of a fail-safe, automatic mechanism to intelligently process data and generate decisions and updates caused this tragedy.

The remainder of this section is organized as follows. Section 3.4.2 details a novel decentralized military C^3 algorithm wherein each entity is provided with sufficient computing power, intelligence gathering facilities, and decision-making aids and is permitted significant autonomy to constitute an effective fighting force. To study its performance characteristics through extensive, fast simulation on a parallel processing testbed, a computer model is developed in Section 3.4.2. Section 3.4.3 presents details on the testbed and the implementation of the model for representative battlefield scenarios. Section 3.4.4 reports on a number of experiments designed to evaluate the decentralized C^3 algorithm and analyzes the performance data.

3.4.2 A Novel Approach to Decentralized Command and Control

3.4.2.1 The Asynchronous, Decentralized Algorithm

There are many motivations for developing a decentralized C^3 algorithm. First, there is ample evidence from military history that a decentralized C^3 approach can constitute a very effective fighting force. The spectacular drives of Generals Patton and Wood, the German blitzkrieg drives, and reported successes in Operation Just Cause are superb examples. In the same spirit, history notes that the lack of decentralized C^3, at appropriate times, may result in failure as witnessed in Operation Desert Storm. Second, unlike in the past, today's military personnel at almost all ranks are highly trained, intelligent, sophisticated, and aided by a host of high-tech systems in gathering, assimilating, and analyzing data and making good decisions. The new French tank design, AMX Leclerc, currently under development, is provided with a dataport or databus to permit the sharing of information such as fuel, ammunition, state of the tank, etc., with other tanks and fighting units. Consequently, it is timely to augment the traditional, centralized approach with decentralized decision making and decentralized execution. The era of exclusive synchronized war at every level is behind us and is being made obsolete by rapid technological changes and renewed emphasis on the value of life of the combat soldier and unarmed civilian. The United States leads and should lead the world in such compassionate philosophy even in war. Third, in actual combat, the outcomes at different instances of time are functions of many parameters, such as enemy strength, self strength, coincidences, and intelligence and cannot be predicted a priori. Because no single combat unit, including the central headquarters, may possess accurate and complete knowledge of the entire battlefield at all instants of time, it is best to permit each combat unit to proceed as fast as it possibly can, without jeopardizing any aspect of the overall mission. Fourth, today's battlefields move rapidly and the weapons are very accurate and extremely fast. As a result, a centralized decision-making unit is highly vulnerable to destruction, and, if destroyed, the entire force may lose coordination, leading to catastrophic failure.

The fundamental and general principles that underlie the decentralized C^3 algorithm, presented here, may be stated as follows. Prior to the start of a mission, every combat unit is aware of the mission's objectives. In addition, every combat unit possesses knowledge of the basic rules of engagement. Examples include sharing intelligence information with peers, assisting friendly units under critical distress, and withdrawing in the face of overwhelming enemy superiority. Once the battle is initiated, every combat unit must recognize that no intelligence data is 100% correct due to confusion, smoke, and the possibility of enemy deception. Also, the battlefield is asynchronous, i.e., firings, sighting, and movements do not occur regularly in time. Therefore, every combat unit must be permitted to execute asynchronously and independently. This will result in the combat units executing concurrently and cooperatively. There must be no unwanted interference from any other combat unit except through messages. Thus, the overall decision-making task must be intelligently distributed among the combat units so as to maximize local computations, minimize communications, and achieve robustness and high throughput. While each combat unit's information database and decisions are private, it may choose to communicate them with the other units through messages. The design of the overall approach and the algorithm that drives each combat unit must be such that the sum total of all decisions, at any time instant, is synergistic and "consistent," where *consistency* refers to the complete absence of all actions that must never occur, such as friendly fire, mutual destruction, and the unnecessary destruction of unarmed civilians. In theory, asynchronous, decentralized algorithms offer the highest benefit from concurrent processing, which promises the use of maximal distributed intelligence from the different combat units. Each unit must note its own precise sightings and evaluation of the enemy location and formation; additional commands from headquarters; intelligence data from GuardRail, satellites, and other friendly combat units; and then it must rate its belief in them. Then it must use its basic doctrine to execute the decision-making algorithm and determine its final decision. Next, the combat unit executes the decision, relays it to the headquarters, and informs other friendly combat units on a need-to-know basis. Thus, the relationship between the mission objective and the actions of the combat units will be subject to continual assessments and adjustments.

In this section, a decentralized C^3 algorithm is presented for a simple, representative battlefield consisting of tanks and artillery. The general principles may be extended to include fixed-wing aircraft, helicopters, rocket launchers, and infantry as well as components from other branches of service, with relative ease. In the traditional centralized scheme, combat units are organized into a hierarchy. In this research, at the lowest level are individual tanks while the highest level is occupied by the company leader. A group of approximately five to six tanks are organized into a platoon that is commanded by a platoon leader. A group of three to five platoons are commanded by the company leader. A long-range artillery unit is attached to every company. In the traditional C^3 algorithm, every tank reports its enemy sightings through the hierarchical command structure, up to the company leader who analyzes the situation and commands the tanks and artillery units to fire. For example, in Operation Desert Storm, there were seven intervening command nodes between General Schwarzkopf, the theater commander-in-chief, and the forward elements of the VII Corps, commanded by General Franks. In the decentralized C^3 algorithm, every tank's awareness of the battlefield results from a fusion of its own sightings of enemy units and the information provided to it by other friendly units. Currently, the fusion of similar sightings, i.e., two sightings of the same enemy tank, is accomplished based on geographic proximity. Whenever a new sighting is determined by a unit, it determines whether to propagate the information to other specific combat units at the same hierarchical level. This decision is based on the position of the enemy unit with respect to the friendly unit and the weapon capabilities of the two units. Thus, instead of propagating raw information to every friendly combat unit, thereby causing data overload, intelligent local data processing achieves in the precise propagation of information to combat units in need of the information, for greater effectiveness. Also, after sighting the enemy, a tank propagates a message directly to its artillery unit, providing it with precise coordinates of the enemy and requesting it to open fire. The artillery unit, after receiving one or more such requests, analyzes the criticality of the situation and directs fire at the appropriate enemy position. When a tank, following enemy sighting, determines that the enemy formation has an N-fold numerical advantage over its own formation, it withdraws and sends messages to withdraw to other friendly tanks to minimize losses. In this effort, N is arbitrarily set at 3, without any loss in generality.

3.4.2.2 Modeling the Decentralized C^3 Algorithm on an Accurate, Parallel Processing Testbed

Given that each combat unit—tank, platoon leader, company leader, and artillery unit—is asynchronous and autonomous, it is labeled as an *individual* node and represented through a concurrent process in the parallel processor. The individual nodes are interconnected based on the command and control strategy and the organization hierarchy. For the decentralized strategy, within a platoon, every tank is connected to its members and to the platoon leader. Every platoon leader is connected to every other platoon leader and the company leader. The artillery unit is linked to every platoon leader and the company leader. In the traditional command and control strategy, only vertical connections are used, i.e., platoon leaders communicate up to the company leader and down to the individual tanks in the platoon.

The software that models the behavior of every individual node is unique to the function of the corresponding underlying combat unit. Thus, while one process may represent a tank within a platoon, another process may model the platoon leader, while still another process may represent the artillery unit. The behavior of a process representing a tank would involve searching its surroundings for enemy vehicles, firing at enemies, and adjusting its course and speed. A platoon leader process would also issue orders to the member tanks of the platoon. Figure 3.68 describes a generic individual node wherein it receives information from other combat units through the incoming links 1 through N and propagates information to other units through outgoing links 1 through M.

The individual nodes interact through interprocess communication links that are established prior to initiating the simulation. The communication is asynchronous. That is, incoming messages may arrive at any time, so a node must periodically check incoming links for new inputs. Similarly, an individual node may propagate an outgoing message on an outgoing link at any time. Figure 3.69 presents the algorithmic behavior of the generic individual node in pseudocode.

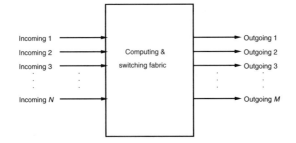

Fig. 3.68. A Generic Individual Node

```
While (not done) do {
  for i from 1 to N do
     check incoming link i for new input
     if input exists
        store in appropriate input buffer
     do internal processing
     place output in appropriate output buffer
     for i from 1 to M do
        if entry in output buffer i exists
           send message on outgoing link i
}
```

Fig. 3.69. Behavior of the Generic Individual Node

The interconnection links between the individual nodes are defined by the underlying command and control strategy. The traditional centralized approach is characterized by *vertical* communication only, i.e., tanks communicate up to the platoon leader who, in turn, communicates up to the company leader. There are no communication links between either the member tanks of a platoon or the different platoon leaders within the same company. In contrast, the decentralized approach inherits all of the communication links of the centralized strategy and adds *horizontal* communication links. Figure 3.70 presents the communication networks for a centralized and a decentralized platoon.

In the battlefield, the human operator of a combat unit detects friendly and enemy units through either visual sighting or infrared detectors. Because processes of a parallel processor, unlike humans, cannot yet see, and as they are independent and concurrent, this ability of every unit is modeled in the simulation through the use of one or more control nodes. A control node maintains accurate global positions for all friendly entities, and this provides a consistent virtual global environment. This is achieved by requiring every friendly unit to propagate new information, following any change to its status such as position, velocity, changes in course, or destroyed or damaged by enemy fire, to the control node. When other nodes require the status of an individual node, they retrieve it from the control node. In addition, the control

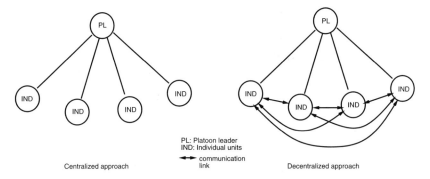

Fig. 3.70. Communications in Centralized and Decentralized Tank Platoons

node automatically determines when a new piece of information is relevant to a specific individual node based on its position and sensor capabilities and propagates the information to it. Consequently, information regarding an individual node is available to other individual nodes on a need-to-know basis. Thus, the control node is only an artifact of the simulation and will not exist in reality. In the simulation, the concept of control node is superior to the broadcasting of changes to the status of an individual node to every other individual node and requiring them to filter and access only information that is relevant. The reason is as follows. Broadcasting information from every node to every other would require enormous and unnecessary communication costs, thereby constituting an inherently nonscalable approach. This effort utilizes a control node for each of the two opposing forces—blue and red—in the virtual battlefield, although additional ones may be used for even larger simulations. In addition, local computation is used, wherever possible, to replace communication and achieve efficiency. For example, when an individual node N_1 contains the position and velocity of a different combat unit N_2, at time t it extrapolates the position of N_2 at a later time $(t+T)$ through local computation, as opposed to retrieving the information from the control node. Clearly, the extrapolation is accurate only if the velocity of N_2 remains unchanged and such information is automatically propagated to N_1 by the control node.

For each force—blue or red—all of the individual nodes are connected to the appropriate control node. The two control nodes are also connected, thereby providing a consistent global view. Any changes to an individual node is immediately propagated to the appropriate control node and to the control node for the other force. As explained earlier, a control node propagates new information to the individual nodes on a need-to-know basis. Figure 3.71 describes the network connectivity for a battlefield with two opposing companies where a company is assumed to consist of three platoons, each with four to five tanks.

In Figure 3.71, three types of communication links are utilized: control node to individual node, control node to control node, and individual node to

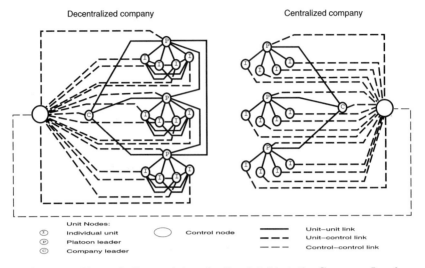

Fig. 3.71. Network Connectivity of a Battlefield at the Company Level

individual node. Of these, the first two serve to maintain a consistent global environment and are artifacts of the simulation. Therefore, they are characterized with 0 propagation delay in the simulation. However, the third type of link models reality and is characterized by propagation delays, analogous to the real-world communication link delays. In this section, every unit-to-unit link is characterized by an identical delay equal to 5 timesteps or 0.5 second.

Unlike SIMNET and CATT [147], where human operators define the speed of progress of the simulation exercise, in this research, the simulation is completely under software control. That is, it does not require human operators and, as a result, it is capable of executing many times faster than real time. Given the basic goal of achieving efficiency through propagating changes, this simulation utilizes the principles of asynchronous, distributed, discrete-event simulation. Discrete-event simulation only allows changes to be propagated and suppresses information identical to what was propagated earlier. Events or causes may occur at any time, subject to a fundamental timestep. A *timestep* is an indivisible basic unit of time that progresses monotonically, governs all combat units including their weapons, and signifies that no event (cause or decision) can occur between any two subsequent timesteps.

The timestep also defines the trade-off between the desired accuracy and efficiency of the simulation. The timestep is selected to be 0.1 second to allow the accurate spatial and temporal modeling of slow- and fast-moving objects. The choice of a 0.1-second timestep will permit the modeling of every major combat unit including infantry, tanks, Bradley fighting vehicles, rocket launchers, anti-aircraft guns, helicopters, GuardRail, satellites, AWACS, and fixed-wing aircraft. While an even smaller timestep would allow even better spatial granularity, it would also slow down the simulation execution. Within the scope of a representative battlefield, assuming that the slow-moving infantry proceeds at 7.2 km/hr, the 0.1-second timestep implies a spatial granularity of 0.2 meter, allowing for reasonably accurate modeling of the infantry position.

A combat unit, at any instant of time, is concerned only with the limited region of the world such that its sensors are capable of detecting other entities should they be in the region. Combat units outside this region are of no interest to the combat unit in question. To facilitate this need for every combat unit, in the simulation, the world is conceptually organized into unique rectangular regions of constant size, termed *sectors*. A combat unit's sensor capability is private information and, as a result, at any time instant it computes its effective sensor range. It then determines one or more sectors that are either wholly or partially overlapped by its effective sensor range and terms it the *sector-set*. The data structures in the simulation are so organized that every sector is aware, at a given time instant, of the combat units that it serves. Next, the combat unit propagates the sector-set to the control node, requesting information on the presence of other units within its sector-set. The control node replies to the request and records the association between the combat unit and the respective sectors. When a control node receives new information, it uses the previously recorded association to quickly determine which of the combat units are affected and automatically notifies them. Conceivably, a given sector may serve multiple combat units at any time instant.

A set of control packets, i.e., specialized messages, are designed in the simulation to assist in accurately maintaining a globally consistent view. These packets are used for individual node–to–control node and control node–to–individual node communication. These are summarized in Table 3.7 and detailed later.

Packet Name	Use	Full Name and Brief Description
REQ_SEC_CNT	Individual node to control node	Request sector contents
SEC_CNT	Control node to individual node	Sector contents
ADD_SEC	Control node to individual node	Add unit to a sector
UPDATE	Control node to individual node Individual node to control node	Update unit
TIME_UPDATE	Individual node to control node	Time update
FIRE	Individual node to control node	Fire
IMPACT	Control node to individual node	Impact
REMOVE	Control node to individual node	Remove unit from the environment
INSERT	Control node to individual node	Insert unit into the environment
STATS	Individual node to control node	End of simulation statistics

Table 3.7. Control Packets for Communication between Control Node and Individual Nodes

- REQ_SEC_CNT: A combat unit requests the physical contents of a specified sector from the control node.
- SEC_CNT: The control node sends the full contents of a sector to the requesting combat unit.
- ADD_SEC: A combat unit, X, has moved into a sector that serves another combat unit, Y, so the control node must notify Y about the presence of X in the sector.
- UPDATE: The status or velocity of a combat unit has changed.
  1. Individual node to control node: First, the combat unit whose status has changed must notify the control node.
  2. Control node to individual node: Next, the control node must determine all other nodes that may be affected by the new information, i.e., all combat units served by the affected sector, and propagate the new information to them.
- TIME_UPDATE: An individual node notifies the control node that it has advanced its internal simulation time counter.
- FIRE: A combat unit notifies the control node that it has fired a weapon and includes the type of weapon fired and the target area.
- IMPACT: The control node notifies a combat unit that it has been hit.
- REMOVE: Used to remove a combat unit completely from the environment because it has been destroyed.
- INSERT: Used to insert a new combat unit or weapons type into the environment.
- STATS: At the end of the simulation, the control node gathers statistics from all individual nodes.

At any time instant, when a combat unit, X, moves into a new sector, it first receives the contents of the sector, i.e., the status of all entities served by the content of X's sector-set. In this work, effective sensor range is set at 2 km, i.e., sighting is considered 100% accurate if the target is within 2 km of X. The report also encapsulates whether the other entity belongs to the blue or red force, the speed, heading, and the type of entity tank, platoon leader, etc.

Following generation of the internal sighting report, the combat unit X compares it with all previous sighting reports to verify whether a new entity sighted was viewed earlier. A sighting of an entity is considered to be identical to an earlier sighting if the two units belong to the same force, are of the same type, and are within a specified distance of each other. If the result of the comparison is affirmative, the two sightings are fused through updating the old sighting report with the new information. Otherwise, the new sighting is declared a new entity.

Thus, either a new or updated sighting report has been generated and it is ready to be acted on. At the level of individual tanks, action may include advancing toward the enemy, firing on the enemy, withdrawing, requesting fire support from artillery, or propagating the sighting report. At the level of the platoon leader, action may mean issuing orders to the member tanks to move toward the enemy, open fire, withdraw, request fire support from artillery, or propagate the report to other platoon leaders and the company leader. An individual tank may propagate a report to a peer tank within its platoon, bypassing the conventional norm. Also, a platoon leader may share the sighting report with a peer platoon leader, bypassing the traditional norm, if it determines that the enemy entity is fast and headed toward the peer. Figures 3.72(a) and 3.72(b) contrast the flow of communication and decisions in the traditional and decentralized schemes for two opposing companies, where each company consists of three platoons, each consisting of a platoon leader and four tanks, a company leader, and two platoon-level artillery units. While the artillery units receive fire support requests directly from platoon leaders in the decentralized approach, in the traditional scheme, they receive the open fire command only from the company leader.

At the level of platoon and company leaders, sighting reports may be fused by a process, termed *grouping* in this effort. Reports from individual tanks that cite sightings of one or a few enemy combat units, or internally generated reports, are merged by platoon or company leaders into a larger sighting report, i.e., one that contains sightings of more enemy combat units. A platoon leader may group enemy combat units in the form of enemy platoon units while a company leader may group enemy entities into enemy company units. Grouping is facilitated by the fact that a platoon leader receives a sighting report from multiple member tanks while a company leader receives reports from multiple platoon leaders. Such fusion of sighting reports constitutes intelligent processing and reduction of data at every level to ensure greater comprehension and manageability.

The execution of every individual node is triggered by three types of inputs: (1) internally generated sightings and sightings received from other friendly combat units; (2) requests from other friendly combat units, propagated in the form of communications messages; and (3) knowledge of short- and long-term objectives. Issue 1 was discussed earlier. Requests from individual tanks may assume the form of withdrawal, fire support, or assistance. Table 3.8 presents the different individual node–to–individual node communication, The long-term objectives, such as engage and destroy the enemy or defend a certain specified perimeter, are acquired statically at the start of the simulation from the highest level of command and are derived from the type of mission. Such objectives may not necessarily be achieved during the simulation exercise. The short-term objectives, aimed at achieving the long-term goals, may assume the form of maneuvering to a specific location and are continually refined. They are either issued periodically by a commander or generated internally within an individual node. Table 3.9 presents a list of the order packets associated with orders from platoon and company leaders.

Armed with timely information, every individual node, including tank units, platoon leaders, and company leader, exercises its share of the decentralized decision making described through the pseudocode in Figure 3.73. The

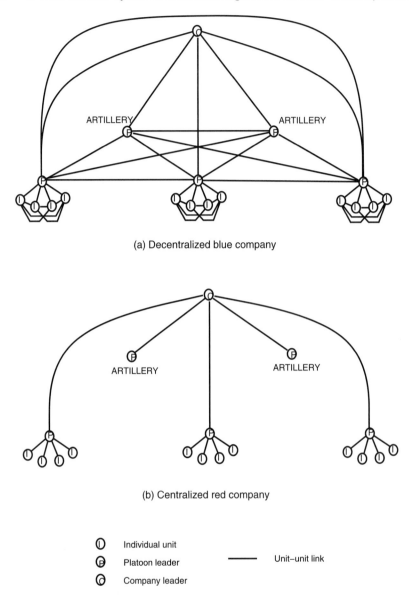

Fig. 3.72. Flow of Communications and Decisions at the Company Level with (a) Centralized C^3 and (b) Decentralized C^3

Packet Name	Description
GEOMETRY	Sets the formation for my subordinate units
STATUS	Informs others about my status (pos, vel, damage, size of group, etc.)
REQUEST	Request supporting fire
ORDER	Direct order to a subordinate unit

Table 3.8. Packets for Individual–Node–to–Individual–Node Communications

Order Name	Description
MOVETO	Move to a specific location
HEADING	Change course to the specified heading
FIRE	Fire at a certain location (indirect fire)
WITHDRAW	Withdraw from the engagement

Table 3.9. Packets to Facilitate Orders from Platoon and Company Leaders

behavior of the relatively stationary artillery unit differs from those of other combat units and is presented in Figure 3.74. It may be noted that a combat unit may choose to supersede a direct firing order from a superior with enemy sighting information from a peer or self, should the sighting require immediate firing.

At times during battle, even an effective fighting force must withdraw from engagement, particularly if the enemy has overwhelming superiority and the chance for survivability is low. The withdrawal criteria is currently established as follows. If a combat unit realizes that the enemy has a threefold numerical advantage over its forces, then the combat unit withdraws. The choice of the factor 3 is arbitrary, without any loss in generality. This requires every combat unit to maintain a fairly accurate count of friendly forces, which is achieved by propagating STATUS packets, shown in Table 3.8, periodically between all interconnected nodes. The STATUS packets also encapsulate the number of combat units being led by the sender. Thus, where the sender is an individual tank, the number is 1, while for platoon leaders, the number equals the number of member tanks. Following several periodic message updates, every friendly combat unit is aware of the current number of units within the force. The number of enemy combat units is obtained from sighting reports and subsequent fusion.

Weapon fire is organized in two forms—direct and indirect fire. *Direct fire* is where the firing unit holds its target in view, as in tank-to-tank fire. A tank unit uses the range and estimated velocity and heading of the enemy unit, the type of weapon it plans to use, and then computes the *lead*, i.e., the spatial point where the weapon is likely to hit the target. Then the tank fires on the enemy unit. In the event of a hit, the impact of the weapon is determined from the type of weapon and the nature of the target. This is

```
Find nearest sighted enemy unit
If found
   If it is in direct sight
      If in range and weapon is loaded and ammunition available
         Fire at enemy unit
   Turn towards the enemy
   If I am a Platoon or Company Leader
      Send MOVETO order to subordinates
      Send REQUEST for artillery support to artillery unit
   Else
      Send REQUEST for artillery support to platoon leader
Count and compare enemy units vs friendly units
   Withdraw if it meets the withdrawal criteria
   If I am a Platoon or Company Leader
      Send WITHDRAW order to subordinates
Process orders
   If received WITHDRAW order
      change course and speed to withdraw
         If I am a Platoon Leader, relay order to subordinates
   If received MOVETO order
      change course to head towards the destination in the order
         If I am a Platoon Leader, relay order to subordinates
   If received HEADING order
      change course to that specified in the order
         If I am a Platoon Leader, relay order to subordinates
   If received REQUEST
      If I am a Platoon Leader, relay request to artillery units
```

Fig. 3.73. Behavior of Decentralized Combat Units, Including Tanks, Platoon Leaders, and Company Leader

modeled in the simulation as follows. Following a tank-to-tank fire, a random number generator, drand48, is executed that is capable of generating a pseudo-random number between 0 and 100. If the actual number generated is less than 20, the enemy tank is assumed to be completely destroyed; otherwise, the enemy tank is assumed undamaged. Thus, on a tank-to-tank fire, there is a 20% probability that the target is destroyed. In contrast to direct fire, *indirect fire* is characterized by the lack of direct visual contact between the firing unit and the target. Indirect fire is typically requested or ordered by another friendly unit and is targeted against a specified geographical area as opposed to a specific enemy unit. Examples of indirect fire include artillery units. They typically use very high velocity shells, and the firing entity is located a significant distance from the target. Clearly, the key factor relative to the accuracy of fire is the time lag between the actual sighting of the enemy unit(s) and the firing of the weapon. While the computed lead attempts to accurately predict a future spatial location for the target, it is contingent on

```
Find nearest reported sighted enemy unit
If found
    If in range and weapon is loaded and ammunition available
        Fire at enemy unit
Count and compare enemy units vs friendly units
    Withdraw if it meets the withdrawal criteria
Process orders
    If received WITHDRAW order
        change course and speed to withdraw
    If received MOVETO order
        change course to head towards the destination in the order
    If received HEADING order
        change course to that specified in the order
    If received FIRE order
        If in range and weapon is loaded and ammunition available
            Fire at location specified in the order
Process requests
    If received fire support REQUEST
        If in range and weapon is loaded and ammunition available
            Fire at location specified in the order
```

Fig. 3.74. Behavior of Decentralized Artillery Unit

the target maintaining its original heading and speed. Unlike tanks, artillery units are relatively immobile. However, they can turn and change the direction of fire.

Figure 3.75 illustrates the advantage of decentralized over centralized C^3 strategy due to the multiple intervening delays between the actual sighting and the firing. Relative to the decentralized strategy, the centralized scheme imposes an additional delay equal to a communication delay plus the company leader processing delay. In general, the communication delay is much smaller than the company leader processing delay; therefore, the latter bears a stronger impact on the effectiveness of the artillery.

Decisions require computing time, whether executed by a human being or a decision-making algorithm on a computer, and this overhead is modeled in every node of the simulation through processing delay. Thus, every decision determined by a combat unit is delayed by the specified processing delay prior to either executing it or propagating it to other entities. Processing delay values are critical parameters because they represent the speed with which decisions may be generated at every level of the command hierarchy. In this research, individual nodes, platoon leaders, and company leader are characterized by fixed processing delays of 10 timesteps (1 second), 25 timesteps (2.5 seconds), and 100 timesteps (10 seconds), respectively. The choice of these values is arbitrary, without any loss in generality, and it reflects the increasing amount of information processing that is necessary as one goes up the military hierarchy. In addition, a dynamic delay component, determined as a function

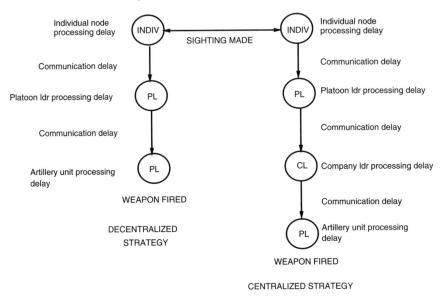

Fig. 3.75. Time Lag between Enemy Unit Sighting and Artillery Fire

of the processing load experienced by the unit at the specific time instant, is added to the fixed component. Thus, where a node is engaged in executing significant decision making, issuing orders, fusing sighting information, and propagating such information, the total processing delay is likely to be very high.

3.4.3 Implementation Issues

The software component of the simulator, coupled with the parallel processing consists of 20,000 lines of ANSI C and runs on a heterogeneous network of 40+ Sun Sparc 1, Sparc 2, Sparc 10, and Sun 4 workstations, configured as a loosely coupled parallel processor. The software includes a Motif-based front end that permits both run-time viewing of the simulation and postmortem replay from a log file. The interface is designed to present either the entire battlefield, analogous to the view from the control node, or from the perspective of a single combat unit. A maximum of 38 concurrent processes have been executed on the network.

3.4.4 Performance Analysis

To evaluate the effectiveness of the proposed decentralized decision making algorithm against the traditional command hierarchy, this section proposes the measure of enemy kill rate relative to the number of friendly units destroyed. These measures are consistent with the measures of force effectiveness

(MOFE), which includes the enemy kill rate, the rate of advance against the enemy, and geographical territory captured. The measures under the Headquarters Effectiveness Assessment Tool (HEAT) are not appropriate for this research for the following reasons. First, the fundamental assumption in HEAT is that all decision making takes place at headquarters. Second, HEAT proposes the measures—completeness, accuracy and consistency—to contrast the accuracy of information held at headquarters to the "ground truth," i.e., those supported by field units and military historians. HEAT is the result of the Defense Communications Agency–commissioned study to measure battlefield performance.

The measures are generated through a number of experiments for two key scenarios: (1) engagement in battle and (2) withdrawal in the face of overwhelming enemy superiority. For each scenario, two opposing forces— blue and red—are cast against each other. In scenario 1, the blue and red forces are identical in all respects, i.e., in the numbers and types of tanks, artillery units, and weapons. The only difference between the two forces is in the underlying command structure—centralized or decentralized. A tank, under decentralized command, has the autonomy of initiating a change in its own course and speed and requesting fire support from artillery units and peer tanks directly. Also, the network interconnection in the decentralized scheme, i.e., one that governs the flow of information and command, is not a fully connected network. Instead, it is a hybrid network that preserves the traditional command network, provides more information to every entity, and avoids the excessive cost of a fully connected network. In centralized command, changes in course, speed, and firings are under strict hierarchical control. For scenario 2, the red force has three times numerical superiority over the blue force, i.e., it has three times the number of tanks, platoons, and artillery units. Military history states that in addition to brilliant command strategy, often the element of surprise, superior weapons, higher ground and strategic positioning, confidence and belief, contributed to one force winning over another. The goal of this effort is strictly to measure the effectiveness of decentralized command over the traditional command structure. Therefore, every care is taken to ensure that both forces have identical intelligence information, tanks, and weapons.

Given that the principal goal of this research is to evaluate decentralized command and control, the individual tanks and artillery units are modeled as simple generic types. The battlefield is modeled as a flat rectangular world with each side extending to 2,500,000 spatial units, where a spatial unit defines the basic grid and is equal to 0.2 meter. For every tank, the sensor range is 10,000 spatial units (2 km), firing range is 3000 spatial units (600 meters), and the effective area of coverage of a weapon is 20 spatial units (4 meters). That is, when a tank shell lands on the ground, it must be within 4 meters of the enemy unit to be effective, virtually requiring a direct hit. The time to reload a shell is 25 timesteps, where a timestep is 0.1 sec. The maximum speed of a tank is 15 spatial units per timestep, or 30 meters/sec, while the speed of its shell is 500 spatial units per timestep or 1000 meters/sec. For s long-range artillery unit, the firing range is 50,000 spatial units (10 km), the area of coverage of an artillery shell once it lands on the ground is 250 spatial units (50 meters), the time to reload a shell is 50 timesteps (5 seconds), and the speed of a shell is 3000 meters/sec. The uncertainty in the battlefield due to smoke and confusion is modeled as follows. When a tank shell strikes a tank, a pseudo-random number generator is executed to generate a number between 0 and 100. If the number is less than or equal to 20, the tank is assumed to receive a direct hit. Otherwise, it is undamaged. When an artillery shell strikes a tank, a pseudo–random number generator is executed to generate a number between 0 and 100. If the number is less than or equal to 50, the tank is assumed to receive a direct hit. Otherwise, it is undamaged. Although the control node sends exact coordinates to an entity, a perturbation error of ± 20 spatial units is deliberately introduced into the positional data. The communication delay between units is modeled at 5 timesteps (0.5 second) while the processing delays at individual tanks, platoon leaders, and company leader are 10 timesteps, 25 timesteps, and 100 timesteps, respectively. The withdrawal factor is set at 3, i.e., withdrawal must commence when the enemy force is determined to possess a numerical superiority of 3.

All of the experiments are executed on a network of Sun Sparc work-stations, configured as a loosely coupled parallel processor. The performance data, reported in this section, are obtained from executing the simulation on eight Sparc 10s executing the Solaris operating system. A total of 38 concurrent processes executing on the network, requires an allocation of four to seven processes per processor. Typical simulation runs execute a total of 600 timesteps within which the battle is decisively over. The 600 timesteps is equivalent to 60 seconds, or 1 minute, of actual battle time. While the simulations do not model the significant time required for maneuver in most actual battles, the fact that a representative battle is over in 1 minute underscores the rapid speed of today's warfare. Typical simulations require 25 to 60 minutes of wall clock time. There are several reasons for the relatively slow speed of the simulation. The most important factor is that the desired accuracy of the position calculations, firings, hits, and granularity in the simulation imposes a great computational burden that slows the simulation. Precision and accuracy are of paramount importance in today's fast battlefields. Second, the C code is not optimized and the repeated searchings through the big, complex, linear linked lists, requires time. Third, the logging of enormous data to facilitate the visual representation of the progress of the battle, given the slow input-output of Sun Sparc 10s, slows down the simulation. Finally, the message passing speed in the 10 Mbit/sec Ethernet-based connectivity is slow, the Solaris operating system is slow, and approximately four to seven processes are allocated to every processor in the simulation.

The performance data reported here are the result of more than 50 full-scale simulation runs, i.e., with 38 concurrent processes, and many small-scale trial simulations to assist in identifying relevant performance parameters.

3.4.4.1 Scenario 1

In Scenario 1, each of the blue and red forces consist of three platoons of five tanks each, a company leader tank, and two long-range artillery units, as was shown in Figure 3.72. Initially, the two forces are not within sensor range but identical intelligence information on both sides propel them to move toward each other. As they move closer, they come within sensor range of one another and initiate maneuver and firing. Figures 3.76 through 3.80 are snapshots of the Motif-based graphical representation of the battlefield at simulation timesteps 2, 35, 98, 228, and 423. They represent the progress of the battle where the blue forces (left) and red forces (right) use decentralized and centralized C^3 strategy, respectively. In Figures 3.76 through 3.80, circles represent individual tanks, PLs adjacent to the circles represent platoon leaders, other PLs represent the artillery units at the platoon level, and CL denotes the company leader. The short lines emanating from each unit represent their velocity magnitude and direction. Figure 3.76 shows the initial positions of the two opposing forces as they begin to move toward one another. No enemy sightings have occurred yet for either side, so all units continue on their initial courses. In Figure 3.77, a few of the individual units of both forces are within each other's sensor range and have spotted each other. Those units within the blue force that have spotted the enemy immediately turn toward them. In contrast, the units of the red force that have sighted the enemy are not allowed to turn immediately toward the enemy. They wait for high-level orders. The unit that sighted the enemy sends the sighting information up to its platoon leader, which then fuses the information into a platoon-sized sighting and relays it to the company leader.

For the red forces, the individual units maintain their course until an order arrives from the company leader guided through the platoon leader. Because centralized decision making is slow, Figure 3.78 shows the red platoons still maintaining their original courses. In contrast, in the blue force, the sighting unit sends the information to the other members of the platoon and the platoon leader. The platoon leader also sends this information to other platoon leaders and the company leader. Other units of the platoon autonomously decide to turn toward the enemy units. Figure 3.78 shows that blue platoons have already begun to converge toward the sighted enemy. For the blue force, the artillery units receive sighting information and request fire support from platoon leaders and open fire immediately. In contrast, the red artillery units await the fire command to arrive from the company leader and are silent at this time instant. The firings are indicated through long blue or red lines on the visual representation and are not shown in Figures 3.76 through 3.80.

Eventually, the company leader of the red force orders the platoon leaders, and the individual tanks to converge on the enemy individual tanks. In Figure 3.79, both the red and blue forces move toward each other with the tanks and artillery units firing at each other. Figure 3.80 represents a snapshot of the battlefield that is very close to the end of the battle, where the blue forces decisively defeat the red forces. Only four tanks of the blue force are destroyed, while 12 red tanks are destroyed.

The advantage of the decentralized C^3 algorithm over the traditional command hierarchy under the stated assumptions is observed in each and every one of more than 50 full-scale simulation runs. It may be noted that the decentralized scheme is realized only through a few changes relative to the traditional scheme, such as autonomy in heading, speed, and firings and communication of intelligence at the horizontal level. Yet, the advantages are consistent, significant, and revealing. The results confirm the earlier stated hypothesis, namely, that today's fast-paced battlefields, involving high-speed and precision weapons coupled with individual fighting units, superbly trained and equipped with intelligence gathering, communication, and computing facilities, despite ever-present smoke and confusion, require effective decentralized command and control.

For consistency, the experiments were designed and executed to test all four combinations: (1) blue force centralized, red force centralized; (2) blue force decentralized, red force centralized; (3) blue force centralized, red force decentralized; and (4) blue force decentralized, red force decentralized. For each of the cases, the cumulative number of friendly units destroyed, the number of tank and artillery firings, the number of enemy units destroyed through tank firings, and the number of enemy units destroyed by artillery firings are reported in Table 3.10.

As expected, where both forces, blue and red, employ the same command and control strategy, i.e., centralized or decentralized, the corresponding numbers of enemy and friendly units destroyed are virtually identical in Table 3.10. Where the two forces employ different strategies, the one that uses the decentralized scheme is the decisive winner. The results for the cases {blue decentralized, red centralized} and {blue centralized, red decentralized} are not identical, primarily due to the stochastic nature of the simulation and the input stimulus.

To understand the nature of the influence of the company leader processing delay on the battlefield performance, the following experiment is designed with blue and red forces using decentralized and centralized schemes, respectively. Clearly, faster information propagation will lower the delay between a sighting and the corresponding artillery firing, thereby increasing the devastating impact of artillery. Thus, for this experiment, the kill rate due to artillery fire is increased to 100% for both forces. That is, when a high-velocity and precision artillery shell lands near an enemy tank that is within its area of coverage, the tank is assumed to receive a direct hit. Additionally, the area of coverage of artillery fire is gradually increased from 250 spatial units to a high value of 750 spatial units. When the area of coverage of artillery fire is 250 spatial units and the company leader processing delay is increased from 0 timesteps, the number of blue tanks destroyed rapidly approaches zero. However, where the area of coverage of artillery fire is 750 spatial units, the red forces achieve finite blue tank kills even with large values for company leader

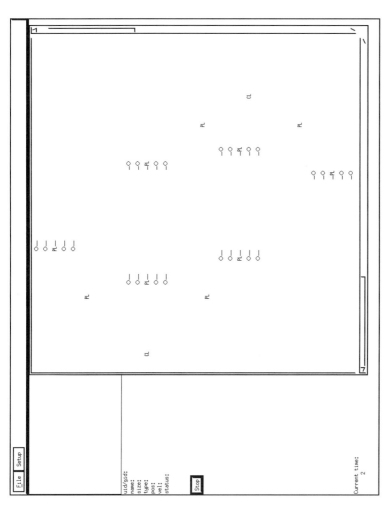

Fig. 3.76. Progress of Simulation: Screen Shot at Timestamp 2 (Blue, Decentralized Force on the Left and Red, Centralized Force on the Right)

158

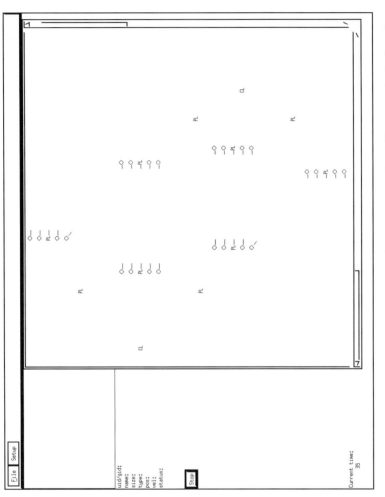

Fig. 3.77. Progress of Simulation: Screen Shot at Timestamp 35 (Blue, Decentralized Force on the Left and Red, Centralized Force on the Right)

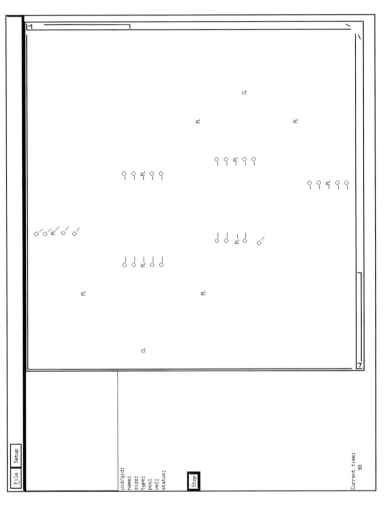

Fig. 3.78. Progress of Simulation: Screen Shot at Timestamp 98 (Blue, Decentralized Force on the Left, and Red, Centralized Force on the Right)

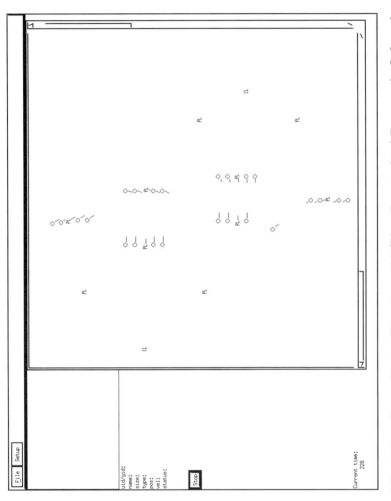

Fig. 3.79. Progress of Simulation: Screen Shot at Timestamp 228 (Blue, Decentralized Force on the Left, and Red, Centralized Force on the Right)

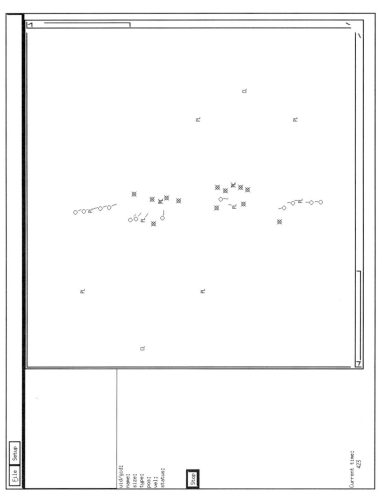

Fig. 3.80. Progress of Simulation: Screen Shot at Timestamp 423 (Blue, Decentralized Force on the Left, and Red, Centralized Force on the Right)

	Blue Force	Red Force
Blue Centralized, Red Centralized		
Units destroyed	7 (39%)	7 (39%)
Times tank weapon fired	37	44
Times artillery fired	14	14
Enemy destroyed by tanks	7	7
Enemy destroyed by artillery	0	0
Blue Decentralized, Red Centralized		
Units destroyed	4 (22%)	12 (67%)
Times tank weapon fired	26	23
Times artillery fired	20	15
Enemy destroyed by tanks	8	3
Enemy destroyed by artillery	4	1
Blue Centralized, Red Decentralized		
Units destroyed	8 (44%)	4 (22%)
Times tank weapon fired	20	21
Times artillery fired	16	20
Enemy destroyed by tanks	3	3
Enemy destroyed by artillery	1	5
Blue Decentralized, Red Decentralized		
Units destroyed	10 (56%)	9 (50%)
Times tank weapon fired	22	13
Times artillery fired	20	20
Enemy destroyed by tanks	6	6
Enemy destroyed by artillery	4	3

Table 3.10. Summary of Performance Measures for Scenario 1

processing delay. Figure 3.81 graphically presents the results of this experiment. The x-axis represents increasing company leader processing delays from 0 to 150 timesteps. The y-axis plots the ratio of red tanks destroyed to blue tanks destroyed and represents the superiority of the decentralized over the centralized scheme. In Figure 3.81, as the company leader processing delay increases, in general, more red tanks relative to blue tanks are destroyed. Clearly, the reaction time increases disproportionately for the red force, diminishing its effectiveness. Where the company leader processing delay is near zero, the centralized scheme closely resembles the decentralized scheme, as corroborated by Figure 3.81. The stochastic nature of the simulation and input stimulus is the primary cause of the apparent aberrations of the graph in Figure 3.81.

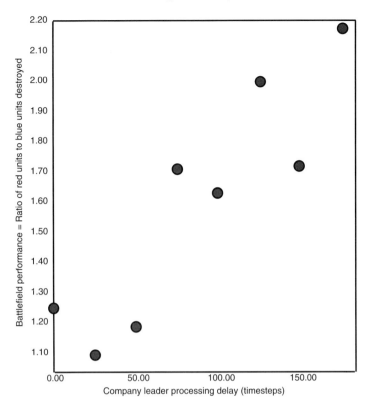

Fig. 3.81. The Nature of Influence of Company Leader Processing Delay on Battlefield Performance

3.4.4.2 Scenario 2

In Scenario 2, the red force utilizes centralized C^3 and consists of three platoons of five tanks each, two artillery units, and a company leader. The blue force consists of one platoon of five tanks and a company leader. As in Scenario 1, both forces are initially outside of each other's sensor range and receive identical intelligence information to move toward the enemy. The goal of this experiment is to study the influence of decentralized C^3 on effective withdrawal, relative to the conventional command hierarchy. In centralized C^3, only the company leader can decide to withdraw. When the withdrawal order is issued by the company leader and subsequently received by the individual units, the latter retreat. In decentralized C^3, each unit is capable of generating the decision to retreat autonomously. In the experiment, first the blue force is designed to utilize decentralized C^3. Second, the blue force employs centralized C^3. The results of the experiment are summarized in Table 3.11. The data reveal that in the decentralized scheme, information regarding the enemy's superior strength is received promptly and, as a result, the blue force is able to retreat at the cost of a single tank, or 17% of strength. In contrast, in the centralized scheme, the company leader takes appreciable time to determine the enemy threat. The individual units of the blue force do not receive the order to withdraw from the company leader in time, resulting in the catastrophic loss of five tanks, or 83% of strength. The advantage of decentralized C^3 is therefore significant under the stated assumptions.

	Blue Force	Red Force (Centralized)
Blue Decentralized		
Units destroyed	1 (17%)	0 (0%)
Times tank weapon fired	0	0
Times artillery fired	0	6
Enemy destroyed by tanks	0	0
Enemy destroyed by artillery	0	1
Blue Centralized		
Units destroyed	5 (83%)	4 (22%)
Times tank weapon fired	6	7
Times artillery fired	0	6
Enemy destroyed by tanks	4	4
Enemy destroyed by artillery	0	1

Table 3.11. Summary of Performance Measures for Scenario 2

3.4.4.3 Observations and Limitations

The performance results reported here are revealing and not obvious. While all information is propagated to a single, centralized, decision maker, in the decentralized strategy, every entity is autonomous and has access to accurate local data, and the decisions are arrived at independently.

This study suffers from the limitation that, terrain data, an important factor in most real-life military engagements, are beyond the scope of this research. Thus, the impact of terrain data on the advantages or disadvantages of C^3, remains an open question. The results reported here, therefore, provide only a general insight into decentralized command and control, and do not claim any military realism.

3.5 An Asynchronous, Distributed Circuit-Partitioning-Based Algorithm for Fault Simulation of Digital Designs on Loosely Coupled Parallel Processors

Fault simulation constitutes an indispensable tool in ensuring the correctness and quality of manufactured digital designs. Traditional uniprocessor-based algorithms for fault simulation have been observed to be agonizingly slow for today's large and complex digital designs. More recently, a few researchers introduced an approach, as evident in the literature, wherein the fault set is partitioned and the digital design fault simulated for each fault subset on separate processors of a parallel processor system. The approach is limited in that it continues to use the traditional uniprocessor-based algorithm and the performance results are not encouraging. This section introduces a distributed algorithm that is capable of fault simulating both combinational and asynchronous sequential digital designs on parallel processors. An underlying assumption of the algorithm is that the digital design, under fault simulation, is partitioned by the user. In this approach, referred to as NODIFS, every component in the circuit is modeled as an asynchronous, concurrent entity that is fault simulated as soon as appropriate signal transitions and fault lists are asserted at its input ports. The circuit partitioning is such that components of every partition are allocated to a unique processor of the parallel processor system. Consequently, a number of components may be concurrently fault simulated on multiple processors in NODIFS, implying significant increase in throughput. This approach promises (1) very high throughput because of its ability, in principle, to utilize the maximal inherent parallelism and (2) scalability. The algorithm is novel in that the overall task of decision making, i.e., fault simulation of the circuit, is distributed into a number of natural, independent, and concurrent entities that execute asynchronously to exploit maximal parallelism. NODIFS's success is the result of the asynchronous distributed discrete-event simulation algorithm, YADDES, and a new approach to fault simulation. The notion of scalability implies that where the problem size increases, the algorithm continues to apply and, by increasing the number of computational engines proportionately, the performance of the algorithm will continue to increase. Furthermore, NODIFS is a natural choice for fault simulation of digital designs at the behavior-level, an eventual reality, wherein the ratio of the computational to communication load for the behavior models may approach a significantly large value. This research also reports on an implementation of NODIFS on Armstrong.

3.5.1 Introduction

Fault simulation [148] constitutes an important tool to ensure the correctness and reliability of manufactured digital designs in the electronics industry. Following its manufacture, a digital design is exercised by a set of external stimuli, termed test vectors, that are determined through a test generation process. Where the results of execution of the design agree with the desired results, the design is considered functionally correct. Otherwise, it is faulty and, as a result, it is rejected. Thus, the accuracy and efficiency of the test vectors are determined through fault simulation. Conceptually, fault simulation consists in the repeated logic simulation of a circuit under investigation for the given test vectors, where each simulation corresponds to a single fault, assumed to have been introduced into the circuit by the manufacturing process.

The earliest known algorithm for fault simulation is the sequential algorithm [149], wherein the entire design is simulated multiple times sequentially, once for each fault. During each simulation run, the circuit is modified to reflect the influence of the fault. This algorithm has been observed to be inefficient even for modestly complex designs. Subsequently, other algorithms have been introduced to address the problem of inefficiency, namely, parallel [149], deductive [150], and concurrent [151] algorithms. Of these, the concurrent approach has been highly favored in the industry. A significant limitation of all of these techniques is that they are limited to execution on a uniprocessor.

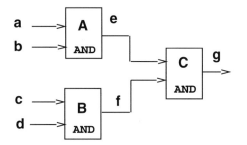

Fig. 3.82. Fault Simulation of a Simple Circuit

Consider the simple circuit in Figure 3.82, consisting of three AND gates A, B, and C. Assume that the input ports a and b of A and c and d of B are primary. The output ports e and f of A and B, respectively, are connected to the input ports of AND gate C. Assume that the test vector used for fault simulation is given by $\{a = 1, b = 1, c = 1,$ and $d = 1\}$. Furthermore, assume the presence of the following faults: a s-a-0, b s-a-0, f s-a-0, and c s-a-0 and that the propagation delays of the gates are 5 ns each. The operation of the uniprocessor-based concurrent fault simulation algorithm may be described as follows. Observe that the entity that schedules the components for fault simulation is a centralized unit that executes sequentially and has access to the global simulation time. Corresponding to the assertion of signal 1 at each of a through d for global simulation time given by $t = 0$ ns, the event queue consists of four entries: execute A for logical 1 at a; execute A for logical 1 at b at $t = 0$ ns; execute B for logical 1 at c; and execute B for logical 1 at d at $t = 0$ ns. Execution of A consists of a good simulation of A followed by simulation of the faults originating at it. The good simulation generates a logical 1 at $t = 5$ ns. Simulation of each of the faults—a s-a-0 and b s-a-0—generates identical output—logical 0 at $t = 5$ ns, at e. These outputs differ from the good values and are, therefore, included in the fault-list at e. Execution of B consists of good simulation of B followed by simulation of the faults originating at it. The good simulation generates a logical 1 at $t = 5$ ns. Simulation of the fault c s-a-0 produces logical 0 at $t = 5$ ns at output f. This output differs from the good value and is, therefore, included in the fault-list at f. The good values and the fault-lists at e and f are both propagated to the component C, which is then executed. The output fault-lists at e and f are organized as input-fault lists of the component C. Execution of C produces a good value of logical 1 at $t = 10$ ns. Simulation of the input fault-list entries corresponding to the three fault effects generate identical output value of logical 0 at $t = 10$ ns at g. The simulation of the fault, f s-a-0, originating at C, causes a logical 0 at $t = 10$ ns at output g. These outputs differ from the good output and, consequently, all four faults are potentially detectable at g at $t = 10$ ns.

In the circuit in Figure 3.82, it may be observed that components A and B may potentially execute in parallel. However, they are simulated sequentially by a single processor. Thus, the uniprocessor algorithm fails to use the parallelism available in the fault simulation process. In fact, a severe limitation of such algorithms is that they are excruciatingly slow for complex designs. For instance, a 5000-gate circuit with 7000 faults required 409 hours, 57 minutes, 20 seconds for fault simulation on a Sun 3/50 workstation at ERC, Bell Laboratories in Princeton, NJ. The fault simulator utilized was the concurrent fault simulator, CSIM [152]. Such large simulation times imply that the usefulness and effectiveness of fault simulation as a tool are significantly reduced in today's world of complex designs.

A few researchers have attempted to speed up the fault simulation process by resorting to special purpose hardware such as IBM's Yorktown Simulation Engine [153] [154], NEC's hardware accelerator [155], or ZYCAD [156]. However, such an approach is expensive and incompatible with the use of different fault simulation algorithms. Furthermore, this approach is confined to fault simulation exclusively at the gate-level representation.

It may be observed that the principal cause for the significant CPU times required for fault simulation stem from the need to simulate every component multiple times, once for every fault originating at it or propagating through it and again for each signal transition received at an input port. At the gate-level representation, execution of a gate requires execution of only a few instructions and is, therefore, relatively quick. Even then, the computational load, corresponding to a single gate, may be significant in a fault simulation system consisting of thousands of faults and test vectors. Furthermore, the computational requirement for simulation at the behavior-level, on a uniprocessor, is clearly formidable given that behavior models are compute-intensive. To address the problem of fault simulation, conceivably, one may adopt the following procedure. The test vector set is partitioned into N sets, $I_1, I_2, \ldots, I_n$, and the process of fault simulation of the entire design is replicated either on a network of N independent workstations [25] or a parallel processor with N processors [157]. Each processor fault simulates the entire design for all of the faults under consideration but only for a fraction of the total test vector set. The key idea is to achieve efficiency through dividing the total computational load on a number of processors; however, this methodology is severely limited to combinational circuits. In sequential circuits, states are affected as a result of execution and, consequently, the final state of the circuit at the conclusion of fault simulation for the test vector set I_{n-1} must be copied prior to initiating fault simulation of the circuit for the test vector set I_n. Thus, the executions for the test vector subsets I_{n-1} and I_n must be done sequentially and parallelism is difficult to achieve.

A second approach consists in partitioning the fault set into N subsets, $F_1, F_2, \ldots, F_n$, and replicating the fault simulation process for the entire design on N independent processors. Each processor is then responsible for fault simulation of the complete circuit for a fault subset F_i and the entire test vector set. A conceptual limitation of this approach may be described as follows. Consider two faults, f_i and f_j, associated with two components A_1 and A_2 of the circuit, and assume a partitioning such that f_i and f_j are allocated to processors P_1 and P_2, respectively. It is conceivable that the effects of both f_1 and f_2 are identical at another component A_3, i.e., the faults f_i and f_j may be considered as a single entry for the purpose of fault simulation. Thus, although f_i and f_j would have coalesced into a single entry in the conventional uniprocessor-based concurrent technique leading to efficiency, in this approach, the simulation of f_i and f_j on P_1 and P_2 beyond component A_3 implies unnecessary duplication. Patil and Banerjee [157] present an implementation of this approach on a Hypercube processor and report that, based on their observations of fault simulation of a number of digital designs, performance improves when the number of processors is increased to four. Where more than four processors are utilized, i.e., the fault set was partitioned into more than 4 subsets, performance degradation is noted, resulting from increased communication and complex control. Markas, Royals, and Kanopoulos [25] report another implementation of this approach on a heterogeneous network of workstations connected through a local area network. While superlinear speedup is observed where a few workstations are utilized, the performance quickly drops for an increase in the number of computational engines, even though the number of components in the circuit greatly exceeds the number of servers. However, the superlinear speedup, from physical and thermodynamic principles, cannot imply that the N servers, each with computational capacity C, deliver a combined power exceeding $N \times C$. One possible explanation is that the uniprocessor implementation is inefficient resulting in excessive page faults due to memory limitations.

Nelson [158] proposes a technique for deductive fault simulation of combinational circuits on Hypercube multiprocessors. In this approach, the circuit is divided into as many levels as the maximum number of gates between the primary input and output ports. The gates in each level are fault simulated by a unique processor of the Hypercube. Corresponding to the input stimulus asserted at the primary input ports at discrete times, conceivably, the components at more than one level are active, resulting in overall improved performance. A principal limitation of this approach is that it fails for sequential circuits.

Daoud and Ozguner [159] propose a parallel fault simulation algorithm for high-speed fault simulation on a Cray X-MP vector supercomputer. While they report significant speedup factors of 50 to 60, their approach is strictly limited to combinational circuits.

A careful analysis of the fault simulation process yields the following observation. Although the large number of test vectors and faults both contribute to the computational load, the primary source of computation is the models. Corresponding to a signal transition at an input port, a model executes a number of times, once for every fault originating at it or propagating through it. Conceivably, an alternate algorithm may be synthesized wherein the independent computational entities may be identified and allocated to unique processors such that they may be executed asynchronously and concurrently, resulting in maximal speedup. Thus, an approach wherein the circuit is partitioned into subsets and the components of each partition allocated to a unique processor of the parallel processor system, may exploit maximal parallelism. The entities that require significant computation, namely, the models, are executed concurrently and asynchronously on multiple processors. The operation of such an approach may be described as follows.

Consider the circuit in Figure 3.82. Assume that the circuit is partitioned into three subsets—$\{A\}$, $\{B\}$, and $\{C\}$—and that the component in each partition is allocated to three unique processors. Given that logical value 1 is asserted at the input ports of A and B, both A and B are simultaneously fault simulated and the output fault lists are propagated to the two input ports of C. Then C is fault simulated. While component C is fault simulated, conceivably, A and B may be fault simulated again, simultaneously, where a second input stimulus is asserted at the input ports $\{a, b\}$ and $\{c, d\}$, respectively. Thus, every computational entity is executed by a unique processor and maximal parallelism is achieved. While it works for combinational circuits, this straightforward approach fails for sequential circuits.

This section presents a novel approach, NODIFS, that successfully addresses the issue of distributed fault simulation of both combinational and sequential circuits and achieves in distributing the computational entities to execute concurrently and asynchronously on unique processors of a parallel processor system. The algorithm is detailed in Section 3.5.2, while Section 3.5.3 discusses the issue of implementation on the Armstrong [160] parallel processor system. Section 3.5.4 presents an analysis of the performance data obtained for a few representative digital designs. The proof of correctness is presented in Chapter 5.

3.5.2 An Asynchronous, Distributed Algorithm for Fault Simulation

The NODIFS approach, proposed in this research, is the result of an integration of the YADDES [118] algorithm and a new approach to fault simulation. YADDES enables the asynchronous distributed simulation of both combinational and sequential digital designs on parallel processors. In the new approach to fault simulation, while the progress of fault simulation for combinational digital components is controlled only by the good events, for sequential components, the progress of fault simulation is controlled by good and faulty events. Thus, consistency is maintained while the fault models execute asynchronously, concurrently, and cooperatively on multiple processors of the parallel processor. NODIFS is based on the philosophy of partitioning the circuit under test and allocating the models corresponding to the components of each partition to unique processors of the parallel processor system. Thus, the computational load is distributed for asynchronous execution on multiple independent, concurrent computational engines to achieve significant speedup. Additionally, in this approach, a model represents each component of the circuit under test. The execution of a model that contains the unfaulted description of the component behavior consists of three phases: the simulation of the fault effects that have been received at the input ports in the form of signal transitions, the good simulation of the component, and the simulation of faults originating at the component. This approach permits the simulation of stuck-at-logical-0 or -1 faults associated with the input or output pins of the component as well as behavior-level fault models [161] [162]. Conceptually, fault simulation is equivalent to the correct execution of events in the system wherein an event consists of a signal transition caused either by the execution of an unfaulted component behavior description in the absence of faults or in the presence of a fault. When an unfaulted component description is executed in the presence of accurate input signal transitions and a new signal transition is generated at its output port, it is referred to as a *good event*. When a component description is executed in the presence of a fault or due to faulty input signal transitions and an output signal is generated that differs from the good output, it is referred to as a *faulty event*.

NODIFS consists of two conceptual subtasks: the control of fault simulation of combinational digital components through the good events and the deadlock-free distributed execution of good and fault-related events for sequential components on a parallel processor utilizing the YADDES [118] algorithm. The circuit under test is first analyzed and the components that constitute cyclic directed graphs (i.e., feedback loops) are identified and preprocessed prior to their fault simulation. The fault simulation of those components that do not constitute feedback loops is less complex and is presented in Section 3.5.2.1. Section 3.5.2.2 discusses the fault simulation of components that constitute feedback loops. NODIFS accepts a user-specified partitioning scheme for the components of the circuit regardless of whether they constitute directed cyclic graphs. Models corresponding to each component of a partition are executed on a unique processor.

3.5.2.1 Distributed Fault Simulation of Combinational Subcircuits

A model (M) representing a component (C) of the circuit consists of a behavior description of C and a list of faults—either stuck-at-type faults associated with its input and output pins or behavior faults [162] [163] originating at C. In addition, associated with every input and output port p of M, except where p is a primary input port of the circuit is a fault-list(p). The fault-list is a linked list of records that contains the effects of faults originating outside C at p. Each record consists of four fields containing the logical value, assertion time, fault identifier, and a pointer to the subsequent record, if any. A record containing f_1 in the fault identifier field refers to the effect, i.e., the logical value and assertion time, of fault f_1 at p. In addition, a temporary value-list(p) is associated with every output port of M that temporarily stores the results of execution of M.

Consider a combinational component, C, shown in Figure 3.83. When a new signal is asserted at one or more input ports $p_1, p_2, \ldots, p_n$ of model M, it is initiated for execution. First, the activation time of the model is computed as the minimum assertion time over all input ports of M through the equation:

$$\text{activation time } (t_1) \text{ of } M = \text{minimum (assertion time of signal at}$$
$$p_i \forall i \in \{1, N\}).$$

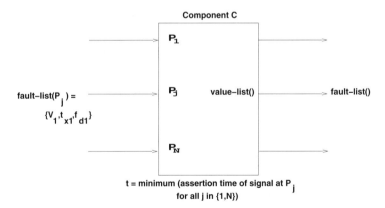

Fig. 3.83. A Combinational Component

The significance of the activation time is that the model may execute at $t = t_1$ with absolute certainty of correctness. Where t_1 exceeds the value of the previous activation time of M, the model is executed. Where an input port p_j of M is not primary, it is conceivable that a nonempty fault list is associated with p_j. That is, faults originating outside M may influence p_j that is recorded in the form of a fault effect, logical value and assertion time. As a part of execution of M, all those fault list entries at $\{p_1, p_2, \ldots, p_N,\}$ with assertion times less than t_1 are identified and simulated, one at a time. For a fault list entry at p_j, characterized by $\{V_1, t_{x1}, f_{d1}\}$ where V_1, t_{x1}, and f_{d1} refer, respectively, to the logical value, assertion time, and fault identifier, V_1 is temporarily forced at p_j and the model behavior description is executed. As a result, an output V_2 is generated at $t = t_{x1} + d$ where d is the propagation delay of M. The output, along with the fault identifier, is stored in the value list of the appropriate output port of M and the corresponding input fault list entry is deleted. Following completion of processing of the input fault list entry, the assertion of V_1 at p_j is undone and the second input fault list entry is simulated. Other input fault list entries whose assertion times exceed t_1, may not be fault simulated at this time because the correct signal transitions at $\{p_1, p_2, \ldots, p_n\}$ of M are yet unknown.

Following the completion of simulation of the executable input fault-list entries, the unfaulted behavior description of M is executed at $t = t_1$ in the presence of correct signal transitions. Where a new signal transition is generated at its output port, it is destined to be propagated to the input ports of other models connected to the output of M. If the generated output signal is identical to the previous value, it may not be propagated to other models. The third phase of the model execution consists of the assertion of the faults originating at M and the execution of the unfaulted behavior description of M for each fault. For instance, corresponding to a stuck-at-logical-0 associated with an input pin p_j of M, fault simulation would consist in the execution of the behavior description of M in the presence of correct signal transitions at $\{p_1, p_2, \ldots, p_{j-1}, p_j, p_{j+1}, \ldots, p_n\}$ and a logical 0 asserted at p_j. The output values are stored in the appropriate value-list of M. In the final phase, all entries of the value-lists associated with the output port(s) of M are examined. An entry whose effect, i.e., logical value and assertion time, is indistinguishable from the good output implies that the corresponding fault is potentially undetectable at the output of M and, as a result, the entry is discarded. When an entry is observed to differ from the good output with certainty, it is moved from the value-list to the fault list at the output port of M. That is, the assertion time of the entry does not exceed that of the good output and their logical values are different. Finally, the good signal transitions along with the entries of the fault-list at the output port of M are propagated to the input ports of other models connected to the output of M, where the output caused by good simulation differs from the previous output value. Where no new signal transition is generated as a consequence of the good simulation, the fault-list continues to remain stored within the model M, and it may be propagated at a later instant of time following a subsequent execution of the model M.

It may be observed that the execution of a model in the fault simulation process involves the multiple execution of the behavior description of the component and is, consequently, compute-intensive.

In the process of fault simulation of the input fault-list entries, described earlier, it was assumed that the fault effects were uncorrelated. Thus, they could be fault simulated independently. This assumption breaks down in those circuits characterized by the presence of reconvergent paths. *Reconvergence* refers to that condition where two or more paths in a circuit originate from the same component and terminate at the input ports of another component in the circuit. As a result, a single fault may simultaneously influence more than one input port of a component. Under such circumstances, the fault effects e_1 and e_2 at input ports p_i and p_j of a model caused by the same fault f_1 must be fault simulated simultaneously. For instance, consider that the two fault effects e_1 and e_2 are characterized by $\{V_1, t_{x1}, f_1\}$ and $\{V_2, t_{x2}, f_1\}$, respectively. Assuming that the model M is activated at $t = t_1$ and that $t_{x1} = t_{x2} < t_1$, the logical values V_1 and V_2 must be asserted at the input ports p_i and p_j simultaneously, followed by the execution of the unfaulted model description. The output constitutes the result of fault simulating the fault effects e_1 and e_2 due to fault f_1.

In the NODIFS approach, the execution of a model is usually associated with the generation of an output signal transition and a nonnull fault-list. Where the execution does not generate a new signal transition at the output, the entries of the output fault-list continue to be stored within the model and are not propagated to the input ports of other models. Thus, conceivably, a model may accumulate a few output fault-list entries that have remained unpropagated and consequently unprocessed by other components of the circuit. The termination procedure of the NODIFS algorithm consists in the propagation of a special termination signal transition at every primary input port of the circuit following the propagation of the last signal transition at that port. When a model receives the termination vector at each of its primary inputs, all unprocessed output fault list entries are propagated at the output prior to the propagation of a termination signal transition. These fault entries manifest as input fault list entries of other components; their simulation was discussed earlier. Every component will eventually receive the termination vector at all of its input ports and, therefore, all outstanding fault-list entries will be processed.

The process of fault simulation of a model may be described through the algorithm presented in pseudocode in Figure 3.84.

3.5.2.2 Asynchronous, Distributed Fault Simulation of Sequential Subcircuits

3.5.2.2.1 Intuitive Overview

The principal cause of deadlock in the traditional approach to asynchronous distributed fault simulation is the presence of feedback loops. That is, the fault

```
read in signal transitions asserted at any input port of a model
read in fault entries into input fault lists
activation time of model = minimum over signal assertion times at
            every input port
if (activation time of model <> previous activation time of model) {
    if (input fault list entries with assertion time equal to
            activation time of models exists) {
        if (two or more input fault list entries possess identical
            fault identifiers)  {
          fault simulate them simultaneously
          include the generated output in the value list at the
            output of the model
        }
        fault simulate each of the remaining input fault list entries
            one at a time
        include the generated output in the value list at the output
            of the model
    }
    execute unfaulted behavior description of component for correct
            input signal transitions
    assert faults originating at the model at activation time and
            fault simulate them, one at a time
    include the output in the value list at the output of the model
    for (every entry in the value-list of model M) {
        if (value-list entry differs from the good output) {
            move entry into fault-list at the output of the model
        }
        else {
          delete entry
        }
    }
    if (output from unfaulted model execution implies a new signal
            transition) {
        propagate signal transition at the output port
        for (every entry in the output fault-list of the model) {
            assert entry at the output port
            delete entry from the fault-list
        }
    }
}
```

Fig. 3.84. NODIFS Algorithm for Combinational Subcircuits

simulation environment represented through models connected by feedback loops is unable to accurately decide the precise execution of events. The second subtask of NODIFS that uses the YADDES [118] algorithm solves this problem through the synthesis of an acyclic circuit of pseudo components based on the original subcircuit under test whose purpose is to enable fault simulation of the subcircuit in a deadlock-free environment. A pseudo component is a mathematical entity and an image of the corresponding component in the original digital design.

To preserve the asynchronous and concurrent nature of the algorithm, each pseudo component represents a decision-making entity whose sole function is to determine when the corresponding model may correctly execute an input event. The second subtask of NODIFS inherits the characteristics of YADDES with one exception. An event in NODIFS refers to either a good or faulty signal transition at an input port for which the model may be executed. Except for important details of YADDES as they apply to fault simulation, for a thorough description of YADDES, the reader is referred to [118]. An event corresponding to a good signal assertion is referred to as a good event while that corresponding to a faulty signal assertion is termed a faulty event. In a model where the smallest assertion time of all good signal transitions is equal to or less than the smallest assertion time of all input fault list entries, the event of the model refers to the good signal transition with the least value of assertion time. Where the model lacks any good signal transitions or the smallest assertion time among all fault list entries is less than that of the good signal, the event of the model refers to the input fault list entry with the smallest assertion time. Execution of a good event consists in the fault simulation of the input fault list entries, good simulation of the unfaulted behavior description, and the assertion and simulation of faults originating at that component. Execution of a faulty event consists only in the simulation of the fault effect in question.

3.5.2.2.2 The NODIFS Algorithm for Sequential Subcircuits

For a given subcircuit containing feedback loops, first, a feedback arc set [103] S given by $S = \{E_1, E_2, \ldots, E_n\}$ of a directed graph corresponding to a digital design is identified such that the graph may be rendered acyclic following removal of all of the edges E_1 through E_n. The proof of correctness of NODIFS is not contingent on identification of the minimal feedback arc set, which is difficult and time-consuming. However, the minimal feedback arc set may imply improved performance. For each $E_i \forall i \in \{1, 2, \ldots, n\}$ in the original directed graph, a new acyclic directed graph is reconstructed, as required by YADDES, by replacing E_i with two unconnected edges E_i^{in} and E_i^{out} as illustrated through Figure 3.85. Figure 3.85(a) depicts a cyclic subcircuit consisting of a two-input AND gate A whose output is connected through edge E_2 to the input of the inverter B. The output of the inverter B is connected through edge E_1 to an input of A. The other input port of A is edge E_3.

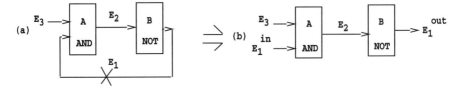

Fig. 3.85. Reducing a Cyclic Directed to an Acyclic Directed Graph

Assume that the feedback arc set for the subcircuit is given by $S = \{E_1\}$. The graph is rendered acyclic in Figure 3.85(b) through the removal of E_1 and replacing it by E_1^{in} and E_1^{out} associated with the input of A and the output of B, respectively. The data-flow network is synthesized utilizing the rules of YADDES and is shown in Figure 3.86.

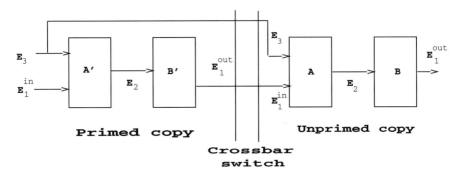

Fig. 3.86. Data-Flow Network Constructed for Cyclic Circuit in Figure 3.85(a)

In Figure 3.86, the pseudo components A' and B' constitute the primed circuit where the input port E_1^{in} of A' is permanently connected to ∞. A' and B' correspond to the AND and inverter gates in the original circuit. Pseudo components A and B constitute the unprimed acyclic circuit. Associated with E_3 are the externally applied signal transitions. Conceptually, these transitions may be included in the good event list of model A, i.e., the list of outstanding input transitions of A. Although the output port E_1^{out} of B defines the rightmost boundary of the data-flow network and is unconnected, in the current implementation of NODIFS, the output of B is connected to a special entity P1 that signifies the rightmost boundary.

Associated with the output port of each of the pseudo components $X' \in \{A', B', \ldots, H'\}$ is a mathematical quantity time of next event that is represented by the symbol W'_X. The mathematical definition of W'_X is presented subsequently. Intuitively, W'_X is the predicted time of the next event at the output of model X. It is computed from the W' values at the input ports of X' and the simulation time of the event of model X. The computation of W'_X is triggered by any changes in the values of its arguments. Any computed W'_X

is propagated to other pseudo components connected to its fanout when it differs from the previous value. Moreover, the propagation process is analogous to a nuclear chain reaction. That is, subsequent components that intercept the W' values are also executed and any change in their output values are further propagated. The chain reaction terminates when either no new W' values are generated or the rightmost component of the network is encountered. The termination is detected through a process of acknowledgments discussed in detail later.

Associated with each of the pseudo components $Y \in \{A, B, \ldots, H\}$ of the unprimed circuit is a similar mathematical quantity represented by the symbol W_Y. The principles of computation and propagation of W' values are shared equally by the W values. However, in contrast to the W' values, the W_Y values are accurate and, as a result, they are used to determine whether an event of a model may be executed. Conceptually, the W values are accessed by the corresponding models in the circuit.

As with any distributed simulator, the signal transitions received at the inputs of a model in NODIFS are stored in an event list for that model. The head of the list refers to the transition with the smallest value of simulation time. This is also referred to as the event of the model, and the value of its simulation time is represented by U_X. U_X refers to a good signal assertion when the assertion time is smaller than or equal to the smallest assertion time for all input fault list entries. Otherwise, U_X refers to the fault list entry with the smallest value of assertion time. In the NODIFS approach, every event of a model may be accessed by the corresponding primed and unprimed pseudo components.

The NODIFS fault simulation environment consists of two major elements, the simulation circuit and the data-flow network. The simulation circuit consists of executable models corresponding to each component of the circuit, and the flow of signals between the models is represented through messages over communication protocols. Signal transitions received at the input ports are executed by the models, and any output transitions generated as a consequence of execution are propagated to other models connected to the output port. The decision regarding the precise execution of an event, however, is generated by the constituents of the data-flow network. The primed and unprimed pseudo components execute concurrently and asynchronously with respect to one another and the simulation models. However, in the current implementation of NODIFS, they are executed round-robin by a processor. The execution of a pseudo component is initiated by either the corresponding model or the propagation of a new W (or W') value at an input port by other pseudo components.

For the formal definitions of the quantities U_X, W'_X, and W_X, the reader is referred to [118]. Initially, every $W_X \forall X$ is set to 0, implying that they are not yet influenced by any event. Fault simulation is considered complete when W_X and $U_X \forall X$ are identical to ∞.

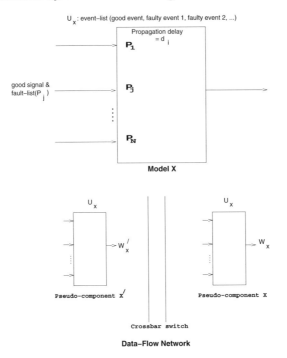

Fig. 3.87. The NODIFS Approach

A description of the NODIFS approach to asynchronous distributed fault simulation is presented as follows. Consider Figure 3.87 that presents a model X contained in a feedback loop of a circuit and its pseudo components X and X'. Assume that a good or faulty signal transition is asserted at an input port of model X either by another model or from the external world. When this event is incorporated in the event queue of X, it may either alter U_X or leave it unchanged. Where U_X is altered as a consequence of the incoming signal transition, model X is initiated for execution. The model X initiates the corresponding pseudo components X and X' of the data-flow network for execution and suspends the execution of the event until those of the pseudo components are completed. X' evaluates W'_X and where its value is observed to be unchanged with respect to its previous value, a message is propagated to the model X signifying that X' has completed its execution. Where the new value of W'_X implies a change from its previous value, X' initiates a chain reaction as described earlier. That is, it propagates the W'_X value to other pseudo components connected to its output port. When a subsequent pseudo component executes as a consequence of a new W' or W value asserted at an input port and generates a new W' or W value at its output port, it propagates the new output value to other pseudo components on the right through the crossbar switch if necessary. The process of computation and propagation of new W' or W values at the output of pseudo components continues until either no new W or W' values are generated or the rightmost boundary of the data-flow network is encountered. Then acknowledgments are initiated by the pseudo components where the chain reaction terminates and are propagated in the reverse direction. When other pseudo components that participated in the chain reaction receive acknowledgments, they take turns propagating them in the reverse direction. Eventually, X' (the primary initiator of the chain reaction) intercepts the acknowledgment and realizes that the process of updating W' or W values in the data-flow network caused by a change in W'_X has been completed. It then sends a message to model X signifying that its execution is complete. It is noted that a pseudo component may be initiated even by new W or W' values asserted at its input port by other such components. The behavior of the pseudo component X following its initiation by model X is identical to that of X' except that the chain reaction is confined only to the unprimed acyclic network. Conceptually, pseudo components X and X' may be initiated concurrently by the model X. Also, multiple models may be executed simultaneously due to signal transitions at their input ports. Consequently, the computations of the W' and W values initiated by multiple pseudo components may overlap. Consistency and correctness are guaranteed because the computations involve a minimum operator and the fact that the W value can never decrease. The issue of correctness is addressed in Chapter 5.

When both pseudo components X and X' have completed execution or the signal transition asserted at an input port of model X does not alter its U value, the model X sends an acknowledgment to the model that propagated the signal transition. If the signal transition was asserted externally, representing a good signal, the acknowledgment implies that the transition is being processed and requires the external world to make available at that primary input port the subsequent good signal transition.

Next, the model X accesses the W or W' values associated with each of the input ports of the corresponding unprimed pseudo component and computes their minimum, K_X. Where $U_X \neq \infty$ i.e., an event exists at X, and K_X exceeds U_X, the model may execute the event corresponding to U_X. Where U_X refers to a faulty event i.e., an input fault list entry, following execution of the model, a faulty output may be generated at $t = U_X + d$, where d is the propagation delay. The good output of X at $t = U_X + d$ must be identical to its previous value given the absence of a good signal assertion at $t = U_X$. Where the faulty output differs from the good output, it is considered a transition. Otherwise, X is assumed to have generated no new transition. Where U_X refers to a good event, execution of A, as detailed subsequently, may generate good output signal—transitions or otherwise—and an output fault-list. Where no new transitions are generated at the output port of model X following its execution, the event corresponding to U_X is deleted from the event queue and a new U_X reflects the time of the new event at the head of the event queue. Once again, U_X may refer to a good or faulty event. Where the event list of model X is empty, U_X is set to ∞.

Execution of the model X for a good event U_X is identical to the execution of a model of a combinational subcircuit at $t = t_1$, described earlier, except for the following. First, because X is included in a feedback loop, one may conceivably assume the presence of a fault-list entry at input port p_j characterized by $\{V_1, t_{x1}, f_1\}$, where p_j is connected to a feedback loop and the fault f_1 originates in X. Under such circumstances, simulation of the fault list entry requires the assertion of f_1 in X in addition to temporarily asserting V_1 at p_j. Where f_1 is a stuck-at fault associated with input port p_j of X, the following analysis is necessary. If V_1 equals logical 0 (or 1) and f_1 is a stuck-at-1 (or -0) fault, an inconsistency in fault simulation is observed and flagged. Second, when the execution of a model has generated a nonempty fault-list but failed to produce a new good signal transition at the input port of X, no good signal is propagated at the output of X but the output fault-list entries are propagated to the input ports of other models connected to the output of X.

The execution of the model X for a faulty event U_X implies the following. The effect of the input fault list entry that corresponds to U_X is asserted, and the good description of the component X is executed. Where the faulty output signal, generated at the output of X, differs from the good output, the faulty output alone is propagated to other models connected to the output of X. The logical value of the good output of X is implicitly identical to its previous value and the assertion time is implicitly identical to that of the faulty output. If a transition is generated at an output port as a consequence of execution of model X, it is propagated by X to other models connected to the output of X. Then, further execution of model X is suspended until it receives acknowledgment from each recipient. Then U_X is removed from the event queue and a new U_X is associated with the event at the head of the queue. The value of U_X is set to ∞ when the number of outstanding transitions at X is nil. Then model X again initiates the pseudo components X and X' for execution and suspends further activity until the pseudo components have completed execution. The process continues until all usable good external signal transitions at the primary input ports are used to fault simulate the model and generate good and output fault-lists.

The precise functionality of a representative model is expressed in Figure 3.88; that of a pseudo component is identical to that in [118].

NODIFS for an example subcircuit is shown in Figure 3.89. In Figure 3.89, NAND gate A is connected to an inverter B through a feedback loop. The output of A is connected to the input of B and the output of B is connected to the second input port of A. The other input port of A is assumed to be primary and a high-to-low good signal transition is asserted at $t = 0$ ns followed by a low-to-high transition at $t = 1000$ ns. The propagation delays of both A and B are 5 ns each and the initial values of the outputs of A and B are assumed to be 0 and 1, respectively. For the given signal transition at the primary input of gate A, the outputs of both A and B change and remain stable thereafter.

```
read in events at input ports- from external ports or other components
update event queue and order events according to time
if (new event alters U value) {
   initiate pseudo components X and X'
   wait till done signal received from X and X'
   send acknowledgement to the sender of the event
}
else if (new event does not alter the U value) {
   send acknowledgement to the sender of the event
}
read W values at every input port of the simulation model X and compute the minimum K
if (K value exceeds U value) {
   execute simulation model and generate output signal
   if (U refers to a faulty event) {
      simulate the corresponding input fault list entry
      if (faulty output != previous good output of X) {
         propagate faulty output at output port of X
      }
   }
   else {
      if (input fault-list entries with assertion time less than or equal to the U value of model) {
         if (two or more input fault-list entries possesses identical fault identifier) {
            fault simulate them simultaneously
            include the generated output in the value-list of model X
         }
         if (a faulty entry possesses a fault identifier that originated at this model) {
            if (the logical value of the fault entry is consistent with the nature of the fault) {
               assert the fault and the fault effect simultaneously and fault simulate
               include the generated output in the value-list of model X
            }
            else {
               flag inconsistency
            }
         }
         fault simulate each of the remaining entries, one at a time
         include the generated output in the value-list of model X
      }
      execute the unfaulted behavior description of model X with good input signals
      assert faults originating at X at the time of U value and fault simulate them, one at a time
      include the generated output in the value-list of model X
      for (every entry in the value-list of X) {
         if (entry differs from good output) {
            move entry from value-list to fault-list of X
         }
         else {
            delete entry from value-list
         }
      }
      if (output from unfaulted model execution implies a new signal transition)
         propagate signal transition at the output port of X
      }
      for (every entry of fault-list of X) {
         assert entry at the output port
         delete entry from fault-list of X
      }
   }
   if (output signal does not differ from previous value) {
      remove U value and update event queue to reflect new U value
      if (event queue is empty) set U to infinity
      initiate X and X' to update W and W' values
      wait till done signals from X and X' are received
   }
   else if (output signal differs from previous value) {
      send output event to all models in the fanout
      wait for acknowledgement from each one of them
      remove U value and update event queue to reflect new U value
      if (event queue is empty) set U to infinity
      initiate X and X' to update W and W' values
      wait till done signals from X and X' are received
   }
}
```

Fig. 3.88. Operations of a Model X

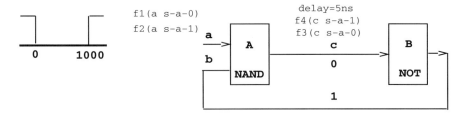

Fig. 3.89. An Example Digital Design for NODIFS

Assume that the faults f_1: a s-a-0 and f_2: a s-a-1 are associated with gate A and faults f_3: c s-a-0 and f_4: c s-a-1 originate at B.

The feedback arc set for the subcircuit in Figure 3.89 is assumed to be the arc from the output of B to the second input of A and the data-flow network is constructed appropriately. Figures 3.90(a) through 3.90(k) represent snapshots of the data-flow network and the execution of the models as fault simulation progresses. The rectangular box above each pseudo component represents the event queue and contains the assertion time and transition for every event. The U value for a pseudo component refers to the assertion time of the event at the head of the queue, i.e., the rightmost entry in the box. The primary inputs of both pseudo components A and A' are connected to the external signal T and the second input port of A' is connected to ∞. The second input port of pseudo component A is connected through the crossbar switch to the output of B'. Also, the computations of the W' and W values at the output of components are shown for each snapshot. Associated with each unprimed pseudo component in Figures 3.90(a) through 3.90(k) is the computation of the symbol K that is equal to the minimum of the W or W' values at the input ports of the component. The K values are computed by the models, and their representations in Figures 3.90(a) through 3.90(k) serve to represent snapshots of the execution of the models as fault simulation progresses.

Figure 3.90(a) describes the initial state where $U_A = U_B = \infty$ and $W'_A = W'_B = W_A = W_B = 0$. Assuming that the signal transitions at the primary input of simulation model A are not yet asserted, the value of K_A is the minimum of W'_B and the W value ($= \infty$) at the primary input of A and computes to 0. The value of K_B is identical to W_A and computes to 0. Figure 3.90(b) represents the scenario where the signal transitions are asserted at the primary input of the simulation model A and are represented through two events, $1000\uparrow$ and $0\downarrow$, of the event list of model A and pseudo components A and A'. The good event $0\downarrow$ is at the head of the event queue and $U_A = 0$. Because the U_A value has changed from ∞ to 0, the model A initiates pseudo components A and A' in Figure 3.90c. Pseudo components A and A' compute W_A and W'_A, respectively, and because they differ from their previous values, a chain reaction is initiated with the consequence that every W' and W is updated, as shown in Figure 3.90(c). When the executions of the components

(a)

U_A 00 U_B 00 T U_A 00 U_B 00

T A 00 B

$W'_A = 0$ $W'_B = 0$

T A B

$W_A = 0$ $W_B = 0$

$K_A = \min(W'_B, T) = \min(0, \infty) = 0$

$K_B = W_A = 0$

Simulation model reads
in transitions at T

(b)

1000 0 U_A 00 U_B 1000 0 U_A 00 U_B

00 A 00

$W'_A = 0$ $W'_B = 0$

A B

$W_A = 0$ $W_B = 0$

$K_A = 0$ $K_B = 0$

Simulation model
initiates A, A'

(c)

1000 0 U_A 00 U_B 1000 0 U_A 00 U_B

00 A B 00 A B

$K_B = 5$

$W'_A = \min(\infty, 5, \infty+5, \infty+5) = 5(\text{change})$

$W'_B = \min(5+5, \infty+5) = 10(\text{change})$

$W_A = \min(\infty, 10) = 10(>0)$

$K_A = \min(10+5, 0+5) = 5(\text{change})$

$W_B = \min(5+5, \infty+5) = 10(\text{change})$

U_A may be executed to produce an L to H transition at t=5 at the output of A

(d)

f1(a sa0)
f2(a sa1)

a A good: 1 at t=5ns
(0,5,f2)

b NAND c B NOT

1

Output event from A is propagated
to B as U_B. B and B' are initiated

(e)

1000 0 U_A 5 U_B 1000 0 U_A 5 U_B

00 A B 00 A B

00

$W'_A = 5$

$W'_B = \min(5+5, 5+5) = 10(\text{no change})$

$W_A = 5$

$K_A = 10$ $K_B = 5$

$W_B = \min(5+5, 5+5) = 10(\text{no change})$

Now, U_A is set to 1000
A and A' are initiated

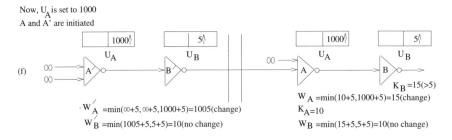

(f)

$W'_A = min(\infty+5, \infty+5, 1000+5) = 1005$ (change)
$W_B = min(1005+5, 5+5) = 10$ (no change)

$K_B = 15(>5)$
$W_A = min(10+5, 1000+5) = 15$ (change)
$K_A = 10$
$W_B = min(15+5, 5+5) = 10$ (no change)

U_B may be executed to produce an H to L transition at t=10 at the output of B

(g)

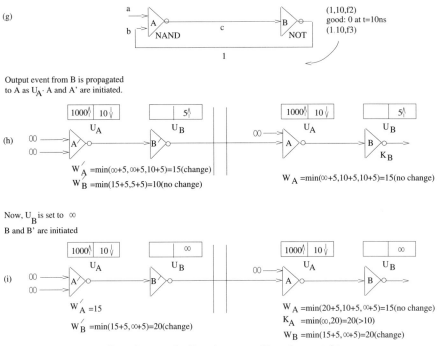

a
b
A
NAND
c
B
NOT
1

(1,10,f2)
good: 0 at t=10ns
(1,10,f3)

Output event from B is propagated
to A as U_A. A and A' are initiated.

(h)

$1000\uparrow\; 10\downarrow$
$5\uparrow$
U_A
U_B

∞
A'
B'

$W'_A = min(\infty+5, \infty+5, 10+5) = 15$ (change)
$W_B = min(15+5, 5+5) = 10$ (no change)

$1000\uparrow\; 10\downarrow$
$5\uparrow$
U_A
U_B

∞
A
B
K_B

$W_A = min(\infty+5, 10+5, 10+5) = 15$ (no change)

Now, U_B is set to ∞
B and B' are initiated

(i)

$1000\uparrow\; 10\downarrow$
∞
U_A
U_B

∞
A'
B'

$W'_A = 15$
$W'_B = min(15+5, \infty+5) = 20$ (change)

$1000\uparrow\; 10\downarrow$
∞
U_A
U_B

∞
A
B

$W_A = min(20+5, 10+5, \infty+5) = 15$ (no change)
$K_A = min(\infty, 20) = 20(>10)$
$W_B = min(15+5, \infty+5) = 20$ (change)

U_A may be executed and it produces no transition at the output of A

A and A' are complete, model A computes $K_A = $ minimum$(\infty, 10) = 10$ which exceeds the U_A value of 0. Consequently, model A is executed for the good event, $0\downarrow$ at $t = 0$ ns as shown in Figure 3.90(d). The good behavior description of model A is executed to generate a logical 0 to 1 transition at $t = 5$ ns. At this instant, model A lacks the presence of input fault-list entries. The effect of fault f_1, originating at A, is logical 0 that is identical to the good logical value at the input port a. Hence, f_1 may not be simulated. The fault f_2 is fault simulated and it causes a logical 0 asserted at $t = 5$ ns at the output of A. Because the fault effect of f_2 differs from the good output and as the

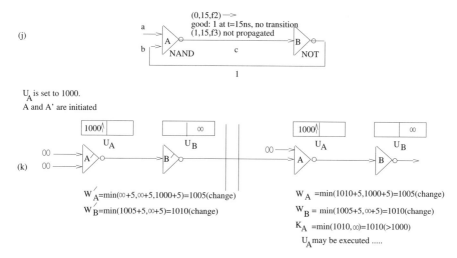

(j)

(k)

U_A is set to 1000.
A and A' are initiated

W'_A=min(∞+5,∞+5,1000+5)=1005(change)

W'_B=min(1005+5,∞+5)=1010(change)

W_A =min(1010+5,1000+5)=1005(change)

W_B = min(1005+5,∞+5)=1010(change)

K_A =min(1010,∞)=1010(>1000)

U_A may be executed .....

Fig. 3.90. Snapshots of the Fault Simulation Process of the Example Design in Figure 3.89

good output implies a transition, both are propagated to model B. The model A generates a good low-to-high transition at $t = 5$ ns at its output. In Figure 3.90(e), the output transition of A is represented as a good event 5↑ of model B. It may be observed that the event of B is a good event, as the assertion time is equal to that of the only input fault-list entry $\{0, 5, f_2\}$.

The model B initiates pseudo components B and B', and as neither W_B nor W'_B changes, the executions of B and B' are immediately complete. Model B sends an acknowledgment to model A in Figure 3.90(f). Then model A removes the already simulated event 0↓ from its event queue and updates U_A. The new value of U_A is 1000 and model A again initiates pseudo components A and A'. The values of W'_A and W_A are updated, but those of W'_B and W_B remain unchanged. The model B computes $K_B = \text{minimum}(W_A) = 15$, which is larger than the U'_B value of 5 and, as a result, the good event 5↑ at B may be simulated, as shown in Figure 3.90(g). Model B contains an input fault-list entry characterized by $\{0, 5, f_2\}$ that is simulated first. The result is a logical 1 asserted at $t = 10$ ns at the output of B. The execution of the unfaulted description of B generates a logical 1-to-0 transition at $t = 10$ ns. The effect of fault f_4, originating at B, is a logical 1 that is identical to the good logical value at the input port c. Hence, f_4 may not be simulated. The fault effect f_3 is simulated to generate a logical 1 at $t = 10$ ns. Both fault effects are distinct from the good output, and the good output implies a transition. Consequently, they are propagated to the input port b of A.

The execution of B generates a good event, high-to-low transition, at $t = 10$ ns at its output that is represented as a good event 10↓ at the input of A as shown in Figure 3.90(h). Furthermore, observe that the event of A is a good event as the assertion time is equal to that of the two input fault list entries, $\{1, 10, f_2\}$ and $\{1, 10, f_3\}$. Model A initiates pseudo components A and A', which compute a new value for W'_A but all other W and W' values remain unchanged. Thus, the executions of A and A' are complete and model A sends an acknowledgment to B. It may be noted that the incoming event $10\downarrow$ at the second input of A displaces the event $1000\uparrow$ as the head of the event queue and forces the new value of U_A to be 10. Model B removes the already executed event $5\uparrow$ and sets $U_B = \infty$ in Figure 3.90(i). It also initiates pseudo components B and B' with the result that none of the W or W' values change. In addition, model A computes $K_A = \text{minimum}(W'_B, \infty) = 20$, which exceeds the U_A value of 10 and, as a result, model A may be executed for the good event $10\downarrow$, as shown in Figure 3.90(j). Model A contains two input fault-list entries associated with the input ports b that must be simulated first. With respect to the entry, $\{1, 10, f_2\}$, it is observed that the fault identifier f_2 originates at model A. The simulation of this entry requires the temporary assertion of logical 1 at b and a, respectively, and the execution of the behavior description of A generates a logical 0 at $t = 15$ ns at the output of A. The second input fault-list entry, $\{1, 10, f_3\}$, is simulated to yield a logical 1 at $t = 15$ ns at the output of A. The execution of the unfaulted description of A causes a logical 1 at $t = 15$ ns at the output of A. The fault f_1, originating at A, may not be simulated as its effect, logical 0, is identical to the good logical value at a. The good logical output does not imply a new transition and, consequently, it is not propagated to B. The fault effect due to f_3 is indistinguishable from the good output and is therefore discarded. Only the fault effect due to f_2 is propagated to B. If the output of model A is assumed primary, fault f_2 is detected and may, therefore, be dropped from further consideration. That is, the fault effect $\{0, 15, f_2\}$ may not be propagated to B.

The model A does not generate a new signal value at its output. Consequently, model A removes the executed event $10\downarrow$ from its event list, updates U_X, and then initiates pseudo components A and A'. The new value of U_A is 1000 and corresponds to a good event. The quantities W'_A and W_A are computed to yield new values, and a chain reaction is initiated with the result that W_B and W'_B values are also altered. Model A recomputes $K_A = \text{minimum}(\infty, W'_B) = 1010$, which exceeds the U_A value of 1000 with the consequence that model A may be executed for the event $1000\uparrow$. Although the entire design has stabilized and no new output values are generated, the data-flow network computes updated values of W and W' that force the outstanding event—the external good signal transition at $t = 1000$ ns—to be simulated. Fault simulation of the subcircuit continues in this manner until all good signal transitions at the primary input ports are used. Where neither of the output ports of A or B are primary, the faulty output, $\{0, 15, f_2\}$, is propagated to B, and given the absence of a good signal assertion, the new value of U_B is 15 and U_B corresponds to a faulty event. Under such circumstances, B will activate the pseudo components B and B' and then U_B may be executed. The event U_A at $1000\uparrow$ will not be permitted to execute by the

NODIFS approach. It is observed that only the fault f_2 will be continuously simulated as it renders the subcircuit oscillatory. Eventually, the external signal transition 1000↑ at the input port a of A will be executed and the fault simulation process will be terminated.

Consider the fault simulation of another example circuit, shown in Figure 3.91. The progress of fault simulation of the models labeled 1, 2, and 3 is expressed in Figure 3.92. For clarity, the snapshots of the data-flow network, as fault simulation progresses, are eliminated. Only the good output and fault lists at the output of the gates are shown in Figure 3.92. It is assumed that the NODIFS approach accurately maintains the order of execution of good events in the process.

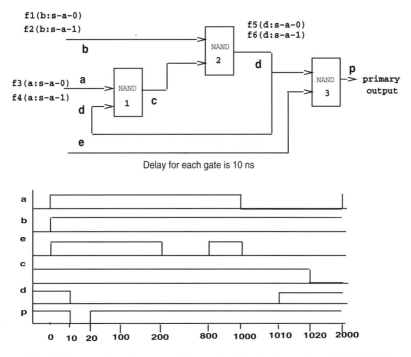

Fig. 3.91. Another Example Design for Fault Simulation in NODIFS

3.5.3 Implementation Issues

The implementation of the NODIFS algorithm is complex and is described as follows. For any given complex circuit, the combinational and sequential subcircuits are identified. For the sequential subcircuit, i.e., a subset of the circuit containing feedback loops, the constituting models are tagged and a

Simulation Time	Gate 1	Gate 2	Gate 3
0	good: v = 1, t = 10 F(c) = {f4, 0, 10}	good: v = 0, t = 10 F(d) = {f1, 1, 10}	good: v = 0, t = 10 F(p) = {f5, 1, 10} f5 has been detected
10	good: v=1,t=20 F(c)={O}		good: v=1,t=20 F(p)={f1,f6,0,20} f1,f6 are detected
100	X good:v=1,t=110 F(c)={O}		
200			X good:v=1,t=210 F(p)={O}
800			X good:v=1,t=810 F(p)={O}
1000		good:v=1,t=1010 f(d)={f4,1,20} + {f2,0,1010}	F(p)={f4,0,30} f4 is detected X good:v=1,t=1010 F(p)={O}
1010	F(c)={O} good:v=0,t=1020 F(c)={f3,f2,1,1020}		
1020		X good:v=1,t=1030 F(d)={O}	
2000		X good:v=1,t=2010 F(d)={O}	good:v=0,t=2010

Fig. 3.92. Progress of Fault Simulation of the Example Design in Figure 3.91

feedback arc-set is determined. For this research, the feedback arc-set is determined through visual inspection, although well-known graph-theoretic algorithms [103] [164] may be utilized for more complex circuits. A user-specified partitioning is provided as an input to NODIFS along with the feedback arc-set information. The total number of processors required for fault simulation equals $N + 2$, where N is the number of partitions. The performance of a fault simulation of a circuit will, in general, depend on the partitioning. While the models of every partition execute on a processor, the primary inputs of the circuit and the output ports of the unprimed data-flow network are modeled as entities P0 and P1, respectively, and are executed on unique processors. The data-flow network is constructed corresponding to the sequential subcircuit, utilizing the feedback arc-set. The entity P1 signifies the rightmost boundary of the data-flow network and participates in the propagation of acknowledgments. Corresponding to every component of the circuit, the final implementation consists of three entities: a fault simulation model that represents the function of fault simulation of the component and the primed and unprimed pseudo components. These are expressed through the C functions: fault-simulate-component, *ppc*-component, and *puc*-component, respectively. Although they are conceptually concurrent entities, in the current implementation on Armstrong, they are executed round-robin on a processor. When a partition includes multiple models, an interconnection between two or more models on the same processor, if any, is expressed through a data structure local to the processor. When the models are located on separate processors, an interprocessor protocol represents the connection between them.

A significant part of the implementation consists of a kernel C description (approximately 3500 lines) that executes on every processor except those that execute the entities P0 and P1. Each processor accepts a unique input file that represents information on the models and pseudo components and their interconnection for the corresponding partition. The input files for the partitions are generated by a preprocessor, "ifigenia" [165], which accepts a description of the circuit in a hardware description language ESL [166] and the user-specified partitions and feedback arc-set. The ifigenia preprocessor is a standard uniprocessor C program that is approximately 4500 lines in length.

The flow of control during execution of the algorithm may be described as follows. The fault simulation models, i.e., the sim-component functions, corresponding to those components that receive signal transitions from the external world at their primary input ports are executed first. A fault-sim-component, in turn, initiates the executions of the *puc*-component and *ppc*-component functions and suspends itself. When the executions of *puc*-component and *ppc*-component are complete, the fault-sim-component is reactivated. The execution of a *puc*-component (or *ppc*-component) is considered complete when either the W (or W') value at the output is unchanged or an acknowledgment is received signifying that the change in the output W (or W') value has been propagated throughout the data-flow network. Additionally, the *puc*-component and *ppc*-component functions may be initiated for execution when a new W (or W') value is received at any of its input ports from the left. Thus, execution of the algorithm continues, the thread of control shifts from one entity to another. Eventually, the fault simulation process terminates when all events have been executed, i.e., all externally supplied (usable) transitions at the primary input ports have been utilized to generate output transitions.

3.5.4 Performance of NODIFS

The principal goal of this research is to present a conceptual development—an asynchronous, distributed fault simulation algorithm that may execute on a parallel processor and exploit the maximal inherent parallelism. NODIFS is implemented on the Armstrong [160] parallel processor system, and several representative digital designs are fault simulated. The principal purpose is to support the mathematical validity of NODIFS along with the proof of correctness.

Armstrong is a loosely coupled parallel processor consisting of 48 MC 68010 processors that may be reconfigured by the user. For the purpose of this investigation, Armstrong is configured as a 5-dimensional Hypercube with 32 processors. Each processor is approximately 5.5 times slower than that of a Sun 3/60 workstation, and the average time required for a guaranteed node-to-node message communication of maximum size 1 Kbyte is approximately 10 milliseconds. The current Armstrong configuration is limited to a maximum of 30 open connections including protocols and file pointers. Additionally, each processor has access to only 370 Kbytes of main memory. Thus, the most distributed instance of fault simulation in this investigation is limited to 16 partitions of the SN74181 arithmetic logic unit that executes on 18 processors. The NODIFS executable code is compiled on a Sun 3/60 workstation under the O4 optimization directive and the execution time is determined through the use of timers associated with each Armstrong node. A total of five example circuits are fault simulated: three are purely combinational and the remaining two are sequential circuits. For each circuit, performance statistics are collected from several fault simulation runs by varying the number of test vectors, number of processors, and the weight factor. Although NODIFS is tested with gate-level circuits in this investigation, a principal goal of NODIFS is to efficiently accelerate the fault simulation of behavior-level models using behavior failures [161]. While the number of processors varies between 1 and 16, the number of vectors chosen varies from 50 to 150. The weight factor is a deliberately introduced delay in the execution process and is designed to mimic the longer execution times that would be associated with behavior-level models. It is expected that behavior models may require between 1 and 10 ms to execute on an Armstrong processor. The results of every fault simulation in NODIFS, i.e., the output fault lists, are verified through comparison against similar results obtained from executing the Bell Labs concurrent fault simulator CSIM [166]. Speedup factors are computed from the performance statistics collected from the simulation runs. For a fault simulation run executed on N processors, the *speedup factor* is defined as the ratio of the CPU time required for executing the fault simulation on a uniprocessor to that on N processors. For the first four example circuits, a simulation run corresponding to a single partition is performed on a single Armstrong processor. For the SN74181 circuit, a single partition is too large for a single Armstrong processor. As a result, for the purpose of comparison, the single partition case for the SN74181 circuit is executed by CSIM on a Sun 3/60 workstation. This demonstrates an additional advantage of NODIFS in that large circuits, which can neither be loaded into a uniprocessor nor fault simulated, may be fault simulated by NODIFS through appropriate partitioning on a parallel processor.

The first example circuit, shown in Figure 3.93(a), consists of eight components organized through three dependent feedback loops. A speedup factor of 2.6 is observed for three processors. Thereafter, an increase in the number of processors does not yield a commensurate increase in speedup, thereby implying that the strong dependency of the three loops limits the inherent parallelism. The second circuit is constructed through adding deliberate feedback links in a two-bit full adder circuit (SN7482). A maximum of four processors yields a speedup factor of 2.8. The third example circuit is a purely combinational 8-1 multiplexer (SN74251) that generates a speedup factor of 3.1 with a maximum of eight processors. The reduced speedup is attributable to the presence of the eight-input NOR gate that must sequentially process all fault lists generated by the remaining components to determine the final fault list at the primary output of the circuit. The fourth example circuit is that of a two-bit adder (SN7482) that yields a maximum speedup factor of 5.1 with a maximum of eight processors. Finally, the ALU circuit is simulated with up to a maximum of 16 processors to generate a high speedup of 12.5. Given the hardware and software limitations of Armstrong, this investigation is unable to exercise fault simulation of larger circuits with more partitions at this time. It may be pointed out that the principal idea underlying the performance measurements is to prove the NODIFS approach as an asynchronous, distributed, circuit partitioning-based fault simulation algorithm and not produce an industrial-grade fault simulator. Also, the current implementation of NODIFS is not optimized for performance. Thus, the results presented here are amenable to further improvement. The performance graphs for the five example circuits are shown in Figures 3.94 through 3.98.

It is expected that the performance of NODIFS will increase significantly with an increase in the message passing speed in future parallel processors.

3.6 A Distributed Approach to Real-Time Payment Processing in a Partially Connected Network of Banks

The payment-processing system in the banking industry consists of deposits, withdrawals, and transfers of monies through the use of cash, checks, magnetic tape, and electronic transactions. Of these, nearly all of the check processing through the United States Federal Reserve System, most of the check processing in the private networks, and a part of the electronic transactions are realized through the use of the principles of batch-mode processing. Batch-mode processing is a conservative and secure means of transaction processing wherein transactions, initiated by users, are stored within the system for a certain length of time, typically a few hours to a day or a week, and are completed during off-hours, i.e., when the bank is closed to users. Batch-mode processing suffers from many limitations, the principal ones being that users are denied real-time access to their money and a user's banking privileges cannot be extended anywhere in the United States, a facility that is increasingly

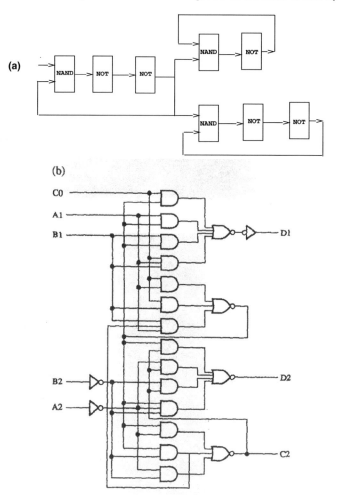

Fig. 3.93. Fault Simulation of Two Sequential Circuits in NODIFS: (a) A Sequential Circuit with Three Feedback Loops, and (b) Modified SN7482 Adder with Feedback

being demanded by users. A centralized banking algorithm, similar to the Swiss Interbank Clearing System (SIC), is inadequate for the United States with more than 12,000 financial institutions and is highly vulnerable to a natural calamity or act of terrorism.

This section proposes a new distributed architecture for payment processing within a network of major banks as an alternative to the Federal Reserve System. This approach distributes the processing operations to multiple concurrent cooperating geographically distributed computers, i.e., at many sites, to achieve real-time transaction processing. It utilizes the principles of an asynchronous, distributed, discrete-event simulation algorithm employing

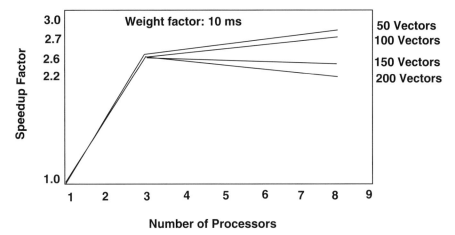

Fig. 3.94. Performance Graphs for the Three-Loop Example Circuit in Figure 3.93(a)

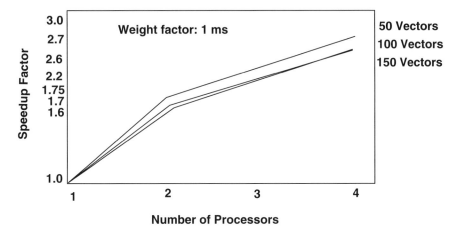

Fig. 3.95. Performance Graphs for the Modified SN7482 Adder with Feedback

pseudotransactions (timestamps) and mathematically guarantees the accuracy of every transaction. Given that the major banks are geographically distributed throughout the entire country, the distributed nature of the algorithm proposed here constitutes a logical choice. It offers the hope of a banking system that is available, transparently, to a user anywhere within the coverage area of the network. In essence, a user's most recent account balance and the banking privileges of withdrawal, deposit, and transfer are available to a user, transparently, anywhere, i.e., at any of the major banks constituting the network. Moreover, the facility to initiate multiple transactions corresponding to a single account simultaneously at different geographical points is permitted

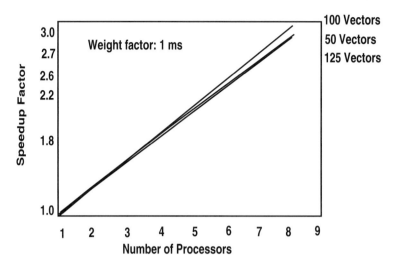

Fig. 3.96. Performance Graphs for the SN74251 Multiplexer

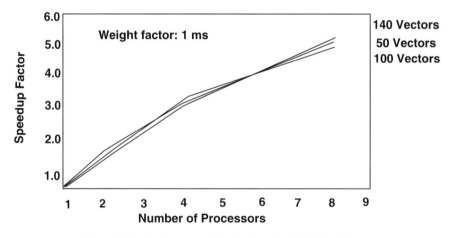

Fig. 3.97. Performance Graphs for the SN7482 Adder

by this approach. The accuracy of every transaction is guaranteed and, as a result, banks are not exposed to the risk of fraudulent or bad credits and users are not denied complete access to their most recent balances. In addition, while the balances of accounts at each of the major banks are owned exclusively by the respective banks, thereby implying privacy and security, any transaction inserted anywhere in the system is guaranteed to be correctly routed to the target bank for execution. This architecture assumes that the banking nodes are partially connected through a broadband-ISDN network. The choice of B-ISDN is timely, given the importance of global electronic banking [167] in the world economy and B-ISDN's unique characteristics. This research also re-

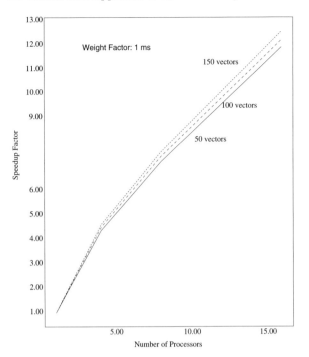

Fig. 3.98. Performance Graphs for the 74181 ALU

ports on an implementation of a model of a network of major banking nodes
on a network of Sun workstations, configured as a loosely coupled parallel
processor system.

3.6.1 Introduction

The payment-processing system in the banking industry uses the basic operations of deposit, withdrawal, and transfer of money. In general, for the
check-processing subsystem, these operations involve two distinct accounts,
which in turn may be associated with two distinct banks in the entire system.
Thus, a deposit of a check, in the amount of M dollars, into an account A^X
associated with bank X, where the check is drawn on another account B^Y
associated with another bank, Y, implies the following. Where possible, B^Y
must be debited by and A^X must be credited with M dollars. The transaction, in general, succeeds when B^Y has a total balance exceeding M dollars
and fails otherwise. Where $X \equiv Y$, i.e., both accounts A^X and $B^{Y=X}$ are
associated with the same bank, the transaction will be executed, correctly, by
a central computer, $C^{X=Y}$, owned exclusively by bank X. In general, such
transactions may be executed immediately, i.e., A^X is debited and B^X is
credited, simultaneously and in real time. The instantaneous nature of this
operation is made possible primarily due to the fact that $C^{X=Y}$ has complete

access to both accounts A^X and B^X. Even where bank X maintains multiple branches, accounts A^X and B^X may ultimately reside on the single centralized computer $C^{X=Y}$.

It is noted in this section that this process may be mathematically modeled as a discrete-event simulation system with feedback loops. When a transaction, say a deposit of a check, is initiated, an electronic stimulus is created and introduced into the system. The stimulus is characterized by the unique identifier of the originating (payee) bank, the distinct identifier of the payer bank, i.e., on which the check is drawn, the dollar amount involved, and a notion of the time at which the transaction is initiated. Evidently, the stimulus is first propagated by the network to the destination bank. Second, the stimulus is processed. That is, if the unrestricted balance of the payer account exceeds the amount of the check, the account is debited and a return acknowledgment is created. The acknowledgment is characterized by an approval or denial in the event that the balance is less than the amount of the check, the dollar amount, and the payee bank identifier. This stimulus is then routed back to the originating bank by the network where, in the event of approval, the dollar amount is credited to the payee account. In this process, the stimuli are constituted by discrete pieces of data, namely, deposit, withdrawal, or transfer of a dollar amount. Furthermore, the stimuli are asynchronous, i.e., they are introduced into the system at irregular intervals of time. Where the accounts concerned reside in the same bank, the process is greatly simplified.

At the present time, the check-processing subsystem of the Federal Reserve system is primarily batch-mode [168]. Much of the check-processing through the private networks also utilize the batch-mode operational techniques. In batch-mode, where a transaction, initiated by a user in a region I (as determined by the Federal Reserve) pertains to a payer bank included in a different region, II, the transaction is queued at the originating bank. Then, at a later time, when the banking system is off-line, i.e., closed to the users, the queued transactions are propagated to the appropriate payer banks where they are processed. The primary reason for this mechanism is security and accuracy, as explained later.

Figure 3.99 describes a partial organizational layout of the United States Federal Reserve system which organizes the country into twelve regions and permits each of the twelve Federal Reserve Banks (FRBs) to extend their jurisdiction over the appropriate regions. The FRB in San Francisco serves the banks in California, Utah, Oregon, Washington, and Hawaii while the FRB in New York serves the banks in the state of New York. Thus, as shown in Figure 3.99, the FRB in San Francisco services Wells-Fargo Bank and Bank of America in California while the FRB in Philadelphia caters to the Meridian Bank, Mellon Bank, and Continental Bank. Similarly, the FRB in New York serves Citibank and the Chase Manhattan Bank, while the FRB in Boston extends its jurisdiction over Bank of Boston and Fleet National Bank. The solid lines interconnecting the FRBs represent the lines through which transactions are propagated. In Figure 3.99, assume that a user of account A_1 at

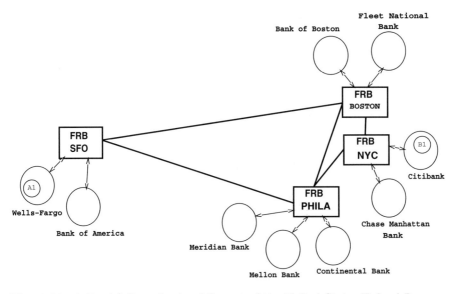

Fig. 3.99. A Partial Organizational Layout of the United States Federal Reserve System

Wells-Fargo Bank deposits a check, C_1, in the amount of M dollars, drawn on an account B_1 at Citibank. The stimulus T_1, created as a result of the deposit, is propagated to the FRB in San Francisco for settlement. The FRB in San Francisco does not maintain an accurate balance for the account B_1 of Citibank and, as a result, it is unable to resolve the issue of settlement immediately. However, to ensure the continuation of the nation's financial system, the FRB in San Francisco advances a credit to Wells-Fargo Bank for M dollars and queues up the transaction in a special queue to be mailed to the FRB in New York. Thus, the Federal Reserve system issues a daylight overdraft in lieu of Citibank and expects Citibank to repay the amount between the time the banks close for business on the current day and reopen the next business day. Other transactions initiated at all of the other FRBs that transcend the jurisdiction of the regional FRB may similarly cause the creation of daylight overdrafts and the appropriate queueing of the transactions. At the end of the banking day, i.e., when the banking system is off-line, the queued transactions are routed to the destination banks, where they are processed. Thus, the transaction T_1 is propagated to Citibank via the FRB in New York, where account B_1 is debited by M dollars, and this money is propagated by Citibank to repay for the overdraft issued earlier by the Federal Reserve system. Because no new transactions are introduced into the system at the end of the day and as each transaction introduced into the system during daytime is guaranteed to be routed by the network to the appropriate bank, the sum total of all transactions will execute accurately. For instance, if transactions $T_1, T_2, \ldots, T_N$ pertaining to the same account B_1 (originating or destination) at Citibank are initiated at N distinct banks at increasing times $t = t_1, t_2, \ldots, t_N$, respectively, during the current day, the network guarantees that the each $T_i \forall i \in \{1, N\}$ will be routed to Citibank. Even if T_i arrives at Citibank prior to T_{i+1}, although T_i was initiated first, the net result, R, given by $R = \sum_{i=1}^{N} T_i$, is guaranteed to be consistent by the commutative and associative laws of mathematics. It may be noted that a T_i may be a deposit in the favor of B_i (i.e., T_i is positive) or a check drawn on B_i (i.e., T_i is negative) in the favor of another account. If the balance of B_i and the net result R are such that all transactions succeed, i.e., none of the transactions fail, then the order of arrival of the $T_i s \forall i \in \{1, N\}$ is unimportant. Where the transitions are, hypothetically, processed in real time, the following scenario may be observed. At an instant of time, due to repeated withdrawals, the account balance for B_1 is reduced to zero dollars. Consequently, subsequent withdrawal transactions fail. At a later time, a large sum is credited to B_1 and subsequent withdrawal transactions are honored. Furthermore, the net dollar amount of the failed transactions is less than the final account balance of B_1. Such a scenario will not be observed given the benevolent nature of the daylight overdraft system supported by the Federal Reserve system and, therefore, the people of the United States.

A benefit of the daylight overdraft system is the possibility of reduced risk to the participating institutions in the event of failure by one of them to settle at the end of the day. However, a limitation of the daylight overdraft system is that, often, the total credit extended by the Federal Reserve system exceeds tens of billions of dollars and occasional glitches, e.g., power failures, compound to create extreme financial risks such as the Bank of New York incident that led to the largest $22.6 billion discount loan window [120]. Perhaps the most notable limitation of the current Federal Reserve system is that it is unable to deliver real-time processing. This manifests in a delay, often arbitrarily imposed by the banks and the network concerned, in the processing of a check. The delay may vary anywhere from one to two days for an intraregion check to a high of six months for international checks. Furthermore, because the FRB in San Francisco maintains account balances for only those banks within its jurisdiction, a difficulty is created when a user of Bank of America tries to access banking privileges through Midlantic Bank during a business trip to New Jersey. This research does not consider the issues of check cashing facilities provided by credit cards to a privileged few, which are based strictly on trust and creditworthiness and not the actual bank balance of the user.

In addition to these limitations, the Federal Reserve system's concern with the current network is amplified by the following possible scenarios. First, while the transaction volume of ACH electronic payments is expected to increase by a factor of 10 over the next 5 years, check transactions are expected to increase by 4% a year, and there is fear that the current system may be incapable of addressing the increase. Second, conceivably, the U.S. Congress, under increasing pressure from users whose businesses experience negative impact due to the payment processing delays, may pass laws mandating real-time performance. Third, banks located within a state in the United States, are subject to strong state regulations that have been carried forward from the days when the union was first established. For instance, until a few years ago, banks in Florida were prohibited from crossing county lines [169]. Thus, mergers of interstate banks are infrequent and, where mergers have occurred, the individual banks have maintained unique identities to their users. There is an increasing possibility that the U.S. Congress may revise the banking rules to permit potential mergers between large interstate banks, say Citibank and Bank of America. Under such circumstances, it is highly likely that a user of Bank of America may demand all of the usual banking facilities through Citibank during a business trip to New York and a user of Citibank may demand similar privileges through Bank of America while vacationing in California. The merger of Manufacturers Hanover Trust and Chemical Bank a few years ago is pointed out in this context. In essence, there may be strong incentives for the banking network to offer a unified transparent view of the entire banking network to the U.S. public and perhaps to the international community. Finally, the Federal Reserve system is acutely aware that a single centralized FRB, which maintains the most recent balances of the banks that it services, is highly vulnerable to natural disasters and artificial catastrophes. The total, or even the partial, loss of data is simply unacceptable given its linkage to the world financial markets and the economies of other nations of the world.

A centralized uniprocessor-based approach to payment-processing may offer the potential of real-time performance with a limited scope. The Swiss Interbank Clearing (SIC) system [121] eliminates the need for daylight overdrafts through real-time processing and achieves this objective through the use of a centralized algorithm. Large multinational companies such as General Motors with business units located in the United States, Australia, and Europe, enjoy real-time performance through dedicated networks, wholly owned or leased, and special banking privileges. Conceivably, a local subset of automated teller machines (ATMs) pertaining to a single bank can potentially offer real-time performance to its local customers. Obviously, under these circumstance, the performance is limited to cash and checks drawn only on the local bank. A principal limitation of this approach is its lack of scalability, i.e., as the size of the system increases, the performance degrades proportionately. As a result, the approach is unsuitable for large countries and communities such as the United States, China, India, Russia, and the EU, and a country with many large financial institutions such as Japan. This section presents a novel approach that offers the potential for real-time payment-processing through the use of multiple concurrent processors that cooperate synergistically through a distributed algorithm.

The remainder of this section is organized as follows. Section 3.6.2 describes the centralized, uniprocessor-based approach. Section 3.6.3 introduces the distributed approach, and Section 3.6.4 details the implementation on a network of Unix workstations configured as a loosely coupled parallel processor. Section 3.6.6 presents the results and analyzes the performance.

3.6.2 A Centralized, Uniprocessor-Based Algorithm for Real-Time Payment Processing

In the centralized approach [121], the most recent balance of every bank must be stored and accessed by a single computational engine. This is referred to as the *reserve account* in the Federal Reserve system. Thus, unlike the current U.S. Federal Reserve network, shown in Figure 3.99, each of the nine banks—Wells-Fargo Bank through Bank of Boston—must communicate directly with a single entity. The single centralized computer (SCC) may be located either near the center of the country, say in Omaha, Nebraska, such that it offers uniform link delays to all of the nation's banks, or near the center of gravity of banking activity. SCC must execute each interbank transaction. Consider that a user of an account at Wells-Fargo Bank deposits a check for settlement that is drawn on the Bank of Boston. The computer at the Wells-Fargo Bank intercepts the transaction and recognizes that the instrument must be forwarded to the SCC for settlement. When the SCC receives the transaction, T_1, it extracts the identifier of the bank that deposited the check and that on which the check is drawn, the dollar amount (M) of the check, and the time at which the check is received. The transaction is first queued at the SCC for processing, in the correct order, at a later time. When T_1 is observed at the head of the queue, it is processed by the SCC. First, the authenticity of the instrument is verified. Then it examines the account balance of the Bank of Boston (BoB_{bal}) with respect to M. Where BoB_{bal} exceeds M, SCC debits the account of the Bank of Boston and credits that of Wells-Fargo by M dollars. Thereafter, an acknowledgment is propagated to the depositing bank, namely, Wells-Fargo Bank. In the event that BoB_{bal} is less than M, the transaction fails immediately and one of two strategies may be adopted. First, the transaction is queued in a waiting queue to be processed later when new deposits are added to the balance of Bank of Boston. Second, a failure message is generated and the transaction is dropped.

Because the SCC has complete access to the account balances for each bank within its jurisdiction and as all interbank transactions are routed to the SCC for settlement, the accuracy of all transactions is ensured. However, the ability to deliver real-time performance is contingent on the fact that the transactions may be processed promptly. Assume that each of the N banks generates an average of T transactions per unit time, destined for the SCC. Assume further that each transaction requires an average of S computer instructions. Thus, the SCC must be capable of processing $N \times T \times S$ instructions per unit time failing which real-time performance is not ensured. For this country, N is approximately 14,000 [120], and the Federal Reserve estimates that T is a monotonically increasing function of time. As a result, this approach is unsuitable. Furthermore, while the scalar speed of expensive and high-performance supercomputers such as CRAY and CDC Cyber are known to have increased steadily over the past decade, this improvement is extremely modest compared to the current magnitude of N and the projected increase in T.

The SIC [121] system, fully operational by January 1989, was designed to settle more than 90,000 payments per hour. The settlement rate was derived from an assumption of a maximum of 400,000 payment transactions on peak days. Although SIC operates on a 24-hour basis, for most transactions entered into the system after 3 P.M. on a bank working day, the value dates are modified to reflect the following day. SIC caters to a total of 156 participating financial institutions in contrast to the Federal Reserve system, which services nearly 14,000 institutions.

Figure 3.100 presents the uniprocessor-based algorithm expressed in pseudocode.

```
receive a user initiated transaction by check
authenticate the transaction
if (check constitutes an interbank transaction) {
   propagate the transaction to SCC
}
else if (check is drawn on the same bank) {
   process the transaction locally
}

            Individual Client Bank

receive a transaction from a client bank
authenticate the transaction and queue it for processing in the future
extract the transaction at the head of the queue
extract identifier of depositing bank (A)
extract identifier of bank on which the check is drawn (B)
extract the dollar amount (M)
if (balance of B is equal to or exceeds M) {
   debit the account B and credit the account A
   propagate an acknowledgment to A
}
else if (balance of B is less than M) {
   transaction fails immediately
   either insert transaction in a waiting queue or
      drop the failed transaction
}
advance the head of the queue to the subsequent entry

         Single, Centralized Computer (SCC)
```

Fig. 3.100. A Centralized, Uniprocessor-Based Approach for Payment Processing

3.6.3 A Novel, Distributed Approach to Payment Processing

In this approach, as an alternative to the Federal Reserve system, the major banks constitute a partially connected network and realize payment-processing directly, without the explicit need of the Federal Reserve banks. This approach assumes that a significant fraction of transactions are local, i.e., confined to limited geographical areas about their origins. Every banking node combines the functions of routing and processing transactions. Only a banking node owns exclusive access to and maintains the most recent balances for all of its accounts. Any transaction introduced into the system is routed by the network to the appropriate target bank where it is executed. Following the execution, an acknowledgment is returned to the originating bank. In addition, every banking node is assumed to possess complete topological knowledge of the network and computes virtual paths to every other node in the network. The notion of virtual paths is similar to that in B-ISDN [170] and is detailed later.

A banking transaction initiated at a node of the network and requiring processing may be viewed as a discrete event in the network. In discrete-event simulation, an event is executed at a node and the execution may trigger the propagation of a piece of information to a subsequent node where it is manifested as a new event. For the case of banking, a transaction initiated at a bank, termed *depositing bank*, may be propagated to a different bank, termed the *payer bank*, on which the instrument of payment is drawn. The information to be propagated is encapsulated as a packet, and given the partially connected nature of the network, a packet may be routed by one or more nodes to the ultimate destination. Following the completion of processing at the payer bank, a new event in the form of an acknowledgment is propagated to the payee bank, which may or may not be identical to the depositing bank. The message may state either that the transaction succeeded or that it failed. Thus, information may flow in a cycle and, consequently, the banking system corresponds to a discrete-event simulation system with feedback loops. Given the fact that the banking network is characterized by geographically distributed, processing nodes, and multiple, concurrent computational engines, and the fact that transactions are asynchronous, i.e., they are introduced at irregular time instants, this approach uses a variation of the discrete-event simulation algorithm [27] to achieve success.

In the Pseudo-Transaction Algorithm (PTA), whenever a banking node processes a transaction represented through a packet—from either the stimulus queue (i.e., from the users at the corresponding node) or incoming queues (i.e., originated at other nodes and routed by the network)—an outgoing real packet may or may not be generated. Under normal circumstances, an outgoing packet is generated with an assertion time value that exceeds the current time value at the node and is propagated to the appropriate destination node. Simultaneously, pseudo packets containing the new assertion time value are propagated on all other outgoing paths from the node. In the event of congestion, the incoming transaction may need to be delayed, i.e., requeued, and, thus, a real packet is not generated immediately. Under these conditions, pseudo packets with assertion times equal to the current time value of the node plus the corresponding link propagation delay are propagated on every outgoing link. A natural requirement for PTA is that an actual event, defined at $t = 0$, must be asserted at every node to signify the start of transaction processing. The proof of correctness for this approach is straightforward and is not presented here.

3.6.3.1 Execution of Events in the Pseudo-Transaction Algorithm

PTA's strategy for selecting an event to be executed, among many candidates, is based on determining the smallest of the assertion times for all incoming packets. The corresponding packet in the appropriate incoming queue or stimulus queue is selected by PTA for processing. This mechanism ensures that the correct order of execution of events and, therefore, causality is consistently honored. Where q_{st} represents the assertion time of the head event associated with the stimulus-queue and q_i through q_n represent the corresponding times for the n incoming queues, the time up to which the node is processed, τ, is given by:

$$\tau = \text{minimum}\{q_{st}, q_i, \ldots, q_n\}.$$

Each queue is arranged in order of increasing assertion times. The basic algorithm of PTA is shown in Figure 3.101.

```
        search, one at a time, over the stimulus-queue and all
                incoming-queues;
label 1: if (head-event corresponds to a pseudo-transaction) {
            if (next-entry is NULL) {
                use the assertion-time associated with the head-event;
            }
            else {
                advance head-pointer to the subsequent entry;
                go to label 1;
            }
        }
        else {
            use the assertion-time associated with the head-event;
        }
```

Fig. 3.101. Algorithm for Determining the Execution of Events in PTA

In addition, where two competing events are characterized by the same value of assertion time, a real packet will always assume precedence over a pseudo packet. Where two or more events with identical assertion times are all genuine or all pseudo, the one that is encountered first assumes precedence over the others. Furthermore, where a real packet, associated with one of its receiving queues, is the event with the least value of time as well as the only event in that queue, it is processed and thereafter replaced by a pseudo packet with the same assertion time.

As an example, consider the simple network shown in Figure 3.102 where three nodes, A, B, and C, are connected by six unidirectional links L_{AB}, L_{BA}, L_{AC}, L_{CA}, L_{BC}, and L_{CB}. The queues associated with the incoming links of the respective nodes are shown in Figure 3.102. Assume that the propagation plus the processing delays for all links are 1 time unit. The contents of the stimulus queues are also shown in Figure 3.102. Also shown with the packets originating at the nodes are the virtual paths along which the packets must be transmitted. A real packet, i.e., one that is actually sent in the network, is represented by XR and a pseudo packet is expressed in the form XP, where X denotes the assertion time of the packet. The body of the packets containing account and bank identifiers, nature and amount of transaction, etc., are not shown in Figure 3.102.

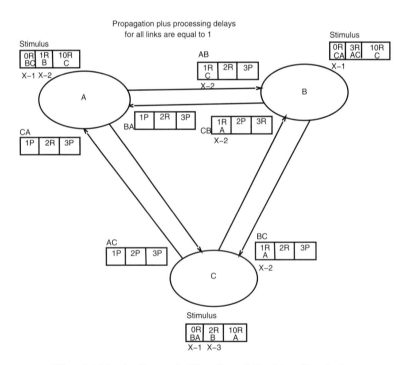

Fig. 3.102. An Example Distributed Banking Simulation

The execution of the distributed banking simulation may be explained as follows. For each of the concurrent banking nodes, a real packet 0R, asserted at $t = 0$, is shown in the three stimulus queues of A, B, and C. When model

A executes for $t = 0$, a real packet 1R is propagated to B and a pseudo packet 1P is sent to C. These packets are incorporated in the receiving queues, AB and AC, respectively. The packets in AB must be subsequently routed to C as per the virtual path. Similarly, when B is executed at $t = 0$, it sends a real packet 1R to C and a pseudo packet 1P to A. After execution at $t = 0$, node C propagates a real packet, 1R, to B and a pseudo packet 1P to A. At this time instant, i.e., $t = 0$, all of the real packets in the stimulus queues at $t = 0$ are utilized and, therefore, they are deleted. The deletions are represented through the symbols, $X - 1$, placed under the corresponding real packets. Each of A, B, and C have packets defined at $t = 0$ at all of their incoming queues. The packets in the stimulus queues are defined up to $t = 10$. When A is executed at $t = 1$, it propagates a 2R to node B and 2P to node C. After execution at $t = 1$, node B propagates two real packets, 2R and 2R, to A and C, respectively. Both of these packets have reached their destinations and, thus, their virtual path information is nil. When node C executes at $t = 1$, it sends a 2R to A and a 2P to B. At $t = 2$, all of the incoming queues of A, B, and C have packets, either real or pseudo, defined at $t = 2$. The real packets, asserted at $t = 1$, that are processed are deleted as identified in Figure 3.102 by the symbols $X - 2$ placed immediately beneath them. As a result, the nodes will execute and generate more packets. The process continues until the contents of the stimulus queues are completely utilized.

3.6.3.2 A Model of the Distributed Banking Network

The distributed banking network architecture is similar to that of the CCITT proposed broadband-ISDNetwork [170] except that every packet represents a unique banking transaction and that packets may not be dropped, regardless of the severity of congestion in the network. In broadband-ISDN, every ATM cell is 53 bytes long with 48 bytes reserved for payload, which appears adequate for encoding banking transactions. A banking node, however, may choose to cluster a set of packets, corresponding to a few transactions, all of which are destined for the same target node, and assert it into the network.

The routing mechanism is unique and similar to that proposed for broadband-ISDN. It differs from that used for existing wide-area packet-switched networks, such as the Internet, in that it incorporates a few of the principles of circuit-switching. This results in the network's ability to provide a measure of its performance in propagating the packets. This may prove essential toward imposing on the banking customers, a fair, tiered charge system for use of the network. The routing algorithm is based on the concept of virtual paths where a virtual path is a route through the network, i.e., through multiple banking nodes, that connects two endpoints in the network. For the transmission of a packet representing a transaction, a route is determined based on several factors such as available bandwidth, cost, and desired performance. A route must be established prior to propagating packets. In this research, a number of standard routes are precomputed during initialization and at discrete points in time during the operation of the network and the allocation of a route to a message is achieved dynamically. Every virtual path is associated with a service type, where a *service type* is a combination of the performance and timing characteristics that the network attempts to guarantee for the packets propagating on the path in question. When packets, representing transactions, are introduced into the network, they are assigned virtual paths by the node. They are then routed through the banking nodes, from the origin to the destination nodes, as dictated by the virtual path. The intermediate banking nodes on a virtual path are aware of the existence of the virtual path information within a packet and use this information for routing.

For all possible pairs of nodes of a given banking network, virtual paths are computed based on the "weighted shortest-path spanning tree" [171] [172]. Every node is assumed to possess complete knowledge of the network topology and computes the virtual paths to every other node. In this scheme, for a given originating node, other nodes are added to a tree structure in order of their increasing distances from the originating node. Thus, when a new node is encountered in the course of traversing through the network for the first time, the algorithm guarantees that the path from the originating node to the node in question is the shortest path. For the banking network, the nodes of the tree correspond to the banking nodes and the weighted paths refer to the links between the corresponding nodes with the appropriate propagation delays. To determine the next-shortest path, one may continue to develop the tree until the node is encountered for the second time. Successive next-shortest paths may be obtained by continuing this process. For a proof of this algorithm, the reader is referred to [172]. In addition to the propagation delay resulting from the limited speed of electromagnetic propagation over fibers, other parameters such as the processing delay at a banking node may be included to influence the choice paths. The determination and selection of shortest-paths in the context of routing are integral to many networks, including TYMNET, ARPANET, TRANSPAC, IBM SNA, and DEC DNA [171].

3.6.3.3 A Distributed Architecture for the Simulation

In the proposed approach, every banking node is expected to require significant computational power to process large amounts of data. Thus, logically, every node is modeled on a unique processor in this approach. That is, the programs, modeling the nodes, are executed on unique workstations of a parallel processor. Each node program consists of two elements: a module that performs the simulation of a single node and a second module that serves as the information server. This division of responsibility is chosen such that only the server needs to parse and process the various network configuration files, thereby removing the need for such complex initial startup code in the node programs themselves and, consequently, reducing its size. The information server contains generic procedures that are essential to reestablish new connections during the actual simulation in the event of link failures.

The node programs communicate with each other on the network through the socket library code provided by the workstation operating system. The nature of sockets is of type stream, where data is treated as a stream of bytes. The node program imposes its own boundaries on the data. The sockets use the Internet standard TCP/IP protocol for flow control and provide reliable point-to-point transmission of data although significant software overhead is implied. Datagram sockets, with low overhead, are fast but they do not guarantee transmission of data. They are used to establish communication between the server and node programs at the initialization of the simulation, given that this communication occurs only once, for a short period of time, at the start of the simulation. However, during many occasions, a few datagrams actually failed to arrive, thus necessitating a restart of the simulation. Clearly, this demonstrates the inappropriateness of datagram sockets because reliable communication is critical, particularly as the simulation itself may generate extremely large numbers of packets in the network.

The important elements of the distributed architecture are elaborated in the following:

3.6.3.3.1 Initialization from Network Configuration Files

As indicated earlier, every node in the network is assigned a distinct workstation. When the model representing a node is executed, initially, it blocks until it receives additional information about its operating characteristics. When all of the nodes reach the blocked state, the server program is executed. The server program first accepts the names of the network configuration files in the form of parameters. It then opens the files, reads and parses their contents, and reconstructs the network configuration in its memory. This process requires extensive computation and graph construction. Following completion of this task, the server program broadcasts the necessary information to the node. The information consists of the following.

3.6.3.3.1.1 Software Operating Characteristics of the Node These characteristics include the network TCP/IP ports that may be used in the simulation, namely, the ports at which to accept connections from its peer switches, the ports at which to connect to its peer switches, and the ports used for communicating routing messages with the corresponding peers. Additional information may be contained where multiple nodes are modeled on a single workstation.

3.6.3.3.1.2 Simulation Characteristics of the Node These characteristics include the processing delay of the node, the number and network addresses of the peer nodes to which it is connected, and the characteristics of the corresponding links such as the speed and length of the links. An additional parameter is included to specify the lifetime of the link that may be used to introduce predetermined link failures during simulation.

3.6.3.3.1.3 Characteristics of the Current Network These characteristics include the nature (type) and identifiers of the virtual paths attached at the ports and the names of the peer nodes at the incoming and outgoing ends of the paths. Only the originating node is aware of the complete specification of a virtual path that is necessary to route the packets. The primary purpose of this philosophy is to minimize the information overhead while achieving a truly distributed system. The author conjectures that the current approach may require modification to address the issues of distributed congestion control and component failures in the network.

3.6.3.3.2 Connection Mechanism at Initialization

For a link in a network connecting two banking nodes, only one of the banking node programs is required to make an active attempt to connect to the other node while the second node program needs to accept the connection passively. Either program may choose to execute a connect and the server makes the actual decision, based on other factors such as CPU identifier. This form of connection is required by the semantics of the networking system calls provided by the operating system. The server instructs a node to execute connect and accept statements corresponding to the links attached to it. Thus, during the initialization phase, while for some links, the node executes an active connect, for others, it executes a passive accept. The system call corresponding to the passive accept will block until the appropriate node executes a corresponding active connect. Because there is a potential threat of deadlock, the following scheme is adopted to ensure the deadlock-free establishment of connections.

Each node maintains a list of connections for which it must perform active connects and the total count of the number of passive accepts. To examine whether a connection is pending, a node uses the well-known system call, select(). The select call checks for pending input on a file descriptor and verifies whether a connection attempt is pending on a descriptor, i.e., a socket. First, it blocks in this call for a random multiple of 10,000 milliseconds, between one and four, and then gives up on waiting. Next, it attempts to establish an active connect from its own list and then again listens for a second random time period for any incoming connections. This cycle is repeated until all of the connections have been established. The randomization of the time intervals is somewhat similar to the random back-off period used in the event of collisions on an Ethernet local area network. In this approach, the randomization helps eliminate the situation where switches A and B both attempt to connect to each other and then listen passively, thereby failing to establish a connection indefinitely.

Given the asynchronous nature of the simulation and that each of the many workstations, running a multitasking operating system, executes with different load factors, the randomization of the waiting interval is probably superfluous. However, its presence is aimed at ensuring logical correctness. For all of the several-hundred simulation runs, this scheme has never failed, thereby guaranteeing that all the connections specified for a test network are established correctly. In practice, it has been observed that the connections for the 50-node network require a maximum of approximately 2 to 3 seconds for completion.

3.6.3.3.3 Assertion of Transaction Packets into the Simulation

Currently, packets representing externally introduced banking transactions may be asserted to the banking network simulation in one of two ways. First, packets may be generated off-line, i.e., prior to the initialization of simulation, and stored in files that are subsequently asserted to the simulation program as input stimulus. The principal content of these files is usually the inter-packet timings and the transaction parameters such as debit/credit, transaction amount, originating bank, payer account, and payee account, all of which are generated through stochastic processes. Second, communication hooks are developed such that the process representing the node may connect to separate processes executing on the same workstation and generating traffic data. The node program receives the packets generated by such processes utilizing special protocols. The basic purpose of permitting simultaneous traffic-generating processes is to enable a study of programs that change their behavior in reaction to changes in the network load while the simulation is executing. Also, the impact and effectiveness of high-level flow-control algorithms to address congestion are facilitated.

3.6.3.3.4 The Notion of Time in the Simulation

An important constituent of the distributed architecture is the concept of time in the simulation. Given that the simulation architecture permits the usage of communication links of different capacities, the fundamental timestep at which the simulation executes is then determined by the time required for a basic packet to be transmitted on the *fastest* link. For example, if the fastest link in the network to be simulated is rated at 800 kbits/second and a packet is 10 bytes (80 bits) in size, the fundamental timestep is 10 microseconds. Slower links are then permitted to receive and send packets at multiples of this fundamental timestep, depending on their speed as a function of 800 kbits/sec. It is pointed out that the time required for a packet to traverse a link depends on the actual physical distance traversed by the link and not the capacity of the link. The use of this philosophy ensures that simulation accuracy is maintained because the simulation proceeds at the finest available chronological precision. In general, it results in a slowdown of the overall simulation because even the presence of a single high-capacity link in a large network of slower links forces the simulation to proceed at the time unit established by this link.

3.6.4 Architecture of the Banking Simulation Program

The simulation program is designed to reflect the functions of each banking node. Figure 3.103 describes a model of a node wherein input packets, generated stochastically, are asserted at the input ports and are stored in the input buffers. The packets may be either generated at the node reflecting user-asserted transactions at the bank or propagated from other nodes. The node examines the destinations of these packets and, under normal circumstances, propagates them to their destinations. Under exceptional circumstances, such as unavailability of channel bandwidth due to heavy traffic, congestion, or link failures, a few packets may be requeued at the node. The issue of link failures is beyond the scope of this book.

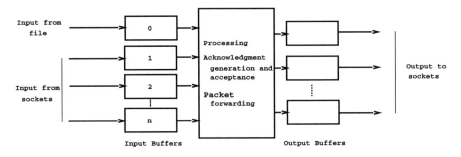

Fig. 3.103. A Graphical Representation of a Banking Node

The basic algorithm for modeling the banking node is straightforward. Associated with every node is the notion of the current local time which is determined to be equal to the minimum of the times up to which all incoming data lines are defined. The model periodically checks for updates on the incoming lines. When a new minimum time is computed, that exceeds the current local time, the program then executes the required number of timesteps until the current local time equals the new minimum time. The algorithm and the node-programs in the simulation guarantee that the timestamps associated with the packets, propagated on every outgoing link, will increase monotonically. That is, for two consecutive packets on a link, C_1 and C_2 with timestamps t_1 and t_2, respectively, t_2 must be either greater than or equal to t_1.

The algorithm that defines the simulation of a node program corresponding to a timestep $t = t_1$ is explained as follows. At local time, $t = t_1$;

1. Check all links for incoming packets. The node blocks until at least a single packet has been received at a link. Input packets are stored in the input buffers corresponding to the link identifier. For every new entry into a buffer, the assertion time is guaranteed to exceed that of the most recent entry in the buffer.
2. The input buffers, including the file that stores input packets asserted at this node (link number 0), are examined and the minimum assertion time over all of the packets is determined. This minimum value is guaranteed to be either equal to or greater than the current simulation time at the node.

When the value of the new minimum time exceeds the current simulation time, the latter is updated to reflect the new minimum time value.

3. For every incoming link, extract from the corresponding simulation buffers all packets with timestamps equal to the current simulation time. These must be processed immediately. For each packet, there are four possible scenarios:

   - The packet is a real packet and is destined for this node. The corresponding transaction is executed that involves updating the balance, where possible, and generating an acknowledgment. The acknowledgment may indicate a success or a failure in the events of adequate and insufficient balances, respectively, and is placed on the output buffer with an assertion time equal to the current time plus the node delay.
   - The packet—a real packet or an acknowledgment—is not destined for this node. Its assertion time is updated by the node delay and it is included in the output buffer for subsequent propagation. The node delay represents the delay arising from the processing of the packets by the switching and computing element of the node. The exact output link at which the packet is asserted is determined based on the virtual path associated with it.
   - The packet is a pseudo packet, representing an update of the simulation time of the originating node. It is utilized in Step 2 and does not cause any output to be placed in the buffers.
   - If the packet is a real packet originating at this node, the node computes the most appropriate virtual path based on the destination. This virtual path is embedded in the appropriate fields of the packet and it is placed in the output buffer.

4. The output buffer is evaluated, i.e., the packets in the buffers are examined. For each packet, the following two scenarios are possible:

   - The packet is successfully propagated and prior to sending it, its timestamp is updated with the propagation delay of the link.
   - The capacity of the link on which the packet must be sent, based on the predetermined virtual path, is exceeded. Then the packet is requeued in the output buffer and its assertion time is incremented as explained later. The capacity of a link Y implies that a packet may be propagated every Y timestep. When a packet is propagated at time t_1, the subsequent packet on the same output link may be sent at $t_1 + Y$, the next packet at $t_1 + 2 \times Y$, and so on. Therefore, for a packet that is requeued in the output buffer with N packets ahead of itself, the assertion time must be incremented by $N \times Y$.

3.6.4.1 The Node Program

The node program consists of three conceptual parts, described in the following.

3.6.4.1.1 Buffering and Processing of Input Packets

The primary need to buffer incoming packets stems from the fact that the simulation proceeds at different speeds on different nodes depending on the load at the individual nodes. When a packet with a timestamp $t = t_x$ arrives at a node where the current local time $t = t_y$ is less than t_x, the packet may not be processed immediately. Such packets have arrived too soon, i.e., they have arrived in simulation sooner than they would in reality. As a result, they are buffered until the current local time increases to a value $t \geq t_x$. When the latter condition is satisfied, the packet is extracted from the buffer for processing by the banking node. The notion of buffering is an artifact of the simulation. In reality, the timestamp of an incoming packet will always equate to its arrival time at the node and, as a result, the phenomenon of packets characterized as arrived too soon is nonexistent.

The process of awaiting input packets is achieved through the use of the select() system call, enumerated earlier. The commonly known principle of polling the input links was not used for two reasons. First, the continuous use of polling is expected to consume significant CPU time, idly. Second, as control is surrendered to the operating system less frequently in the event of polling, it contradicts the author's desire to execute the simulation as a background job on the workstation without seriously affecting other users of the machine. Instead, a mechanism is used wherein, for a specified maximum time interval, the system call listens for incoming packets only for a time interval equal to the specified time. Thereafter, the operating system returns control from the system call to the node program. Where a packet arrives at the link within the specified time interval, the operating system immediately returns control to the node program. As initially hypothesized, this approach was highly efficient. That is, under normal conditions, the node program executed at normal priority, consuming less than 20% of the available CPU time, and the normal interactive usage of the machine by other users was not noticeably affected.

3.6.4.1.2 Switching Packets through the Node

Currently, packets that are deemed executable at a particular simulation time instant are extracted individually from the pool in any random order for the purpose of processing by the node. Thus, except for their timestamp values, the packets are not prioritized with regard to their execution order. A packet, extracted from the pool, is forwarded to the proper send queue following processing, and the process continues until the pool is empty. The send queues are accessed by the packet transmission routines on a first in first out (FIFO) basis.

3.6.4.1.3 Transmission and Buffering of Outgoing Packets

When permitted, any of the multiple packets ready for transmission is selected at random, extracted from the appropriate send queue, and transmitted over the proper link. When multiple packets compete for transmission, one or more of them may need to be requeued.

3.6.4.2 Limitations of the Proposed Approach

As with any simulation, the banking simulation program is an attempt to model a real banking system as accurately as possible. The principles of the simulation, as outlined in this section, may be applied directly to an actual banking system with one exception, namely the issue of pseudo packets. The notion of pseudo packets is solely an artifact of the distributed implementation of the approach, proposed here, on a loosely coupled parallel processor. First, different processors may execute and communicate at different speeds. Second, the clocks associated with the different processors of the parallel processor are not synchronized. Third, in the current implementation, all external customer-introduced transaction packets to a banking node are synthesized prior to the initiation of simulation and stored in a queue. In reality, however, the clocks at all banking nodes will be synchronized to the Coordinated Universal Time, UTC [126], such that each will refer to the same Universal Time at the same instant. Every transaction packet will be ordered in time, i.e., timestamped, by the absolute (UTC) value of its arrival time at a banking node. Therefore, events, i.e., transaction packets, will be executed in the correct order and the need to send pseudo packets to synchronize, i.e., align the different banking nodes to the same simulation time, is eliminated.

A fundamental assumption in this section is that transaction packets are never lost; they use the connection-oriented mode, and their performance is characterized by acceptable delay between their introduction into the network and arrival at the destination. Although these packets may be assigned service class C, in the context of broadband-ISDN [173], and while the guaranteed delivery of a packet, in general, is achieved through a combination of higher-level protocols and retransmission, the issue of link failures in broadband-ISDN and the consequent loss of packets and impact on the performance of the proposed approach are beyond the scope of this research.

3.6.5 Implementation Issues

The distributed simulator is written in C and consists of approximately 2100 lines of code. It is compiled utilizing the Sun ANSI standard C compiler, acc without optimization. The simulator is executed on a network of 50+ Sun Sparc station1 (Sun 4/60) workstations, each with 16 MB of main memory and CPUs rated at 12.5 MIPs. All the workstations are connected through Ethernet, with most of the file systems mounted remotely off two Sun 4/490 file servers using Sun's Network File System (NFS).

The simulations are run under the condition that the node programs, representing the banking nodes, execute in the background at low priority while the workstations are in regular use by other users at the consoles. The priority is adjusted such that the CPU usage by a node program at any of the workstations is limited to approximately 20%.

The input stimulus to the banking network is realized through packets that are generated off-line and prior to the initiation of the simulation. A transaction packet has several parameters—debit or credit, amount of transaction, payer account identifier, and payee account identifier, all of which are determined stochastically, i.e., through the use of pseudorandom generators. Given that the fastest link in the network is 155.52 Mbits/sec and that each packet in broadband-ISDN [170] is 53 bytes long, the basic unit of simulation time, referred to as a timestep, is 2.83 μseconds. In theory, a transaction may be asserted at a banking node by external customers every timestep. This would correspond to a 100% transaction volume and the interpacket time interval would correspond to 2.83 μseconds. For the simulation experiments, the number of transaction packets per 100 timesteps and hence the interpacket time interval is determined stochastically. For a given desired transaction volume M, approximately M transaction packets are selected at every node in a pseudo-random manner. The assertion time of every transaction packet corresponds to an integer timestep value. The seeds for the pseudo–random generators that are responsible for the selections at the different banking nodes are also selected stochastically. It may be further noted that while the exact number of transaction packets within any 100 timesteps may not equal M, the transaction packet generation algorithm continuously monitors and adjusts the number of transactions within every successive 100 timesteps to ensure an average transaction volume of M.

3.6.6 Performance of Banking Network Simulation

3.6.6.1 Experimental Banking Networks

This section reports the results of simulation using three banking networks consisting of 10, 20, and 50 nodes. In the absence of a standard network for banking nodes, the banking networks in this research are constructed assuming hypothetical nodes and stochastically generated geographical distances between them. The construction of the networks is unbiased except that local nodes are connected through a relatively higher number of low-capacity links while farther nodes are connected through fewer higher-capacity links. The assignment of link capacities to the links that interconnect the nodes of the partially connected network is also stochastic. For the networks, a total of 50,000, 100,000, and 250,000 input packets, respectively, are employed to obtain the simulation results reported in this section. The 10-, 20-, and 50-node networks are presented in Figures 3.104 through 3.106. In Figures 3.104 through 3.106, the node names are arbitrary. Associated with every link is the value of the propagation delay, computed from dividing the length of the link by the speed of electromagnetic transmission in optical fibers. Every link is assumed to be bidirectional. The second quantity, associated with every link, refers to its capacity as a fraction of the basic 155.52 Mbits/sec (B-ISDN) link. Thus, given that the capacity of a link is 6, the link is six times slower than the basic 155.52 Mbits/sec link. In addition, every node is characterized by a queueing delay that arises because every transaction requires computations (CPU time) at the node. This delay is actually modeled in this research through a unique processing delay or node delay associated with every banking node. In each of the three experimental networks, the node delay is assumed as a static parameter.

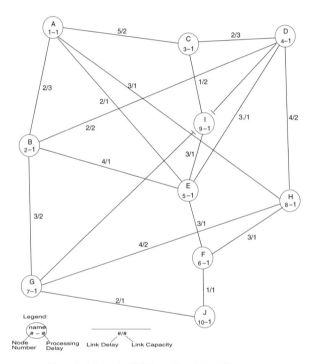

Fig. 3.104. A 10-Node Banking Network

3.6.6.2 Results

Execution Times

Table 3.12 presents the total simulation times required for the simulations of the different networks, using the appropriate number of workstations as a function of the input packets. The data are obtained for the case of 50% transaction volume, where transaction volume is defined as follows. At each node, packets representing banking transactions, generated at that node, may be asserted at every timestep, and this corresponds to the case of 100% transaction volume. Where transactions are asserted at the average rate of

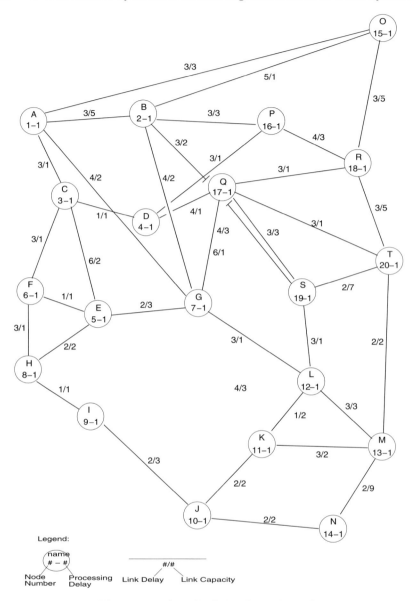

Fig. 3.105. A 20-Node Banking Network

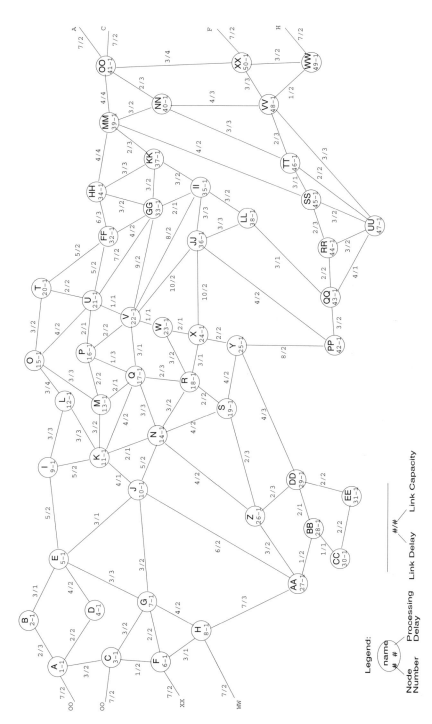

Fig. 3.106. A 50-Node Banking Network

M $(0 \leq M \leq 100)$ per 100 timesteps, the transaction volume is defined as $M\%$. Given that multiple workstations execute simultaneously, the total simulation time is computed as the maximum of the CPU times of all participating workstations. The last column in Table 3.12 presents the average time required for processing a transaction for each of the three networks that is graphically shown in Figure 3.107. Because increased transaction volume is likely to imply slower processing speed, the average transaction time is likely to be lower for lower transaction volume values. The nature of the graph in Figure 3.107 reveals that, even as the size of the network increases fivefold, the average time to process a transaction in the network of Sun workstations increases only by 26%. While the increase reflects the increased average node processing, link delays, and overhead, the size of the increase attests to the algorithm's scalability. That is, as the banking network grows in size, the number of available processors in the system also increases and, as a result, the total system throughput increases without adversely affecting the processing time of individual transactions.

It is pointed out that the performance of the distributed simulation, reported here, is pessimistic because pseudo packets will be completely absent in an actual banking network. Furthermore, given that a significant fraction of the transactions are likely to be confined to a limited geographical area, for efficiency, the overall network may be structured hierarchically. At the lowest level, a limited number of banking nodes, say 50 to 100, are organized into groups where the nodes are connected through intragroup networks and deliver fast performance. High performance is essential at this level because most transactions are local to their respective groups. At the next higher level, groups are interconnected through an intergroup network that offers slightly reduced but acceptable performance since relatively few transactions cross group boundaries.

No. of Banking Nodes (No. of Processors)	Transactions Asserted	Elapsed Time (sec)	CPU Time (ms) per Transaction
10	50,000	203.49	4.07
20	100,000	520.54	5.21
50	250,000	1237.05	4.95

Table 3.12. Simulation Execution Times as a Function of Input Transactions and Network Size

The evidence of scalability is observed across different values for the transaction volume factor, as shown in Figure 3.108. In Figure 3.108, the elapsed time is divided by the total number of transactions that includes both real and pseudo packets. While the size of the network increases fivefold, the average time to process a transaction increases by 86%, 48%, and 36%, corresponding

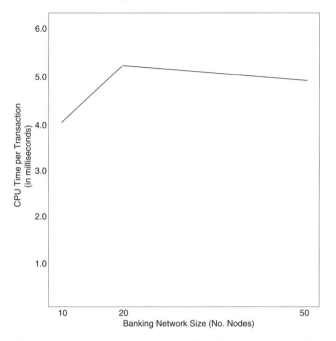

Fig. 3.107. CPU Time (ms) per Transaction (Real) as a Function of Network Size

to the transaction volume values of 10%, 30%, and 50%, respectively. Note that the values along the y-axis are expressed in units of microseconds.

Figure 3.109 presents the average size of the output queues of node 1 for the 20-node banking network, obtained from dividing the cumulative sizes of all the queues of node 1 divided by the total number of output queues. The data are computed every timestep and are plotted against the transaction assertion time for different values of transaction volume. At relatively high values for transaction volume, namely 40% and 50%, the queue size increases linearly with time, implying that transactions are queued faster than they are serviced by the network. For lower values of transaction volume, namely less than 35%, the size of the queue is constant with time, implying that the transactions are processed as fast as they are added to the system.

The graphs in Figure 3.110 present the completion times of the transactions for the 20-node banking network as a function of the transaction volume. The graphs correspond to the transactions between nodes 1 and 5. The choice of the node pair $\{1, 5\}$ is based on the fact that it corresponds to the worst-case scenario in that the completion times of the transactions are the highest among all other possible pairs of nodes. A transaction is complete when it has been routed to its destination by the network, executed at the destination bank, and an acknowledgment has been returned to the originating banking node. A total of five scenarios are considered corresponding to 5%, 10%, 11%, 12%, and 15% transaction volume values. The x-coordinate of a trans-

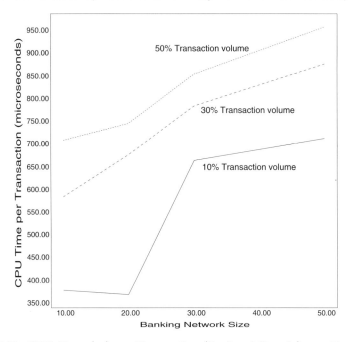

Fig. 3.108. CPU Time (μs) per Transaction (Real and Pseudo) as a Function of Network Size

action refers to the simulation time, in timesteps, at which it is asserted into the network. The y-coordinate refers to the simulation time required for the transaction to complete. Transactions are asserted into the system, between 0 and 10,000 timesteps. However, given that they are produced stochastically, the assertion of transactions for a case may terminate prior to the simulation time being equal to 10,000 timesteps. All of the transactions asserted into the system are verified to execute to completion. The values for the mean, standard deviation, and minimum, and maximum completion times are extracted from Figure 3.110 and presented in Table 3.13.

For the given link delays in the network, the minimum time that a transaction may require between nodes 1 and 5 is 16 timesteps. In the course of the simulation, a few transactions are actually observed to require 16 timesteps. However, the minimum completion time for the 15% transaction volume scenario is a high of 85 timesteps. On the other hand, in the event of high transaction volume, a few transactions are observed to require significant completion time. The maximum of the completion times are presented in the last column of Table 3.13. In general, as the value of the transaction volume increases, i.e., as more transactions are asserted into the system, the mean and standard deviation values increase, with one exception. For the 5% transaction volume case, a few transactions are delayed significantly due to excessively

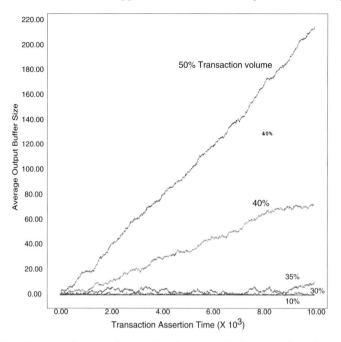

Fig. 3.109. Average Output Queue Size between Nodes 1 and 13 for a 20-Node Banking Network, as a Function of Transaction Assertion Time

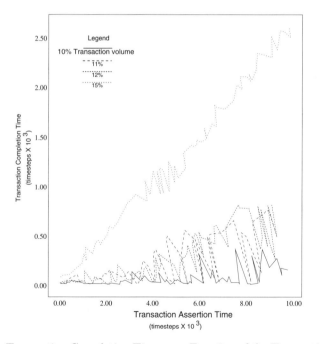

Fig. 3.110. Transaction Completion Times as a Function of the Transaction Volume

Congestion Level	5%	10%	11%	12%	15%
Mean Completion Time (timesteps)	95.9	76.4	269.4	288.0	1260.2
Standard Deviation (timesteps)	174.3	83.8	243.9	250.6	720.0
Minimum Completion Time (Ideal)	16	16	16	16	85
Maximum Completion Time (timesteps)	859	368	761	819	2608

Table 3.13. Transaction Propagation Measures as a Function of Transaction Volume for 20-Node Banking Network

low capacity of an intermediate link, and this contributes to high values for the mean and standard deviation.

In a banking network, one of the major concerns is likely to be the value of the factor F, where F is defined as the ratio of the maximum completion time to the lowest possible completion time. The values of F are observed to be 53.7, 23, 47.5, 51.2, and 163 for the 5%, 10%, 11%, 12%, and 15% cases, respectively. The value of F reflects the degradation of performance, compared to the ideal, due to the high volume of transaction traffic and the consequent congestion. The exact value of F that may be tolerated is a function of many factors, economic, political, etc.

Figure 3.111 presents the completion times of the transactions for high levels of transaction volumes—10%, 30%, 50%, and 70%. While transactions require significantly larger completion times, unlike the graphs in Figure 3.110, it may be noted that the slopes of all of the curves are modestly positive with one exception. For the 10% scenario, the slope is nearly zero, implying that as transactions continue to be asserted to the system, they are continuously and promptly completed. Under this scenario, transactions are rarely accumulated at different nodes due to congestion, and the system may be sustained, relatively, on a continuous basis. In contrast, for increasing levels of congestion—30% to 70%—more transactions are requeued locally, and the time for completion, even when the assertion of transactions into the system is discontinued, continues to increase. The different curves in Figure 3.111 may serve as a model for different qualities of banking service with appropriately tiered charges. Furthermore, although the assertion of transactions into the system is discontinued at $t = 3,000$ timesteps, the graphs for the 10% and 70% cases do not extend up to 3,000 timesteps, implying that the input traffic is discontinued even sooner. The simulation continues to run for an additional 8,000 timesteps, without any input stimulus, to allow completion of all transactions in the system.

To study the impact of priorities on the performance, transactions are classified according to the following scheme. Transactions of types A, B, and C

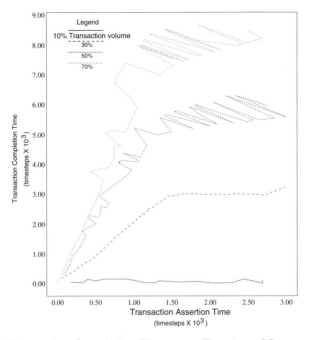

Fig. 3.111. Transaction Completion Times as a Function of Increased Values of Transaction Volume

represent highest, intermediate, and lowest priorities. For each class of transaction, a separate subbuffer is maintained, and transactions of a certain priority are not processed until any transaction with a higher priority remains outstanding. Similarly, when the outgoing link is capable of propagating a new transaction, preference is given to the one with the highest priority. The performance results are presented in Figure 3.112 for the case of 70% transaction volume, transactions asserted to the system for more than 10,000 timesteps, and the following distribution of priorities: 15% class A, 35% class B, and 50% class C. While transactions for class A required small yet constant completion times, those of B and C betray the effects of congestion for the high value of transaction volume. In Figure 3.112, although the simulation executes up to 10,000 timesteps and all transactions of class A are completed, not all transactions of classes B and C are completed. The last of the transactions of type class C that completed successfully were introduced into the system at 750 timesteps, and they required a maximum of 5200 timesteps. That is, those transactions that were asserted into the system after 750 timesteps failed to complete. Figure 3.113 presents a similar behavior for the case of 50% transaction volume.

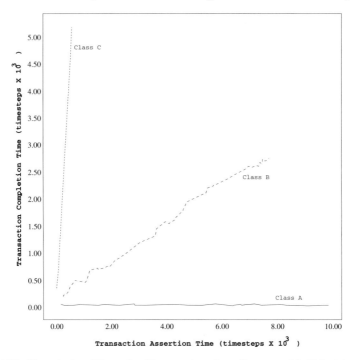

Fig. 3.112. Completion Times for Transactions in a System with Priorities Corresponding to 70% Transaction Volume

3.7 Hierarchical, Distributed, Dynamic Inventory Management

This section presents HDDI as an ADDM algorithm for highly efficient inventory management. HDDI comprises four key components. The first is the concept of emergency replenishment, wherein a retail unit is permitted to request the transfer of items from another retail unit in the neighborhood when, despite an outstanding reorder request from the warehouse, the demand continues to rapidly deplete the inventory level and the latter falls below an emergency threshold value. The aim is to satisfy local demand fast because, in general, the time to transfer from a retail unit is shorter than that from the warehouse. Second, for HDDI to be effective in today's environment of rapid price changes stemming from competition and fast-paced consumer demand, the cost function must be dynamic, i.e., reevaluated with current system parameters whenever the inventory level falls below the threshold. Consequently, HDDI is expected to track the dynamic consumer demand closely, resulting in a lower cost function than the traditional schemes. Third, frequent cost function evaluation is likely to require significant computation. Therefore, HDDI proposes the distribution of the overall inventory management computation among all of the retail units. Each retail unit determines the reorder point,

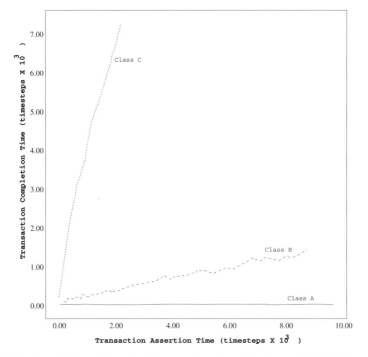

Fig. 3.113. Completion Times for Transactions in a System with Priorities Corresponding to 50% Transaction Volume

which includes the (1) source of items, warehouse or a specific retail unit; (2) order quantity; and (3) lead time, where (2) and (3) are determined by the nature of the source. Fourth, HDDI organizes inventory management networks into a region-based multilevel hierarchy where one or more retail units and warehouses are grouped into a region based on state boundaries, geopolitical, and other considerations. HDDI is modeled for a few representative inventory management networks and simulated on a Linux-based Pentium testbed and 17+ multiple, concurrent Sun workstations, configured as a loosely coupled parallel processor. Extensive simulation experiments are performed with stochastically generated demand functions and for different sets of values of the key parameters.

3.7.1 Introduction

The principal goal of inventory management is to optimize the flow and distribution of goods and items among retail and warehouse units to maximize monetary gain. This may be achieved through minimizing a cost function that takes into consideration the inventory status and cost of holding items at the retail and warehouse units, the size of reorders, cost of reordering, annual demand, unit purchase price, frequency of orders, delivery time from warehouse to retail unit, and other relevant parameters. The underlying basis of a cost function is an inventory management decision model. Of the many inventory management decision models that have been reported in the literature, the fundamental traditional inventory decision model is the classic economic-order-quantity (EOQ), which assumes a constant demand rate that is known a priori. It also assumes that inventory is replenished when it drops below the predetermined threshold; the lead time is a nonzero constant; and the ordering cost, unit price, and holding cost are all constants. This permits the analytical determination of the reorder point, quantity, and frequency of reorders.

The computations of the reorder point and the reorder quantity are both static, i.e., they are executed either yearly or at some fixed interval of time, using historical data, projected demand, and other known parameters. Also, the computation is performed by a single centralized decision-making entity that maintains the relevant parameters such as the reorder point, the reorder quantity, the holding costs at retail and warehouse units, the forecast demand functions for every item at every retail store, the ordering cost, back-order cost per item, and lead time. The centralized decision-making entity, implemented through a computer, receives information at regular intervals of time regarding the changes to the inventory status of every item at every retail and warehouse unit. When the inventory level of an item at a retail store falls below the predetermined threshold, the computer triggers a reorder from the warehouse to the appropriate retail unit. Given that the consumer purchases are asynchronous in time and the demand distribution stochastic, the central computer is likely to initiate reorders irregularly in time.

Figure 3.114 presents a retail network consisting of a warehouse W1 that supplies to the retail units R1, R2, R3, and R4 and the centralized decision maker, CU. During actual operation, consumer purchases are executed at each of the respective retail units as asynchronous discrete events. At regular time intervals, determined a priori by the decision maker, each of R1, R2, R3, and R4 propagates its current inventory status of every item to CU. The CU compares the inventory levels of the items against the corresponding analytically predetermined thresholds and, when the reorder point is reached, it orders the warehouse to supply items to a specific retail unit. The warehouse fills the order after a delay, given by the lead time. In Figure 3.114, the dashed lines represent the flow of information from the warehouse and retail units to the CU and commands from CU to the warehouse, and the solid lines describe the flow of goods and items from the warehouse to the retail units. The absence of communication links between the retail units is pointed out as a characteristic of the traditional approaches.

The literature on inventory management is rich. Mendelson, Pliskin, and Yechiali [174] describe a centralized approach wherein the only objective is to maximize the time interval between successive reallocations. While this is rarely the only goal of today's inventory management, it is counterintuitive to the current needs arising from dynamic and fast-changing consumer de-

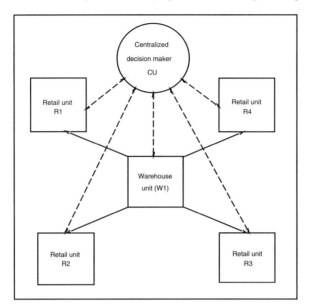

Fig. 3.114. A Traditional Inventory Management Network

mands. Simpson [175] presented a theory of "one-supply–many-outlet" stock allocation and proposed emergency handling in which special treatment is given when regular ordering is impossible. Zheng and Zipkin [176] attempt to simplify the computational burden on the centralized decision maker through a simple discrimination policy that gives priority to decisions potentially associated with larger gains over those related to smaller gains. Evidently, in this approach, the basic goal of inventory management is sacrificed for computational efficiency. Variations of the centralized approach are presented by Eppen and Shrage [177], Eppen [178], and Gross [22]. Wagner [179] proposes new decision-making rules for determining the reordering time and the amount of reorder for a particular retail store. However, it fails to address the issue of item reallocation.

Roundy [180] develops an allocation policy for one-warehouse-multiretailer systems, but makes an unrealistic assumption of instantaneous reorders and has no provision for back-orders. In addition, this study is limited to a small system. Song and Zipkin [181] have proposed an inventory model where the demand varies with an underlying state-of-the-world variable such as economic variables or stages in production life cycle. Roundy [182] presents a model of a multistage, multiproduct inventory system in discrete time. In the model, delivery is instantaneous and external demand for a component is assumed to be nonconstant yet deterministic and the demand must be satisfied without backlogging. Nielsen and Zenios [183] propose an algorithm wherein multiple scenario subproblems are executed concurrently on a CM-2 SIMD processor.

Most inventory models reported in the literature assume a limited number of retail units, a much more limited number of warehouses, and identical demand functions at retailers to provide analytic solutions for fixed and probabilistic demands. In reality, however, retail networks may consist of up to hundreds of retail units and up to tens of warehouses, distributed over a wide geographical area. In a recent report, Axsater [184] reports exact and approximate evaluation of batch-ordering policies for two-level inventory systems, assuming a single warehouse and N identical retailers. To address the severe computational needs of the centralized approach, particularly in today's environment of many product types and rapidly changing consumer demand, contemporary retailers including Wal-Mart Stores Inc., Kmart Corp., and Macy's are resorting to expensive supercomputers such as Cray Inc. More recently, Wal-Mart has off-loaded a part of its inventory computation by requiring that its vendors log into Wal-Mart's computer and track the sales of their products, store by store, and day by day to anticipate orders and, if necessary, adjust production weeks before Wal-Mart issues an order. Wal-Mart's objective is to "get the right merchandise at the right price on the shelves quicker so as to achieve higher volume of sales per square foot."

The notion of "just in time" (JIT) manufacturing [185] requires that the right units are produced in the right quantity at the right time, such that the need for inventory is drastically diminished, if not completely eliminated. Ideally, the number of parts produced or purchased at any one time should be just enough to produce one unit of the finished product. While the strategy has been successfully used by Japanese manufacturing companies and has been effective in dramatically lowering costs and improving quality, its value is reduced when holding costs are low and back-order costs are high. In addition, the risk of customer dissatisfaction due to lack of adequate inventory and high backorders may be predominant in the warehouse/retail industry.

A number of researchers propose the use of transshipments, i.e., transfer of items between retail units [186], in their inventory models. While some use transshipment as an alternative to ordering from the warehouse, others describe transshipment as a means to redistribute inventory among retail units in the final period before they are restocked. A few researchers permit transshipment between retail units at the same echelon level while others propose to review the inventory positions of all retail units and execute transshipment decisions synchronously, i.e., at the same time, at regular intervals.

It is clear that analytical solutions to realistic inventory management networks, wherein each retail unit is subject to unique and stochastic demand functions for every stocked item, item prices are subject to rapid fluctuations, reorder costs and times are variable, and multiple sources of items are available, are virtually impossible [187]. Given the current trend of fierce competition, rapidly changing prices, and consumer demand curves, the need for accurate and precise inventory control is increasingly becoming critical. Centralized decision making is inefficient, and while supercomputers such as Cray may help, it only serves to postpone the problem, not to mention the exorbitant cost of supercomputer usage. Given the limitation of the CPU speed of a uniprocessor and the increasing size of large retail networks, the centralized approach can only deliver poor performance. Failure to address the problem may result in the inability to stock high-demand items at critical times.

The remainder of this section is organized as follows. Section 3.7.2 reviews the traditional inventory management and elaborates the importance of key system parameters, while Section 3.7.3 introduces the HDDI approach. Section 3.7.4 presents the performance of HDDI.

3.7.2 Review of the Traditional Inventory Management Model

The traditional, static inventory management model consists of the lot-size control model wherein items are ordered in lot sizes because it is more economical to do so than order on an as-needed basis to satisfy demand. A few reasons for this choice include the availability of quantity discounts and reduced order or setup costs. The fundamental aim is to reduce the cost of managing inventory, expressed in the form of a cost function, while maximizing profit. The key components of the cost function are holding cost, ordering cost, and back-order cost, where backorder is permitted. When a retail unit runs out of an item and a consumer wishes to purchase it, the item is ordered and the consumer's request is filled when the shipment arrives. Thus, the sale is not considered lost, although some overhead is associated with the process of backordering.

Figure 3.115 presents the typical behavior of a traditional, static inventory model, also referred to as the EOQ model. While the x-axis represents the time line, in timesteps, the y-axis shows the variation of the inventory level at every timestep. While the traditional model is shown through solid lines in Figure 3.115, the dotted lines mark the threshold corresponding to the emergency replenishment and will be elaborated subsequently. In Figure 3.115, the low trigger level, L, determines reorders and is more common than the rare high trigger point, H, wherein items are returned to the warehouse. Given that the coefficients of the three components are constant, the cost function [188] for a single item type for a year or any other fixed time period, is expressed as

$$\text{total cost} = \text{order cost} + \text{holding cost} + \text{back order cost},$$

$$T_c(Q, B) = \frac{C_o D}{Q} + \frac{C_h (Q - B)^2}{2Q} + \frac{C_b B^2}{2Q} \tag{3.11}$$

where C_o, C_h, C_b, D, Q, and B represent, respectively, the ordering cost per order, holding cost per unit of the item type per fixed time period, backordering cost per unit per fixed time period, consumer demand in units in the time period, lot size or order quantity, and maximum permitted back-order amount.

To determine the optimal values for Q and B, represented by Q^* and B^*, respectively, first, the partial derivatives of the cost function with respect to Q and B are obtained as follows:

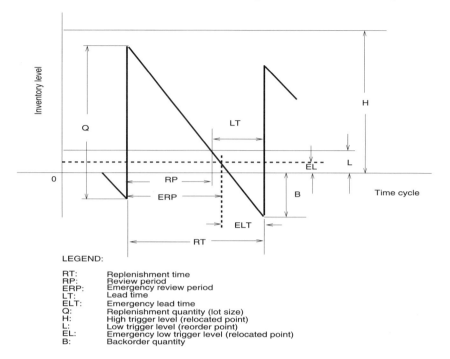

LEGEND:

RT: Replenishment time
RP: Review period
ERP: Emergency review period
LT: Lead time
ELT: Emergency lead time
Q: Replenishment quantity (lot size)
H: High trigger level (relocated point)
L: Low trigger level (reorder point)
EL: Emergency low trigger level (relocated point)
B: Backorder quantity

Fig. 3.115. Traditional Inventory Model and the Proposed Emergency Replenishment

$$\frac{\partial T_c}{\partial Q} = \frac{C_h(Q - B)}{Q} - \frac{C_o B^2 + C_h(Q - B) + 2C_b D}{2Q^2}, \tag{3.12}$$

$$\frac{\partial T_c}{\partial B} = \frac{C_o B}{Q} - \frac{C_h(Q - B)}{Q}. \tag{3.13}$$

Then the partial derivatives, represented through equations (3.12) and (3.13), are set to zero, resulting in two simultaneous equations which are solved to yield the optimal values;

$$Q^* = \sqrt{\frac{2DC_o}{C_h}} \sqrt{\frac{C_h + C_b}{C_b}}, \tag{3.14}$$

$$B^* = \sqrt{\frac{2DC_o}{C_b}} \sqrt{\frac{C_h}{C_h + C_b}} = Q^* \frac{C_h}{C_h + C_b}. \tag{3.15}$$

Upon substitution of the optimal values obtained in equations (3.14) and (3.15) in equation (3.11), the minimum cost within the fixed time period is obtained as

$$T_c^* = \sqrt{2DC_o} \sqrt{\frac{C_b C_h}{C_b + C_h}}. \tag{3.16}$$

Without back order, if no sales are to be lost, the reorder point is defined as follows: The inventory level at reorder is equal to the daily consumer demand multiplied by the lead time. The latter is referred to as the lead time demand. Mathematically,

$$\text{reorder point}, L = \text{lead time} \times \text{demand} = LT\frac{D}{N} \qquad (3.17)$$

where D represents the consumer demand over the fixed time period, N units, and therefore the $\frac{D}{N}$ shows the average daily consumer demand. The lead time, LT, represents the duration between placing the order and the actual arrival of the lot.

With back orders, the reorder point is defined as follows. The inventory level at the reorder point is equal to the lead time demand minus the back-order amount. Thus, equation (3.17) is modified to equation (3.18):

$$\text{reorder point}, L = \text{lead time demand} - \text{back orders} = LT\frac{D}{N} - B^* \qquad (3.18)$$

The issue of the impact of back orders on the overall cost function is the subject of investigation in this research. In general, if back orders incur no costs, i.e., C_b is much less than C_h, equation (3.15) dictates that B^* will tend to be large and equal Q^*. That is, in the extreme case, no inventory is held and all demand is back ordered. Where back orders are prohibitively expensive, C_b is much larger than C_h and the number of back orders, given by equation (3.15) approaches zero in the extreme case. In reality, however, the back order cost is somewhere in between and, as a result, it is possible to incur back orders particularly toward the end of the inventory cycle. It is also possible for the reorder point to go negative, when the back-order quantity exceeds the lead time demand in equation (3.18) and the impact of this scenario on the cost function will be studied.

A few key characteristics of the traditional system follow from the preceding equations and are noted as follows:

1. If C_o decreases, then Q^* will decrease according to equation (3.14). Given that the number of orders per year equals the total demand divided by Q^*, the frequency of ordering will increase. Similarly, a decrease in C_o will imply reduced ordering frequency.
2. For high holding cost, C_h, and $C_b \gg C_h$, Q^* will decrease, which implies that the inventory level cannot reach a high value. When C_b is very low, which is very unlikely, Q^* is virtually independent of C_h according to equation (3.14).
3. It also follows from equation (3.14) that a high value for C_b will mean that Q^* is virtually independent of C_b and B^*, according to equation (3.15), will approach zero as C_b approaches ∞.
4. In equations (3.11) through (3.13), all of the parameters are assumed time-invariant. Even if a probabilistic demand function is used, most of the key parameters including C_o, C_h, and C_b, will continue to remain time-invariant. In addition, most traditional approaches fail to include

some form of emergency replenishment, which is introduced and formally investigated under this research, and one that may prove very important in today's highly competitive market and the era of customer satisfaction.

3.7.3 The HDDI Approach

The design of the HDDI approach is triggered by the realizations that (1) consumer demands have become highly dynamic, (2) many of today's key system parameters are time-dependent, being driven by competitive market forces, and (3) some form of emergency replenishment is very important to address the current drive toward customer satisfaction. While dynamic recomputations of the reorder point imply significant computational demand, current advances in asynchronous distributed algorithms offer the promise of effective solutions.

The HDDI approach assumes that the total inventory management system consists of a number of geographically distributed retail and warehouse units. It organizes them into a few neighborhoods, where the choice of a neighborhood and the constituent entities are dictated by geographical proximity, state boundaries, and social, economic, and other political factors. A neighborhood typically consists of one or more warehouses and several retail units. The retail units and warehouses are connected through full-duplex communication links between themselves and they maintain bidirectional transportation routes to send and receive goods. HDDI reasons that much of the decision making involved in the inventory management system is localized, i.e., it predominantly affects the local retail and warehouse entities. Thus, all inventory-related decisions, including reorders from warehouses and emergency replenishments from neighboring retail units, are first addressed within the retail unit's immediate neighborhood. Only when a neighborhood experiences shortage of an item, does the warehouse seek items from other neighborhood warehouses.

Within a neighborhood, every retail unit and warehouse have access, at all times, to the thresholds, parameters, inventory level, and relative distance and location of all other units in the neighborhood. Although many of the system parameters are likely to be similar across the retail units in the neighborhood, the dynamic consumer demand functions are unique to every retail unit and these, in turn, will manifest in unique reorder points for the retail units, as evident from equation (3.18). The parameters for the warehouse(s) are likely to differ from those for the retail units, because the warehouses neither sell items nor make any profit. However, every warehouse maintains knowledge of the locations of all other warehouses in the entire network and may access their key system parameters. Every entity is provided with a dedicated processor, and it executes its share of the inventory management task, independently, concurrently, and asynchronously. At every retail unit, consumer interactions are modeled through events. While the events occur at regular intervals, the demand levels are stochastic, ranging from 0 to a predetermined maximum value, and this emulates a realistic scenario where the probabilistic consumer demand drives the inventory level up or down, asynchronously. In turn, the rise and fall of the inventory level, relative to the reorder point, trigger the execution of the decision-making algorithm at the corresponding entity.

This research effort acknowledges that a realistic inventory management system, consisting of many retail units and warehouses, is complex, and estimation of its performance is difficult. It argues that the traditional approaches that aim to use analytical techniques are generally based on simplifying assumptions and are inaccurate. In contrast, this effort focuses on the nature and impact of key system parameters on the performance of representative inventory management systems, through extensive distributed simulation. The expression for the cost function is complicated by the presence of a number of system parameters and a great number of possible values for each of the parameters. The plan is to select representative values for each of the key parameters, perform simulation experiments, and estimate their impact on the system performance.

In HDDI, stochastic demand values for items are generated at the retail units corresponding to every timestep. Timesteps are time values along the time axis that are selected by the inventory management system to reflect significant changes in the inventory system including appreciable changes in consumer demand, filling an order from the warehouse, receipt of items from another retail unit, etc. Thus, no significant changes occur within a timestep. In HDDI, the timestep is set to one business day, without any loss in generality. In addition to the high and low trigger levels of the traditional EOQ model, HDDI proposes the emergency replenishment technique wherein an emergency threshold level is defined at a level lower than the low trigger level. The cost function computation is triggered whenever the inventory falls below the low trigger level, and it is likely followed by a reorder from the warehouse. Given the delay in filling the order from the warehouse, if the consumer demand continues to be strong, the inventory level may fall below the emergency threshold. At this point, the cost function is triggered again and an emergency replenishment request to a neighborhood retail unit is likely. HDDI argues that during its slide below the emergency threshold, the inventory level must have already crossed the low trigger level, thereby causing a reorder from the warehouse. At the time the inventory level just falls below the emergency threshold, the reorder from the warehouse must be on its way and is delayed by the customary lead time of the warehouse filling the order. The placement of a second order from the warehouse at this time will not relieve the current situation. Therefore, it is not meaningful for the inventory computation to issue another order from the warehouse. Instead, the transfer of items from a neighborhood retail unit is preferred and may arrive in time to meet the anticipated consumer demand. Figure 3.115 presents the emergency threshold through dotted lines. At a timestep, a retail unit subtracts the demand value from its inventory level from the previous timestep, and adds any items that it receives from the warehouse or other retail units to update its current inventory level. When the current inventory level falls below the emergency threshold, the following procedure is executed.

The retail unit in question, say R_i, propagates a request to a local warehouse or retail unit, say R_1, selected arbitrarily, requesting it to send its current inventory level for item x, its holding cost, its ordering cost, consumer demand in the subsequent timestep, profit (revenue minus cost) from the sale of a piece of item x, and cost to place a back-order. For a warehouse, the consumer demand and profit parameters are irrelevant. HDDI assumes that no potential sales are lost and that they are back ordered. Next, R_i evaluates the cost function dynamically, for three possible scenarios:

1. assuming that z pieces of item x are transferred from R_i to R_1
2. assuming that z pieces of item x are transferred from R_1 to R_i, and
3. assuming that no transfer takes place.

While the value of z, say z_1, is identical for all retail units, its value may be different for the warehouse, say z_2. Of course, the first and second scenarios are meaningless if the inventory levels at R_i and R_1, respectively, are less than z. The general form of the dynamically computed cost function, evaluated for a single retail unit, is given by

$$f_{R_1}^{R_i}(d) = \{\text{holding cost per piece of item } x * \text{ (posttransfer inventory of item } x$$
$$- \text{ number of pieces predicted by the demand function)}\}$$
$$+\{\text{back-order cost per piece of item } x *$$
$$\text{(number of pieces predicted by the demand function}$$
$$- \text{ posttransfer inventory of item } x)\}$$
$$-\{\text{profit from selling each piece } * \text{ minimum (number of pieces pre-}$$
$$\text{dicted by the demand function, posttransfer inventory of item } x)\}$$
$$+\{\text{ordering cost}\}.$$

In the preceding expression, the cost function equals the sum of the holding cost, back-order cost, and ordering cost minus the profit. The parameter d may be $-$, $+$, or 0, representing the three scenarios just described. In the expression for the cost function, (1) the holding cost is nil if the mean of the consumer demand distribution is equal to or exceeds the posttransfer inventory and (2) the back-order cost is nil where the posttransfer inventory is equal to or exceeds the mean of the demand distribution. The consumer demand distribution is assumed to be stochastic [189] and is elaborated in section 3.7.4. It is noted that, in general, the cost function will evaluate to a negative value and the goal of inventory management is to minimize this value. Also, unlike a retail unit, a warehouse cannot engage in selling and, therefore, the profit parameter is nil. In reality, transfer of items from a retail unit to the warehouse is rare. The ordering cost includes the cost of transportation and the time lag resulting from the limited speed of transportation. It is finite for the cases $d = +$ and $d = -$ and nil for the case of $d = 0$. For each of the three scenarios, R_i determines $f_{R_1}^{R_i}(d)$ for itself as well as for R_1 and then computes the sum.

Following its interaction with R_1, R_i interacts similarly with the subsequent local retail unit, R_2, then with R_3 and all other local retail units, and finally with each of the local warehouses, $W_1 \dots W_m$. Eventually, R_i examines the values obtained from evaluating the cost functions, $f_{R_1}^{R_i}(d), \dots, f_{W_m}^{R_i}(d)$, for all possible values of d and selects the one with the lowest value. R_i initiates the inventory process corresponding to the selected value. Where more than one choice is indicated, any may be selected arbitrarily. Despite emergency replenishment from another retail unit, the outstanding reorder from the warehouse to the retail unit in question will be filled in due time, thereby increasing the inventory position.

The difference in the execution of the cost function corresponding to low trigger and emergency threshold may be described as follows. Corresponding to the inventory level sliding down the low threshold, reordering from the warehouse is likely to result in lower cost because the reorder cost is low, the reorder amount is relatively high, and there is no immediate threat of stock-out. In contrast, when the inventory level falls below the emergency threshold, the threat of stock-out coupled with the relatively longer delay associated with ordering from the warehouse, is likely to imply lower cost for emergency replenishment request from other retail units.

Within a neighborhood, a warehouse W_j is, in general, passive. That is, it merely recomputes its inventory level following a transfer to or from a local retail unit. When it receives a request for its parameters and inventory level or a transfer of specific pieces of an item from a warehouse in another neighborhood, W_j complies with the request. When the inventory level for an item falls below the low threshold, a reorder from the manufacturer is likely. However, when the inventory level of an item falls below the emergency threshold, W_j requests the parameters and inventory levels from other neighborhood warehouses, uses its knowledge of the ordering cost from the factory or manufacturer and the delay, and then computes the cost function, similar to the retail unit but with respect to other neighborhood warehouses, determines the lowest value, and requests emergency replenishment from the appropriate neighborhood warehouse.

Given that HDDI is asynchronous and distributed, conceivably two or more local retail units, R_i and R_j, may simultaneously request another warehouse or retail unit R_1 for its parameters and inventory level for the same item y and then evaluate their respective cost functions. Assume that R_i determines that the lowest value of the cost function is achieved when R_1 transfers z pieces of item y to itself and issues that request. Conceivably, should Rj subsequently request R_1 to also transfer z pieces of item y, R_1's inventory level for y may have fallen short of z pieces and it may be unable to comply with the request. Under these exceptional circumstances, R_j may have to reselect the next best alternative.

As an example, consider the neighborhood shown in Figure 3.114. Where the retail unit, R_1, is engaged in decision making, it interacts, sequentially, with each of the three remaining retail units—R_2, R_3, and R_4—and the warehouse unit, W_1. For each interaction, R_1 computes the cost function three times, as shown in Table 3.14. In general, for a given neighborhood consisting of S units, the cost function is evaluated, at a retail unit, for a total of $(S-1)*3$ times, which for Figure 3.114, amounts to $(5-1)*3 = 12$ evaluations.

	From R_1	To R_1	No Transaction
R_1/R_2	$f_{R_2}^{R_1}(\text{-})$	$f_{R_2}^{R_1}(+)$	$f_{R_2}^{R_1}(0)$
R_1/R_3	$f_{R_3}^{R_1}(\text{-})$	$f_{R_3}^{R_1}(+)$	$f_{R_3}^{R_1}(0)$
R_1/R_4	$f_{R_4}^{R_1}(\text{-})$	$f_{R_4}^{R_1}(+)$	$f_{R_4}^{R_1}(0)$
R_1/W_1	$f_{W_1}^{R_1}(\text{-})$	$f_{W_1}^{R_1}(+)$	$f_{W_1}^{R_1}(0)$

Table 3.14. Cost Function Evaluations by R_1s during Its Decision Making

In an actual implementation of HDDI, every entity continues to execute in an asynchronous, independent, and concurrent manner. When the inventory level falls below the appropriate threshold, the entity first issues requests to other units, as described earlier. Upon receiving the requested responses, the units execute the decision-making processes that, in turn, generates either reorder requests from the warehouse or emergency replenishment requests from other retail units.

As an example, consider Figure 3.116 which shows a retail inventory management system consisting of two neighborhoods, in this instance two southern New England states, Connecticut and Rhode Island. While the Connecticut neighborhood has a single warehouse, labeled WCT, and three retail units, CT1, CT2, and CT3, the Rhode Island neighborhood consists of two retail units RI4 and RI5 that are served by warehouse WRI. While the dashed lines describe the intraneighborhood bidirectional flow of information and goods, the solid line relates to the interneighborhood flow of information and goods between the warehouses.

Unlike the traditional inventory management systems whose slow performance is caused by the sequential execution on a centralized computer, HDDI recognizes the trend toward increasingly powerful yet inexpensive computers and decreasing local-area communication costs. Coupled with localized decision making through asynchronous distributed algorithms, HDDI promises fast inventory decisions that will track dynamic consumer demands better, generate higher customer satisfaction, and realize greater efficiency and profit. In addition, HDDI will facilitate the initiation of price reductions on selected

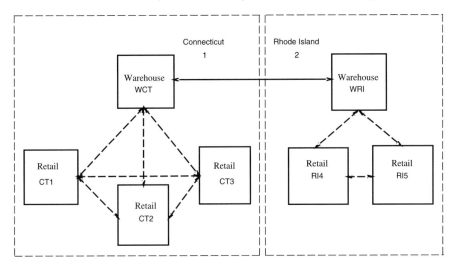

Fig. 3.116. An Example Inventory Management System Consisting of Two Neighborhoods

items and in selected geographical areas, based on past sales analysis. The predominance of local computations in HDDI is also likely to realize scalability. That is, as the inventory management system grows, adding more retail units, warehouses, and neighborhoods, the number of computing engines increases proportionately and the algorithm will continue to function and yield monotonically increasing performance. By distributing the overall decision making to a number of geographically dispersed entities, HDDI realizes greater reliability and less vulnerability to catastrophic failures.

3.7.4 Simulation Results and Performance Analysis of HDDI

Given that the key parameters of a representative inventory management system include the order size, threshold, lead time, and holding, order, and back-order costs, HDDI's performance is likely to be influenced by them. Each of these parameters may assume a wide range of values; this section details the efforts to understand the impact on HDDI of different combinations of parameter values.

Table 3.15 shows the key parameters used in this study. While the reorder quantity, holding cost, ordering cost, low and high triggers, lead time, and profit relate to all inventory management systems, emergency order, emergency trigger, and emergency lead times are specific to HDDI. To facilitate comprehension, in Table 3.15, sets of two related but independent parameters are encapsulated through a ratio. Thus, the ordering and holding costs are encapsulated through a single ratio o_h, while the holding to back-order cost is expressed through the ratio h_b. The emergency lead time is assumed to be unity while the conventional lead time is expressed through the ratio r_l.

Key Parameters	Symbol Used Here	Usage in Simulation	Notes
Reorder quantity	Q_r^*	Equation 3.14	Q_w^* used for warehouse
Holding cost	C_{hr}		C_{hw} used for warehouse
Ordering cost	C_{or}	Expressed through o_h = ratio of ordering to holding cost	C_{ow} used for warehouse
Back-order cost	C_{br}	Expressed through h_b = ratio of holding to back-order costs	C_{bw} used for warehouse
Low trigger	L_r	Equations 3.18 and 3.22	L_w used for warehouse
High trigger	H_r		Occurs rarely
Lead time	LT_r	Expressed through r_l = ratio of lead time to emergency lead time	w_l used for warehouse
Emergency order size	Q_{re}	Expressed through r_p = ratio of regular to emergency order size	w_p used for warehouse
Emergency order cost		Expressed through r_c = ratio of regular to emergency order cost	w_c used for warehouse
Emergency trigger	EL_r		
Emergency lead time	ELT_r	Set to unity	Units received next day
Daily profit	d_p		Irrelevant for warehouse

Table 3.15. Key Parameters in HDDI

The corresponding ratio at the warehouse level, i.e., the ratio of the time to access items from a neighborhood warehouse to that from the manufacturer, is expressed through w_l. The emergency to regular ordering cost is expressed by r_c, while the regular to emergency order size is represented by r_p. The corresponding symbols at the warehouse level are w_c and w_p, respectively. The daily profit d_p reflects the profit from selling one item. HDDI models and simulates representative inventory management systems for a number of representative values of the key parameters.

Corresponding to a choice of parameter values, the initial inventory level is set at the value obtained from equation (3.14), and the low and high trigger points are also computed. HDDI also sets the size of the regular order from the warehouse to that determined by equation (3.14). The consumer demand function is assumed to be stochastic and, to model reality closely, at every retail unit, it is given by a normal distribution with unique mean and standard deviation values. The value of D in equation (3.14) is set equal to the mean of the normal distribution function. A discrete Poisson distribution could have been used for the demand function. However, while the Poisson distribution lends itself to easy mathematical manipulation, simulation of the HDDI model is greatly facilitated by the readily generated tables from normal distribution. It is also pointed out that our simulation assumes a typical scenario, i.e., the items are consumed year-round as opposed to seasonal consumption. Thus, the continuous normal distribution is utilized in this study without any loss in generality. Furthermore Kreyszig [190] notes that, for large n, i.e., the number of independent performances of an experiment, a binomial distribution may be approximated by a normal distribution, while it is well known that the Poisson distribution may be derived as a limiting case of the binomial distribution.

At a given retail unit with identifier uid, the mean and standard deviation (s.d.) values used are given through equations (3.19) and (3.20). The use of the sin function is aimed to reflect representative demand fluctuations among the different geographically distributed retail units:

$$\text{mean(uid)} = a + b \sin\left(12\pi \frac{\text{uid}}{\text{MAX\_NODE\_NO}}\right) \tag{3.19}$$

$$\text{s.d.(uid)} = \frac{a}{5} + \frac{b}{5} \sin\left(12\pi \frac{\text{uid}}{\text{MAX\_NODE\_NO}}\right) \tag{3.20}$$

where a and b are constants with initial values 15 and 10, respectively, and MAX_NODE_NO reflects the cumulative sum of all retail units and warehouses in the inventory management system. Using the mean and s.d. values and the relation $z = ((x - \text{mean})/\text{s.d.})$, where z refers to the standard units for the corresponding standard normal distribution curve, a demand table is constructed. In the demand table, entries for the consumer demands, x, are obtained for z values ranging from -3 to $+3$ at intervals of 0.05. Using the standard statistical table that lists the probability that a random variable, having the standard normal distribution, takes on a value between 0 and z, the probability values corresponding to the z values in the demand table are recorded in the demand table. Thus, the demand table relates the probability of a stochastic demand value to the demand value itself. In the course of simulation, HDDI generates a random number that is used as an index into the demand table to obtain the corresponding random demand value. Consider the following example. At a retail unit, a random number value of 0.4167 is generated for item x. The mean and s.d. of the normal distribution are 25 and 5, respectively. For the 0.4167 value, the standard normal distribution table yields a z value of -0.2. Therefore, the demand is computed as $(-0.2 * \text{s.d.} + \text{mean}) = 24$.

While a warehouse does not interact directly with the consumers, its demand function solely depends on the reorders from the constituent retail units. The mean for the warehouse demand function, w_mean, is assumed to be derived from the sum of the means of the demand functions associated with the retail units. In equation (3.21), nid refers to the neighborhood identifier, n the total number of retail units in the neighborhood, and mean (uid) the respective means of the distributions of the retail units. The synthesized demand function is used to substitute for the value of D for the warehouse in equation (3.14).

$$\text{w\_mean(nid)} = \sum_{\text{uid}=1}^{n} \text{mean(uid)}. \tag{3.21}$$

HDDI modifies equation (3.14) by setting D to w_mean, as shown in equation (3.21), and using a multiplicative factor to compute the reorder size, Q_w^*. Although the warehouse is likely to receive demands from the individual retail units at discrete times, relative to the frequent consumer demands imposed on the retail units, there is a slight chance that 2 or more retail units may issue reorders simultaneously. Therefore, the reorder quantity for the warehouse, Q_w^*, should include a multiplicative factor. In this effort, the number of retail units in the neighborhoods ranges from 2 to 4 and, therefore, the multiplicative factor is set at 2. For neighborhoods with large n, i.e., many retail units, a higher value for the multiplicative factor is recommended.

The low trigger point for the warehouse in the neighborhood with identifier nid, L_w(nid), is defined as the average of the reorder points for the individual retail units, as shown in equation (3.22). The reasoning underlying the factor 2 in equation (3.22) is similar to that given earlier. It is also pointed out that although the reorder point for the warehouse is not too far from those for the retail units, the reorder size for the warehouse is significantly larger than those for the individual retail units:

$$L_w(\text{nid}) = 2 \, \frac{\sum_{\text{uid}=1}^{n} L_r(\text{uid})}{n} \tag{3.22}$$

Following initialization, the consumer demands, in the form of customer purchases at every retail unit, are asserted at regular time intervals, termed timesteps. The size of the timestep is chosen based on the desired resolution of the inventory management process and is identical across the entire inventory management system. However, despite demands asserted at regular time intervals, the occurrence of reorder points and emergency replenishment scenarios may be asynchronous, i.e., they occur at irregular time intervals. As noted earlier, both the initial inventory level and the subsequent reorder sizes are given by equation (3.14). The principal focus of this section is in calculating the cost function dynamically, i.e., using the current parameters, including inventory levels, to determine the reorder points for both regular reorders and emergency replenishments.

3.7.4.1 Overview of HDDI's Performance Behavior

Figure 3.117 presents a representative inventory management system that is modeled and simulated under HDDI. It consists of six neighborhoods, labeled after the six states in the northeast United States: Maine, New Hampshire, Vermont, Massachusetts, Connecticut, and Rhode Island. A total of 16 retail units and 6 warehouses defines the system. The consumer demand functions for the retail units are derived using equations (3.19) and (3.20), while those for the warehouses are obtained using equation (3.21) and the discussion toward the beginning of Section 3.7.4. Figures 3.118(a) and 3.118(b) present graphical views of the consumer demand functions in the regions labeled Rhode Island and Massachusetts, respectively, and they reveal the familiar bell-shaped curve for normal distributions. Even within the same neighborhood, the use of different mean and s.d. values causes the individual distributions to assume different shapes. While the x-axis represents the demand for an item, the y-axis refers to the number of occurrences of this demand value corresponding to the simulation extending from 0 to 2000 timesteps. Consider retail unit 8 in the region labeled Massachusetts, where the demand function corresponds to a mean value of 25 items/day as evident in Figure 3.118(b).

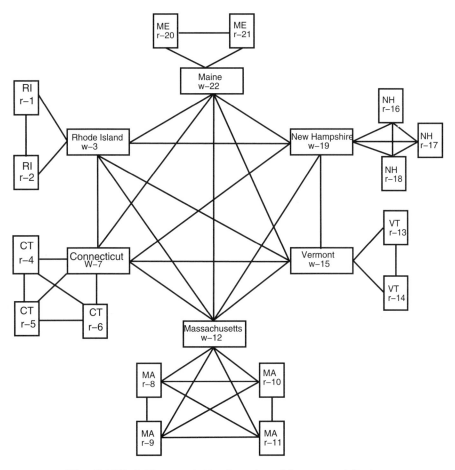

Fig. 3.117. A Representative Inventory Management System

Where unique values are assigned to each of the parameters in Table 3.15 for every retail unit and warehouse, the simulation is likely to become very complex and the results are difficult to comprehend. To facilitate an overview of HDDI's performance, this section assumes the following values of the parameters throughout the network. The values of r_p, r_c, and r_l are 20, 3, and 5, respectively. Clearly, the emergency replenishment order size from a neighbor retail unit is significantly lower than the regular order from the ware-

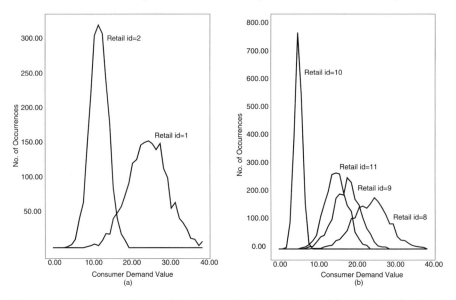

Fig. 3.118. Consumer Demand Functions for Retail Units in (a) a RI Neighborhood and (b) a MA Neighborhood.

house, while the cost for emergency reorder is higher and the lead time for emergency replenishment significantly shorter than that from the warehouse. At the warehouse level, reorders from the manufacturer and interneighborhood warehouse are analogous, respectively, to reorders from the warehouse and emergency replenishment requests from neighborhood retail units. The values for w_p, w_c, and w_l are 20, 4, and 7, respectively. For the retail units, the ratio of the holding to back-order cost, h_b, is 0.1 while the ratio of the order to holding cost o_h is 10. These are based on the realistic assumptions that back-ordering is significantly more expensive than ordering, which is more expensive than the holding cost. The d_p value is 10.

A representative value of the ratio of cost of ordering from the warehouse to holding at the retail unit o_h is 10 [188]. At the warehouse level, the ratio refers to ordering from the manufacturer to holding at the warehouse, and a representative value is 10. While the ordering cost, C_o, is stated in cost per order, the holding cost, C_h, refers to the holding cost per unit per year. Orders are typically specified relative to a year. Assuming that the holding cost at the warehouse is $1/x$ per day, its value per year is $365/x$. Assuming $C_o = 50$, we obtain, $10 = 50/(365/x)$, which yields $x = 73$. At the retail level, the cost of ordering is generally higher, and it is assumed to be 73. Using o_h = the daily holding cost is obtained as $y = 365 * 10/73 = 50$. These figures are employed in the cost function computation.

The graphs in Figure 3.119(a) present the variation of the inventory levels in the retail units, retail_8 through retail_11, in the Massachusetts neighbor-

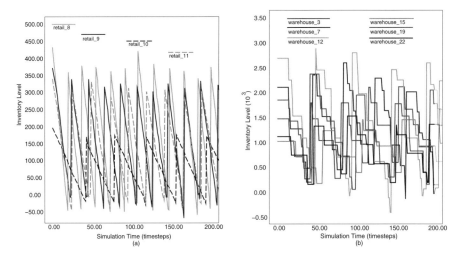

Fig. 3.119. Overview of HDDI's Performance Behavior: Inventory Levels for (a) Retail Unit #8 in the Massachusetts Neighborhood, and (b) All Warehouses

hood as a function of timestep. While the progress of the simulation ranges from 0 through 2,000 timesteps, Figure 3.119(a) only plots the data for 200 timesteps for clarity and to facilitate comprehension. Figure 3.119(b) presents the behavior of the inventory level in all warehouses as functions of the progress of simulation. An analysis of the graphs in Figure 3.119(a) reveals the following. First, despite dynamic computations of the reorder points, the sawtooth behavior of the inventory levels closely resembles the EOQ model. Second, the inventory level for retail_8 is consistently higher than the others, reflecting its high demand distribution. Third, given that back orders are permitted at 10 times the holding cost, conceivably, a lower cost function may be achieved through back orders while the inventory level is pushed into the negative territory. Last, the frequency of the rise and fall of the inventory level is unique to every retail unit, reflecting their unique stochastic demand functions.

Unlike Figure 3.119(a), the graphs representing the warehouse inventory levels in Figure 3.119(b) are more abrupt, reflecting the fact that the warehouses receive reorder requests at larger time intervals than the continuous stream of consumer demands incident on the retail units. The differences in the rise and fall of the inventory levels reflect the unique sizes of the warehouses and the unique demand distributions of the constituent retail units.

The graphs in Figures 3.119(a) and 3.119(b) present the gross-level behavior of HDDI. In the following sections, a number of simulation experiments are conducted to analyze the individual impact of each parameter on the performance of HDDI. The aim is to identify critical elements in the inventory management system. A parameter is identified as the control variable, and

HDDI is simulated for different representative values of the variable while all other parameters are held at a fixed set of values.

3.7.4.2 Performance Evaluation of HDDI Relative to Its Parameters for the Inventory Management Network

3.7.4.2.1 The Parameter r_c, Ratio of Emergency to Regular Reorder Cost

At the retail level, r_c refers to the ratio of the emergency reorder cost from a neighborhood retail unit to the cost for regular reorder from the warehouse. At the warehouse level, the ratio of the cost of reordering from a warehouse in a different neighborhood to ordering from the manufacturer, is represented through w_c. Given that the demands are stochastic and regular and emergency reorders may occur asynchronously, for a fair comparison of the results from HDDI simulations corresponding to different choices of r_c and w_c values while all other parameters are held constant, the total demands asserted at the retail units and the cumulative number of cost function computations for the different simulations must lie within a narrow margin. Here, the margin of error is arbitrarily set to less than 1% for the entire simulation ranging from 0 to 2,000 timesteps, and the results indicate that the tolerance is not violated.

Figure 3.120(a) presents a plot of the cumulative cost function value as a function of time, expressed through timesteps, for retail unit #8 in the Massachusetts neighborhood. The cost function value reflects the cumulative value of the cost function at each timestep, starting with timestep 1 up to the current timestep. The three graphs in Figure 3.120a correspond to three sets of choices of r_c and w_c values, {3.0, 4.0}, {10.0, 12.0}, and {∞, ∞}, while the following parameters are held at the fixed values: $r\_p = 20$, $w\_p = 20$, $r\_l = 5$, $w\_l = 7$, $h\_b = 0.1$, $o\_h = 10.0$, and $d\_p = 20$. Figure 3.120(a) reveals that as r_c and w_c decrease, the cumulative cost function value also decreases, implying efficiency and superior performance for HDDI. The ability to address stock-outs through emergency replenishment clearly implies financial gain. When $r\_c = w\_c = ∞$, the cost for emergency replenishment is set too high, zero items are transferred between neighboring retail units, and the cumulative cost function is worse.

To gain a better insight into HDDI's behavior, Figures 3.120(b) and 3.120(c) measure and plot the behavior of four quantities as a function of simulation time, one corresponding to the presence of emergency replenishment and the other assumes the total absence of emergency replenishment. The simulation is executed for 2,000 timesteps although, for clarity, the data presented here range through 200 timesteps. The four quantities include back orders, demands, refusals, and number of items transferred under emergency replenishment and are represented in Figures 3.120(b) and 3.120(c) through lines of different styles. The cumulative values of the parameters throughout the entire simulation are also shown on the figures. The total demand values between Figures 3.120(b) and 3.120(c) differ only by ±0.5% which is negligible, as per prior assumptions. The irregular shapes of the individual plots attest to the stochastic nature of the demands. In Figure 3.120(b), the total number of items transferred among neighbor retail units is 1092, which is high relative to the total back order of 3055. Clearly, 36% of the back orders are compensated very quickly through emergency replenishment from neighbor retail units. Given the random rise and fall of the inventory levels in the retail units, as evident in Figure 3.119(a), refusals are likely to be low. In fact, Figure 3.120(b) records only two refusals. When the cost of emergency replenishment is high, the nature of the variation of the graphs changes very little, except that the cost increases. In the extreme case, when r_c = w_c = ∞, the total replenishment is zero, the cost increases, and the back orders must wait until a regular order is filled. Figure 3.120(d) highlights the relationship between the number of items transferred under emergency replenishment and the variation of the cost function, for different values of r_c, ranging from 1 to 100. As the cost for emergency reorders increases at the retail level, the number of items transferred decreases sharply while the cost function rises rapidly. As expected, a similar behavior is exhibited at the warehouse level. Thus, the value of emergency replenishment is not simply in achieving customer satisfaction, but are strong economic advantages in today's dynamic markets.

3.7.4.2.2 The Parameter r_p, Ratio of Regular to Emergency Order Size

Figure 3.121(a) presents the normalized cumulative cost function values corresponding to different values of r_p (and w_p) ranging from 10 to 30 and for three simulation snapshots: timestep 1 to 500, timestep 500 to 1000, and timestep 1500 to 2000. For each snapshot, the number of occurrences of the inventory level falling below the emergency threshold determines the number of times the cost function is computed, which determines the cumulative cost function value. For uniformity in comparison, the cumulative cost function values in the three snapshots are normalized with respect to the number of occurrences of cost function computation. Assume that the unnormalized cumulative cost function values in the three snapshots are C_1, C_2, and C_3, while the number of computations of the cost function are K_1, K_2, and K_3, respectively. Assume that K_2 is the minimum of all K values. Then the normalized cumulative cost function values are $C_2{}^*K_2/K_1$, C_2, and $C_3{}^*K_2/K_3$. The use of the three snapshots is aimed to facilitate analysis of the behavior of HDDI at different stages of the simulation. It is noted that the behavior of the three graphs is similar, implying that the ratio r_p influences the cost function uniformly throughout the simulation. The data presented here use constant values for the parameters, r_c = 10, and w_c = 12. Figure 3.121(a) shows that for low emergency order size, the cost function value is high. Where the emergency reorder size is high, i.e., the value of the ratio r_p is low, the cost function value is low, implying superior performance of emergency replenishment. For r_p values less than 25, emergency replenishment plays a finite role

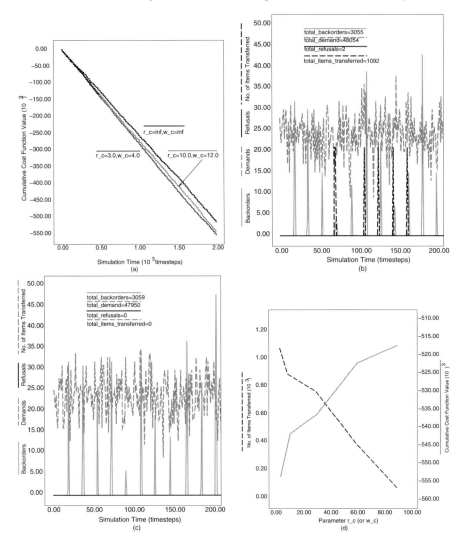

Fig. 3.120. (a) Cumulative Cost Function as a Function of Simulation Time, for Different Values of r_c; (b) Plot of Four Measures—Back orders, Demands, Refusals, and Number of Pieces Transferred—as a Function of Simulation Time, for r_c = 3 and w_c = 4; (c) Plot of Four Measures—Back orders, Demands, Refusals, and Number of Pieces Transferred—as a Function of Simulation Time, for r_c = w_c = ∞; (d) Variation of Cumulative Cost Function and Number of Pieces Transferred as a Function of r_c and w_c Parameter Values

and influences the behavior of the cost function. For r_p values greater than 25, the emergency reorder size is too small for the replenishment strategy to play any role in the behavior of the cost function. Thus, the graphs in Figure 3.121(a), for r_p values beyond 25 appears to gradually saturate. The graphs in Figure 3.121(b) correspond to different values of r_c ($= 20$) and w_c ($= 20$) and further amplify this finding. While the x-axis represents different values of r_p, the cumulative cost and number of items transferred under emergency replenishment are plotted along the y-axis. For small values of r_p, the number of items transferred is high, coupled with lower cost function value. For larger values of r_p, the number of items transferred is negligible and the cost function value is high.

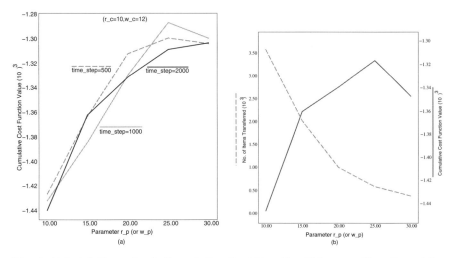

Fig. 3.121. (a) Normalized, Cumulative Cost Function Value as a Function of the Ratio, r_p; (b) Cumulative Cost Function Value and Number of Items Transferred under Emergency Replenishment as a Function of r_p

3.7.4.2.3 The Parameter h_b, Ratio of Holding to Backorder Cost

Figure 3.122(a) presents the normalized cumulative cost function values corresponding to different values of h_b ranging from 0.1 to 1.0 and for three simulation snapshots: timestep 1 to 500, timestep 500 to 1000, and timestep 1500 to 2000. For each snapshot, the cumulative cost function values are expressed as a ratio of the cost function value at the corresponding starting timestep value. The use of the three snapshots, as with Figure 3.121(a), is aimed to facilitate analysis of the behavior of HDDI at different stages of the simulation. The behavior of the three graphs is similar, implying that the ratio h_b influences the cost function uniformly throughout the simulation. Where the holding cost is held constant, an increase in the value of h_b implies a corresponding decrease in the value of back-order cost. Figure 3.122a shows that the normalized cumulative cost function value increases with decreasing back-order cost. This investigation hypothesizes that the reduced cost of back orders triggers a significant increase in back orders. As a result, the holding cost decreases but the commensurate decrease in the revenue drives the total cost function higher. Figure 3.122(b) plots four measures—back orders, demands, refusals, and number of pieces transferred—as a function of the simulation time. The simulation corresponding to the data in Figure 3.122(b) sets h_b at 1.0, implying very low back-order cost. Figure 3.122(b) also notes the totals for the measures throughout the entire simulation. It is observed that the total back order of 22,296 is nearly half of the total demand of 47,701, which supports the hypothesis.

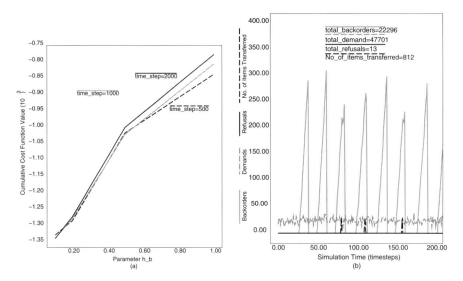

Fig. 3.122. (a) Normalized, Cumulative Cost Function Value as a Function of the Parameter, h_b; (b) Plot of Four Measures—Back orders, Demands, Refusals, and Number of Pieces Transferred—as a Function of Simulation Time, for Low Back order Cost Given by h_b = 1.0

3.7.4.2.4 The Parameter r_l, Ratio of Normal to Emergency Lead Time

An important parameter underlying the concept of emergency replenishment is the value of the normal lead time, relative to the emergency lead time, r_l. Figures 3.123(a) and 3.123(b) present the plot of four measures—back orders, demands, refusals, and number of pieces transferred—as a function of simulation time, for $\{r\_l = 3, w\_l = 5\}$ and $\{r\_l = 1, w\_l = 3\}$, respectively. Figures 3.123(a) and 3.123(b) also note the totals for the measures throughout the entire simulation. For $r\_l = 3$, a realistic value, the data in Figure 3.123(a) reveal the occurrence of emergency replenishments with a total of 399 pieces transferred. However, when r_l decreases to 1, an unlikely pragmatic scenario, regular reorders are filled the following day, eliminating any need for emergency replenishment.

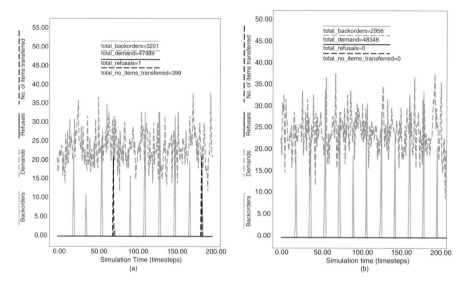

Fig. 3.123. Plot of Four Measures—Back orders, Demands, Refusals, and Number of Pieces Transferred—as a Function of Simulation Time, for (a) r_l = 3 and w_l = 5, (b) r_l = 1 and w_l = 3

3.7.4.2.5 The Parameter d_p, Daily Profit

In all of the graphs presented thus far, the value of profit per item, d_p, is assumed to be 20. Figure 3.124 presents a plot of the cumulative cost function value as a function of simulation time, for different values of d_p, ranging from 20.0 to 1.0. The values of other parameters are set at: r_p = 20, w_p = 20, r_c = 3, w_c = 4, r_l = 5, w_l = 7, h_b = 0.1, and o_h = 10.0. As expected, for decreasing value of the profit per item, the revenue declines and the cumulative cost function value increases, until the cost function assumes positive values for d_p values less than 1, which implies that the cost exceeds the gain from the profit margin.

3.7.4.2.6 Performance Comparison of Four Scenarios

To understand the scope of performance of HDDI, this research generates the graphs in Figure 3.125(a) that present the cumulative cost function values for four distinct scenarios. In Scenario 1, while demands are random, emergency reorders are permitted and the regular to emergency lead time, r_l, is set to

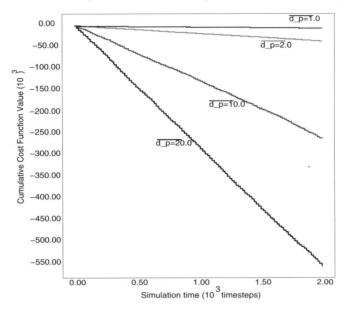

Fig. 3.124. Cumulative Cost Function Value as a Function of the Daily Profit per Item, d_p

3. Other parameter values are identical to those in Figure 3.120. The HDDI approach is representative of this scenario, and the reader is referred to Figure 3.120(b). In Scenario 2, the demands are random, and although emergency reorders are not permitted, the normal lead time is unity. All other parameters are identical to those for Scenario 1. The classic EOQ model with a fixed demand equal to the mean of the random demand constitutes Scenario 3. All other parameters are identical to those in Scenario 2. Scenario 4 is an ideal case with normal lead time of unity, zero back orders, and a priori known fixed demand. Thus, Scenario 4 is similar to Scenario 3 except that back orders are not absent. In Figure 3.125(a), the cost function for Scenario 4 is lowest, implying its superiority over the other three scenarios. However, it is impractical. The cumulative cost function value for Scenario 1 is lower than those for both Scenarios 2 and 3, implying that any form of emergency replenishment is likely to achieve superior performance. Although the EOQ model predicts that the use of fixed demand generally yields performance equal to or greater than when random demand is utilized, the performance of Scenarios 1 and 3 appears very close. While this may be the result of the narrow band, normal distribution, it is revealing that HDDI's performance with emergency replenishment and random distribution rivals that for fixed demand. Figures 3.125(b) through 3.125(d) highlight the behaviors of the measures—back orders, demands, refusals, and number of pieces transferred— as functions of the simulation time for Scenarios 2 through 4.

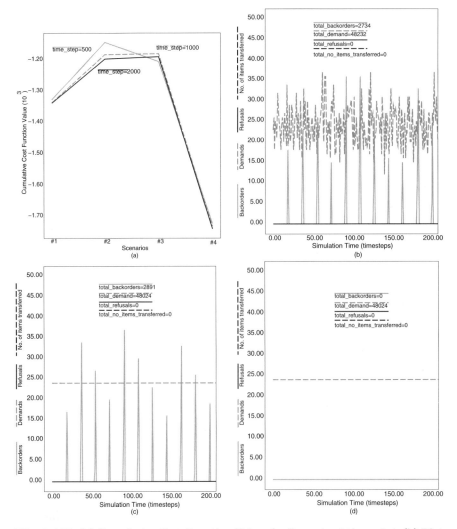

Fig. 3.125. (a) Cumulative Cost Function Values for Scenarios 1 through 4; (b) Plot
of Back orders, Demands, Refusals, and Number of Pieces Transferred, as a Function
of Simulation Time, for Back orders and Random Demand; (c) Plot of Back orders,
Demands, Refusals, and Number of Pieces Transferred, as a Function of Simulation
Time, for Back orders and Fixed Demand; and (d) Plot of Back orders, Demands,
Refusals, and Number of Pieces Transferred, as a Function of Simulation Time, for
Fixed Demand and Absence of Back orders

3.7.4.3 Performance Analysis for Different Inventory Management Networks

In addition to the key parameters discussed in Table 3.15, HDDI's performance is likely to be influenced by the size and composition of the underlying inventory management network. This section focuses on evaluating two additional performance measures: (1) the execution time required to complete the simulation from timestep 1 through 2000 as a function of the size of the network and (2) the cumulative cost function value as a function of the network size. Unlike the traditional EOQ model that executes serially on a centralized computer, HDDI executes on a number of concurrent computers and is expected to yield both fast decisions and higher throughput. Also, unlike the traditional approach, where all units communicate serially with the single computer, communication among the entities in HDDI are primarily local and, therefore, significantly faster.

A total of five representative inventory management systems are selected, modeled in HDDI, and then simulated on two platforms, an Intel Pentium-based computer from Micron executing the public domain Linux operating system, and a network of Sun Sparc 1, Sparc 1+, Sparc 2, and Sparc 10 machines configured as a loosely coupled parallel processor. Figures 3.126(a) through 3.126(d) present the four networks, while the largest network used in this study was presented in Figure 3.117. The total number of entities in the five networks are 5, 8, 12, 16, and 22, respectively. The network in Figure 3.126(a) consists of a single neighborhood, termed Massachusetts, with one warehouse and four retail units while the network in Figure 3.126(b) consists of both the Rhode Island and Massachusetts neighborhoods.

Given that each retail unit and warehouse is represented through a process and that a centralized process synchronizes all other processes, the total number of independent concurrent processes is given by the total number of entities plus 1. On the Linux-based Pentium testbed, all of the processes are physically executed, round-robin, on a single processor. Thus, assuming that the processes require approximately identical execution times, the execution time for a single process is equal to the total wall clock time divided by the number of entities, where the execution requirement of the centralized process is ignored.

The first set of simulation experiments are executed on the Linux-based Pentium testbed. Figure 3.127(a) presents both the total wall clock time (in milliseconds) and the normalized execution time (in milliseconds) for each of the five networks, for the following set of parameter values—$r\_p = 20$, $w\_p = 20$, $r\_c = 3$, $w\_c = 4$, $r\_l = 5$, $w\_l = 7$, $h\_b = 0.1$, $o\_h = 10.0$, and $d\_p = 20$. As expected, the wall clock time increases with growing network size. The reason for the relatively higher wall clock time for network 1 is that the overhead of the centralized synchronizing process dominates the execution. In contrast, the normalized execution times, i.e., per process, initially decreases with increasing network size, and then remains uniform. The reason is that

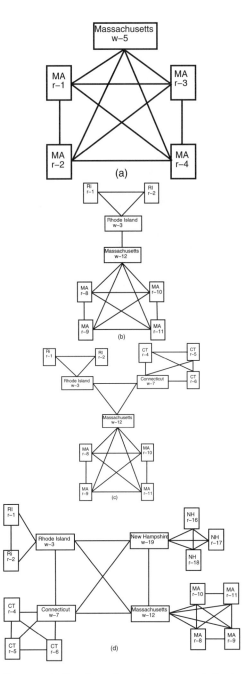

Fig. 3.126. Four Representative Inventory Management Systems: (a) Network 1 with 5 Entities; (b) Network 2 with 8 Entities; (c) Network 3 with 12 Entities; and (d) Network 4 with 16 Entities

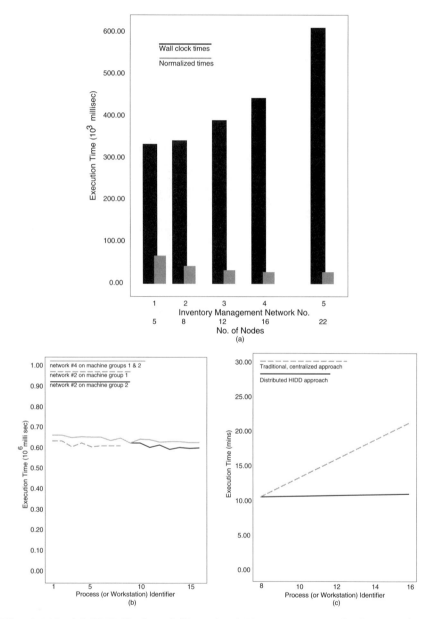

Fig. 3.127. (a) Wall Clock and Normalized Execution Times (milliseconds) for Different Networks, on Linux-Based Pentium Testbed; (b) Execution Time (milliseconds) of Network 2 and Network 4 on the Collection of 17 Sun Sparc Machines Configured as a Loosely Coupled Parallel Processor; and (c) Total Measured Execution Times (milliseconds) for Networks 2 through 4, in HDDI and Projected Execution Time for the Traditional, Centralized Approach

the dominance of the overhead of the single centralized synchronizing process diminishes with increasing number of entities and network size. Thus, the data allude to the scalability of HDDI.

The second set of simulation experiments are executed on the collection of 17 Sun Sparc 1, Sparc 1+, Sparc 2, and Sparc 10 workstations, configured as a loosely coupled parallel processor. The lack of availability of 23 Sun workstations precluded the simulation of network 4. Network 2, with 8 entities, and network 4, with 16 entities, are simulated with each entity executing on a unique workstation. Given that the machines differ in their execution speeds, they are grouped into two groups of 8 machines each, and one experiment is repeated on each group, in an effort to eliminate any undue influence on the performance behavior of HDDI. For a given experiment, the total execution time is determined as the longest of the execution times on all of the workstations. Figure 3.127(b) presents the execution times (in milliseconds) of every entity of (1) network 4, executing on both groups of machines and (2) network 2, executed twice on each of the two machine groups. Analysis of the data shows that the execution times for network 2 on both machine groups are similar, implying negligible impact of the actual machine speed on the performance of HDDI. Analysis also reveals the lack of appreciable difference in the execution times for network 2 and network 4, attesting to the scalability of HDDI. For a larger inventory management network, while the total computational task is high, HDDI achieves in equitably distributing the computational load among the proportionately larger number of available processors. The slight increase in the execution time for a larger network is primarily caused by the increased demand for communications between the entities.

Figure 3.127(c) presents the total execution times for each of network 2, network 3, and network 4. Corresponding to the simulation of each network, the cumulative sum of the execution times of all of the constituent processors represents the approximate execution time that would have been required by the traditional inventory management schemes. Clearly, the data in Figure 3.127(c) reflect the scalable nature of HDDI in sharp contrast to the deteriorating performance of the traditional approach corresponding to increasing inventory management system size.

To understand the relationship between the cost function value and the size of the inventory management system, the following experiment is executed. During the simulation, the cumulative cost function value is obtained for three simulation time windows–{timestep 1 through timestep 500}, {timestep 500 through timestep 1000}, and {timestep 1500 through timestep 2000}–and then normalized relative to the cost function value at the beginning of the time window. Each of the five networks is simulated on the Linux-based Pentium testbed, using the same values of the parameters as in Figure 3.119, and the data presented here pertain to retail unit #8 in the Massachusetts neighborhood. Furthermore, identical mean and s.d. values are utilized for the demand function at retail unit #8 in the Massachusetts neighborhood in each of the

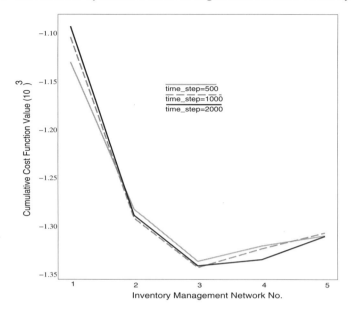

Fig. 3.128. Normalized, Cumulative, Cost Function Value as a Function of Network Size

five networks. Figure 3.128 presents the normalized, cumulative, cost function value as a function of network size. The data reveal that the smallest network incurs the highest cost function value, the cost reduces dramatically for increasing network size, and that it asymptotically reaches a saturation value. Clearly, at the warehouse level, the lack of neighborhood warehouses in the smallest network implies the inability to take advantage of transfer of items between neighboring warehouses. For larger networks, the transfer of items under emergency replenishment increasingly helps reduce the cost function, until the gain with increasing network size becomes minimal.

4

Debugging Network-Centric Systems

4.1 The Difficulty in Debugging NIT Systems

The key difficulty in debugging implementations of NIT systems stems from the fact that they are large-scale, distributed, and asynchronous. Given that the geographically dispersed nodes behave autonomously and interact with each other asynchronously, at any time instant, each of the nodes may reside in a unique execution state, making it difficult to trace the chain of cause and effect to the source of error following an incorrect execution result. From actual experience, as a result of the complex interactions, often an error appearing at a node was caused at a very different node in the system.

This chapter describes a new approach—behavior modeling coupled with asynchronous distributed simulation [14], which has been developed to address the challenges of debugging NIT systems and tested. Under this approach, first, the constituent entities of the NIT system are modeled in an appropriate language, generally C/C++ and possibly nVHDL [191] in the future. The level of detail of the model is defined by the desired resolution of behavior. The behavioral models and their interconnection topology are then integrated into the simulator, ensuring that fundamental principles, including causality, are honored. Next, the simulator is executed on a testbed network of workstations, interconnected as a loosely coupled parallel processor, to yield results that are cross-checked against the desired NIT system behavior for consistency and performance estimation. There are several advantages to this approach. First, modeling and simulation offer a relatively inexpensive way of validating NIT systems prior to developing and testing prototypes. Second, the approach is flexible in that it permits encapsulating into the simulator a wide range of key parametric variations of the underlying processes. Experience dictates that the need to modify the asynchronous distributed simulator—both simple and complex changes—is very strong, even as late in a study as performance analysis. The need stems from the fact that such simulations often yield unexpected results, and performance analysis reveals unforeseen relationships between key system parameters. Third, the input stimuli density generally bears a direct relationship to system use. Because efficiency is a goal, the desire to increase the input stimuli density is obvious. However, when the choice of the input stimuli density is high, the system will experience increased stress and congestion, resulting in one or more of its key metrics to incur a continuous increase in performance degradation with increasing simulation time. Because such large-scale real-world NIT systems are designed to operate continuously, i.e., 24 hours a day and 365 days a year, the performance degradation will eventually reach a critical point beyond which the system becomes virtually unusable and may be considered practically broke. We will characterize this system behavior as unrealistic, unstable, and unreliable, and we will label the input stimuli rate as unacceptably high.

To realize an operational system that is driven to its maximum efficiency, just short of instability, the input stimuli density must be decreased to a point where the key performance metrics start to exhibit a continuous and uniform behavior with increasing simulation time. This operating point is termed the *stability point*, the corresponding input stimuli density is labeled *critical input stimuli density*, and this method of indirectly determining the input stimuli density is referred to as the *stability criterion*. The stability criterion method is logically sound because it strikes a balance between two extremes—the desire to increase the input stimuli density and drive the system efficiency high on one hand and the effort to maintain a reliable and accurate operational system on the other. The method also reflects solid engineering because the stability point serves as a reference point, a precise demarcation line between two characteristic and clearly differentiable states of the system operation. Currently, the stability criterion is the only known practical technique to determine an appropriate input stimuli density for use in large-scale system design. Fourth, where the NIT system, like most real-world systems, is asynchronous, the use of a loosely coupled parallel processor testbed, the distribution of the constituent entities of the system among the processors, the independent execution of the entities, and the use of an asynchronous distributed simulation algorithm that lacks a global clock, will yield a simulation environment closely resembling the operational system. Similar to an operational NIT system, the simulation system will incur the occurrence of events at irregular, a priori unknown time instants, exposing the behavior models to a realistic environment. Errors in the behavior models, if any, are likely to be magnified, and timing errors and races are likely to be manifested by the asynchronicity of the testbed. Their detection and subsequent removal will help ensure a more reliable system design. Where such errors are not exorcised in the simulation, they may remain undetected, implying a potentially unreliable system design. For further details on the approach, how to develop, debug, and execute such simulations, as well as the software architecture for constructing a debugger for a loosely coupled parallel processing testbed, the reader is referred to [14]. The following two sections present the principal reasons underlying the difficulty in debugging NIT systems and a representative debugging experience, respectively.

4.1.1 Principal Reasons Underlying Debugging Difficulties

In a typical uniprocessor programming effort, one organizes the task into independent modules with clean interfaces, writes each of them out, tests them with dummy intermodule calls, and then assembles them together. The assembled code generally functions correctly immediately or requires, at most, a straightforward and modest debugging effort. In contrast, with ADDM algorithms, this process is not guaranteed to lead to success. Even after each module is tested and passes, and the code is then assembled, the program may not execute correctly. In a uniprocessor scenario, fundamentally, there is a single thread of control manifested through a single program counter. Even if multithreaded programming is employed, control is dictated from a centralized entity. Under ADDM algorithms, however, the number of independent and concurrent program counters may be significantly large. As a result, any effort to comprehend the execution of the NIT system by monitoring the execution of the nodes is rendered extremely difficult. Furthermore, the asynchronous nature introduces races, delays, and highly complex interdependencies, making debugging a real challenge. If an error occurs, when tracing it back to the source, one encounters convoluted dependencies, fundamentally stemming from data dependency but manifested in the form of temporal and internode dependencies. From experience, the best and, perhaps the only technique is to start with an exceptionally clear, sincere, and thorough understanding of the entire program, including all of its components, and then to exercise the simultaneous execution threads in one's mind. The errors must be rectified in the order of their importance, and no error, regardless of how insignificant it may appear, should be permitted. Simple errors have been observed, based on actual experience, to assume gigantic effects, distracting one from the really important and often subtle errors.

When the testbed consists of a network of workstations, one may either open one window per process, employing LPdbx [14] or GNU gdb debuggers or trace messages, or exploit visual monitoring and debugging tools, as described in Section 4.2.

4.1.2 A Representative Experience in Debugging NIT Systems

In debugging the ADDM algorithm for decentralized command and control, described in Section 3.4, the asynchronous, distributed, and autonomous nature of the algorithm introduces a formidable debugging task that far exceeds the task of debugging the equivalent of $20,000 \times 38 = 760,000$ lines of C code. The principal reason is the timing races that vary from intermittent to permanent and are excruciatingly difficult to reproduce. At any instant of time, each of the 38 processes may be in unique execution states, triggered by unique input messages and correlation between them is difficult. The complexity is further coupled by the fact that each simulation run requires 30 to 40 minutes of wall-clock time.

For instance, during the development of the simulator, it was observed that the blue forces appeared to fire more accurately than the red forces, regardless of whether they used a centralized or decentralized strategy. The problem would surface, intermittently, once every 5 or 6 simulation runs. Added complexities included the fact that the error would not occur for smaller-scale simulations, the overhead of starting up 38 processes was significant, and each simulation run required approximately 35 minutes of wall-clock time. After many repeated simulation runs and analysis of intermediate data, it was determined that a few of the red combat units were occasionally firing at nonexistent blue units. Careful analysis eventually revealed that the red control node would occasionally corrupt parts of its internal representation of the world which would then be propagated to all other individual nodes that requested that information, and it would eventually corrupt the entire system.

The visual display is an invaluable tool to assist in ensuring the validity of the simulation; it helps to confirm that all of the nodes are executing correctly. In addition, the processes generate very specific log files, which may be analyzed for errors. The log files include data on all sighting-related events, communications with other entities, communication with control nodes, weapon-related events, and information relative to what, when, and why decisions were made. However, the fundamental technique to successfully debug this decentralized command and control algorithm and other asynchronous, distributed algorithms lie in one's ability to maintain a high level of comprehension relative to the simulation execution, at both the conceptual and detailed levels.

The visualization software permits both a postmortem replay of the battlefield simulation and a concurrent display of the execution of the battlefield simulation. To achieve postmortem display, a single control node necessarily logs all changes to the physical environment, i.e., the initial positions of all individual nodes, every velocity and course change, every weapon firing event, weapons impacts, changes in status to the individual nodes, and the insertion and removal of weapons. When replay is initiated, the logged events are displayed sequentially. First, the starting positions of the nodes are used in constructing the initial battlefield. Every velocity and course change results in a change in the previously constructed velocity vector. Firing events are always accompanied by Insert events, which draw the weapon. These either cause Impact on a target or land harmlessly in the battlefield. In either case, a Remove event is caused subsequently that results in the weapon being erased from the display. If an individual node has been destroyed by the weapon, the Status change is logged, which causes the node to be redrawn with the destroyed image.

While the concurrent display of the execution of battlefield simulation is analogous to the postmortem replay in appearance, there are important differences in their executions. The display program is located on top of the control and individual nodes and has direct access to their data structures. Corresponding to a control node, the display shows the complete physical environment. However, corresponding to an individual node, the display is limited by the node's actual knowledge of the environment. The display can show the contents of the node's sector set, the node's own sighting, or the sightings received from other nodes. This allows the programmer to view the exact information that is used by the node to generate its decisions. This architecture also permits the programmer to alter, interactively and dynamically, the physical status of the node, i.e., the fuel, ammunition, etc., as well as the decision-making algorithms of the nodes, i.e., the sensor capabilities, withdrawal criteria, and so on.

4.2 Visual Aids in Debugging: DIVIDE

4.2.1 Introduction

The issue of monitoring the execution of ADDM algorithms on loosely coupled parallel processor systems is important for the purposes of (1) detecting inconsistencies and flaws in the algorithm, (2) obtaining important performance parameters for the algorithm, and (3) developing a conceptual understanding of the algorithm's behavior, for a given input stimulus, through visualization. Given multiple processors executing concurrently and cooperatively and exchanging information asynchronously to solve a problem under ADDM algorithm control, the task of conceptualizing the algorithm's behavior is generally difficult. The amount of information generated in the course of such executions in the form of textual lists of values, is generally large and, conceivably, a visual representation [192] of the data may greatly facilitate comprehension. For such high-level representation, the high-resolution data are coalesced into user-specified coarse-grain information through extensive computation. This section introduces a new approach, DIVIDE, that consists of distributed visual display of the execution of ADDM algorithms on loosely coupled parallel processors. It distributes the tasks of analysis, computation, and graphical display of the data among multiple workstations to achieve significant speedup.

4.2.2 Visual Display of Parameters

In the course of execution of asynchronous, distributed algorithms, a visual display of one or more parameters, as a function of time, may greatly assist in the comprehension of an algorithm's behavior. For instance, consider the distributed simulation of a broadband-ISDN network [193] on a number of concurrent processors. A display of the average time required by an ATM cell for propagation between a given pair of nodes may provide a good clue to the state of congestion in the network. Other parameters of interest include the size of the output buffers of a B-ISDN node and the link utilizations. For a given algorithm, the parameters of interest are selected and embedded into the program by the user. Data, corresponding to the parameters of interest, are generated during execution and intercepted by DIVIDE.

In general, the data generated during simulation correspond to the basic simulation timestep and are thus at a very high resolution. While a visual display of such detailed data is necessary for comprehending small-scale effects such as local congestion, for large-scale effects such as link utilization and average ATM cell propagation times, the data may need to be coalesced to yield average values over longer user-defined time periods. Thus, for the simulation example, the original data, with a resolution of a microsecond, are condensed by DIVIDE using a user-specified time period of, say, a second. The design of DIVIDE calls for fast visual display to permit the user to specify new values for the time period and view the display almost immediately. This, in turn, mandates fast condensation of the original data.

In the current implementation of DIVIDE, the original data are stored in a file through a few distinct entries, some of which are elaborated as follows. Each line of data in the file corresponds to a change in the value of the parameter.

- An integer identifier representing the time of the change. The time refers to the simulation time and the specification is with respect to the unit of the basic timestep.
- A flag indicating the direction, i.e., increasing or decreasing, of the change associated with the parameter. The absolute value of the change is always unity.
- A set of integers identifying the physical entity, such as the link or node in the B-ISDN network, associated with the parameter.

Assuming that the condensation process includes the computation of the average value of a parameter, for a user-specified time period, the new value is computed as follows. The products obtained from multiplying the value of the parameter at every sampled time with the length of the sampled time, over the entire time period, are added together and then divided by the length of the time period. Conceivably, a parameter's value may remain unchanged over a number of basic timesteps. In Figure 4.1, the average value of the parameter over the user-specified time period of 20 basic timesteps is determined to be 3.85.

The standard deviation for this time period is computed analogously to the mean. Unlike for the case of the mean, the difference between the value of the parameter and its average is computed for every sample point and then squared and added. The intermediate value is then divided by the width of the time period, and finally, its square root yields the desired standard deviation. While the traditional method of computing these values uses addition rather than a combination of multiplication and addition, the technique used here promises faster speed, particularly where the parameter changes slowly with time. In general, for asynchronous distributed algorithms, the parameters of interest are expected to change slowly with time. For the algorithm detailed in

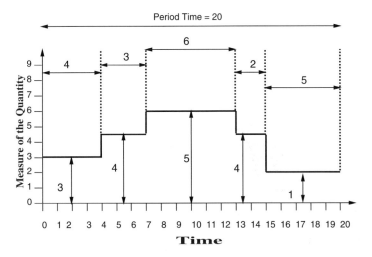

Fig. 4.1. Computing the Average of a Parameter over a User-Specified Time Period

[193] that DIVIDE uses for testing, the average time between two subsequent changes of a parameter is 3.1 timesteps.

In the course of execution of a typical algorithm, the impact of several parameters on the performance of the algorithm may be of interest to the user. For each of these parameters, a significant amount of computation is necessary to determine the mean and standard deviation values. Thus, to achieve high performance, the overall task of DIVIDE is distributed among multiple processors.

In Figure 4.2, the top two windows, constituting a partial display of a 50-node network simulation, are physically located on the respective workstations W_1 and W_2. The visual network display is located at the top of each window, while the buffer graphs are positioned near the bottom. The control window, situated immediately beneath the first display window on workstation W_1, dictates the execution of all of the display windows.

4.2.2.1 Issues in User Interface Design

4.2.2.1.1 Movement Controls

Following analysis of the data, the result consists of an array data structure in the main memory that contains the values of the mean and standard deviation for every output buffer for every time period. The issues in user-interface design include (1) whether to display the values simultaneously or serially and (2) the nature of control over the display that the user may be permitted. In DIVIDE, the user selects the parameters of interest such as the specific output buffers to be displayed, and DIVIDE displays both the mean and the standard deviation values as a function of time. Additionally, DIVIDE permits the users

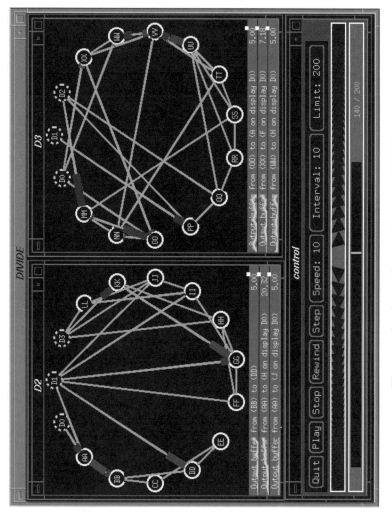

Fig. 4.2. An Actual Screen Display in DIVIDE.

to move to any position, in time, within the result, quickly and accurately. The *position* refers to the specific time period that is currently displayed by DIVIDE. This promises to harness the user's intelligence to determine the time periods of importance, move to examine them, compare them with those corresponding to other time periods, and look as little or as much as necessary at any particular time period's results. The more control a user has over the visual display, the more comfortable one is likely to feel and the more one can accomplish [194].

To permit the user to move within the results, three mechanisms for movement control are developed in DIVIDE. The first technique consists of a group of tape-player-type buttons and are labeled **Play**, **Step**, **Stop**, and **Play Period**. Following activation of the **Play** button, the display windows on the workstations are updated periodically with monotonically increasing time period, until the **Stop** button is depressed. The duration of the pause between the displays of two subsequent time periods may be adjusted through the **Play Period** button. The user is prompted to enter the value in milliseconds. To freeze the display, the user may depress the **Stop** button. The visual display resumes from the most recent time period when the **Play** button is depressed again. The **Step** button permits the user to advance only to the next time period and display the corresponding result.

The second mechanism consists of the Jump Bar, which is designed to alter the current position within the data. Thus, unlike the absolute Position Bar, detailed later, the Jump Bar is a relative positioning system. This mechanism is analogous to the Jog Shuttle dial available on expensive editing videocassette recorders. The Jump Bar is implemented on a rectangular area of the screen, with arrows pointing left and right. While the right arrow permits forward movement, the left arrow allows backward movement, relative to the current time period. The amount of jump, selected by the user by clicking the mouse, is exponentially proportional to the distance of the cursor from the center of the jump bar. This permits the user to exercise fine control over the jumps, i.e., while large jumps may be achieved by clicking at the far ends, smaller jumps are realized through clocking near the center of the Jump Bar.

The final technique consists of the Position Bar, which is implemented through a long horizontal rectangle with a short vertical rectangle located on the bar. While the long rectangle represents the entire data set, the vertical rectangle, referred to as the Position Indicator, represents the location within the set that corresponds to the current visual display. To move the display of the simulation results anywhere in time, one may click at an appropriate location within the horizontal rectangle. In addition, a number of the form "T/E," where T represents the current simulation time in timesteps and E the maximum simulation time, in timesteps, of the data, is shown at the left of the bar. Thus, the Jump Bar and the Position Bar offer the user a far greater degree of control, and its design, therefore, is superior to that of the traditional scroll bar.

Although the three positioning systems enjoy a degree of redundancy, their design is intended to facilitate the user's choice of visualization. For constant monotonic forward steps, one may choose the tape-player-style controls. For large absolute jumps, one may choose to use the Position Bar controls. For relative jumps of arbitrary amounts in either the forward or backward direction, one may use the Jump Bar.

4.2.3 Issues in the Design of the Graphical Display

The principal components of DIVIDE include the network display, buffer graphs, layout design, dynamic scaling, and the allocation of visual images and related tasks to the processors of the parallel processor testbed.

4.2.3.1 Network Display

The mean sizes of the buffers associated with pairs of nodes are represented through the length of elongated rectangles placed along the axes of the corresponding links in DIVIDE. The statistical deviation is expressed, for efficiency, through the color of the rectangle [195]. While pure red represents a value of unity or greater than unity for the deviation, pure blue indicates zero deviation, and the intermediate values are expressed through different shades of purple (between red and blue).

To update the visual display quickly, DIVIDE implements the following basic steps efficiently:

- For every buffer, where the size is smaller than at the last update, the difference is erased by redrawing it in background color.
- Redraw the lines interconnecting the nodes.
- For each buffer, the new buffer rectangle is redrawn with its correct size and color over that of the old one.

4.2.3.2 Buffer Graphs

In addition to the visual display of the simulation network, termed network display, DIVIDE graphs the variation of the mean and standard deviation, as a function of time, of important parameters such as output buffers for the Broadband-ISDN simulation [193]. At the bottom of the network display, each of the three boxes corresponds to an output buffer selected by the user.

While the mean of a parameter is represented through the height of the graph, the horizontal axis represents time. Whenever the simulation time proceeds forward by one time period, a yellow line is extended from the previous to the current mean value and a vertical orange line is appended to the graph. The length of the orange segment reflects the value of the standard deviation for the current time period. All three graphs in the boxes are maintained in sync, i.e., the corresponding vertical positions of the graphs are placed directly beneath one another. This facilitates visual analysis of the behaviors of and the interactions between the quantities.

When a buffer between a pair of nodes is selected by clicking in the network display, the corresponding graph is immediately displayed in the uppermost of the three boxes. The graph that may have been resident in this box is pushed down to the middle box, while that in the middle box will be shifted to the lowermost box. Thus, the user may select all three graphs for visual analysis quickly, with three clicks. It is argued that such convenience and speed will greatly encourage users to examine many different relationships.

To alter the size of a box, the user may click on the square grip to the right of the box and drag the grip up or down. An upward drag will increase the size of the box, while a downward drag will decrease its size. Where one of the boxes is deemed more important than the others, it may be extended in size to eclipse other boxes. Following any change, an automatic mechanism will scale the graphs to ensure a constant ratio between the upper limit of the graph and the size of the box. Where necessary, the user may pull one or more boxes toward the lower part of the screen using the grips and thereby allow more room for the network display. Thus, DIVIDE allows the user to manipulate the visual display directly, and research [196] supports this approach to intuitive user interfaces.

4.2.3.3 Issues in Layout Design of the Graphical Images of the Concurrent Processes

The autonomous and concurrent entities of an asynchronous, distributed algorithm are represented in DIVIDE through circles on a two-dimensional layout. The connections between the entities are modeled through lines between the appropriate circles. The identifiers of the entities are expressed through texts within the circles. This choice is primarily influenced by the speed and efficiency of redrawing on the computer screen.

An important issue in DIVIDE is to place the nodes on the layout so that no link between any pair of nodes is eclipsed by any node. For reasons of simplicity and efficiency, a circular layout with circles to represent nodes and straight lines to model communications links is chosen. In a circular layout, given sufficient spacing between the geometric objects along its circumference, no three nodes will be collinear. The choice of a rectangular layout is eliminated, given that where nodes represented through geometric objects A, B, and C are collinear, a link from A to C may be eclipsed by node B. The choice of the size of the circles is based on the limited size of the layout and the desire to express important information, pertaining to the node, within the circle. Where a larger network must be represented, a large value for the radius of the circular layout and a smaller size for the circles representing the nodes may be chosen. For a smaller network, the circles may be larger and the radius of the circular layout may be chosen to be small. For a circular layout of a given maximum radius R (Figure 4.3), maximum width of a link L, the maximum number of circles that may be placed along the circumference, each of radius r, is computed as the greatest integer $\leq \dfrac{2\pi}{\cos^{-1}(1-\frac{r+L/2}{R})}$.

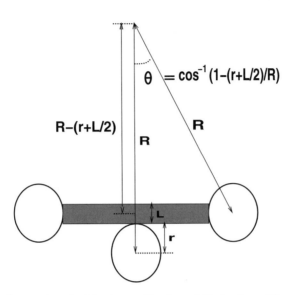

Fig. 4.3. Computing the Maximum Number of Nodes for a Circular Layout

Where $r \ll R$ and $L \ll R$, the maximum number of nodes is approximately proportional to R. Because the area of the layout is proportional to the square of R, the size of the display grows as the square of the number of models to be displayed. Given this quadratic dependence, for efficient display of simulations of large systems, the displays in DIVIDE are distributed over multiple heterogeneous workstations that are configured as a loosely coupled parallel processor.

4.2.3.4 Dynamic Scaling

As time progresses, many of the graphs in DIVIDE may exhibit a tendency to grow, reflecting the increase in the value of a parameter. To limit the graphs from exceeding the bounds of the rectangular box, DIVIDE implements an automatic scaling mechanism. When a graph reaches the maximum measure, the scale is reset so that the new maximum value of the scale is approximately 130% of the current maximum value. When a graph reaches the extreme right edge, it is cleared and restarted from the extreme left edge. A graph is also cleared when the user uses either the Position Bar or the Jump Bar to move by more than one time period. This ensures that the graph is always nonoverlapping and contiguous.

DIVIDE lacks a formal mechanism to modify the scales of the graphs. To achieve reduction of scale, the user may reselect the buffer and play the simulation until the graph reaches the limit of the scale. Additionally, to avoid repeated scaling, the user may first play the relevant periods of all of the displayed graphs where they reach their maximum values. This will establish the appropriate scales. Then the user may replay the simulation from the start.

The dynamic scaling strategy suffers from two limitations. First, a single large value associated with a buffer may imply that the remainder of the buffer sizes are scaled down to near invisibility for the entire duration of the simulation. Second, based on the placement of the nodes on the screen, the maximum length for the display of the buffer sizes corresponding to each node pair is not constant. However, this section recognizes that a scaling mechanism is essential because, without it, a buffer size may increase greatly thereby causing the corresponding bar to extend beyond the length of the underlying link and erase other parts of the screen.

In DIVIDE, the mean values of the buffer sizes for every node pair are represented through rectangles along the links. At every time period, all buffer sizes are scaled with respect to a scaling factor and the choice of the factor is such that the rectangle corresponding to the most constrained buffer is nearly maximum. For every node pair X and Y, a ratio of the sum of the buffer sizes at X and Y to the length between X and Y on the screen is computed. This ratio corresponds to a measure of the density of the mean buffer size with respect to the display length. The maximum of the ratios of all node pairs is determined and is referred to as the *scaling factor*. The buffers of the corresponding nodes are referred to as *constrained*. Thus, for a different node pair M and N, the length of the corresponding rectangle is given by the sum of the buffer sizes for M and N, divided by both the distance between M and N and the scaling factor. In reality, the scaling factor is chosen to be slightly smaller than the maximum ratio for the following reason. For a node pair $\{P, Q\}$, where the density is close to the scaling factor and the buffer size for P is extremely small relative to that for Q, a discontinuity between the linear display from Q to P and that from P to Q will distinguish the individual mean buffer sizes.

Conceivably, the scaling factor may change abruptly from one time period to the next. The presence of this discontinuity is a limitation of DIVIDE. While the present mechanism reacts well to impulse spikes in the mean buffer sizes, automatic adaptive mechanisms to smooth the abrupt changes, currently under investigation, may exhibit the limitation of reduced dynamic range.

4.2.3.5 Distributing the Visual Images of the Concurrent Processes

It has been observed that for visualization of large networks, a single processor suffers from limited screen space and extensive computational requirements, associated with the calculations of the displayed variables—mean and standard deviation values of the buffers. For typical workstations with screen size capable of displaying 1000 pixels on an edge, the maximum number of legible nodes that may be displayed while honoring the restrictions outlined in Section 4.2.3.3, is approximately 15 to 20. Most implementations of complex distributed algorithms involve many processors—20 to 60—implying that a single workstation is inadequate. In DIVIDE, the complete network is decomposed into smaller subsets of nodes, each of which is displayed and executed on a unique workstation. DIVIDE designates one of the workstations to assume the role of a central command that issues and propagates the appropriate analysis and display commands to the respective workstations. While a user's interaction with a centralized command is facilitated, the computations underlying the visualization are executed locally on the corresponding workstations.

To facilitate the understanding of the interactions between the regular nodes displayed on a workstation with the remainder of the network, DIVIDE represents the nodes on each of the other workstations through a dotted circle, termed the *gateway node*. Additionally, a *gateway line* between a regular node N_1 on a workstation, W_1, and a dotted circle (corresponding to a workstation W_i) signifies the link between N_1 and one of the nodes of W_i. Thus, in general, a workstation may display multiple dotted circles and multiple gateway lines may interconnect the regular nodes of the workstation with any of the dotted circles. For each gateway line, an associated bar can only represent the characteristics of the buffer from the regular node to one of the nodes in the gateway node. The gateway lines cannot display the buffer characteristics from a gateway node to a regular node for an otherwise significant amount of data must be transferred from other workstations. This approach, however, is limited in that only a single gateway line connects a regular node to a gateway node even though the regular node is connected to two or more nodes of the workstation represented by the gateway node. Thus, the bar displays the cumulative characteristics of the corresponding buffers.

The workstation, designated central command by DIVIDE, communicates the analysis and display commands to other workstations via the use of Internet stream sockets. To establish a connection between the central command and other workstations, the following steps are executed. First the user executes the control program, specifying the number of other workstations that will be connected as a command line argument. Then, each process on the other workstations is executed. The host name of the command workstation is specified, along with the view name, as command line arguments. This machine will announce each connection from other workstations as it is established. When all of the connections have been established, DIVIDE pops up the control panel window with buttons and positioning tools, described earlier. Next, the user must choose and specify the analysis period to enable the processing of the data in the respective machines. As a part of this step, the user depresses the button marked **Analysis Period: Unknown**. DIVIDE prompts the user to type in the desired analysis period in the control panel. Upon the user's specifying, control messages are propagated from the control panel to every other workstation requesting analysis and visualization. Finally, the user may adjust the positioning controls to view the display.

The command messages are very compact, small enough to fit into a single packet and typically requiring no more than 1 to 25 milliseconds for propagation between the control command workstation and the display workstations. In general, a command message contains a command code and one or more integer arguments. For instance, imagine that the user wishes to reanalyze the data, entering a new value for the time period and the time value up to which data must be analyzed and displayed, to the control command workstation. The control command workstation propagates the new values to all other workstations. Every workstation receives the new values, updates the value of the time period, quickly analyzes the data corresponding to the supplied values, and returns a message to the control command informing the amount of data that has been analyzed. Conceivably, the quick analysis, implying faster response of the display workstations to the user's commands, permits the user to exercise greater control and make better decisions than a system that responds slowly [197].

4.2.4 Implementation Details

DIVIDE is written in C and implemented on Sun workstations. It uses the Athena widget set to create subwindows and collect input events. Except for the buttons, all of the subwindows are Athena form widgets to which customized translations are added to call the routines that redraw and choose input events that correspond to the mouse clicks in the window. DIVIDE is organized through two executable subprograms—control and display—which are further decomposed into six and seven modules, respectively. This organization permits fast recompilation and better access to specific code segments.

DIVIDE requires that the topology of the network be specified in an input file, the default name of which is topology.dat. The format of the file is specified later.

```
<number of views> <number of nodes> <number of links>
<view #0 name>
<view #1 name>
...
<node #0 name> <number of view that node #0 exists on>
<node #1 name> <number of view that node #1 exists on>
...
<name of from node in link #0> <name of to node in link #0>
<name of from node in link #1> <name of to node in link #1>
...
```

During execution of the algorithm, output files are generated for each node of the network. These output files store the behavioral characteristics of the

buffers connected to it and serve as input files to DIVIDE. Each file is named
<X>.out, where <X> refers to the corresponding node name. It consists of
textual information encapsulated in the following format:

```
<time> <flag> <0> <to-node>
<time> <flag> <0> <to-node>
<time> <flag> <0> <to-node>
...
```

The individual fields of the file imply the following. The <time> field is
the integer time value at which a simulation output is asserted. When the
field <flag>, contains C, it implies that the output buffer has grown in size
by unity. In the event that the field contains D, the buffer has shrunk by unity.
The field <0>, is reserved for future enhancements to DIVIDE and is not used
in the current version. The last field <to-node> refers to the destination node
of the buffer. That is, where the file is designated to be B.out, implying that
the data pertain to node B and the <to-node> field in the current line of the
file is C, then the data refer to the buffer from node B to node C. The actual
value of the field is an integer that is translated into a node identifier using
the position of the nodes in the topology file for node B.

For each subset of the network that is displayed on a workstation, the node
output files for all of the nodes in the subset are coalesced into a corresponding
merge file. These files are generated by simultaneously opening the relevant
node files, reading the entries, and sorting them based on the value of the
<time> field. The format of the merge files is presented later and differs from
those of the individual files as follows:

```
<end-time>
<time> <from-node> <flag> <0> <to-node>
<time> <from-node> <flag> <0> <to-node>
<time> <from-node> <flag> <0> <to-node>
.....
```

The <end-time> field refers to the time of the last event in the merge file.
This is required because the merging process accepts partial contents of the
<X>.out files, particularly the subset of the data that has been subject to
coalescence. When a merge file needs to be generated for reanalysis of the data,
this field is examined first. Where the desired time of reanalysis exceeds the
value of the <end-time>, thereby requiring more data from the individual
node output files, the merge file is automatically extended. Otherwise, the
current merge file is used. The <from-node> field refers to the source node
of the line of data. The default name for a merge file is <view name>.mrg.
Figure 4.4 presents the architecture of DIVIDE.

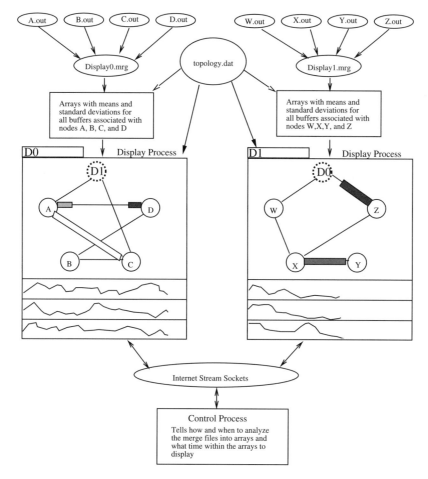

Fig. 4.4. Architecture of DIVIDE

4.2.5 Performance of DIVIDE

The architecture of DIVIDE permits individual workstations to accept short messages from the command workstation and then execute the computations locally and independently. Each workstation accesses the data, in read-only mode, for the nodes that it displays. In addition, once the workstations start analyzing the data, no further communication is required between them and this asynchronism implies efficiency of resource usage. DIVIDE has been executed for broadband-ISDN simulation [193] and a distributed, real-time banking algorithm (Chapter 3). The overall task of visual display is decomposed into subtasks of nearly equal sizes through allocating an equal number of nodes among the workstations. Experimental results indicate that for the visual display of the algorithms in [193] and in Chapter 3, the variation in the completion times of the display activities on the workstations is less than 10%. In addition, the overall execution time is observed to be nearly inversely proportional to the number of workstations used for a given network.

In an experiment to determine the performance of DIVIDE, relative to a uniprocessor, the data from an algorithm requiring 50 nodes of a loosely coupled parallel processor, are analyzed for the purpose of visual display. The analysis included 1000 timesteps and a time period of 10. The overall visual display task requires 44 CPU seconds when implemented on a single Sun sparc 2 workstation. When the same task is completed in DIVIDE, using four identical workstations, the overall task requires 13 seconds. Thus, a speedup of $44 \div 13 = 3.4$ is achieved for a fourfold increase in the number of computational engines.

5
Proofs of Correctness of ADDM Algorithms

5.1 The Need for Proofs of Correctness of ADDM Algorithms

The accurate, reliable, and precise operation of NIT systems will underscore the public acceptance and success of the information age, given that they will be increasingly more encompassing, powerful, highly capable, and greatly beneficial in the future. The stakes for NIT systems will be increasingly high and even the slightest error may not be tolerable. For example, should a design error in a nationwide patient medical record network accidentally release the medical records of thousands of patients even once, irreversible damage will result, causing the public to lose confidence in the system. Logic dictates that the precision of an NIT system will depend, in turn, on the functional accuracy of the underlying ADDM algorithm, which implies the indispensable need to construct proof of correctness of the algorithm. In the absence of a proof, there is the strong likelihood of the algorithm executing erroneously.

ADDM algorithms are characterized by a significant number of interactions between the constituent entities. The asynchrony and distributed nature of these interactions manifest in the form of complex timing relationships between the events and complex system states. While the precise execution of the events is crucial to the overall correct functioning of the system, for the system to manifest in any of the states in the course of its operation is a distinct possibility. Where the correctness of every conceivable state and event is not proven, freedom from errors cannot be guaranteed. From experience with ADDM algorithms, anything that can potentially go wrong in an NIT system actually does go wrong. The simple reason is that NIT systems are so vast that even events with very low probabilities of occurrence do occur. In reflecting on the mishap in *Apollo 13*, the crew later revealed that they would have revolted had NASA insisted on confronting them with the three simultaneous subsystem failures—a very very rare occurrence—during their simulator training exercise. Of course, the rare event did occur, causing many experts to believe that, in Nature, anything can happen. Queueing model-based proofs, used for communication systems in the past, are too simple and unrealistic for today's NIT systems, given that they lack the ability to encapsulate complex timing interactions between the large number of distributed entities.

The key difficulties posed by the need for proofs of correctness of ADDM algorithms are twofold. First, the key principles of the traditional mathematical techniques may be traced back to the 1800s when they were invented to address sequentially executing processes and the underlying reasoning paradigm also followed a single thread of control. Today's NIT systems consist of hundreds or even thousands of processes executing concurrently, asynchronously, and at geographically dispersed locations. The underlying computational intelligence that enables the NIT system to function clearly does not follow a single thread of control. Thus, the traditional formal proof techniques are simply inadequate for today's NIT systems. What the future needs is a new mathematical framework that can address, with the same degree of rigor as the conventional mathematics, real-world systems that consist of multiple autonomous processes executing concurrently, while employing a reasoning process that is also distributed. Second, driven by the difficulty in synthesizing sound algorithms for complex systems, the tendency in the research community has been to address academic-type, toy problems while the system development community has relied on the use of the time-out policy realized through the use of timers. Real-world systems may run into deadlocks, stemming from any number of reasons. In the absence of an algorithmically correct algorithm that can prevent the onset of deadlocks, the only option left is to employ time-outs. Apart from their lack of elegance, there are two difficulties with this policy. First, it is not a true solution and its success is never guaranteed in every situation. Second, it is practically difficult to determine the actual value of a time-out parameter for a given problem. Invariably, the reason is the lack of a scientific basis. For example, in a recent international standards meeting, the choice of whether a specific time-out parameter for a communication network protocol should be 15 or 30 minutes, was decided based on the audience's feeling, not on any objective science. The fact that a billion packets may be transported in this time-out period was not even a factor in the decision process. In essence, the use of timers is symptomatic of a deeper issue, the lack of a complete and true understanding of the underlying problem.

5.2 The Nature of the Proofs of Correctness of ADDM Algorithms

Given that the behaviors of the constituent processes of the NIT system, under algorithmic control, are asynchronous, autonomous, concurrent, underlie highly complex timing, and pose difficulties to the centralized mathematical tools, the proof of correctness must first enumerate every conceivable scenario; second, identify from them the scenarios that are unique and significant; and third, employ logical reasoning integrated with classical mathematical proofs, to prove the following. For the unique and significant scenarios, the ADDM algorithm must generate consistent and accurate results, remain free from deadlock, terminate in finite time (not necessarily known a priori), and ensure the correct order of execution of the underlying discrete activities, also termed events. The proofs must be grounded in reality, i.e., they must reflect, where applicable, physical laws and realistic parameters of the NIT system design. The proofs must never assume information not available to the constituent entities in the underlying NIT system. For instance, the existence of a global entity with instantaneous access to all information from every geographically dispersed constituent entity of the NIT system may not be assumed.

5.3 Proof of Correctness of the NODIFS Algorithm

The proof of correctness of the NODIFS algorithm, introduced in Chapter 3, is presented here. The proof consists of three parts: correct order of execution of events, freedom from deadlock, and termination of simulation in finite time, applied to both combinational and sequential subcircuits.

5.3.1 Combinational Subcircuits

The proof of correctness of the NODIFS algorithm requires that the fault-free circuit be good simulated in the presence of the given external signal transitions and that each of the faults originating in the components of the circuit is fault simulated correctly. The good simulation of the entire circuit, i.e., in the absence of all faults, consists of the independent, asynchronous, concurrent execution of the models corresponding to either the good events or signal transitions asserted at the primary input ports of the models. The simulation of a fault f_1 consists in (1) the assertion of f_1 at the component C_1 where it originates and the subsequent execution of C_1 in the presence of f_1 and (2) the execution of the components $\{C_2, C_3, \ldots, C_n\}$ in the presence of f_1 should f_1 cause an assertion of a logical value at an input port of $\{C_2, C_3, \ldots, C_n\}$.

For the set of components $\{C_1, C_2, \ldots, C_r\}$ of a circuit constituting an acyclic subcircuit, the correct execution of the good events is ensured by the execution of the unfaulted behavior description of a component $C_i \in \{C_1, C_2, \ldots, C_r\} \forall i \in \{1, r\}$ at $t = t_{i1}$ given by the minimum of the assertion times of signals at every input port of C_i. The issue of correctness of execution of an unfaulted description of a component is limited by the accuracy of description of the component. Because every component is executed only up to $t = t_{i1}$, where the complete knowledge of all of the input signals is available, execution of the unfaulted description of the component and any output generated thereof must be accurate.

Consider a component C_l such that all of its input ports are primary. Thus, C_l is characterized by the complete absence of any input fault list entries. The execution of the model C_l for a time given by $t = t_{x1}$ is characterized by the execution of the unfaulted description of C_l at $t = t_{x1}$ followed by the assertion and subsequent simulation of each of the faults $\{f_1, f_2, \ldots, f_r\}$ originating at C_l. The good simulation of C_l at $t = t_{x1}$ may generate a good output signal at $t = t_{x1} + d$, where d is the propagation delay of C_l. The simulation of a fault $f_i \in \{f_1, f_2, \ldots, f_r\} \forall i \in \{1, r\}$ may cause a faulty output signal at $t = t_{x1} + d$. Where the logical value of the output signal differs from that of the good output, the faulty output is stored in the fault list at the output of C_l and f_i is potentially detectable at the output of C_l. Where the two outputs are indistinguishable, the faulty effect is discarded. Finally, the good output and the entire output fault list of C_l are propagated at the output of C_l. With reference to the execution of C_l at $t = t_{x1}$, it is guaranteed that a future execution of C_l at $t = t_{x2}$ $(t_{x2} > t_{x1})$ will generate neither an inconsistent good output signal nor an inconsistent faulty output signal due to any of the faults originating at C_l. An inconsistent output signal is one that has an assertion time smaller than or equal to the assertion time of the previously generated output, i.e., $t_{x1} + d$.

For any other component $C_j \in \{C_1, C_2, C_{l-1}, C_{l+1}, \ldots, C_r\}$, the good signal transition and the fault list entries at any instant of time cannot be inconsistent with the good signal transitions and the fault list entries asserted at C_j at a future time instant. Thus, a faulty output, generated as a consequence of execution of an input fault list entry, must be accurate. Similarly, a faulty output, generated as a consequence of fault simulation of a fault originating at a component, must necessarily be correct. Although the fault simulation process is limited to the assertion of a single fault at a time, the fault effects contained as input fault list entries of a component may not all be independent. Thus, where two or more entries at different input ports of the component are dependent, they are necessarily caused by the presence of reconvergence. However, two or more entries—e_1, $\{V_1, t_1, f_1\}$ and e_2, $\{V_2, t_2, f_1\}$—at the same input port p_i of a model pertaining to the same fault identifier f_1 must be independent. Otherwise, $t_1 = t_2$, which implies that the result of the simulation of a single fault due to two distinct causes (i.e., input stimuli), will occur at the same time. This contradicts the assertion stated herein. The dependent fault effects are identified by NODIFS and fault simulated simultaneously, guaranteeing accuracy.

In the fault simulation process, eventually all of the components $\{C_1, C_2, \ldots, C_r\}$ must execute to use all of the external signal transitions asserted at the primary input ports of $\{C_1, C_2, \ldots, C_r\}$ and other signal transitions asserted at the remaining input pins. Where a component has not received a legitimate good signal assertion at any of its input ports for a substantial fraction of the length of fault simulation, the model may contain a number of entries in the input fault lists that are not yet fault simulated. In the NODIFS approach, a special signal transition that marks the final signal is propagated by the external world at every primary input port. When a model receives such vectors at all of its input ports, all of the outstanding input fault list entries are simulated and the output fault list is propagated at the output port of the model along with a special signal transition. Thus, eventually, all of the outstanding input fault list entries are simulated and fault simulation terminates for the component set $\{C_1, C_2, \ldots, C_r\}$.

5.3.2 Sequential Subcircuits

For the subcircuit that consists of those components connected through feedback loops, the proof of correctness of the NODIFS algorithm is more complex. In the NODIFS algorithm for combinational subcircuits, discussed earlier, events in the fault simulation system pertain only to the good signal transitions. The simulation of fault effects and faults originating in a component are considered internal to the execution of the model. In contrast, in the NODIFS algorithm for sequential subcircuits, an event may refer to either a good or faulty signal transition. The execution process corresponding to a good signal transition differs from that related to a faulty signal transition. Thus, the proof requires the correct execution of the unfaulted component description, execution of the good and faulty events in the correct order, absence of deadlock in fault simulation, and the termination of fault simulation in finite time. The issue of correctness of execution of an unfaulted description of a component is limited by the accuracy of the description of the component.

The correct order of execution of events implies the following. Where e_1 and e_2 are two events associated with components C_x and C_y with assertion times t_1 and t_2 $(t_2 > t_1)$, respectively, e_1 must execute prior to the execution of e_2 should there exist the possibility that execution of C_x due to e_1 may generate an output that may potentially influence the events associated with C_y. This is necessitated not only where e_1 and e_2 are both good events but even for the case where e_1 and e_2 are good and faulty events, respectively, as explained later. Consider a simple sequential circuit consisting of a NAND gate A whose output is connected to an inverter B and the output of B is connected to the second input of A. Assume that A and B each has a propagation delay of 10 ns. Assume that a fault $f1$: s-a-X, originates at the first input of A, where X refers to either logical 0 or 1. Corresponding to a signal transition at $t = 0$ ns at the first input port of A, model A executes to generate an output fault list entry $\{V_1, 10, f_1\}$ but no good signal transition. Thus, B contains a faulty event at $t = 10$ ns. Assume that A receives a second good transition at the first input port at $t = 20$ ns. If the model A were to be executed for this good event at $t = 20$ ns, regardless of the faulty event at $t = 10$ ns associated with B, erroneous results may be generated. Assume that the faulty event at B were to generate a faulty output—$\{V_2, 20, f_1\}$ that differs from the good output and is consequently propagated to the second input port of A. The execution of model A corresponding to the good event at $t = 20$ ns would consist of the assertion of the fault identifier f_1, originating at A, and its subsequent simulation. That is, a value $x \in \{0, 1\}$ would be asserted at the first input port while the good logical value would be assumed to be asserted at the second input port. This should have been erroneous because the correct execution of fault identifier f_1 must include the assertion of logical value V_2 at the second input port of A. Thus, the correct order of execution of good and faulty events is a necessary condition for the NODIFS approach.

When a component X with input ports $\{p_1, p_2, \ldots, p_n\}$ is characterized by a good event U_X that relates to a signal transition asserted at the input port p_i, U_X is the smallest assertion time of all signal transitions asserted at $\{p_1, p_2, \ldots, p_n\}$. Furthermore, if $\{e_1, e_2, \ldots, e_k\}$ refers to the input fault list entries associated with X, the U_X must be equal to or smaller than the assertion times associated with $\{e_1, e_2, \ldots, e_k\}$. The execution of model X for U_X may generate a good signal output and faulty outputs corresponding to the simulation of each entry of some subset $\{e_i, \ldots, e_j\} \in \{e_1, e_2, \ldots, e_k\}$ and faults originating at X, where the assertion times of $\{e_i, \ldots, e_j\}$ equal U_X and those of $\{e_1, \ldots, e_{i-1}, e_{i+1}, \ldots, e_j\}$ exceed U_X. The faulty outputs may now be compared against the good output to determine which of the corresponding fault identifiers are potentially detectable at the output of X. These faulty outputs are included in the fault list at the output of X.

When a component X is characterized by a faulty event U_X that relates to the input fault list entries $\{e_m, \ldots, e_n\}$, all of which possess the same assertion time U_X, the implication is either that X lacks a good event or the assertion time of the good event exceeds those of $\{e_m, \ldots, e_n\}$. Given that X lacks a good signal transition at U_X, NODIFS guarantees that the good logical values at $\{p_1, p_2, \ldots, p_n\}$ are unchanged at U_X and, consequently, the good output of X is unchanged at $U_X + d$ with respect to its previous value, where d is the propagation delay of X. Thus, the faulty outputs resulting from the simulation of $\{e_m, \ldots, e_n\}$ may be compared with the previous value of the good output signal to determine which of the corresponding faults are potentially detectable at the output of X.

The proofs of correctness that events execute in the correct order and that they execute deadlock-free in NODIFS are analogous to that for YADDES [101]; the reader is referred to [198] [14].

5.3.2.1 Termination of Fault Simulation

A fault simulation system terminates when the number of outstanding events is nil and consequently, every W', W, and U value is ∞. Assume that a system with a finite number of externally applied transitions never terminates. Because it was proved that a system may not deadlock, it must therefore execute continuously. The execution of a model involves receiving messages from or transmitting messages to other models that require finite time, execution of the model description which must terminate in finite time, and the computation of the W and W' values in the data-flow network, that must also terminate in finite time because the computations are unidirectional and limited by the finite number of pseudo components in the data-flow network. Consequently, models must continuously receive incoming messages as events.

Because the K and W values increase monotonically, subsequent events must be associated with increasing assertion times. In the expression for any W or K, the external events appear, along with events that may have been generated by the models. Because the minimum operator is involved in the computation of W or K, the assertion times of externally asserted transitions must eventually approach ∞, which is contradictory. Consequently, the fault simulation system must terminate in finite time.

Eventually, all events are executed and the fault simulation process terminates. That is, all externally applied signal transitions are used and as faults originating in the entire circuit are simulated for the externally applied set of signals. Conceivably, where all faults are detected at a primary output earlier that the maximum simulation time and thus dropped from further consideration, the fault simulation process degenerates into good simulation until all external signals are completely used. Conversely, should the good simulation of the circuit stablize, i.e., no new good events are generated, one of two possibilities are implied. First, all faults may have already been detected at a primary output port and thus dropped from consideration, implying process termination. Second, the fault effects of a subset of the faults may continue to be fault simulated until the simulation halts, i.e., when the assertion time of the fault effects exceeds the maximum assertion time of the external signal transitions.

5.4 Proof of Correctness of P^2EDAS

The proof of correctness of the P^2EDAS algorithm, introduced in Chapter 3, is presented here. The proof consists of three parts: correct order of execution of events, freedom from deadlock, and termination of simulation in finite time.

5.4.1 Execution of Events in the Correct Order: Monotonicity in W_h Values

The conservative nature of P^2EDAS requires that events be executed in the correct order. That is, if an input event with assertion time t_z is executed by a model, the model may not execute any event with assertion time t_y in the future, where $t_y < t_z$. Similarly, if an output event with time t_z is asserted at the output, the model may not assert any output event with time t_y at the output in the future, where $t_y < t_z$. Because models are executed asynchronously and concurrently on different processors, the propagation of events from one model to another may require arbitrary time, and as output events may be rendered inconsistent requiring deletion, it is critical that P^2EDAS guarantees the execution of input and output events in the correct order. It is assumed, using the guaranteed end-to-end message delivery in TCP/IP, that if two events with assertion times t_a and t_b $(t_a < t_b)$, respectively, are propagated from model A to model B, the event with the smaller assertion time,

t_a, will arrive at B prior to the event with assertion time t_b. Also, it is given that at the primary inputs of the models, events are asserted in the order of increasing assertion time values.

In P^2EDAS, where multiple input events are available at a model, C^N, the clock^N advances successively to the input event with the smallest assertion time, provided that clock^N does not exceed the t_{win}^N value. Also, if the assertion time of an output event is less than or equal to the value of clock^N, the output event is asserted at the output. Therefore, if it can be shown that the t_{win}^N for every model only increases successively as the simulation progresses, i.e., it is a monotonically increasing function, then the execution of events in the correct order is guaranteed.

The t_{win}^N value for a model was given by equation (3.7) and is computed from the W_i values at the input ports of the corresponding head pseudo component in the event prediction network. Consider the circuit in Figure 5.1 and the corresponding event prediction network in Figure 5.2. In Figure 5.1, the input pin 1 of every model A through N is primary. While t_1^1 represents the event with the smallest assertion time associated with model 1, t_1^N refers to the input with the smallest assertion time at model N. The event queues corresponding to the second input pin of each of the models 1 through N contain events generated as a result of execution of the models. For compactness in representation, the $minimum\_inertial\_delay(i, o, S_o)$ is referred to as $d(i, o, S_o)$ in this section. Therefore, to guarantee the execution of events in the correct order, it is adequate if it is proved that the W_i values at the inputs of head pseudo components and W_{oh} values at the output of the head pseudo components increase monotonically.

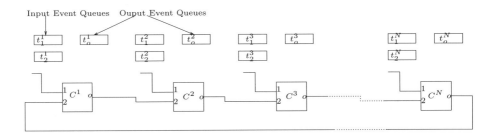

Fig. 5.1. An Example Circuit to Illustrate the Monotonicity in the W_h Values

In Figure 5.2, the W value at the output of the pseudo component 1 in the tail event prediction network, is computed as follows.

$$W_{ot}^1 = \text{minimum}(t_o^1, t_1^1 + d^1(1, o, S_o^1), d^1(2, o, S_o^1) + W_1^1)$$
$$= \text{minimum}(t_o^1, t_1^1 + d^1(1, o, S_o^1), d^1(2, o, S_o^1) + \infty)$$

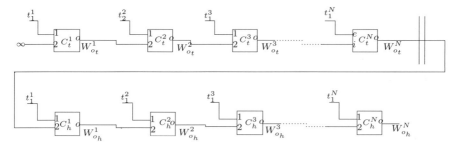

Fig. 5.2. Event Prediction Network for a Circuit in Figure 5.1

$$= \text{minimum}(t_o^1, t_1^1 + d^1(1, o, S_o^1), \infty)$$
$$= \text{minimum}(t_o^1, t_1^1 + d^1(1, o, S_o^1)). \quad (5.1)$$

The W value at the output of the pseudo component 2 in the tail event prediction network, is computed as follows.

$$W_{ot}^2 = \text{minimum}(t_o^2, t_1^2 + d^2(1, o, S_o^2), t_2^2 + d^2(2, o, S_o^2), d^2(2, o, S_o^2) + W_{ot}^1). \quad (5.2)$$

Substituting equation (5.1) in equation (5.2), we get

$$W_{ot}^2 = \text{minimum}(t_o^2, d^2(1, o, S_o^2) + t_1^2, d^2(2, o, S_o^2) + t_2^2, d^2(2, o, S_o^2) + t_o^1,$$
$$d^2(2, o, S_o^2) + d^1(1, o, S_o^1) + t_1^1, d^2(2, o, S_o^2) + d^1(2, o, S_o^1) + t_2^1). \quad (5.3)$$

The W value at the output of the pseudo component 3 in the tail event prediction network is computed as:

$$W_{ot}^3 = \text{minimum}(t_o^3, t_1^3 + d^3(1, o, S_o^3), t_2^3 + d^3(2, o, S_o^3), d^3(2, o, S_o^3) + W_{ot}^2). \quad (5.4)$$

Substituting equation (5.3) in equation (5.4), we get

$$W_{ot}^3 = \text{minimum}(t_o^3, d^3(1, o, S_o^3) + t_1^3, d^3(2, o, S_o^3) + t_2^3, d^3(2, o, S_o^3) + t_o^2,$$
$$d^3(2, o, S_o^3) + d^2(1, o, S_o^2) + t_1^2, d^3(2, o, S_o^3) + d^2(2, o, S_o^2) + t_2^2,$$
$$d^3(2, o, S_o^3) + d^2(2, o, S_o^2) + t_o^1, d^3(2, o, S_o^3) + d^2(2, o, S_o^2)$$
$$+d^1(1, o, S_o^1) + t_1^1,$$
$$d^3(2, o, S_o^3) + d^2(2, o, S_o^2) + d^1(2, o, S_o^1) + t_2^1). \quad (5.5)$$

While equation (5.1) contains three terms, equation (5.3) contains six terms and equation (5.5) has nine terms in it. The expression for W_{ot}^N will contain $3N$ terms in it and may be derived through analogy as

$$W_{ot}^N = \text{minimum}(t_o^N, d^N(1, o, S_o^N) + t_1^N, d^N(2, o, S_o^N) + t_2^N, d^N(2, o, S_o^N) + t_o^{N-1},$$
$$d^N(2, o, S_o^N) + d^{N-1}(1, o, S_o^{N-1}) + t_1^{N-1}, \dots,$$
$$d^N(2, o, S_o^N) + d^{N-1}(2, o, S_o^{N-1}) + \dots + d^1(2, o, S_o^1) + t_2^1). \quad (5.6)$$

The W_{ot}^N value is the input W value to the first pseudo component in the head section of the event prediction network. It influences the computation of t_{win}^1 for model 1, which will determine the execution of the input and output events of model 1. It will also affect the expressions for W_{oh}^1 through W_{oh}^N. The expression in equation (5.6) takes into account the influences of every input transition and output event, if any, that may affect its value and, therefore, the execution of events by model 1. Thus, the terms in the expression in equation (5.6) represent the transitive closure over the t_1 values and t_o of all models. This section will show that W_{ot}^N is a monotonic function, i.e., its value only increases as a function of the progress of simulation.

The proof focuses on all worst-case scenarios that create the possible appearance of decrease in the value of W_{ot}^N between two successive computations and shows that they are false. The values of t_o^1 through t_o^N, t_1^1 through t_1^N, and t_2^1 through t_2^N changes as simulation progresses.

Scenario 1. Following execution of an input transition at a primary input, say t_1^X, of model X, it is deleted and replaced by the subsequent event at that input, if any, which has a higher value of assertion time. Because the models and pseudo component execute asynchronously and potentially on different processors, P^2EDAS first propagates the resulting t_o^X value, if different from the previous value, to the corresponding pseudo components, and then deletes the executed input event. This prevents a potential race condition that may momentarily cause a decrease in the W_{ot}^N value. When all transitions are consumed, the t_1^X value will be set to ∞. Also, when an output event is asserted at the output port, prior to deleting it, P^2EDAS ensures that the output event is propagated to the input event queues of the models connected to the output and the corresponding pseudo components in the event prediction network. Clearly, between any two successive values of W_{ot}^N, none of the t_1^X values will not decrease and will not contribute to lowering the value of W_{ot}^N.

Scenario 2. Next, assume an input event, t_{2a}^X, of model X. Assume that $\text{clock}^X = t_{2a}^X$ and t_{2a}^X is less than t_{win}^X. Therefore, t_{2a}^X is executed and say that an output event, t_{o2}^X, is generated at the output of model X. Clearly the assertion time of t_{o2}^X exceeds that of t_{2a}^X. The output event is included in the output event queue which already contains an event t_{o1}^X. Following its execution, the event t_{2a}^X is deleted. Assume that the W_{ot}^N value is now determined by t_{o1}^X. Now assume that there is a second transition at the same input pin, t_{2b}^X, such that t_{2b}^X is less than t_{win}^X. Thus, the clock^X is first advanced to t_{2b}^X. Assume that the entry t_{o1}^X in the output event queue satisfies the condition that t_{o1}^X is less than or equal to the new value of clock^X. Therefore, the output event t_{o1}^X is asserted at the output and the logical value, S_o^X, changes. The entry t_{o2}^X now occupies the head of the output event queue and assume that it controls the value of W_{ot}^N. Next, the input event t_{2b}^X is executed and an output event t_{o3}^X is generated. The generation of t_{o3}^X uses a different delay value compared to the generation of t_{o2}^X and assume that t_{o3}^X is less than t_{o2}^X. Therefore, the output event t_{o2}^X will be preempted and event t_{o3}^X will become the head of the output event queue. If the value of W_{ot}^N has been controlled by the output event queue, the value of W_{ot}^N appears to suffer a decrease. This appearance is false for the following reason. Immediately preceding the execution of the input event t_{2b}^X, the value of W_{ot}^N was computed as the minimum of $t_{2b}^X + \text{delay}()$, t_{o2}^X, and other factors. Clearly, because t_{o3}^X is equal to $t_{2b}^X + \text{delay}()$ and it is smaller than t_{o2}^X, the value of W_{ot}^N must have been determined by $t_{2b}^X + \text{delay}()$ and not t_{o2}^X. The value of W_{ot}^N does not change when the output event t_{o2}^X is preempted. Therefore, the W_{ot}^N does not decrease.

Scenario 3. Consider the following situation, which differs slightly from Scenario 2. Consider that the two input events are associated with two different input pins of model X, i.e., t_{2a}^X and t_{1b}^X, where t_{2a}^X is executed prior to event t_{1b}^X. Also assume that the assertion time of the output event, t_{o3}^X, corresponding to t_{1b}^X is less than that of the event t_{o2}^X generated from the execution of t_{2a}^X. This is easily conceivable, because the generation of t_{o2}^X uses a delay value different from the one used for the generation of t_{o3}^X, regardless of whether there is a previously generated entry in the output event queue t_{o1}^X or not. Clearly, output event t_{o2}^X will be preempted. Under these circumstances, a proof may be constructed, similar to the preceding one, to show that the value of W_{ot}^N will be controlled by $t_{1b}^X + \text{delay}()$ and not by t_{o2}^X. Therefore, W_{ot}^N will not decrease despite the incidence of preemption.

Scenario 4. Consider the following situation, which also differs slightly from Scenario 2. Consider that the two input events are associated with the same input pin 2 and that the output event queue is empty. Following execution of the first input event, t_{2a}^X, the output event t_{o2}^X is generated. Because both input events are less than the current value of t_{win}^X, the comparison of the output event t_{o2}^X with the t_{win}^X is deferred until the second input event t_{2b}^X is executed. Following the execution of t_{2b}^X, output event t_{o3}^X is generated. Because the logical value at the output of model X, S_o^X, has not changed between the two consecutive executions of X, the same delay value is used in the generation of t_{o2}^X and t_{o3}^X. Because t_{2a}^X is less than t_{2b}^X, t_{o3}^X cannot be less than t_{o2}^X. Thus, there is neither preemption nor any decrease in the value of W_{ot}^N.

It may be proved, analogously, that the values of W_{oh}^1 through W_{oh}^N, associated with the pseudo components 1 through N of the head section of the event prediction network in Figure 5.2, will also increase monotonically. The assertion that W_{oh}^X values increase monotonically may be proved for any digital circuit with any number of feedback loops.

5.4.2 Proof of Freedom from Deadlock

The principal characteristics of P^2EDAS that ensure freedom from deadlock include the following. A change in any input event queue of any of the models will trigger the initiation of the event prediction network. Changes in the event queue may arise as a result of new events asserted at the primary inputs or assertion of output events of a model at its output that subsequently alter the input event queues of other models connected to the output. During execution, the event prediction network propagates any and all changes to W_t and W_h values such that all necessary and sufficient W_t and W_h values are updated leading to the computations of correct values of t_{win}. Also, the execution of the pseudo components of the event prediction network is unidirectional, i.e., from left to right, and asynchronous and concurrent with respect to each other and the models.

Assume, on the contrary, that P^2EDAS deadlocks. First, consider the scenario where there are no outstanding input or output events. Thus, all external events are executed, implying that all input event queues are empty. Similarly, the output event queues are empty. As a result, all W_t, W_h, t_{win}, and clock values are set to ∞. Clearly, the simulation has terminated.

Next, consider the scenario wherein a model, C^X, contains an event in the output event queue, represented by t_o^X. The simulation is in deadlock and the output event t_o^X continues to remain unasserted at the output of X indefinitely. Therefore,

$$t_{\text{win}}^X \leq t_o^X. \tag{5.7}$$

In the event prediction network, t_o^X is the only event. Therefore, the W_h^{X-1} value at the output of the preceding model, C^{X-1}, must be given by

$$W_h^{X-1} = \min(t_o^X + d^{X+1}(2, o, S_o) + \ldots + d^1(2, o, S_o) + \ldots + d^{X-1}(2, o, S_o)). \tag{5.8}$$

Now, t_{win}^X is computed as the minimum over all incoming W_h values, as per equation (3.7), and is given by

$$t_{\text{win}}^X = \min(t_o^X + d^{X+1}(2, o, S_o) + \ldots + d^1(2, o, S_o) + \ldots + d^{X-1}(2, o, S_o)). \tag{5.9}$$

Because the delay values are nonnegative, it follows from equation (5.9) that t_{win}^X is greater than t_o^X, which contradicts equation (5.7). Thus, the assumption of deadlock leads to a contradiction, which implies that the assumption is false. Therefore, deadlock may not occur relative to the event. In the proof, if two or more events exist with the same assertion time, each event will independently lead to a contradiction.

The proof of freedom from deadlock is similar for the scenario where there are multiple outstanding input events and multiple events associated with the output event queues of models. The event, input or output, if any, with the smallest assertion time that must be executed first, in accordance with the correct order of execution of events, is identified. A proof is constructed similar to the one described earlier to prove that deadlock may not occur for this event. Then the event with the next larger assertion time is identified, and it is shown that deadlock may not occur for this event. This process is continued successively to show that deadlock cannot occur for any input or output event. Thus, deadlock cannot occur in P^2EDAS.

5.4.3 Termination of Simulation

A simulation system terminates when the number of outstanding events is nil and consequently, every t_{win}, t_o, and W value is ∞ and t_{E_i} for every primary input of the circuit is ∞. Assume that a system with a finite number of externally applied transitions never terminates. Because it was proved that a system may not deadlock, it must therefore execute continuously. The execution of a model involves receiving messages from or transmitting messages to other models that require finite time, execution of the model description which must terminate in finite time, and the computation of the t_{win}, t_o, and W values in the event prediction network, which must also terminate in finite time because the computations are unidirectional and limited by the finite number of pseudo components in the event prediction network. Consequently, models must continuously receive incoming messages as events. Because the t_{win} and W values increase monotonically, subsequent events must be associated with increasing assertion times. In the expression for any W or t_{win}, the external events appear along with events that may have been generated by the simulation models. Because the minimum operator is involved in the computation of W or t_{win}, the assertion times of externally asserted transitions must eventually approach ∞, which is contradictory. Consequently, the simulation system must terminate in finite time.

A Mathematical Framework for Synthesizing ADDM Algorithms

6.1 Review of the Current Literature

This chapter presents a formal approach to synthesizing ADDM algorithms, the underlying motivations being the need to coordinate the decisions of the entities to achieve global optimal behavior for the overall system and to establish a scientific basis to rate the quality of their decisions. The literature on synthesizing decentralized decision-making algorithms and evaluating the quality of distributed decision making, is sparse. Rotithor [51] proposes distributing the overall tasks—system state estimation and decision making—of a decentralized decision-making system among independent decision-making processing elements and attempt to improve the overall performance of the system by optimizing the performance of the individual decision makers. Rotithor models the problem of load balancing in distributed computing and notes substantial performance improvements. Tsitsiklis and Athans [52] consider the distributed team decision problem wherein different agents obtain different stochastic measures related to an uncertain random vector from the environment and attempt to converge, asymptotically, on a common decision, and they derive the conditions for convergence. In [53], Tsitsiklis and Athans study the complexity of basic decentralized decision problems that are variations of team decision problems and conclude that optimality may be an elusive goal. It is noted that in contrast to the problems studied in [52][53], here, each entity derives its own decisions—possibly different from those of other entities—while attempting to achieve global optimal behavior.

This chapter is based on the distributed hybrid control paradigm of Kohn and Nerode [199][200] in that every entity of the decentralized decision-making system is designed to optimize a Lagrangian [201][202], a local dynamically evolving nonnegative cost criterion, subject to the constraints imposed by the global objectives and principles. Thus, the notion of Lagrangian here is more general in that it reflects the usage in the most general calculus of variations. In the literature on mathematical programming, the term objective function is used synonymously with Lagrangian, merely reflecting the fact that both the linear and nonlinear programming cases are, in essence, special cases of the calculus of variation problem of Bolza on a manifold [202]. Every entity uses its local information, encapsulated through an internal state vector, its local goals, and appropriate coordination information obtained from other entities, to determine its decisions autonomously and asynchronously, yet cooperatively, to achieve the desirable global performance. Compared to the centralized control system, the distributed decision-making system can process information faster and react to dynamic changes to the environment quicker. However, because each entity computes decisions autonomously, key system information including the global goals must be made available to them. This is precisely the objective of the distributed Lagrangians. The distributed system is expected to exhibit robustness, i.e., resistance to catastrophic failure and scalability. That is, as the system grows due to an increasing number of entities, the number of computing engines will increase proportionately and the system is expected to continue to deliver undiminished performance. The joint state of all entities is the operative evolving state of the entire system and is referred to as the carrier manifold state in [203].

6.2 A Representative Military Command, Control, and Communication Problem

The scenario presented here is a simulated battlefield with two opposing forces. Both forces consist of a number of identical tank units. However, while one uses a centralized command and control structure, the other utilizes a decentralized structure. Under centralized control, each tank gathers information on the environment—detection and classification of enemy objects, tracking, etc.—stores them in its internal state vector, and propagates the vector to the centralized decision maker, a tank commander. Upon receiving the state vectors from all its constituent tanks, the commander processes the information, assesses the threats, computes the decisions, and propagates them to the individual tank units, which fire on the enemy. Under decentralized command and control, every tank uses the locally obtained data, coordination information from its peers, assesses threats to itself, and computes its own decisions, subject to the global goals that are manifested through its local goals. An entity is also capable of propagating information, including threats, to a peer, especially when the enemy is outside the field of view of the peer. All units, friend and enemy, are assumed to be identical and, therefore, the threat function is proportional to the distance between the friend and enemy units. This chapter does not use predictive mechanisms to estimate and track enemy positions, for two reasons. First, the objective here is to contrast the performance of the decentralized algorithm with the traditional centralized scheme. Second, predictive techniques are beyond the scope of this chapter.

6.2.1 Component Vectors of the Entities

Each entity necessarily maintains a vector that consists of three component vectors to capture movement, sensor, and targeting information.

6.2.1.1 Movement State Vector

The movement state vector contains information pertaining to the movement of this entity. It includes the current position of the unit, (x, y), its velocity, (v_x, v_y), and the amount of fuel remaining. Also included is the *status* of the unit, which can be either *OPERATIONAL* or *DESTROYED*. The *mode* field represents the unit's mode of operation. While the mode is normally *ENGAGE*, it may also be *RETREAT* or *SEARCHING*. When an entity is under enemy fire and is unable to see enemy units, it enters the *SEARCHING* mode, which triggers its sensor management decisions in an attempt to place its field of view over the enemy unit:

$$V_m = [status, fuel, mode, x, y, v_x, v_y]^\top,$$

where $\top$ represents the transpose operation such that V_m is expressed as a column vector.

6.2.1.2 Sensor State Vector

Each entity possesses sensor capability to view a limited area of its surroundings. This ability is defined through a cone originating at the unit and extending out for a finite distance. The distance is directly related to the unit's sensor range but is unrelated to its weapons range. The cone is defined through two angles that form it, α and β, in a given coordinate system. The sensor axis for the cone is derived from the α and β, as shown in Figure 6.1.

Thus, the sensor state vector consists of the (α, β) pair that describes the orientation of the sensor arc:

$$V_s = [\alpha, \beta]^\top.$$

6.2.1.3 Target State Vector

The target state vector contains information on the state of the unit's weapon system and the position of its current target. This section assumes that a unit is supplied with a single antitank weapon and that it may engage a single target at a time. While the *weapon status* can be either *READY* or *RELOADING*, the *ammunition* field reflects the number of shells (rounds) remaining, if any. The symbol τ represents the time at which the unit will open fire on its target. The purpose of using τ is elaborated later in the chapter. The target itself is identified by its current coordinate position, (t_x, t_y).

$$V_t = [weapon\ status, ammunition, t_x, t_y, \tau]^\top.$$

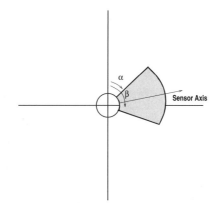

Fig. 6.1. Sensor Arc and Sensor Axis for an Entity

6.2.2 State Vectors of the Entities

The state vector for an entity encapsulates its total knowledge of the system; its components include the self, friend, and enemy state vectors. It is noted that while only the leader unit in the centralized paradigm must maintain the status of all friendly and sighted enemy units, every unit in the decentralized paradigm is a decision maker and must contain similar information.

6.2.2.1 Self State Vector

The self state vector contains the state of this unit. Because the unit always has immediate access to its own status, this information is accurate up to the current time:

$$X_s = [V_m, V_s, V_t].$$

6.2.2.2 Friend State Vector

Given n friendly units, the friend state vector must contain the state of each of them. Because this information is obtained from the respective friendly units, it is necessarily delayed by a communication delay, τ_c. Thus, at the current time, T, the friend state vector represents the states of the friend units at time $T - \tau_c$:

$$X_f = [V_{m,1}, V_{s,1}, V_{t,1}, \ldots, V_{m,n-1}, V_{s,n-1}, V_{t,n-1}].$$

6.2.2.3 Enemy State Vector

Where p enemy units are sighted, the enemy state vector contains the states of p enemy units. This information constitutes a fusion of what this unit can see through its own sensor and the enemy sighting reports that it has received from other friend units. Consequently, while a part of the information represents the enemy state at the current time T, the remainder of the vector represents the enemy state at time $T - \tau_c$:

$$X_e = [V_{m,1}, V_{s,1}, V_{t,1}, \dots, V_{m,p}, V_{s,p}, V_{t,p}].$$

6.2.3 Complete Internal State Vector of an Entity

Thus, the complete internal state vector of every unit in the decentralized paradigm and the leader unit in the centralized approach, representing the unit's entire knowledge of the world, may be expressed as a collection of the self, friend, and enemy state vectors:

$$X = [X_s, X_f, X_e].$$

6.2.4 Decision Vectors of Entities

A unit's decision vector captures the decisions computed by each unit in the decentralized case or the orders enforced on a unit in the centralized scheme by its leader. The decision vectors are to take effect subsequently. The components relate to movement decision, sensor management, and target management.

6.2.4.1 Movement Decision

A unit's physical movement is specified through two velocity components, v_x and v_y. The time rate of change of these vectors represents the acceleration of the unit, and it is governed by its maximum acceleration or deceleration capability:

$$U_m = [v_x, v_y]^\top.$$

6.2.4.2 Sensor Management

As described earlier, the sensor arc is represented through α and β and is characterized by the sensor axis. Sensor management consists in changing the sensor axis, where the rate of change of the arc, in degrees per second, is subject to a maximum value. The sensor decision vector, however, is expressed as:

$$U_s = [\alpha, \beta]^\top.$$

6.2.4.3 Target Management

Each tank unit has a turret-mounted gun that is used to engage targets. This section also assumes that a unit can open fire at an enemy unit only when the latter is within its field of view. Following target selection, it may be necessary to choose an optimal time, τ, to open fire. The cost function corresponding to the target decision will be described in section 6.3.1. If the distance between the unit and the target is decreasing, then delaying the firing would increase the probability of hitting the target. However, this delay also increases the threat that the enemy unit presents to this unit and possibly other friendly units. In contrast, when the distance between the unit and the target is increasing, it may be necessary to open fire immediately. Assuming target location at (t_x, t_y), the target decision vector is written as:

$$U_t = [t_x, t_y, \tau]^\top.$$

6.3 Modeling the C^3 Problem under the Centralized Paradigm in MFAD

In the centralized paradigm, each individual unit communicates exclusively with the leader unit—logically the centralized decision maker—and there is a total absence of communication between the individual tanks. Information relative to the environment flows from the individual units to the leader, which computes the decisions for all other units and propagates them in the form of orders. Thus, the individual subordinate tanks need not maintain either friend or enemy state vectors and are not permitted to modify their own decision vectors. The leader unit must determine its own decision vector, U_m^1, U_s^1, U_t^1, where superscript 1 relates to the leader unit, and the decision vectors, U_m^i, U_s^i, and U_t^i for each of its $i = 2$ to n subordinate units. The complete decision vector is expressed as:

$$U = [U_m^1, U_s^1, U_t^1, \ldots, U_m^n, U_s^n, U_t^n].$$

6.3.1 Synthesizing Decision Vectors through Cost Functions

To enable comparative analysis of the two paradigms, the respective decision vectors must be translated into real or scalar values. To achieve this goal, Lagrangians or cost functions, i.e., nonnegative real-valued functions, are developed corresponding to each of the component decision vectors of the entities: movement, sensor, and targeting. Unless otherwise noted, the component decisions are independent of each other. That is, U_t and U_s, for instance, may be calculated independently, with no dependence on the values of each other. As a result, a unit's decision to move its sensor is independent of the enemy unit it may choose to target. The cost functions for both U_t and U_s, however, incorporate information on currently sighted enemies, so there is a shared dependency on the state information. Nonetheless, the optimization of U_s does not impact the optimization of U_t because this state information remains unchanged during the decision-making period. In summary, therefore, the optimal choices for each component of U may be obtained through minimizing the corresponding cost function.

6.3.1.1 Cost Function Corresponding to the Movement Decision

The cost function corresponding to the movement decision, J_m, is synthesized from (1) the distance D^i between the ith friendly unit and all sighted enemy units, for all friendly units; (2) the threat rating T^i of all sighted enemy units against the ith friendly unit, for all friendly units; and (3) the deviation V^i of every ith friendly unit from the movement axis, which is defined as the preferred direction of movement for all friendly units, as defined prior to the battle. Thus,

$$J_m(X, U_m) = \sum_{i=1}^{n} J_m^i(X, U_m^i), \text{ where} \tag{6.1}$$
$$J_m^i(X, U_m^i) = \alpha_m^i * D^i + \beta_m^i * T^i(X) + \gamma_m^i * V^i, \tag{6.2}$$
$$D^i = \sum_{j=1}^{p} \text{ distance from the } i\text{th friendly unit to the } j\text{th enemy unit,}$$
$$T^i = \sum_{j=1}^{p} \text{ distance from the } i\text{th friendly unit to the } j\text{th enemy unit,}$$
$$V^i = |\text{Actual Direction of the } i\text{th friendly unit} - \text{Movement axis}|,$$

and α_m^i, β_m^i, and γ_m^i are constant weights that are assigned initial values at the beginning of the simulation and may be altered to influence the behavior of the ith friendly unit. As stated earlier, in this research, all units, friend and enemy, are assumed to be identical and, therefore, the threat function is proportional to the distance between the friend and enemy units. Thus, $T^i = D^i$. However, should the need arise to model enemy units differently from the friend units, the threat presented to the ith friendly unit by an enemy unit may be modified in the cost function. It is also pointed out that there are p enemy units.

6.3.1.2 Cost Function Corresponding to the Target Decision

The Lagrangian for the target decision, J_t, is synthesized from two factors:

- the threat rating T^i posed by all sighted enemy units to the ith friendly unit, and
- the probability P^i of the ith friendly unit securing a direct hit on its selected target and destroying it. Thus,

$$J_t(X, U_t) = \sum_{i=1}^{n} J_t^i(X, U_t^i), \text{ where} \tag{6.3}$$
$$J_t^i(X, U_t^i) = \alpha_t^i * T^i + \beta_t^i * P^i; \tag{6.4}$$

T^i, the threat rating, is defined earlier; and α_t^i and β_t^i are constant weights that are assigned initial values at the beginning of the simulation and may be altered to influence the behavior of the ith friendly unit.

6.3.1.3 Cost Function Corresponding to the Sensor Decision

The sensor decision cost function, J_s, is derived from four factors and a special case:

- the degree of overlap between the friendly sensors;
- the deviation of the sensor axis from a predefined threat axis, which is the expected direction of arrival of the enemy;
- a friendly unit's preference to include the nearest sighted enemy unit, not currently targeted by any friendly unit, within its sensor arc; and
- an ith friendly unit's preference to include the nearest sighted enemy unit, currently targeted by another friendly unit, within its sensor arc. When the ith unit is also the current targeting unit, the preference is stronger and this scenario is one where the sensor decision is linked to a previous targeting decision.
- In addition, there is a special case when the unit has been fired on by an unseen enemy, as described earlier, and it enters the *SEARCHING* mode. Given that all units are assumed to possess identical range, this guarantees the presence of an enemy unit within the range of the unit's weapon system but probably not within the sensor range. The *SEARCHING* mode encourages the unit to undergo maximum change in its sensor arc to see new areas and locate the enemy. Thus,

$$J_s(X, U_s) = \sum_{i=1}^n J_s^i(X, U_s^i), \text{ where} \tag{6.5}$$
$$J_s^i(X, U_s^i) = \alpha_s^i * O + \beta_s^i * S + \gamma_s^i * W + \delta_s^i * V + \epsilon_s^i * D; \tag{6.6}$$

O is an estimate of the degree of sensor overlap; S is the deviation of the sensor axis from the threat axis; W is the angle between the nearest sighted engaged enemy and the sensor axis; V is the angle between the nearest sighted unengaged enemy and the sensor axis; and α_s^i, β_s^i, γ_s^i, δ_s^i, and ϵ_s^i are constant weights that are assigned initial values at the beginning of the simulation and may be altered to influence the behavior of the ith friendly unit. In *SEARCHING* mode, the parameter D is assigned a very high value. At all other times, D is assigned the value 0.

6.3.1.4 Centralized Lagrangian

Thus, the overall cost function under the centralized paradigm, referred to as the centralized Lagrangian, is expressed subsequently, and the combinatorial optimization problem is to minimize it:

$$J(X, U) = J_m(X, U_m) + J_s(X, U_s) + J_t(X, U_t). \tag{6.7}$$

After inspection, the overall minimization effort, $\min\{J(X,U)\}$, may be rewritten in terms of simultaneously minimizing the n cost functions corresponding to the n individual friendly entities, as shown in equation (6.8). The result of minimization, according to the traditional centralized optimization schemes, may yield the global minimum:

$$\min J(X,U) = \min\{\sum_{i=1}^{n} J^i(X,U^i)\}. \qquad (6.8)$$

The expression for minimizing the cost function of each entity may be elaborated to $\min J^i(X_s(t), X_f(t), X_e(t), U^i(t))$, with all of its components and the time dependency shown. The minimization effort for every entity is carried out by the leader unit, under the centralized paradigm. At a given time $t = T$, given the geographical separation between the leader and other entities, the leader unit is only aware of a friendly entity's state up to $t = T - \tau_c$, where τ_c represents the communication delay between the leader and the entity in question. Thus, the peer state information suffers a latency of τ_c. While the state information for the entity itself is current, the enemy state information, implied by the term $X_e(T, T-\tau)$ in equation 6.9, is a combination of information from its own sensors at $t = T$ and information sent from its peers at $t = T - \tau_c$. Therefore, the minimization effort corresponding to every entity is given by

$$\min J^i(X_s(T), X_f(T - \tau), X_e(T, T - \tau), U^i(T)). \qquad (6.9)$$

Following minimization, the decision vectors U^i that are generated must be propagated as orders to the subordinate units that execute them at $t = T + \tau_c$.

6.4 Synthesizing Distributed Lagrangians for the C^3 Problem in MFAD

Under the distributed paradigm, every entity is granted autonomy to determine its own decision vector, locally. The computations for the individual entities are carried out locally, using locally obtained data and appropriate information that is propagated from other sites. The aim of MFAD is for each entity to minimize a Lagrangian, asynchronously, concurrently, and independent of other entities, with the expectation that, ultimately, global optimal behavior is achieved. For the decisions to be effective, each entity must maintain state vectors for each of the friend and enemy units. This requires every unit to communicate directly with its peers and with the leader unit. Thus, the status and sighting reports are exchanged directly between peers and with the leader unit. As noted earlier, information from a peer will suffer latency due to finite communication delay. Also, the leader unit is no longer responsible for computing and communicating the decision vectors to the subordinate units.

Under MFAD, which uses the Kohn-Nerode [199][200] distributed hybrid control paradigm as its basis, the Lagrangian corresponding to the ith entity is synthesized analogous to expression (6.9), except for three significant differences that are elaborated later. The differences arise as a result of the decentralization of autonomy. The Lagrangian for the ith entity is presented in expression (6.10) where X_s^i, X_f^i, and X_e^i represent its internal state, its knowledge of the states of its peers, and its knowledge of the states of the enemy units:

$$J^i(X_s^i(T), X_f^i(T - \tau), X_e^i(T, T - \tau), U^i(T)). \qquad (6.10)$$

The first difference is that, under the centralized paradigm, the leader unit must determine the decision vectors for each of the n subordinates. Despite significant computational cost, the decision vectors are consistent, subject to the latency of the information from the subordinate units, because the leader has access to the state of the total system. In contrast, in the decentralized paradigm, every entity must compute only its own decision vector, using accurate knowledge of its state at the current time, knowledge of its peers' states up to time $t = T - \tau_c$, and the knowledge of the states of the enemy units acquired through its own sensors at the current time and from its peers at time $t = T - \tau_c$. None of the entities has access to the entire system state. Thus, while the computational cost is lower for each unit relative to the centralized decision maker, the units' decision vectors, computed at $t = T$, are not guaranteed to be coordinated.

Second, while there is execution latency in the centralized paradigm stemming from the need to propagate the decision vectors from the leader unit to the subordinates, the decision vector is executed immediately by the corresponding unit in the decentralized paradigm.

Third, the interpeer connectivity and the messages exchanged between peers, subject to the controlling parameter INFORM_RANGE, reflect a significant increase in communication of the decentralized paradigm over the centralized paradigm, as evident in Figure 6.2(b). Only when an enemy unit is sighted within INFORM_RANGE of the last known position of a friendly unit i, will the sighting friendly unit j propagate its sighting information to unit i.

6.5 A Representative Battlefield Scenario and the Simulation Architecture

A representative battlefield is constructed from blue and red forces, each of which consists of a total of six entities. While all entities correspond to generic tanks, five are assumed to form the lowest hierarchy of the command, subordinate to the leader, the sixth unit. Each entity is modeled in the simulation as an autonomous, concurrent process. The processes are executed on a mix

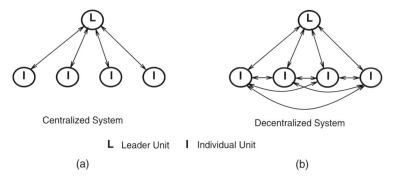

Centralized System   Decentralized System

L Leader Unit   **I** Individual Unit

(a)   (b)

Fig. 6.2. Interconnection under the Centralized and Decentralized Paradigms

of available processor platforms, connected through a 10 Mbit/sec ethernet, including the Sun sparc stations under SunOS 4.1 and Solaris 2.4 and Intel 486DX2/66- and Pentium-based machines under the freely available Linux operating system. Interprocess communication is achieved through TCP/IP.

To ensure a consistent view of the battlefield among peer entities, despite the corresponding autonomous, concurrent processes, each unit maintains a point-to-point connection with its peer and leader, and two control nodes are introduced into the simulation corresponding to the blue and red forces. A control node is merely an artifact of the simulation and has no counterpart in the real world. It maintains an accurate picture of the entire system and propagates information to entities on a need-to-know basis. That is, the control node will not propagate change information relative to an entity, E_1, to a different entity, E_2, if E_2 cannot possibly see or interact with E_1. Whenever the status of an entity changes, the control node requires an automatic update. Relative to positional information, only the change in the velocity vector needs to be propagated because the control node is capable of computing the final position. In turn, after a request from an entity, whose field of view is limited by its sensor, a control node propagates the corresponding subset of the view of the entire battlefield. For convenience, the entire battlefield is organized into square sectors. Using the knowledge of its sensor capabilities, an entity specifies its sector set, i.e., the set of sectors of the entire battlefield, such that the entity can see or detect other units in each individual sector. Figure 6.3 presents the organization of the interconnection network in the battlefield. For a comparative evaluation of the centralized versus decentralized paradigms, the blue force, on the left, implements the decentralized paradigm, while the red force, on the right, is organized under the centralized paradigm.

The accuracy of the simulation results are governed by the spatial and temporal resolutions, i.e., the smallest changes in the location and time that may occur atomically. The finer the granularity, the more accurate the simulation at the cost of increased simulation time. In this chapter, the spatial and temporal units are set at 0.2 meter and 0.1 second, respectively, so that the

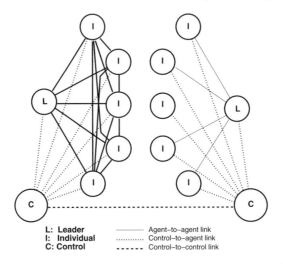

L: **Leader**   ——— Agent–to–agent link
I: **Individual**   .... Control–to–agent link
C: **Control**   ‒ ‒ ‒ ‒ Control–to–control link

Fig. 6.3. Interconnection Network for the Blue and Red Forces in the Simulation

weapon travel times and communication delays are registered through multiple timesteps. The battlefield is defined to be a flat terrain, 2,500,000 units square. Each entity is a generic tank type with the characteristics detailed in Table 6.1. At simulation initiation, the initial locations of the entities are generated randomly to fall within squares of length 15,000 spatial units. Furthermore, the leader units are placed farther apart from other units so that they are not engaged in firing. The initial sensor axes for the entities are also generated stochastically. That is, at the start of the simulation, the values of α and β are chosen at random, subject to the constraint that they constitute a 45° angle, as noted in Table 6.1. While the sensor cone must be constrained for practical reasons, the choice of the 45° arc reflects a reasonable value for the sensor cone. While each tank carries a total of ten shells and only one shell is fired at a time, the fuel capacity values are unconstrained. The study reveals that neither ammunition nor fuel runs out prior to the completion of the battle for any tank in any simulation, representing desired battlefield conditions. The damage incurred by a tank after intercepting an enemy shell is governed by a statistical probability that is defined by the entity and the type of weapon. The damage assessment is binary, i.e., it is either destroyed or left operational, and the probability that the tank is destroyed is set at 30%.

In addition, the simulation models two delays: (1) the leader–to–entity and peer entity–to–peer entity communication delay and (2) decision computing delay. For simplicity and without any loss in generality, this chapter assigns the same value, a positive integer, τ_c, to the leader–to–entity and peer entity–to–peer entity communication delays. While the leader is expected to incur higher computation and communication than the subordinates, the difference in their

Characteristic	Value
Movement	
Maximum velocity	15 units/timestep
Maximum acceleration	$\pm\sqrt{2}$ units/timestep^2
Sensor	
Arc size	$45°$
Rate of change	$\pm 10°$/timestep
Targeting	
Weapon range	3000 units
Weapon velocity	500 units/timestep
Weapon reload time	25 timesteps

Table 6.1. Generic Characteristics of Each Entity

communication delays is likely to be significant under the centralized scheme and less significant in the decentralized paradigm. The decision computing delay, τ_p, models the computing time needed to minimize the cost function and assumes that the minimization may require several timesteps. While τ_p may equal several timesteps for the centralized paradigm, τ_p is zero if the decision time is less than a single timestep.

Minimizing a cost function is difficult. The literature reports a number of algorithms that require reasonable computational costs to generate approximate solutions. However, the goal here is to synthesize a decentralized algorithm under the MFAD framework, corresponding to a centralized decision-making algorithm, and to measure the effectiveness of MFAD. Therefore, this chapter limits every independent variable in the cost functions to a finite number of integral values and computes exact solutions for both centralized and decentralized paradigms, relatively quickly. Corresponding to the movement cost function, each entity is only permitted to alter each component velocity vector by ± 1 and the value of the acceleration is assumed constant. The sensor cost function is expensive to compute, stemming from the desire to minimize sensor overlap between peers. Conceptually, the problem is equivalent to computing the area of overlap of multiple cones. A simple numerical approximation method is chosen to yield rough estimates of sensor overlap quickly. Also, the maximum change of the sensor axis is limited to $10°$ and successive increments are limited to 5-degree intervals.

The simulator is written in C; is approximately 18,000 lines long; and implements both centralized and decentralized paradigms. A Motif-based graphical interface has been included to allow for both real-time and post-mortem viewing of the simulation. Figure 6.4 presents a screen shot where the small circles represent the individual units and identifiers 2 through 6 and 9 through 13 represent the blue and red units, respectively. The arcs originating at each entity reflect the current sensor arc while the short lines of different lengths emanating from the circles represent the magnitude of the current velocity vector.

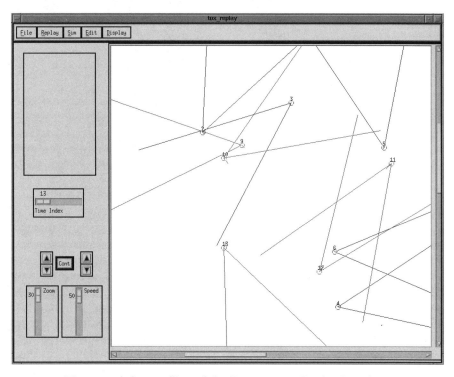

Fig. 6.4. A Screen Shot of the Post-mortem Replay Interface

6.6 Comparative Performance Analysis of the Centralized and Decentralized Paradigms under MFAD

To evaluate the effectiveness of the MFAD framework, this section reports the results from executing the centralized and decentralized command and control algorithms, corresponding to the representative battlefield scenario. A number of experiments are designed, as described later.

In every experiment, a number of simulation runs are executed corresponding to a number of different initial locations of the entities, generated stochastically. The distribution function used is uniform and is generated by the Unix function drand48. In addition, for every experiment, two sets of simulation runs are executed—one with the red force centralized and blue force decentralized and another with the red force decentralized and blue force centralized. The aim is to eliminate any bias resulting from geographic advantages. Each simulation is executed for a total duration of 600 timesteps, which allows sufficient time for the two forces to engage, eventually leaving only one of the two forces with the surviving entities. Both of the paradigms are assigned identical units with identical weapons, similar initial geographic locations for the entities, and identical number of units. The parameter τ_p, which normally provides an advantage for the decentralized paradigm, is assumed to be zero. Thus, the key remaining factor to discriminate between the two paradigms in MFAD is the communication delay, τ_c, which assumes the form of the independent variable and is assigned values ranging from 1 to 9 timesteps, i.e., 0.1 sec to 0.9 sec, that reflect relatively large communication distances in representative battlefields. The parameter INFORM_RANGE is set to 30,000 spatial units.

A set of five measures are obtained and reported in this section: (1) the average number of enemy units destroyed by each of the decentralized and centralized paradigms; (2) sensor and movement error measures for the two paradigms relative to the perfect decision vector; (3) average sensor error over all entities as a function of the communication delay; (4) average movement error over all entities as a function of the communication delay; and (5) quantitative evaluation of the communication requirements imposed by the two paradigms.

Figure 6.5 presents the first measure, namely, the average number of enemy units destroyed by the decentralized and centralized paradigms, as a function of τ_c. For the entire range of τ_c and for the large number of initial locations (approximately 50) of the blue and red forces, Figure 6.5 reveals that the decentralized paradigm is superior to the centralized scheme. For the lowest delay value $\tau_c = 1$ timestep, the decentralized paradigm exhibits an advantage of 1.3. The advantage increases to 3.667 for $\tau_c = 9$ timesteps, i.e., 5 enemy units are destroyed by the force using the decentralized paradigm for a loss of only 1.333 of its units.

While the results in Figure 6.5 clearly demonstrate the performance superiority of the distributed over the centralized paradigm, they lack insight into the quality of the decisions under the distributed paradigm. While the underlying algorithms of the decision-making entity in the centralized paradigm have access to the entire system state, the combination of (1) latency of the information received from its subordinates, (2) the delay resulting from the significant computational need, and (3) the latency of transmission of the decisions hinders generation of high-quality decisions. In contrast, while the decentralized paradigm successfully addresses issues (2) and (3), the lack of access to the total system state limits the quality of its decisions. To provide insight into the quality of the decisions, this chapter proposes a hypothetical entity, the Perfect Global Optimization Device (PGOD), which is capable of generating perfect decisions. By definition, PGOD transcends time in that it is capable of acquiring any and all knowledge at any spatial location in the system instantaneously, i.e., unaffected by the finite rate of propagation of

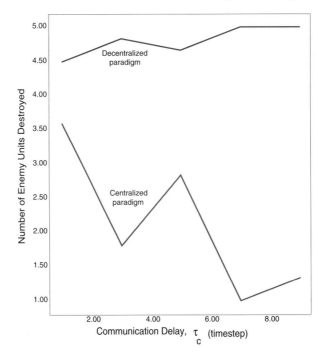

Fig. 6.5. Number of Enemy Units Destroyed under the Centralized and Decentralized Paradigms, as a Function of τ_c

information that characterizes the physical world. Thus, PGOD uses the perfect information and generates perfect decisions and while they may never be realized in the real world, they serve as the absolute standard for comparing the effectiveness of the distributed and centralized paradigms.

A series of experiments are designed with the blue and red forces implementing the decentralized and centralized paradigms. The decision vectors, computed by each of the n entities of the blue force at every timestep, $UD^i(t)$, are logged, and the overall decision vector for the entire system under the decentralized paradigm is expressed through $UD(t)$,

$$UD(t) = \sum_{i=1}^{i=n} UD^i(t) = \sum_{i=1}^{i=n} [UD_m^i(t), UD_s^i(t), UD_t^i(t)].$$

While the overall decision vector for the entire system for the centralized paradigm may be obtained from the leader of the red force, the sequence of decisions for the two paradigms is likely to be different, given the asynchronous nature of the decentralized paradigm. For consistency in comparing the decision vectors from the two paradigms, this chapter uses the sighting reports sent to the leader of the blue force by the friendly units to compute the corresponding centralized decision, $UC(t)$, at every timestep. However, in a true centralized paradigm, the decisions generated by the leader must be propagated to the individual entities for execution and, therefore, the corrected overall decision vector is given by $UC(t = T - \tau_c)$, where the delay from the leader to each of the entities is τ_c timesteps.

For the hypothetical entity PGOD, located at the blue leader, the state vectors of every entity and the sighting reports from the entities are assumed to be available to it instantaneously at time instant t, i.e., without incurring any propagation delay. PGOD employs the same algorithm as the centralized paradigm and computes the decision vector for each entity. These vectors are considered ideal because they are not subject to the latency inherent in the centralized paradigm and the decision process uses PGOD's knowledge of the total system state unlike the decentralized paradigm. The perfect decision vector is labeled $UI(t)$.

The second set of measures in this section consists of error measures for each of centralized ($E_c(t)$), corrected centralized ($E_{cc}(t)$), and decentralized ($E_d(t)$) decision vectors, relative to the perfect decision vector, as presented through expressions (6.11), (6.12), and (6.13), respectively. Thus, contrary to common belief that the traditional centralized paradigm generates globally optimum results, the PGOD analysis reveals the fundamental limitation that is inherent when a centralized algorithm controls an asynchronous, distributed, decision-making system.

$$E_c(t) = \sum_{i=1}^{i=n} E_c^i(t) \quad \text{where} \quad E_c^i(t) = \left| UI^i(t) - UC^i(t) \right|, \quad (6.11)$$

$$E_{cc}(t) = \sum_{i=1}^{i=n} E_{cc}^i(t) \quad \text{where} \quad E_{cc}^i(t) = \left| UI^i(t) - UC^i(t - \tau_c) \right|, \quad (6.12)$$

$$E_d(t) = \sum_{i=1}^{i=n} E_d^i(t) \quad \text{where} \quad E_d^i(t) = \left| UI^i(t) - UD^i(t) \right|. \quad (6.13)$$

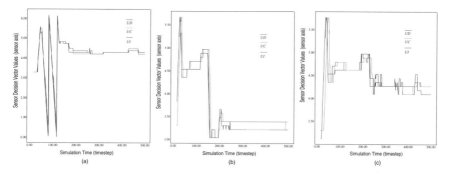

Fig. 6.6. Sensor Decision Vector Graph for an Entity under the Centralized and Distributed Paradigms and PGOD, as a Function of Time, for (a) $\tau_c = 1$ Timestep, (b) $\tau_c = 5$ Timesteps, and (c) $\tau_c = 9$ Timesteps

Figure 6.6(a) presents the sensor decision vector graph for an entity computed under each of the centralized and distributed paradigms and by PGOD,

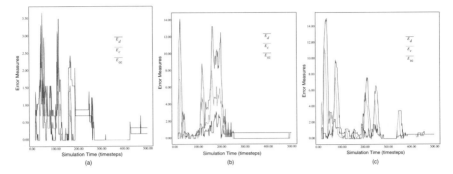

Fig. 6.7. Sensor Error Measures for an Entity for Centralized, Corrected Centralized, and Distributed Scenarios, as a Function of Time, for (a) $\tau_c = 1$ Timestep, (b) $\tau_c = 5$ Timesteps, and (c) $\tau_c = 9$ Timesteps

as a function of time, between 15 and 500 timesteps. The value of τ_c is set at 1 timestep. Figure 6.6(a) reveals that the graphs corresponding to $UD^i(t)$ and $UC^i(t)$ closely follow that of PGOD. Thus, the sensor decision vector graph for the decentralized paradigm closely tracks the perfect decision vector graph. The graph for the corrected centralized paradigm may be obtained by shifting the graph for $UC^i(t)$, shown in Figure 6.6(a), by one timestep, and would differ from that of PGOD.

As the value for τ_c increases from 5 to 9 timesteps, shown through Figures 6.6(b) and 6.6(c), the $UC^i(t)$ graph lags the $UI^i(t)$ graph considerably. The corrected centralized graphs that may be obtained through shifting the $UC^i(t)$ graph by 5 and 9 timesteps, respectively, would differ substantially from that of $UI^i(t)$. That is, the decision vector graph corresponding to the corrected centralized paradigm differs significantly from that of PGOD. In contrast, the decision vector graph corresponding to the decentralized paradigm, closely follows that of PGOD for large shifts in the sensor axis and differs only slightly for small and rapid changes in the sensor axis. A likely cause of this behavior is the relatively high communication delay value.

The data in Figure 6.6(a) through 6.6(c) are replotted in Figure 6.7(a) through 6.7(c) to present the sensor error measure for the centralized, corrected centralized, and distributed scenarios, also as a function of time. The graphs reveal that the error for the corrected centralized is larger than that for the decentralized paradigm and that the magnitude of the error margin increases with increasing values for τ_c.

Figure 6.8 presents the third measure, average sensor error over all entities, as a function of the communication delay, τ_c. The average error for the decentralized paradigm is observed to be relatively uniform, implying that the decentralized decisions closely track the perfect decisions. In contrast, the quality of decisions in the centralized paradigm deteriorate with increasing values of the communication delay.

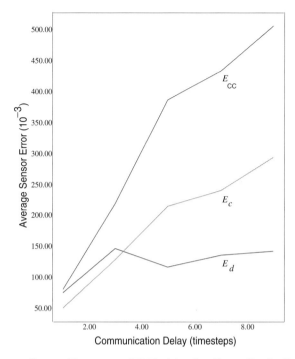

Fig. 6.8. Average Sensor Error over All Entities for Centralized, Corrected Centralized, and Distributed Scenarios, as a Function of τ_c

Figure 6.9 presents the fourth measure, average movement error over all entities, as a function of τ_c. The behaviors of the corrected centralized and distributed paradigm graphs are similar to that in Figure 6.8, further confirming the observation that the decentralized decisions closely track the perfect decisions.

Given that an integral component of the distributed paradigm is increased communication, the fifth measure aims at a quantitative evaluation of the communication. Measurements from the simulation indicate that the average number of bytes on the communications links are 289 and 292 per timestep for the decentralized and centralized paradigms, respectively. These correspond to link throughputs of 2.89 and 2.92 Kbytes/sec, respectively. The maximum throughputs required on any link in the decentralized and centralized paradigms are 16.08 Kbytes/sec and 21.44 Kbytes/sec, respectively. Thus, despite requiring additional communication links, the decentralized algorithm does not impose a higher average link throughput. The key reason is that, unlike the centralized algorithm where the communication is concentrated around the centralized leader, the communication subtask is distributed among all the links in the decentralized algorithm.

The results reported through the graphs up to Figure 6.9 assumed a constant value of 30,000 spatial units for the parameter INFORM_RANGE.

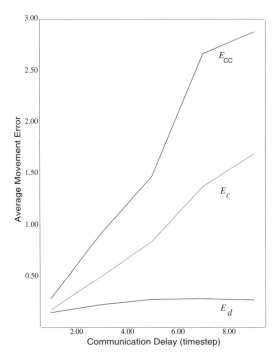

Fig. 6.9. Average Movement Error over All Entities for Centralized, Corrected Centralized, and Distributed Scenarios, as a Function of τ_c

When an enemy unit is sighted within INFORM_RANGE of the last known position of a friendly unit i, the sighting friendly unit j will propagate its sighting information to unit i. Therefore, as the value of the parameter IN-FORM_RANGE is decreased, the effective area of interest of the battlefield diminishes and communication is likely to decrease. However, the limited visual field of the battlefield is expected to increase the total sensor error. A set of experiments are designed wherein the value of INFORM_RANGE is decreased from 30,000 to 15,000 and 5,000 spatial units. For the decentralized paradigm, while the required average link capacities decrease from 2.89 Kbytes/sec to 2.71 Kbytes/sec and 1.94 Kbytes/sec, the total sensor error increases from 0.143126 to 0.140849 and 0.223081. Even at a relatively low value of INFORM_RANGE = 5,000 timesteps for $\tau_c = 5$, the error for the decentralized algorithm is less than the error of 0.2609 for the centralized algorithm.

As indicated earlier, the value of τ_p is set to 0 for all of the experiments in order to focus on the impact of communications delay on the quality of decisions. The assumption implies that the time to compute the cost function corresponding to a timestep is completed in less than a single timestep. Such an assumption may be realistic for the decentralized algorithm wherein the overall decisions are shared among the concurrent entities. However, for the centralized algorithm wherein the leader unit solely executes the cost function, the assumption may be inappropriate, particularly where the leader unit has to compute the decisions for a large number of subordinate entities. A nonzero value for τ_p would effectively require the graph for the corrected centralized algorithm to be shifted even further to the right by τ_p, thereby increasing the error. An informal estimate of the computational costs in the simulations using the Unix ps command reveals the following. For a total of 600 timesteps of the simulation run, the ratio of the computational time required by the centralized leader unit to that for each of the entities in the decentralized paradigm is 15:1.

7

Performance Analysis of ADDM Algorithms

7.1 Review of the Current Literature in Performance Analysis

The use of centralized algorithms to control systems has been well documented in the literature. In this paradigm, data from one or more sources are collected at a central site and a single processor uses it to compute the systemwide decisions through sequential execution. The range of centralized decision-making algorithms extends from the battlefield [20], scheduling trains in a railway network [21], inventory management [22], and highway management [23] to distributed federated databases [24]. However, with increasing system complexity, the computational burden on the central processor continues to increase, eventually leading to lower throughput and poor efficiency. In contrast, distributed algorithms promise higher throughput and efficiency through sharing the overall computational task among multiple concurrent processors. Markas, Royals, and Kanopoulos [25] report a distributed implementation of fault simulation of digital systems and note throughput improvements over the traditional centralized approach. The classification of distributed algorithms into synchronous and asynchronous categories was discussed in Chapter 1; the key principles are briefly recapitulated here. The synchronous distributed approach is characterized by the presence of a single control processor that schedules executions of all of the remaining processors. The presence of the sequential control node theoretically limits the performance advantage of the synchronous approach. As the number of processors is increased, the synchronization requirement imposed by the control node will effectively counteract the potential advantages of the multiple concurrent processors. ADDM algorithms permit, in theory, the exploitation of the maximal inherent parallelism of any given system. Therefore, it is critical to design and compute performance measures for ADDM algorithms in order to facilitate algorithm redesign to achieve the highest performance for the given system.

The concept of performance is well understood and enjoys widespread use. A general commonsense definition is presented by Ferrari [204], who defines performance as an indication of how well a system, already assumed to be correct, works. Tron and colleagues [28] argue that in parallel systems the performance metric must reflect the program, the machine, and the implementation strategies because it depends on each of them. Ronngren, Barriga, and Ayani [29] cite the need for a common benchmark suite to evaluate parallel algorithms. Gupta and Kumar [30] note that while the parallel execution time, speedup, and efficiency serve as well-known performance metrics, the key issue is identification of the parallel processing overheads, which sets a limit on the speedup for a given architecture, problem size, and algorithm. For their study in optimal overheads, they propose [30] minimization of the parallel execution time as the principal criterion. Brehm, Madhukar, Smirni, and Dowdy [32] propose to expand the list of metrics with computation and communication times. Kushwaha [33] proposes the use of expected user response time, system throughput, and average server utilization as metrics toward evaluating the performance of multiclient multiserver distributed systems. Braddock and colleagues [34] claim system availability and system throughput as two key metrics to characterize operational distributed systems. While Lecuivre and Song [35] suggest response time and resource load as the performance parameters, Kumar et al. [36] propose throughput, subject to minimal total cost for execution and interprocess communication. Arrouye [37], Clement and Quinn [38], and Kremien [39] stress scalability as a performance criteria for parallel systems. However, while Arrouye [37] fails to define the exact type of the parallel systems for the proposed criteria, the efforts of Clement and Quinn [38] are confined to data-parallel distributed algorithms, i.e., single-instruction multiple-data (SIMD) type programs, whose range of practical application is limited. Furthermore, unlike speedup, which is quantitative, scalability is a quasi-quantitative measure and it refers to the continued application of the core algorithm as the system grows. Performance scalability may be measured semiquantitatively for NIT systems, as reported by Iyer and Ghosh [72], through tracking a specific performance measure while all of the entities in the system are doubled, quadrupled, etc.

Speedup has been proposed in the literature as a metric for estimating the performance of parallel and distributed algorithms [27] [205] [30], parallel processor architectures [40], and networks [41]. The most common definition of speedup is the ratio of the execution time of the best known serial algorithm to the execution time of the parallel algorithm on a given number of concurrent processors. The execution time corresponding to a parallel execution is the longest of the CPU times required by any of the concurrent processors. For stochastic analysis of a distributed system [42], a number of serial and parallel executions are carried out, one for each stochastic input set, and for the speedup computation, the numerator and denominator are determined from the arithmetic mean of the corresponding individual execution times. For details on the issue of determining stochastic yet representative input traffic, the reader is referred to [14]. Frequently, for a given problem of constant size, a speedup graph is obtained by first partitioning the problem for a number of different sets of concurrent processors, executing them, and then computing the ratios of the serial execution time to the execution time from each parallel execution. The speedup graph may be used to study the overheads for a given problem and project the maximum number of processors that may be exploited advantageously. Ertel [43] complains that use of the mean execution time during stochastic simulation of parallel systems causes the loss of variance information relative to speedup. Ertel suggests the use of functional speedup. Barr and Hickman [44] claim that the effectiveness of speedup factor is eroded by testing biases, machine influences, and the effects of the tuning parameters. Wieland, Jefferson, and Reiher [45] show empirical evidence of bias in speedup and report its magnitude at 3.1 for concurrent theater-level simulation. Yan and Listgarten [46] state that the presence of software instrumentations to measure performance invariably exert adverse influence on the measures.

The efforts reported in [28] through [46] and [49] through [50] are generally applicable to data-parallel, i.e., SIMD, and synchronous-iterative distributed programs [47], both of which have a limited range of practical application in the real world that largely comprises asynchronous systems. In addition, the efforts in [28] through [46] are based on either pure theoretical assumptions or small-scale implementations, and they fail to address the unique characteristics of large-scale NIT systems. Capon [48] observes that understanding the behavior of asynchronous parallel programs is extremely difficult and is chiefly responsible for the limited parallelism reported in the literature. This chapter presents a fundamental framework for NIT systems. While it recognizes that diversity among NIT systems may require the development of novel and unique performance criteria, the framework in this chapter requires that absolute performance measures must be available for every such measure. The development of the framework reflects the author's experience in the design and development of large-scale NIT systems.

7.2 The Traditional Performance Metric: Speedup and Its Limitations

Speedup is defined as the ratio of the sequential execution time of the best known serial algorithm to the execution time of the parallel algorithm on a given number of concurrent processors. Although speedup may be measured and reported for a given number of concurrent processors, the greatest utility is derived from constructing the speedup graph, which is a plot of the speedup values corresponding to different numbers of concurrent processors used, subject to the problem size held constant. The speedup graph reflects the amenability of the problem to higher speedups by employing more concurrent processors.

In SIMD or data-parallel distributed programs, at each timestep, each of the concurrent processors simultaneously executes the same instruction or operation on different parts of the same data set. The task of design rule checking in a VLSI layout is ideally suited for SIMD programming. The results generated from the executions are usually exchanged between the processors prior to the next timestep. While increased performance is provided over sequential algorithms, the forced synchronization at each timestep, in general, lowers the performance significantly relative to an asynchronous algorithm. Furthermore, the practical application domain of SIMD programs is usually limited. In synchronous-iterative programs, although one or more subtasks may be executed concurrently by the processors, all processors must synchronize at the end of every timestep. Finite element analysis enjoys increased performance over sequential execution when performed utilizing synchronous-iterative algorithms. In both data-parallel and synchronous-iterative distributed programs, however, an increase in the number of processors to obtain higher speedup is generally confronted by increased synchronization overhead, thereby limiting the speedup in most problems.

This chapter observes that most physical processes and many man-made large-scale processes are asynchronous in nature. In such processes, the entities execute independently and interact asynchronously, i.e., at irregular intervals of time. The use of asynchronous algorithms to model such systems offers the potential of exploiting the maximal parallelism inherent in the problem. Unlike the data-parallel and synchronous-iterative algorithms, there is no forced synchronization in asynchronous algorithms. In the field of computer-aided design of digital systems, simulation of behavior models [27] and fault simulation of digital systems [206] employ asynchronous, distributed algorithms. Speedup values are determined relative to a uniprocessor implementation and speedup graphs are reported for both [27] and [206]. Iyer and Ghosh [72] and Ghosh [125] report, respectively, the design of asynchronous, distributed algorithms for railway networks and national-level banking and present the corresponding speedup graphs.

The key limitations of the notion of speedup are fourfold. First, in all of the research efforts [27] through [72] and [206], the uniprocessor implementations required significant CPU times and were observed to be excruciatingly slow for large-scale problems. In addition, significant difficulty was experienced with the uniprocessor implementations of the large-scale problems due to their severe memory requirements, leading to failure in a few cases. In a distributed simulation of a large-scale BISDN network [193], wherein a total of 3.2 million ATM cells propagate through the network, a uniprocessor implementation was deemed impractical to design and execute. Second, in a number of complex real-world NIT systems, including the command and control of military battlefields and navigation of vehicles on highways, the entities are distributed geographically. Clearly, the design and implementation of the corresponding uniprocessor approaches are unnatural and, therefore, the notion of speedup is irrelevant. In a feasibility study of centralized traffic management in White

Plains, New York, Nynex [23] noted that route guidance required an average cellular phone call of 5 to 10 minutes, where the system included a limited set of test cars. Nynex concluded that while it was already too costly, the cost for route guidance would be even higher for a realistic system with thousands of vehicles. Third, the notion of speedup uses as its basis the uniprocessor implementation. Because the evidence that the uniprocessor implementation is either optimal or the absolute best is not obvious, the speedup factor conveys only a relative sense of improvement. Fourth, while speedup reflects a ratio of the execution times, it conveys no information relative to other characteristics of the distributed system. For instance, the quality of the choice of the routes by the individual trains in the distributed railway scheduling scheme [72] is an important performance criteria but is not reflected in the speedup graph.

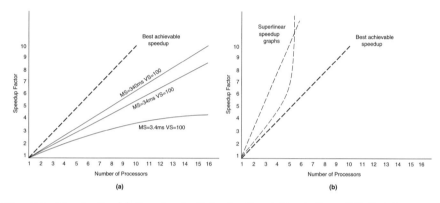

Fig. 7.1. Graphs for (a) Speedup in Behavior-Level Simulation of Digital Systems, (b) Superlinear Speedup

Figure 7.1(a) presents the reported speedup graphs for asynchronous, distributed, behavior-level simulation of a digital system [27]. Figure 7.1(b) presents the best achievable speedup graph and representative superlinear speedup graphs. Clearly, in Figure 7.1(a), the speedup graph lies between the X-axis and the best achievable speedup graph. Markas, Royals, and Kanopoulos [25] report superlinear speedup values during fault simulation on a heterogeneous network of workstations connected through a local area network. Mechoso, Farrara, and Spahr [207] propose to develop global climate models and achieve superlinear speedup on the gigabit network testbed through masking communications latency with computations. Gropengiesser [208] reports superlinear speedups using a master-slave parallelization scheme to search for the ground state energy. Kim and Nang [209] report superlinear speedups during distributed simulation of a parallel genetic algorithm model based on the Island Population Model (IPM) and the Stepping Stone Population Model (SSPM), on a Fujitsu AP1000, a distributed-memory multiprocessor.

To establish the theoretical range of speedup values, we will start with an analysis of the basic behaviors of distributed algorithms. Real-world problems may permit the design and development of two major classes of distributed models. There is a third class of models, which will be discussed later. In the first class, the distributed model may consist of N decomposed concurrent tasks $(N \gg 1)$, where the tasks do not require any communication among themselves. Because the longest execution time of the concurrent tasks determines the parallel execution time, this chapter assumes identical computational load for all tasks and identical computational power for all processors to achieve the shortest possible execution time. The tasks may be executed by N concurrent processors, yielding a speedup graph that consists of a straight line through the point coordinates (1,1), with a slope of 45°. This is the best speedup achievable and, contrary to the claim by Mechoso, Farrara, and Spahr [207], it may not be superseded even if all essential intertask communication is masked successfully through computations. Most practical problems, however, will invariably require intertask communication, with the degree of communication defined by the nature of the problem. Thus, the second class of distributed model includes intertask communication. As the number of decomposed concurrent tasks (N) increases, the intertask communication overhead may either increase or decrease, although it has been generally observed to increase. Even if communication exhibits a decreasing trend with an increase in N, the overhead will never fall below zero, implying that the best achievable speedup may not be exceeded.

Assume for the moment that superlinear speedup, as reported in [25] [207] [208] [209], is achievable and that the standard definition of speedup has been applied consistently. That is, the execution time from the best available sequential algorithm has been used in the numerator. This chapter extends the philosophy embedded in the standard definition of speedup to speedup graphs in that every distributed implementation, i.e., for $N = 2, 3, \ldots$ reflects either the same underlying distributed algorithm or the best available distributed algorithm. The second law of thermodynamics, which encapsulates the law of conservation of energy, implies that heat (or some form of energy) is needed to perform work and eliminates the possibility of a perpetual motion machine. In a direct analogy with the thermodynamic world, computers draw electrical energy from the power supplies and deliver computational work in the form of executing high-level programs and microinstructions. It is reasonable to assume that computer designers are committed to maximizing the efficiency of conversion of electrical energy into computational work. This chapter also makes the logical assumption that the uniprocessor and each of the concurrent processors are characterized with the same potential efficiency, all other factors being identical. In general, faster devices implying faster computation require greater energy. For example, emitter coupled logic (ECL) devices are faster and consume more energy than complementary metal-oxide semiconductor (CMOS) devices. Consider a distributed system with two concurrent processors, i.e., $N = 2$. A superlinear speedup exceeding 2.0 implies that the distributed scheme generates greater than twice the computational work while consuming only twice the electrical energy of that of the uniprocessor. This implies one of the following possibilities: (1) the distributed scheme generates computational work without the corresponding consumption of electrical energy or (2) each processor delivers a higher efficiency than the uniprocessor. Possibility (1) implies the existence of a perpetual computing machine, which violates the fundamental law of conservation of energy. Therefore, the assumption that superlinear speedup is achievable is wrong. Consider possibility (2). Given complex large-scale problems, conceivably, the uniprocessor implementation may experience increased swapping and paging stemming from main memory limitations, which may lower its net efficiency. In contrast, as a result of the sharing of the computational task by the two concurrent processors of the distributed implementation, the individual processors of the distributed scheme may not experience the swapping and paging problem of the uniprocessor, despite similar main memory sizes. The experience related by Markas, Royals, and Kanopoulos [25] fits this scenario precisely. They report superlinear speedup values corresponding to a limited number of processors, which gradually decays as the number of processors is increased. However, as the value of N is increased, there will exist a value of N such that the main memory limitation will affect two consecutive distributed implementations corresponding to $N = i$ and $N = 2i$ ($i \gg 1$) similarly, implying identical efficiencies for both implementations. Thus, possibility (2) may not be sustained and, again, the assumption that superlinear speedup graphs are achievable is wrong.

There is the third class of distributed model, where the real-world problem includes significant communication and the nature of the communication undergoes major changes as one migrates from the uniprocessor to a distributed paradigm. In railway networks [72], every train communicates with a central dispatcher in the centralized scheduling scheme. The efficiency of the centralized processor is slow, given that it has to connect, one at a time, to each train. In addition, on the average, the trains are likely to be far from the dispatcher, implying long communication delays and, consequently, a slower rate of decisions generated by the dispatcher. Assume that the single central dispatcher is represented by C_1. Consider a hypothetical distributed scheme where two dispatchers, D_1 and D_2, are used in one implementation and three dispatchers, K_1, K_2, and K_3, are used in a different implementation. While all trains communicate with C_1 in the centralized scheme, in the first distributed scheme, select subsets of trains communicate with each of D_1 and D_2 in addition to the communication between D_1 and D_2. Similarly, in the second distributed scheme, K_1, K_2, and K_3 interact among themselves in addition to select subsets of trains communicating with each of K_1, K_2, and K_3. The communication delays between the trains and the corresponding dispatchers may decrease progressively, due to closer proximity, as the number of dispatchers increases, thereby lowering the communication overhead. In contrast, the increased interactions between the dispatchers are likely to add higher overhead.

The trade-off between the opposing forces will determine the exact nature of the linearity of the speedup graph.

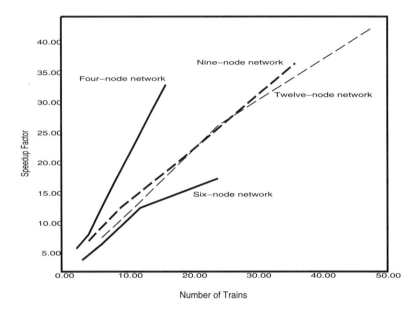

Fig. 7.2. Performance of DARYN, a Distributed Scheduling Approach for Railway Networks

DARYN [72] may be viewed as the ultimate hypothetical distributed scheme wherein the notion of central dispatcher is completely eliminated and the trains communicate with the local stations, as they navigate autonomously toward their ultimate destinations. As a result, the communication overhead is lower in DARYN relative to the central dispatcher scheme, and this gives rise to superlinear speedup plots. Figure 7.2 presents speedup plots for a total of four systems, 4-node, 6-node, 9-node, and 12-node networks. Although the number of trains inserted into a system is shown along the x-axis, the number of processors utilized by a system equals the corresponding number of nodes. Uniprocessor implementations are developed corresponding to each system and, for a given DARYN system, the parallel execution time divides the corresponding uniprocessor execution time to generate the speedup measures plotted along the y-axis. Thus, the plots are not strictly speedup graphs because the problem size differs between the 4-node, 6-node, 9-node, and 12-node DARYN implementations. In Figure 7.2 a speedup exceeding 45 is obtained for the 12-node implementation, which employs only 12 processors. The apparent superlinearity is merely a reflection of the strategic change in the nature of communications; it does not imply free computational work, i.e., without the corresponding expenditure of energy. It is argued that for a real-world NIT system, such as railway networks, it is natural to employ ADDM algorithms such as DARYN. Such algorithms have transcended speedup as a performance metric. The comparison with a central dispatcher scheme and the computation of the speedup plots are both unnatural and without meaning.

7.3 A Fundamental Framework for Evaluating Performance of NIT Systems

Under control of the ADDM algorithm, the constituent entities of the NIT system collectively and cooperatively solve the challenges posed by the NIT problem through decentralized decision making. The potential benefits include scalability, high throughput, and robustness. Given our current knowledge and experience, although all NIT systems bear a common set of traits enumerated earlier, there is great diversity among such systems, and every NIT system is unique. For a given problem, the corresponding ADDM algorithm must be designed and developed, where possible, from first principles. It is, therefore, logical to expect the performance criteria for each ADDM algorithm to be unique. This chapter proposes a fundamental framework that recognizes the need to develop novel performance criteria, possibly unique, for every NIT system. A designer's criteria for a given problem may be very different from the parallel execution time, speedup, efficiency, and computation and communication times. Chow, Bicknell, McCaughey, and Syed's [210] proposal to use user's desires, such as restoration time and the use of fewer spares during link restoration in a communication system as the important performance metrics, is very appropriate. Conversely, the proposal to implement a common benchmark suite [29] may not be relevant.

For instance, consider the proposed decentralized approach to military command, control, and communications against the traditional command hierarchy Lee and Ghosh [20] propose, and utilize the measure of enemy kill rate relative to the number of friendly units destroyed. Although not proposed in [20], a conceivable measure may consist of minimizing the length of engagement. The measures are generated corresponding to two key scenarios: (1) engagement in battle and (2) withdrawal in the face of overwhelming enemy superiority. The simulation casts two opposing forces—blue and red—against one another, where the blue and red forces implement, respectively, the decentralized and centralized approaches. Each force consists of three platoons of five tanks each, a company leader tank, and two long-range artillery units. Because both approaches execute for the same length of simulation time, the traditional speedup metric is irrelevant. Table 7.1 presents the cumulative number of friendly units destroyed during a deliberate engagement, the number of tank and artillery firings, the number of enemy units destroyed through tank firings, and the number of enemy units destroyed by artillery firings. Table 7.2 presents corresponding data during withdrawal in the face of overwhelming enemy superiority. The contents of Tables 7.1 and 7.2 constitute the performance of the system. The absolute best performance would consist of killing all 15 enemy tanks without losing any friendly tanks in Scenario 1 and sacrificing no friendly tanks in Scenario 2.

	Blue Force	Red Force
Units destroyed	4 (22%)	12 (67%)
Times tank weapon fired	26	23
Times artillery fired	20	15
Enemy destroyed by tanks	8	3
Enemy destroyed by artillery	4	1

Table 7.1. Summary of Performance Measures for Decentralized Military Command and Control during Deliberate Engagement

	Blue Force	Red Force
Units destroyed	1 (17%)	0 (0%)
Times tank weapon fired	0	0
Times artillery fired	0	6
Enemy destroyed by tanks	0	0
Enemy destroyed by artillery	0	1

Table 7.2. Summary of Performance Measures for Decentralized Military Command and Control during Withdrawal in the Face of Overwhelming Enemy Superiority

The framework requires that corresponding to each criterion, the absolute or ideal performance standard must be computed. The standard must be an intrinsic function of the problem, independent of the computing infrastructure. It may be obtained through a comprehensive set of two approaches, A or B, as elaborated later.

A. For many NIT systems, the ideal performance standard, theoretically possible, may be determined automatically, based on the inherent nature of the problem and regardless of whether the underlying system employs a centralized or ADDM algorithm. For instance, consider the behavior-level simulation of digital designs [27], where the length of execution of a distributed system, expressed through speedup, is a performance metric. The absolute performance standard refers to the best achievable speedup graph. As a second example, in the DICAF [11] system for autonomous route guidance, the ideal travel time for each vehicle using its desired speed of travel, from origin to destination, in the absence of any other vehicle in the system, serves as the absolute performance metric.

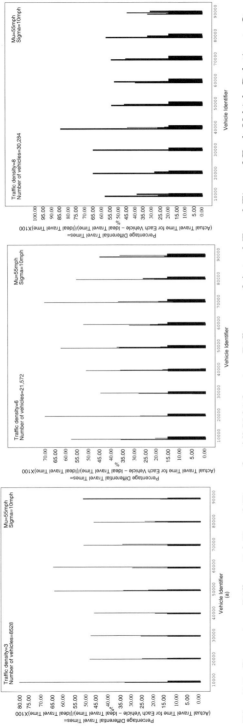

Fig. 7.3. Percentage Differential Travel Times for All Vehicles, i.e., Difference of Actual Travel Time of Each Vehicle Relative to Its Ideal Travel Time as a Fraction of the Ideal Travel Time, for (a) Density 3, (b) Density 6, and (c) Density 8.

Figure 7.3(a) through 7.3(c) plot the percentage differential travel time along the y-axis for every vehicle in DICAF, for density values 3, 6, and 8, respectively. A total of more than 30,000 vehicles corresponds to the density value of 8. The x-axis represents the unique vehicle identifiers that range from 10,000 to 90,000. The percentage differential travel time for a vehicle is computed as ((actual travel time for a vehicle − ideal travel time)/(ideal travel time) × 100). For a vehicle, the actual travel time is the cumulative sum of the travel times between every distributed traffic management center (DTMC) pair in its route during the simulation. By definition, the percentage differential travel time for every vehicle must be a positive percentage, i.e., greater than or equal to 0%, and it reflects the travel time that the corresponding vehicle requires in excess of the absolute minimum. The average and standard deviation value pairs for density values 3, 6, and 8 are obtained as {1.89%, 6.09%}, {1.85%, 5.71%}, and {2.12%, 6.14%}, respectively. Thus, with more than 30,000 vehicles inserted into DICAF, the average vehicle's travel time is only 2.12% higher than the absolute best, attesting to DICAF's extraordinary performance.

A third example refers to the RYNSORD approach, detailed in Chapter 3. A brief description is recapitulated here. RYNSORD is a novel decentralized algorithm with soft reservation for efficient scheduling and congestion mitigation in railway networks. In it, every train employs lookahead to dynamically replan its route. Thus, a train, currently at position X and headed for the ultimate destination position Y first requests and reserves N tracks, i.e., the lookahead, ahead of its current position for use at appropriate future times. The N tracks are chosen either along the shortest path or an alternate shortest path where the tracks of the two paths are mutually exclusive. The train issues two sets of requests concurrently for the tracks on the two paths. After it has been granted reservations, the train selects the path that promises the quickest arrival time at the final destination. The train moves through the N tracks and, upon completion, it again requests and reserves N subsequent tracks ahead of itself. The process continues until the train reaches its destination, Y. When a train issues a request, it propagates a time window to the appropriate station as opposed to a specific time instant in the traditional case. The time window is based on many factors, including the speed of the train, the length of tracks, and the train's expected sequential progress through the path. The station arbitrates, taking into consideration requests from other trains, and grants reservation for the most appropriate time slot. Thus, the reservation process may be characterized by less abruptness and greater flexibility in negotiation between the trains and stations. This characteristic is termed *soft reservations* here, in contrast to the traditional, rigid, *hard reservations*. Under hard reservations, a train may fail to acquire reservations for all N tracks and, in that case, it either has to try alternate paths or retry the failed path later. Under soft reservations, a train negotiating for N tracks will, in general, always succeed because it accepts reservations of individual tracks as long as the time instants for the corresponding tracks are within the specified time window and monotonically increasing. In negotiating and reserving N tracks, a train competes for resources with other trains in the vicinity at that time, in essence, utilizing the most recent congestion information. Furthermore, at intervals of N tracks, every train dynamically refines its route toward Y using the most recent information available to itself at the time of decision making.

To measure the effectiveness of RYNSORD, the absolute standard refers to the computation of the ideal path that the train would take, from origin to destination, if every train was assumed to be the only one in the system. Clearly, in the presence of other trains in the system, a specific train may not succeed in acquiring reservation for and traveling on the tracks along its ideal shortest path. RYNSORD chooses to use the following performance criteria. It compares the number of hops in the actual path taken to that in the ideal path. Figure 7.4 shows a plot of the hop (track) distribution of trains, i.e., the number of tracks, ranging from 1 to 20, that are used by the trains to reach their destinations, corresponding to low input traffic density. Figure 7.4 shows three graphs, one corresponding to the ideal scenario and two relative to RYNSORD for lookahead values of 2 and 4. The graphs corresponding to RYNSORD, show that the hop distribution closely follows the ideal scenario. That is, despite 484 trains competing for tracks, RYNSORD's distributed dynamic routing with soft reservation yields results that are close to ideal.

B. A fundamental issue with NIT systems, in contrast to centralized systems, may be expressed as follows. The underlying algorithm of the decision-making entity in the centralized system has access to the entire system state. However, the combination of (1) the latency of the data received from the geographically dispersed entities at the central decision maker, (2) the delay resulting from the significant computational need, and (3) the latency of execution of the decisions by the geographically dispersed entities, hinders the generation of high-quality decisions under the centralized paradigm. In contrast, under control of the ADDM algorithm, each geographically dispersed entity determines and executes the decisions concurrently. Thus, while issues (2) and (3) are addressed successfully, the lack of access to the total system state is likely to adversely impact the quality of the decisions in NIT systems. To provide insight into the quality of the decisions, the concept of a Perfect Global Optimization Device (PGOD), a hypothetical entity capable of generating perfect decisions, was introduced in Chapter 6. Here, a subset of the discussion from Chapter 6 is briefly reproduced for the purpose of comparative analysis. By definition, PGOD transcends time in that it is capable of acquiring any and all knowledge at any spatial location in the system instantaneously, i.e., unaffected by the finite rate of propagation of information that characterizes the physical world. Thus, PGOD utilizes the perfect information and generates perfect decisions, and while they may never be realized in the real world, they serve as the absolute standard for comparing the effectiveness of NIT systems and even centralized systems.

Under MFAD, the overall decision task is distributed among the individual tanks, which are geographically dispersed in the battlefield. In contrast, in the centralized paradigm, all tanks send sighting data to the centralized commander and first receive and then execute the decisions propagated from the commander. A series of experiments are designed with the blue and red forces implementing the MFAD and the centralized approach, respectively. The decision vectors computed by each of the n entities at every timestep are logged, and the overall decision vector for the entire system is expressed through $UD(t)$. $UD(t)$, in turn, is synthesized from its subcomponents—movement and sensor decision vectors. For consistency in comparing the decision vectors from the two paradigms, the sighting reports sent to the leader of the blue force by the friendly units are used to compute the corresponding centralized decision, $UC(t)$, at every timestep:

$$UD(t) = \sum_{i=1}^{i=n} UD^i(t) = \sum_{i=1}^{i=n} [UD_m^i(t), UD_s^i(t), UD_t^i(t)].$$

For the hypothetical entity PGOD, the state vectors of every entity and the sighting reports from the entities are assumed to be available to it instantaneously at time instant t, i.e., without incurring any propagation delay. PGOD employs the same algorithm as the centralized approach and computes the decision vector for each entity. These vectors are considered ideal because they are not subject to the latency inherent in the centralized paradigm and the decision process uses PGOD's knowledge of the total system state, unlike the decentralized paradigm. The perfect decision vector is labeled $UI(t)$.

Figure 7.5 presents the sensor decision vector for an entity computed under each of the centralized and distributed paradigms and by PGOD, as a function of time, between 15 and 500 timesteps. The value of τ_c, is set at 1 timestep, where τ_c represents the communication delay between the leader and the entities in the centralized paradigm as well as the delay between the peer entities in the decentralized paradigm. Figure 7.5 reveals that the graphs corresponding to $UD^i(t)$ and $UC^i(t)$ closely follow that of PGOD. Thus, the sensor decision vector for the decentralized paradigm closely tracks the perfect decision vector. The graph for the corrected centralized paradigm may be obtained by shifting the graph for $UC^i(t)$, shown in Figure 7.5, by one timestep, and would differ from that of PGOD.

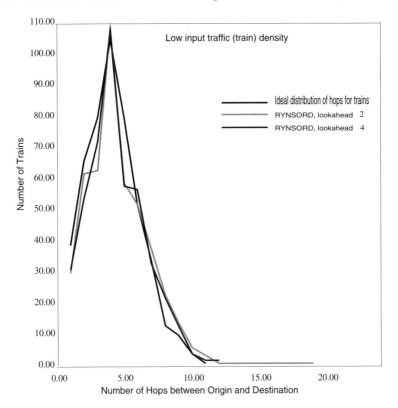

Fig. 7.4. Distribution of Actual Number of Hops for Trains in RYNSORD vs. Ideal Distribution

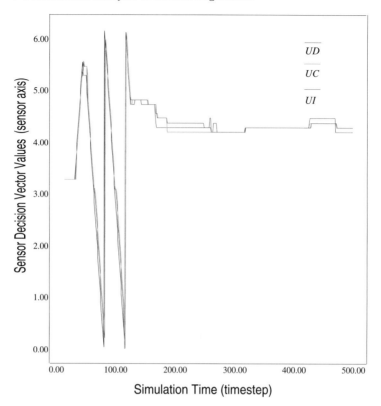

Fig. 7.5. Sensor Decision Vector for an Entity under the Centralized and Distributed Paradigms and PGOD, as a Function of Time, for $\tau_c = 1$ Timestep

Stability of ADDM Algorithms

8.1 Review of the Current Literature in Stability of Distributed Systems

In the literature, the most comprehensive treatment of stability occurs in the disciplines of physics and control systems. The motivation for defining stability is well stated by Stewart in the foreword of the 1992 translation of A.M. Lyapunov's *The General Problem of the Stability of Motion* [211] by editor A.T. Fuller. Stewart notes that Lyapunov recognized that there are many distinct concepts of stability—different ways to formalize the idea that small disturbances lead to small changes in the motion of a physical body. This general concept has applied to a wide range of disciplines, from engineering to political science. In each case, however, the definition has been adapted to the area to which it is being applied. This chapter will take the same liberties and apply it to complex software and hardware systems. However, it will remain motivated by the concept that small disturbances lead to small changes in the motion.

Chen [212] describes three types of stability in control theory: (1) bounded-input bounded-output; (2) marginal stability; and (3) asymptotic stability. Control theory defines them in terms of differential equations, state-space, and transfer function models.

8.1.1 Bounded-Input Bounded-Output Stability

Bounded-input bounded-output (BIBO) stability is defined as stability where for every bounded input the output is also bounded. A bounded function has a magnitude less than some constant for all time.

8.1.2 Marginal Stability

Marginal stability is generally referred to as Lyapunov's definition of stability, and Fuller [211] notes in his introduction that this stemmed from his interest in astronomical problems. For many problems, a perturbation may not be fully dissipated, but it continues to persist, within some bounds, for all time. For example, a particle in a circular trajectory around a point continually oscillates around it and is, therefore, marginally stable. This definition of stability is analogous to the definition of marginal stability adopted here.

8.1.3 Asymptotic Stability

In contrast to marginal stability, *asymptotic stability* is stability where the perturbation is eventually dissipated. Letov [213], in explaining Lyapunov's second theorem, notes that, under asymptotic stability, the disturbed motion converges to an undisturbed state as time progresses to infinity. Control systems engineers find this definition most appealing and it constitutes the basis of the definition of *strong stability* here.

Casavant and Kuhl [214] regret that it is difficult to apply control theory directly to distributed systems in that the mathematical methods generally used are difficult to apply to distributed systems. The difficulty lies in the complex interactions within a distributed system, which defy attempts to describe their generally nonlinear behavior through a set of differential equations or transfer functions unless significant simplifications are assumed. In contrast, this chapter adopts the approach that control theory is a valuable step in analyzing the properties of distributed systems, even if the accuracy of the evaluation depends on the impact of the simplifications. Many of the basic concepts of control theory apply even where the rigorous mathematical foundations fail to apply.

In the discipline of distributed systems, the issue of stability is discussed relative to the properties of self-stabilization, correctness, i.e., absence of deadlock, robustness, fault-tolerance, and quality of service.

8.1.4 Self-Stabilization

The study of self-stabilization in distributed systems was introduced by Dijkstra in 1973. He wrote: "I call a system 'self-stabilizing' when, regardless of its initial state, it is guaranteed to arrive at a legitimate state in a finite number of steps" [215]. Thus, self-stabilization implies that the system is robust enough to recover from an illegal state. *Legitimate state* is defined by Dijkstra [216] in terms of *privileges*, which are predicates based on a process's own state and that of its immediate neighbors. There are four requirements for a legitimate state:

1. One or more privileges are present.
2. Each possible move brings the system to another legitimate state. A *move* is the act of going to a new state based on the previous state and the states of one's neighbors.
3. Each privilege must be in at least one legitimate state.

4. For any pair of legitimate states there is a sequence of moves from one to the other.

Thus, a self-stabilizing system is one in which legitimate and illegitimate states have been identified and the system obeys the preceding definition. There is a difficulty in finding realistic systems that conform to this definition of legitimate states and privileges. Work has been done in areas such as self-stabilizing approaches to the dining philosophers problem [217], using only two-state machines for self-stabilization [101], applying self-stabilization to other areas [218] [219], and on the communication and computational cost [220]. The definition of privileges as predicates lends itself to mutual exclusion-type problems. While this includes a range of problems that are of interest, it is somewhat restrictive. An additional problem is that this definition is based on the identification of specific states and the identification of which global states are legitimate and which are not. This is a very difficult problem, as the set of possible states can be enormous for a large and complex system.

A more general definition, without the specific definition of privileges, is given by Awerbuch and Varghese [221]. They wrote: "Self-stabilization formalizes the following intuitive goal: *despite a history of catastrophic failures, once catastrophic failures stop, the system should stabilize to correct behavior without manual intervention.*" A catastrophic fault is defined as where the global state has been arbitrarily corrupted. This definition is a much more practical one, yet it goes well beyond Dijkstra's definition. They only become the same if we define "correct behavior" to be a legitimate state. The definition proposed here espouses this intuitive goal but is not limited to corruptions in state. Awerbuch's work focuses on noninteractive systems and approaches self-stabilization through periodically checking correctness and performing a reexecution whenever a fault has been found. In contrast, the RYNSORD system continuously interacts with the environment and may not be stopped and reexecuted due to practical considerations.

8.1.5 Stable Properties

Related to this model of a distributed system is the definition of *stable properties* by Chandy and Lamport [222]. They note that if y is a predicate and a stable property of a distributed system D, then in a computation of D, once y is true, it remains true for the remainder of the computation. Other researchers including Venkatesan and Dathan [223] and Garg and Waldecker [224] use stable "predicate" rather than property. The two examples provided in [222] are that "computation has terminated" and "the system is deadlocked." Additionally, a stable property can be defined for only a phase of an algorithm, that is, a subset of the entire execution of the program. An example of this is an algorithm that requires computation in one phase to terminate before commencing the next phase. So detection of this termination, a stable property, would be a critical element of the algorithm. The detection of stable properties, especially for termination and deadlock detection, has been the subject of considerable research. However, this definition of stable properties is very different in that it deals with properties defined as predicates of the system while the definition proposed here deals with stability in a systemwide perspective. For instance, deadlock is considered to be a stable property in [222]. In contrast, in this chapter, if a system were to deadlock, it would result in the system being unstable. This apparent contradiction reflects the view that system stability is based on bounding the error in a system and that a deadlocked system is a case of infinite error. The assumption here is that the system is not designed to deadlock, as is the case with RYNSORD and most practical systems, so this is a characteristic of an unstable system.

8.1.6 Robustness

Robustness is the ability to maintain correct behavior despite changes in the system. Schreiber [225] makes the distinction between robustness and fail-soft behavior by the types of errors; for robustness they are errors in the inputs and for fail-soft behavior they are faults in the system. Stankovic [226] offers a different definition, stating that "in the computer science literature, robustness normally refers to the ability of a system to handle failures." The disagreement lies in the scope of the definition. Schreiber's definition is limited to errors in the input while Stankovic describes it in terms of "failures." Meyer [227] identifies four properties for distributed real-time systems: (1) concurrency, (2) timeliness, (3) fault-tolerance, and 4) degradable performance in the presence of faults. In control theory, a robust system is one that performs correctly despite perturbations in its state. This chapter is concerned with the performance impact of both failures as well as changes in input patterns. Perturbations do not necessarily imply a failure but represent any changes in the normal operating environment, and therefore, the definition proposed here encompasses robustness, fail-soft behavior, and degradable performance.

8.1.7 Fault-Tolerance

Fault-tolerance is concerned with making the system resilient against failures, which is fundamentally different from the concerns of this chapter. The concern of stability is the performance after the fault, not how to recover from the fault. For example, suppose a system uses a replicated database to provide fault-tolerance. If the original primary unit fails, then the secondary takes over once the failure is detected. The period of time between the original failure and the recovery is considered the *perturbation duration*. However, the secondary unit may provide a degraded level of service; thus the overall performance of the system, while adequate, may be less than it was before the failure. This is defined as *marginally stable*. If the system, while using the secondary database, is able to provide the same performance as with the primary, then the system is *strongly stable*. Finally, if the secondary database is unable to handle the workload and the performance degrades as some function of time, it is declared *unstable*.

8.1.8 Quality of Service

In [228] Garg et al. have defined stability for distributed applications. They have also adopted a performance perspective for stability and have chosen to use the quality of service (QoS) provided to the user as their performance index. They define a stable distributed application as one where the QoS is bounded for all time, including during the perturbation. The definition is limited in that QoS attributes do not relate to RYNSORD and other systems and the error during a perturbation may be unbounded.

This chapter derives inspiration from marginal and asymptotic stability. Its aim is to present a conceptually different definition of stability, one based on the issue of performance, not correctness. The objective is to provide a practical methodology to aid in the advancement of NIT systems.

8.2 Formal Definition of Stability in NIT Systems

This section introduces the concept of stability and presents a definition. Although it may apply to a broader range of distributed systems, the proposed definition is restricted strictly to NIT systems. While the nature of the computation and interaction in every NIT system may be unique, the computational model for all systems includes two fundamental inherent characteristics, asynchronicity and concurrency. The combination of these characteristics strongly resists any attempt to develop accurate and realistic characterizations of NIT systems using the current mathematical structures. Given this difficulty, this chapter adopts an engineering approach and presents a definition of, or equivalently, a methodology for measuring the stability of NIT systems based on performance and that is practically usable. As discussed earlier, the current definitions of stability either do not apply to NIT systems or yield metrics that have limited practical use.

The intent here is to define stability in terms of performance criteria to provide performance guarantees for the system in a dynamically changing environment. Ferrari [204] defines performance as an indication of how well a system, already assumed to be correct, works. Typical examples would include the output rate and system delay. Thus, a critical concept for NIT systems is a need for a quantitative error measurement, which is referred to as a user-defined measurable quantity. The three requirements for the error criteria are as follows: (1) it is a quantifiable value; (2) conceptually, it represents the deviation of the system from some ideal, so the ideal must also be quantifiable; and (3) the user desires to minimize the error quantity, a logical goal. The definition of error will depend solely on the application problem. Therefore, it is loosely defined as a user-defined measurable quantity; an exact definition is not presented here.

Although the notion of convergence time may provide valuable information on how fast the perturbation dissipates, it is not included in the definition of stability here, for two reasons. First, the concept of strong stability is based on Lyapunov's asymptotic stability, which requires the perturbation to disappear as time progresses to infinity. The inclusion of a time bound, T, would imply that a system that converges at $T + 1$ or later instead of within T is unstable, which would contradict the premise of asymptotic stability. Second, the objective of this effort is a metric where the difference between a strongly stable and an unstable system is clearly pronounced in an engineering sense. The introduction of time bounds would cause stability to assume a more subtle nature. The aim of this chapter, in essence, is to address the question, Will the system ever recover from the perturbation? If it partially recovers, it is marginally stable. If it recovers completely, it is strongly stable. If it will never recover, it is unstable. The author hopes that this definition will serve as a good starting point and stimulate further discussion within the community.

Definition 1. *Error quantity*: a quantitative measurement of the system's performance, expressed as $error = |ideal - actual|$. Both *ideal* and *actual* must be measurable or computable.

Definition 2. The *equilibrium* or *steady state* for a distributed system is defined simply as the operational environment, i.e., a set of inputs and system resources, under which the system operates when the error is bounded by some finite constant for all time. The exact magnitude of this bound is unspecified except that it must be less than some constant, which is less than infinity.

Definition 3. The *equilibrium* or *steady state* (a quantitative representation of the preceding definition): if a system exists in a steady state then the error of the system, e, is defined by $e < K < \infty$ for all time where K is an arbitrary constant.

The primary focus of defining stability is in what happens to the system, in a steady state, following a change in the environment, termed perturbations, that are inevitable in a real-world environment. The changes are classified into two categories: system-level perturbations and input perturbations. System-level perturbations are generally those considered faults or failures. These include all forms of hardware failures and the arbitrary corruption of local states. Input perturbations are changes in the manner or rate of the input into a system as in the RYNSORD system.

A perturbation is described in terms of the *assumption* it has violated. An assumption is described as a characteristic of the steady-state operating environment. Although multiple perturbations may conceivably affect the system simultaneously, here, a perturbation is limited to a single change in the environment.

Definition 4. A *perturbation* is a violation of an assumption specified by the nature of the violation, the magnitude when applicable, and two time values: t_{pert} is the time at which the perturbation occurs and $t_{\text{pert\_end}}$ signifies the end of the changes to the system. Also $t_{\text{pert\_dur}} = t_{\text{pert\_end}} - t_{\text{pert}}$, is defined as the perturbation duration.

Although the definition of perturbation duration, presented earlier, is logical, it may appear confusing under special scenarios. Under such scenarios, $t_{\text{pert\_dur}}$ is assigned the symbol ϕ. This chapter is generally interested in measuring the steady-state system behavior prior to the initiation of perturbation and following the termination of the perturbation, to quantify the impact of the perturbation. The chapter is generally not interested in the system behavior while the system is under the influence of perturbation because a number of transient processes may be at play, including automatic recovery mechanisms. However, this chapter is interested in stability analysis for permanent perturbations. Therefore, under such circumstances, the assignment of ∞ to $t_{\text{pert\_dur}}$ would require one to wait up to time ∞ before obtaining measurements, i.e., preclude one from analyzing stability. The assignment of ∞ to $t_{\text{pert\_dur}}$ signifies this special case, and measurements are obtained for an NIT system while it is permanently perturbed.

Definition 5. *Stability*: if a system is in a steady state and a perturbation occurs, it will return to a steady state as $t \to \infty$. Let K_1 be the bound on the original steady state and K_2 be the bound on the final steady state. If $K_2 \leq K_1$ the system is *strong stable*, otherwise it is *marginally stable*.

The final steady state, as per Lyapunov's asymptotic stability, refers to the final steady state in the asymptotic sense. The distinction between strong and marginal stability is an important one. Given a strongly stable system, its steady state, and a perturbation, following repeated applications of the perturbation, the system will eventually return to a steady state that is either better than or equal to, in terms of the error bound, its original steady state. In contrast, following a perturbation, a marginally stable system may result in a steady state with a worse error bound. Furthermore, repeated applications of the perturbation may exhibit a growing error bound. In the worst case, a periodic perturbation may either drive the system into instability or the error may oscillate between consecutive perturbations. Thus, whether marginal stability is acceptable is dependent on the application and the user. Conceivably, a specific error may be bounded by a finite value for a given problem. This is true for the MFAD system, described later, where the maximum sensor error is restricted to $180°$. Therefore, while the system will always remain in steady state and therefore be deemed marginally stable, the key question for such systems is whether it is strongly stable.

This chapter defines two related classes of stability, distinguished by the perturbations to which they correspond: input stability and system-level stability.

Definition 6. *Input stability*: stability related to input perturbations, i.e., input rate, distribution, or magnitude.

Definition 7. *System-level stability*: stability related to system-level perturbations. The definition is inclusive of anything other than input perturbations, examples being component failures, i.e., links and nodes, and component degradation, i.e., dropped messages.

8.3 Stability Analysis of MFAD, a Decentralized Military Command and Control Problem

Chapter 6 described the decentralized military command and control decision-making problem under MFAD in detail.

8.3.1 Modeling and Assumptions for Stability Analysis

Unlike in MFAD in Chapter 6, where the weapon range is assumed to be 3000 spatial units, in this chapter, the range is deliberately limited to 300 spatial units. While this reduces the probability of entities being destroyed, the increased number of decisions determined by them during the simulation constitutes a higher quality of input data to the computation of stability. The stability measure reflects the quality of the decisions, not the number of entities destroyed. The MFAD simulation models two delays: (1) the peer entity-to-peer entity communication delay and (2) the decision computing delay. For simplicity and without any loss in generality, this section assigns the same value, a positive integer, τ_c, to every peer entity-to-peer entity communication delay. The decision computing delay, τ_p, models the computing time needed to minimize the cost function. Given that MFAD is a decentralized system where the overall decision task is shared by all entities, each entity is expected to compute decisions quickly, implying $\tau_p = 0$.

In MFAD, the sensor data acquired by every entity, along with information received from its peers, constitutes its input. Therefore, the input perturbation may assume the form of reduced sensor capability, which may correspond to, for instance, reduced visibility from smoke and confusion in the battlefield. The system-level perturbation may consist of communication failures between the entities that, in turn, may be caused by enemy jamming. Conceivably, the initial conditions, including the locations and orientations of the entities, will affect the results of the analysis. This chapter, however, is limited to a single set of stochastically generated locations and orientations for the entities.

8.3.2 Steady-State Analysis

In MFAD, the movement and sensor error criteria are intrinsically bounded. The errors are computed at each timestep which is equal to 0.1 second. The sensor error, computed as the absolute difference between the ideal sensor axis and the actual sensor axis, is bounded by 180°. The maximum error of 180° occurs when the ideal and actual sensor axes are pointing in exactly opposite directions. For simplicity, the movement error is computed as the difference of the magnitudes of the actual and ideal velocity vectors, and it does not reflect the direction component of velocity. The absolute value of the error in the movement decision vector is bounded by 30 units, given that the maximum magnitude of any velocity vector is limited to 15 units. Given that the errors are always bounded in time, by definition, MFAD is permanently in steady state and marginally stable. However, unqualified marginal stability may be of little value in the battlefield, given that a tank looking in a direction opposite to that of the approaching enemy is likely to be killed. Therefore, the conditions of either strongly stable or marginal stability with a restricted error bound are of greater value in MFAD.

8.3.3 Input Stability Analysis

Given that the input to every entity comprises the data acquired through its sensors, input perturbation may be emulated through degrading the sensor performance, i.e., limiting their effective range, either temporarily or permanently. The perturbations correspond to the inevitable smoke and confusion in the battlefield and is dynamic. Table 8.1 tabulates the average sensor error prior to, during, and following sensor perturbations, corresponding to temporary and permanent perturbations that reduce the effective sensor range to 33% and 66%, respectively, of its original value. Under normal conditions, the key system error values are obtained for either prior to or following perturbation. However, the permanent perturbation, i.e., for infinite duration, scenario is considered an exception, and the error value following the perturbation is measured immediately following the assertion of the perturbation.

Sensor Degradation (%)	Perturbation Duration (timesteps)	Average Error before Perturbation	Average Error during Perturbation	Average Error after Perturbation
33	50	0.509	0.686	0.733
66	50	0.509	0.529	0.501
33	∞	0.509	—	0.715
66	∞	0.509	—	0.513

Table 8.1. Average Sensor Decision Error Values Corresponding to Sensor Perturbations

The results in Table 8.1 reveal that when the effective sensor range is degraded to 33% of its normal value, either for a temporary duration of 50 timesteps or permanently, the average sensor error following the perturbation is relatively high. Figure 8.1 presents the average sensor error magnitude as a function of the simulation time, for sensor range degraded to 33% of its normal value, and contrasts it against the sensor error without perturbation. The graphs in Figure 8.1 reveal that the primary contribution to the error occurs between timesteps 100 and 170. The perturbation is asserted at 50 timesteps. Thus, severe sensor perturbations result in serious sensor errors. Conceivably, during a serious sensor perturbation, the tank unit fails to sight an enemy, and when the sensor range is restored following the termination of the perturbation, the enemy unit may have moved out of the field of view, leaving behind the lingering effect of the sensor error well past the perturbation duration. Where the sensor range is degraded to only 66% of its original value, the sensor error returns, at the end of the perturbation duration, close to the value prior to the initiation of the perturbation.

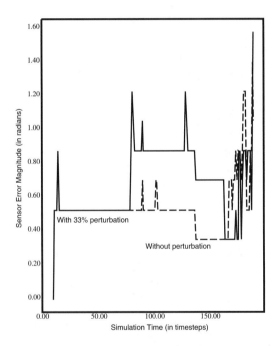

Fig. 8.1. Average Sensor Error as a Function of Simulation Time, for Sensor Range Reduced to 33% and No Sensor Perturbation

Table 8.2 presents the average movement decision error values prior to, during, and following a perturbation, for sensor ranges degraded to 33% and 66% of their original values, respectively, and for temporary and permanent degradations. A comparative analysis of the data, i.e., average errors before and after perturbations, in Tables 8.2 and 8.1 reveal that the impact of sensor

Sensor Degradation (%)	Perturbation Duration (timesteps)	Average Error before Perturbation	Average Error during Perturbation	Average Error after Perturbation
33	50	5.762	5.880	5.670
66	50	5.762	6.000	5.875
33	∞	5.762	—	6.015
66	∞	5.762	—	5.938

Table 8.2. Average Movement Decision Error Values Corresponding to Sensor Perturbations

perturbations on movement decision error is less severe than on the sensor decision error.

8.3.4 Perturbations to System Characteristics and Stability Analysis

The basic infrastructure of MFAD assumes that every entity is able to communicate with its peers. However, enemy jamming and hardware failures in the battlefield may cause communication failures, and this section presents an investigation into the stability of MFAD under such failures. In a set of experiments, communication failures are asserted systemwide at timestep 50, for two separate durations, 50 timesteps and permanent. The results of the perturbation analysis are shown in Tables 8.3 and 8.4. While Table 8.3 records the average sensor decision error values prior to, during, and following the temporary and permanent perturbations, the data in Table 8.4 correspond to the movement decisions. The results indicate that communication perturbations bear a slightly greater impact on the movement decision errors relative to the sensor decision errors. In contrast, recall that the sensor perturbation had a greater impact on the sensor error than the movement error. Figure 8.2 presents the movement and sensor decision errors as a function of the simulation time for both sensor and communication perturbations. Given that the perturbations are asserted at timestep 50, the behaviors of each graph relative to its value prior to timestep 50 corroborate the conclusions derived from Tables 8.1, 8.2, 8.3, and 8.4.

8.3.5 Summary of Stability Analysis of MFAD

MFAD is observed to exhibit strong stability for perturbations of finite duration. Although it is intrinsically marginally stable, the final steady states following certain perturbations may be fatal and, therefore, unacceptable. The results of analysis may be used to uncover potential weaknesses for the most likely perturbations and to suggest corrective measures.

Perturbation Duration (timesteps)	Average Error before Perturbation	Average Error during Perturbation	Average Error after Perturbation
50	0.509	0.658	0.490
∞	0.509	—	0.676

Table 8.3. Average Sensor Decision Error Values Corresponding to Communication Perturbations

Perturbation Duration (timesteps)	Average Error before Perturbation	Average Error during Perturbation	Average Error after Perturbation
50	5.762	7.160	6.100
∞	5.762	—	7.577

Table 8.4. Average Movement Decision Error Values Corresponding to Communication Perturbations

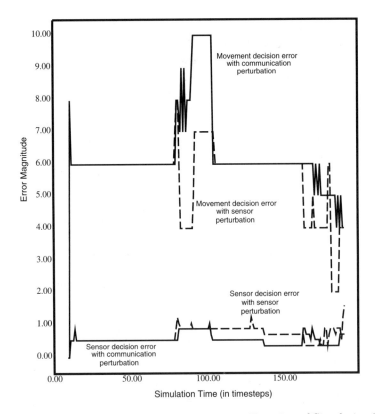

Fig. 8.2. Movement and Sensor Decision Errors as a Function of Simulation Time, Corresponding to Communication and Sensor Perturbations of Finite Durations

8.4 Stability Analysis of RYNSORD

Chapter 3 described the decentralized railway network control algorithm, RYNSORD, in detail. An important detail is recapitulated here, briefly.

In RYNSORD, a railway network is assumed to consist of a set of railroad stations, also termed nodes, connected by lengths of railroad tracks. Every station is equipped with a computing engine and communication facilities. For every pair of stations connected by a track, there exists a bidirectional communication link between the stations. Every track is bidirectional. Furthermore, every train is equipped with an onboard computing engine and facilities to initiate communication with the computing engine of the corresponding node when it is located at a station. RYNSORD does not require train-to-train communication or train-to-station communication while the train is moving. Each track segment is characterized by its length and the station node that owns it exclusively. A track between nodes X and Y is owned either by X or Y, and the owner is solely responsible for negotiating the use of the track with the competing trains. This characteristic is crucial to guaranteeing safety and collision avoidance in RYNSORD.

8.4.1 Modeling and Assumptions for Stability Analysis

The key performance measures in RYNSORD are the travel times required by the trains to reach their destinations and the average number of trains waiting at each station. Because stability is measured through performance behavior, this chapter proposes two error criteria designed to capture the deviation of the performance measures from standard benchmark values. In the discipline of distributed systems, centralized algorithms corresponding to the distributed algorithms usually serve as the standard benchmarks. This chapter proposes a novel benchmark, ideal performance measures. The ideal travel time for each train is the time required for the train to travel the shortest path from origin to destination, in the total absence of any competing trains. The ideal number of trains waiting at any time instance at any station is zero. While these ideal values may be achieved in the total absence of any competing trains and are impractical, they are absolute minimum values and are ideally suited as benchmarks. The reasons for selecting the ideal performance values are as follows. First, the ideal measures serve as absolute benchmark values. Second, a centralized algorithm-based system for RYNSORD may not be practically feasible. Error criterion 1 is expressed as

$$error = |\text{actual travel time} - \text{ideal travel time}|,$$

where the actual travel time of a train is computed as the time elapsed between the time the train is asserted into the system in the presence of other competing trains and the time the train reaches its destination. Error criterion 2 is expressed as

$$error = |\text{actual number of trains waiting at a station}|.$$

Although both error criteria aim to achieve the best overall performance, they may be at odds under certain scenarios. The errors are computed every timestep, which is equal to 1 minute. To minimize the travel times of trains, the first error criterion may encourage a train to wait at a specific station along an optimal route until a track from it becomes available for travel. In contrast, the second error criterion may encourage the train to keep moving while the optimal routes are occupied, through selecting longer and slower routes. Although RYNSORD selects routes based on minimizing travel time and does not directly consider the time spent waiting at the stations, both error criteria exhibit similar stability properties, reflecting the fact that the average waiting queue size and travel time for each train are related.

A real implementation of RYNSORD is a continuously running system. However, here, the simulation maintains both start and finish. Simulation is initiated with no trains in the system and the timestep set to one. The system is then executed until the end time, which for most of the experiments in this analysis corresponds to 17,280 timesteps or 12 operational days. Following initiation of the simulation, the trains asserted into the system experience very little contending traffic, which appears to extend superior performance for these trains. These trains are not considered in the performance analysis of RYNSORD. Following the termination of the simulation corresponding to a predetermined timestep, there may be trains still in progress in the system. These trains are marked as having been asserted but never having reached their destinations and are not considered in the performance data. In computing the results, RYNSORD only considers those trains that have successfully completed their journeys.

8.4.2 Steady-State Analysis

Because any error analysis of a system, caused by perturbations, is relative to its normal behavior, it is imperative to first identify the steady-state behavior of the system. This section presents a steady-state analysis of RYNSORD and identifies a key criterion as the input traffic distribution. Given that freight trains dominate passenger trains in RYNSORD, this section assumes that the assertion of trains into RYNSORD follow a uniform distribution over time. Unlike a bursty traffic model, a uniform distribution is likely to imply a constant level of network usage, leading to efficient use of resources. At every station, the probability of a train originating at that station at each timestep is defined as the *input rate*. For every train originating at a station, train speeds are generated stochastically, ranging from 60 to 100 mph. The final destination is also generated stochastically by assigning equal weight to every station except the originating station and selecting a station at random. Geographic proximity plays no part in the selection process. Because major stations, corresponding to major urban centers, are more likely to encounter high traffic densities, a set of nine high-traffic stations are identified—Chicago, Detroit, St. Louis, Philadelphia, New York, Washington, Pittsburgh, Columbus, and Cincinnati. For the stations corresponding to these cities, the input train traffic density is set at 0.3, which, as shown later, is well above the maximum steady-state rate for the system. However, as the steady-state analysis will show, the presence of these high traffic stations does not prevent the system from achieving a global steady state. Also, during the process of selecting final destinations of trains, these cities are assigned twice the weight of other stations.

A trial-and-error approach is used to determine the steady-state conditions. RYNSORD is simulated corresponding to different input rate values. Table 8.5 summarizes the average number of input trains that are generated corresponding to different input rate choices. Analysis reveals that, corresponding to an input rate of 0.125, shown in Figure 8.3, the error does not continue to increase as time increases, and as a result RYNSORD is considered to exhibit steady-state behavior corresponding to the input rate of 0.125. In contrast, for an input rate of 0.175, the error clearly grows as a function of time, reflecting nonsteady-state behavior. For the input rate of 0.140, RYNSORD exhibits *both bounded behavior and growth, depending on the specific stochastic input, reflecting that this input rate marks the boundary between bounded and unbounded error. As expected, different steady-state conditions exhibit different error bound values, as revealed in Figure 8.4 for error criterion 2 corresponding to steady-state input rates ranging from 0.05 to 0.125.

Input Traffic Density	Total Trains Introduced	Total Trains Finishing	Average Error for Completed Trains (timesteps)	Maximum Error (timesteps)
0.050	453	439 (97%)	67.95	439
0.100	858	822 (96%)	183.18	822
0.125	1,093	1,048 (96%)	309.65	1,387
0.140	1,250	1,156 (92%)	710.25	3,207
0.175	1,506	1,292 (86%)	1,115.62	5,324

Table 8.5. Input Traffic Parameters for Steady-State Analysis of RYNSORD

8.4.3 Perturbations to the Input Rate and Stability Analysis

As with any real-world system, RYNSORD is designed to execute in steady state but is likely to encounter periods of rapid fluctuation of input rates arising from any number of unforeseen circumstances. Thus, the most logical perturbation to the input rate in RYNSORD consists of an abrupt increase

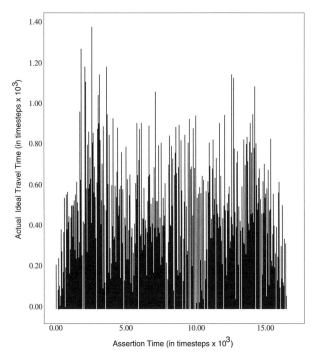

Fig. 8.3. Error Criterion 1 for Each Train as a Function of the Assertion Time, for Input Rate = 0.125

in the input traffic rate, sustained for a short duration. Along with the magnitude of the increase in the input rate and the length of duration of the perturbation, the choice of the steady-state operating point of RYNSORD is likely to influence the stability. It is desired that the RYNSORD design reflect a strongly stable system, i.e., it returns to the original steady state, at least, within finite time, following termination of the perturbation. A number of experiments are designed and executed wherein first a steady-state RYNSORD system is exposed, one at a time, to different perturbations, under different original steady-state operating points. Second, the error criteria 1 and 2 are measured as simulation progress and are analyzed.

Input Rate	Perturbation Magnitude	Perturbation Start Time (timestep)	Perturbation Duration (timestep)	Total Trains Introduced	Total Trains Finishing
0.05	+0.5	5,760	720	1,230	1,219 (99%)
0.125	+0.5	5,760	720	2,955	2,911 (99%)
0.125	+3.0	5,760	720	3,755	3,443 (92%)

Table 8.6. Perturbations to Input Rate and System Characteristics

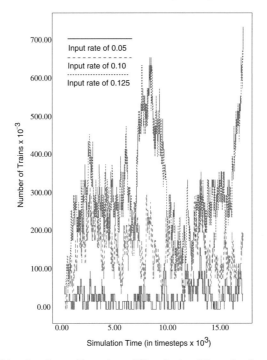

Fig. 8.4. Error Criterion 2 as a Function of Simulation Time, for Steady-State Input Rates

Table 8.6 summarizes the system characteristics under three different input rate perturbations. The magnitudes of the three perturbations are designed to push RYNSORD further beyond the steady-state point. The graphs for error criterion 1 are not shown here. Figure 8.5 presents error criterion 2 for each of the three scenarios, as a function of the simulation time. In the graphs for error criterion 1, the error magnitudes increase immediately following the perturbations. However, as time progresses, the error magnitudes decrease, with RYNSORD ultimately returning to the original steady-state point for all three cases. Thus, RYNSORD is strongly stable with respect to input perturbations.

8.4.4 Perturbations to System Characteristics and Stability *Analysis

The basic infrastructure of RYNSORD assumes that every train is able to communicate with an appropriate station and that stations can communicate between themselves. Although the RYNSORD algorithm does not explicitly take into consideration the possibility of track failures, trains are capable of determining alternate routes when one or more tracks are in use or unavailable.

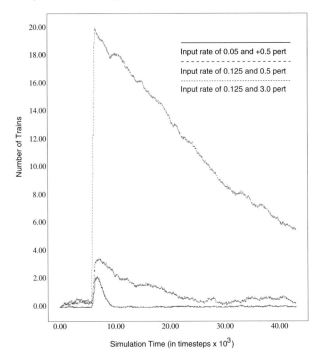

Fig. 8.5. Error Criterion 2 as a Function of Simulation Time, for Different Input Perturbations

This section presents an investigation into the stability of the RYNSORD algorithm under such failures.

8.4.4.1 Perturbations to Interstation and Train-to-Station Communication

Interactions between stations and between a train and a station constitute the key communication in RYNSORD without which trains can neither succeed in reserving tracks nor travel toward their destinations. The correctness requirement prevents a train from traveling on a track segment unless it has been granted explicit reservation. Should a reservation request, initiated by a train, remain unanswered, the train will never attempt to use the track in question. Thus, perturbations that are deliberately introduced in this chapter to affect the reservation process will bear no impact on RYNSORD's correctness.

The characteristics of the perturbations are as follows. A message propagated from one station to another never arrives at the destination. Also, a communication between a station and a train does not reach the receiver. Under such scenarios, the behavior of a train in RYNSORD is as follows. When a train does not receive a reply to its reservation request, it decides to travel on the alternate path, where available, rather than to wait indefinitely for the response. When responses to both of its requests for reservation fail to arrive, the train temporarily alters its lookahead to unity and renews its reservation effort. Unless both communication links along which the train propagates its reservation requests are down, which is unlikely, the most recent action by the train ensures at least one reservation response. When the unlikely event occurs, the train waits at the station and renews its reservation effort at the subsequent timestep with the restored lookahead value. Conceivably, computer communication failures are relatively short-lived and this chapter reasons that it is logical to wait for a single timestep within which the communication link is likely to be restored as opposed to engaging in a very roundabout detour. It is pointed out that a communication failure between two stations does not eliminate all uses of the corresponding track segment. The failure only affects those trains that attempt reservation through the nonowner station because the messages never arrive at the owner, which has sole capability in committing the reservation. Trains traveling from the station that owns the track are able to request and use the track.

A number of experiments are designed to measure stability. A number of different communication links are subject to failure, different failure durations are selected ranging up to permanent failure, and different values for the input traffic rate are used. The objective is to analyze the impact of communication perturbation on RYNSORD and to determine a traffic input rate for which RYNSORD is stable under perturbations. In the first experiment, two sets of three and eight links are forced to fail separately. The links are identified through the stations at either end. Care is exercised to avoid failing a link that is the only communication path from any station to the remainder of the network. While the set of three links is a suspected high-traffic link, the choice of the set of eight links reflects the desire to distribute failures throughout the network. The simulation is executed for 17,280 timesteps for steady-state input rates of 0.05 and 0.125, respectively. The failures are asserted at timestep 5760 and last for a duration of 1440 timesteps. Thus, $t_{pert} = 5760$, while $t_{pert\_end} = 5760+1440 = 7200$. The choice of the failure duration of 1440 timesteps, which corresponds to one full day of actual operation, reflects adequate time for repairs. In another set of experiments, the links are forced to fail permanently, i.e., $t_{pert} = 5760$ and $t_{pert\_end} = \infty$.

Set of three links:Baltimore(34):Washington(33); Detroit(9):Toledo(10); and Roanoke(48):Lynchburg(47).
Set of eight links: Cleveland(11):Columbus(12); Rochester(27):Syracuse(28); St. Louis(5):Detroit(9); Wilson(40):Raleigh(41); Charlottesville(35):Richmond(36); New York(31):Philadelphia(25); Knoxville(18):Bristol(20); and Parkersburg(44):Huntington(45).

Table 8.7 summarizes the performance results and reveals that RYNSORD is strongly stable with respect to failures of finite duration. Given the higher

No. of Links Failed	Base Input Rate of System	Perturbation Time (timestep)	Perturbation Duration (timesteps)	Stability Class
3	0.05	5,760	1,440	Strongly stable
3	0.125	5,760	1,440	Strongly stable
3	0.05	5,760	∞	Marginally stable
3	0.125	5,760	∞	Unstable
8	0.05	5,760	1,440	Strongly stable
8	0.125	5,760	1,440	Strongly stable
8	0.05	5,760	∞	Marginally stable
8	0.125	5,760	∞	Unstable

Table 8.7. Performance Results for Communication Perturbations

probability of communication failures repaired quickly, the results are encouraging. However, for permanent perturbations in both sets of links, RYNSORD is observed to be marginally stable and unstable under input traffic rates of 0.05 and 0.125, respectively. Clearly, the boundary between marginal stability and instability is a function of the input traffic rate, the number of tracks failed, and the specific tracks failed. Error criterion 2 mirrors the behavior of error criterion 1. The results for the set of three tracks failed are similar to those for the set of eight tracks and are not presented here.

However, a comparative analysis of error criterion 2 for the two sets of tracks failed reveals the following. While RYNSORD is marginally stable for both cases, the final steady-state point for the set of three links is worse, i.e., higher error bound value, relative to that for the set of eight links. The result clearly underscores the importance of the specific links failed over the number of links failed, and a likely cause is the degree of congestion. Further, off-line analysis, i.e., following the termination of simulation, reveals that a total of 201 trains used one or more of the set of three links in their shortest paths. In contrast, only 167 trains utilized one or more of the set of eight links. Thus, stability analysis may contribute toward identifying communication links whose failure is more likely to adversely affect the performance.

8.4.4.2 Perturbations Relative to the Track Segments

A track may become unavailable following an accident, breakdown, or sabotage or due to routine maintenance. Although RYNSORD, by design, lacks an elaborate mechanism to handle such failures, on occurrence of a failure, the stations at the two endpoints of the track segment become aware within a single timestep, i.e., 60 seconds of actual operation. Also, a train already traveling on a track segment at the time of the failure will continue to travel and reach the other end safely. The stations at the endpoints will prevent future trains from using the track by canceling all reservations and forcibly initiating reroute computations for all affected trains.

No. of Links Failed	Base Input Rate of System	Perturbation Time (timestep)	Perturbation Duration (timesteps)	Stability Class
3	0.05	5,760	1,440	Strongly stable
3	0.125	5,760	1,440	Strongly stable
3	0.05	5,760	∞	Marginally stable
3	0.125	5,760	∞	Unstable
8	0.05	5,760	1,440	Strongly stable
8	0.125	5,760	1,440	Strongly stable
8	0.05	5,760	∞	Marginally stable
8	0.125	5,760	∞	Unstable

Table 8.8. Performance Results for Track Perturbations

An experiment is designed wherein the tracks corresponding to the two sets of three and eight links, described earlier in Chapter 3, are subject to failure. The performance results, presented in Table 8.8, are identical to those for the communication perturbations (Table 8.7). The error criteria graphs are also similar in behavior to those for the communication perturbations but there are key differences. Consider the failure of the eight links for a finite duration of 1,440 timesteps, under high input traffic rate. While RYNSORD is strongly stable relative to both kinds of perturbations and the behaviors of the error criterion 2 graphs corresponding to communication link failures and corresponding track failures are similar asymptotically, the magnitude of the error for communication perturbation is significantly worse than for track perturbation. In contrast, consider the permanent failure of the eight links under low input traffic rate. While RYNSORD is observed to be marginally stable for both communication link failures and corresponding track failures and their asymptotic behaviors are similar, the error magnitude corresponding to communication perturbation is considerably higher than for track perturbation. A possible explanation lies in the fact that while only the failed track becomes unavailable to a train, a communication link failure may impair a train's ability to compete for reservation, and therefore, travel access, for multiple tracks.

8.4.5 Summary of Stability Analysis of RYNSORD

The stability analysis of RYNSORD has revealed that it is strongly stable with respect to perturbations of finite durations to the input traffic rate and track segment failures. For permanent perturbations, the stability measure is dependent on the input traffic rate prior to the onset of the perturbation. However, it is weak with respect to communication link failures, and the underlying algorithm needs redesign for superior immunity to perturbations.

—

9

The Need and Art of Interdisciplinary Thinking

Given the versatility of its constituent components, computing engines and networking infrastructure, the scope of NIT systems is vast, extending into many diverse applications and disciplines, limited only by our imagination. Consider, for example an NIT system, shown in Figure 9.1, that integrates the tasks of a new, free-flight, air travel system with global telemedicine, automated precision farming over a wide geographical area, forest management, and natural resource protection.[1]

The combination of the versatility, the intrinsic complexity of NIT systems, and the NIT design tools including modeling, simulation, debugging, MFAD mathematical framework, stability analysis, and performance estimation that were presented earlier in the book, implies the following. ADDM algorithm designers must not only possess knowledge of the interdisciplinary fields but also a high quality of interdisciplinary thinking. The rationale behind including the case studies in Chapter 3 was to expose the reader to diverse ADDM algorithm designs from a number of different application domains. The expectation is that the reader will internalize the general and particular concepts, develop an intuitive understanding, and synthesize innovative ADDM algorithms for new problem domains. Thus, while the need for interdisciplinary thinking follows from logic, its practice is far more complex and, to date, has been more of an art. This chapter undertakes a systematic analysis of the creative discoveries and inventions in the history of engineering and science and aims to discover, where possible, a quasi-objective approach to train designers to generate innovative ADDM algorithms for NIT problems.

9.1 The Notion of Computational Intelligence

To understand the nature of interdisciplinary thinking, it is logical to first examine the requirements posed by the design of ADDM algorithms. In essence,

---

[1] Courtesy of Dr. Norm Sorensen of the Aerospace Corporation.

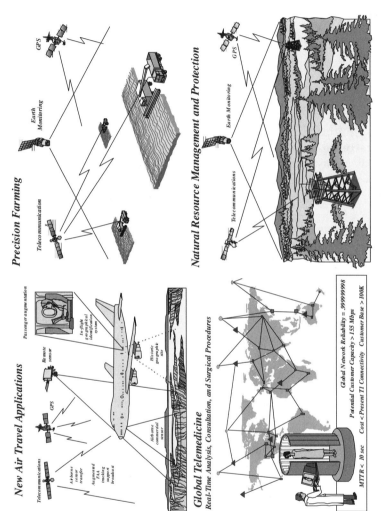

Fig. 9.1. Interdisciplinary Nature of Information Technology Systems

ADDM algorithms constitute computationally intelligent (CI) solutions to NIT problems. That is, the computers at the nodes of the NIT system successfully solve the underlying problem, through reasoning, systematic application of rules on a system of facts, and logical decision making. The networking infrastructure facilitates interactions between the nodes. Although these tasks are normally reserved for intelligent human beings, computing engines are employed because they are orders of magnitude faster, virtually fatigue-free, exceptionally precise, ultrareliable relative to human beings, and, most important, a computer may be used to emulate, through careful programming, any physical or thought process with incredible faithfulness. As computers become faster and our ability to exploit computers improves, problems that were previously considered intractable will finally yield to CI techniques. Fundamentally, however, the CI solution must originate in the human mind. The computing engine merely serves to amplify the human mind. Thus, the challenge for the ADDM algorithm designer is the translation of a real-world NIT problem into an algorithm that, on execution on a computing node, yields a solution to the underlying NIT problem.

9.2 Reflection as a Catalyst in Triggering Creativity

In the recent literature [229], creativity has been clarified as a phenomenon that categorically differs from intelligence in that the ideas that result from it may not be deduced by applying current reasoning techniques on the state-of-the-art knowledge. Thus, creativity clearly transcends intelligence. Despite this new perspective, by its very nature, creativity defies a true and complete definition, and the issue of how to arrive at a creative solution for a given problem continues to remain an open question. This section represents an effort to gain insights into the nature of creativity. It is motivated by the desire to develop, where possible, a quasi-systematic approach to foster creative solutions to challenging real-world engineering and scientific problems, today as well as in the future. This section begins by observing (1) documented manifestations of creative discoveries and inventions by leading scientists and inventors, (2) records of creative flashes in many day-to-day ordinary activities, and (3) instances of creativity in Nature. It then critically analyzes these observations to uncover what mechanisms trigger the processes that eventually lead to creative solutions to problems. Three hypotheses are submitted for cases (1) through (3), and it is claimed that reflection constitutes the underlying mechanism in each, serving as a catalyst for creativity. The first hypothesis is that, in many of the highly creative scientific and engineering discoveries, reflection has played an explicit role in catalyzing the onset of creativity in the scientists and inventors, leading to spontaneous solutions. Examples include Nobel's invention of the blasting-cap which led to the discovery of dynamite, and Dolby's discovery of the noise-reduction system in sound recordings. The second hypothesis is that creativity may be triggered by resorting to implicit reflection. The underlying mechanism consists of highly experienced professionals who report arriving at decisions and diagnoses, almost instantaneously, through intuitive flashes that later turn out to be precisely correct. Examples include experienced firefighters whose spontaneous and lightning-fast actions prevent fires from spreading and veteran nurses who can predict soon after birth whether a prematurely born baby will survive, weeks before all medical tests are exhaustively completed and long before the highly trained pediatricians deliver their prognoses. The third postulate is that Nature is guided by reflection, while using the enormous resources and knowledge at her disposal, to play her meta-level role in introducing creative traits, selectively, in one or more individuals of a specific animal colony. The resulting collective behavior of the entire colony represents a spontaneous, creative behavior, very different from that of a pure, homogeneous colony. Examples include defense tactics deployed against predators by schools of fish while in synchronized motion and preemptive strategies employed by select bee colonies against predatorial wasps. Five experiments are presented here, incurred in industrial and academic research environments and pedagogical settings, to demonstrate the occurrence of creativity, deliberately triggered by reflection. In essence, the contributions are threefold. First, although the exact definition of creativity continues to elude us, the use of explicit and implicit reflection constitutes two approaches that are potentially useful in triggering creativity at will in ordinary scientific and engineering personnel to achieve quantum leaps in our knowledge and achievement. *Reflection* is defined as introspective contemplation or meditation on a thought or idea, quietly or calmly, with a view to understanding it in its right relation to all other concepts. The role of reflection is that of a catalyst. Reflection also appears to underlie the inner workings of Nature. Second, from the perspective of engineering pedagogy, these approaches may constitute a tried-and-tested mechanism for inducing creativity in ordinary students through practice. Third, the combination of the definition of creativity and our recognition of its presence in us guarantees that human beings will always remain superior to any man-made machine.

9.2.1 Introduction

It is common knowledge that while creativity is elusive, its impact on the advancement of civilization, arts, science, and engineering, is definite and profound. By definition, creativity transcends current knowledge and reasoning. As a result, its complete nature is difficult, if not impossible, to comprehend. Despite the difficulty, this section constitutes an effort to understand its nature in as self-consistent, scientific, and systematic a manner as possible. In the recent literature, Heck and Ghosh [229] showed that while most constituent entities of an organization should follow the established normal behavior to yield a reasonable level of basic system performance, the inclusion of a limited few entities that possess nonconformal creative traits may enable an organization to achieve, in some cases, extraordinary, unexpected, and highly innovative behavior. Such achievement may be characterized as transcending the rote, getting out of the local minima, or breaking the deadlock. The issue of fostering creativity in a few entities of an organization while encouraging conformity in the majority, is a real challenge. It is well known that it is easy to destroy creativity through discouragement and other means, while to cultivate creativity requires a significant, disproportionately higher degree of effort. In their studies, Heck and Ghosh [229] showed that the energy expenditure is significant among creative entities, partially corroborating common knowledge.

In the discipline of psychology, the effort to define creativity relates principally to human behavior and problem-solving ability. Creativity is viewed as "the production of a novel and socially useful object, process, or idea" [230]. Although creativity appears to be linked to intelligence in that a reasonable amount of intelligence is necessary for creativity, "intellectual giftedness does not guarantee that an individual will be creative" [230]. Creativity involves the ability to produce original and ingenious solutions to problems [231]. A subtle distinction between creativity and originality may be expressed as follows. While originality refers to the tendency to produce unusual solutions to problems, the extent to which a solution is creative depends significantly on the quality and usefulness of the solution [231]. Psychologists distinguish convergent thinking from divergent thinking as follows. Convergent thinking, usually associated with intelligence, emphasizes memorization, recognition, and repetition. It is logical and is used when there is only one correct answer that can be reached by logical inferences [231]. In contrast, divergent thinking, associated with creativity, uses existing information to produce new information. This kind of thinking involves nonlogical processes, and there may arise several relevant answers [231]. The techniques used by individuals to evoke creativity have been described by many psychologists [231] [232] [233]. They argue in favor of the four stages in the creative process:

- Preparation: The problem is identified and knowledge about the problem domain is acquired.
- Incubation: The problem is set aside while other tasks are accomplished.
- Illumination: The solution emerges as a consequence of a sudden insight.
- Verification: The solution is analyzed and validated, i.e., examined to show that it really works.

The most difficult and least understood aspect of the creative process is the period of incubation where the creative individual works on the problem unconsciously with little or no linear progress toward the ultimate goal. More importantly, the greatest challenge in understanding is posed by the illumination phase, where there is recognition of a potential solution that appears to arise out of nowhere. Eysenck [231] believes that illumination may involve manipulating information in three basic ways. First, a creative individual may use *selective encoding*, which involves identifying crucial information from the total available information. Second, *selective combination* may be used, which involves realizing how relevant pieces of information fit together. Third, the problem may be solved by analogy, using *selective comparison*, where information from a different problem is related to the current problem. Luderer's view on incubation and illumination [5] is as follows. The brain is a multiprocessing engine in that when an individual is in the conscious state, a number of processes may be started, some of which continue to function in the lower, subconscious state. Each process attempts to converge toward a state in which no contradictions with the real world are present. While some of these controls are switched off during dreaming, illumination is the result of at least one such process finally hitting the jackpot. Richard Hamming, famed inventor of the Hamming code, observes [234], creativity comes out of your subconscious. Hadamard [235] describes the notion of illumination in the field of mathematics through a number of examples and links it to unconsciousness. The issue of illumination is the key focus of this section.

9.2.2 Reflection as a Catalyst in Triggering Creativity

9.2.2.1 Scientific Discoveries and Engineering Inventions

Analysis of the circumstances leading to profound scientific discoveries and engineering inventions throughout history reveals a familiar pattern. While attempting to solve an unknown challenging problem, a scientist or engineer first exhaustively explores every known principle and technique. After all attempts fail, the individual engages in deep contemplation for a period of time, which may vary considerably, at the end of which an innovative solution drops, literally, from somewhere into the individual's mind. The most famous example is the classical story of Archimedes who, while deeply immersed in thinking of a solution to determine the purity of a gold ornament during his bath, was suddenly struck by the answer we now understand as Archimedes' principle. In trying to conceive of a structure for benzene, molecular formula C_6H_6, the father of organic chemistry, Kekule, applied every atomic bonding principle known at the time and failed. Then, while engrossed in deep contemplation, he fell asleep and dreamed of a snake attempting to bite its tail. Kekule woke up with the inspiration that the six carbon atoms in benzene must form a closed hexagonal structure but he could not offer an acceptable reason. Today, we understand it in the form of a resonance structure for C-C bonding. In the late nineteenth century, the unpredictable dangers of black powder (gun powder) and nitroglycerine coupled with the enormous economic potential of safe explosives motivated Alfred Nobel to search for ways to package nitroglycerine safely. Despite years of study, all of his efforts based on current knowledge ended in failure. Finally, while engaged in deep thinking, the solution fell into Nobel's lap in the form of two concepts—a stabilized nitroglycerine paste and a very low-powered blasting cap that could safely set off an enormously powerful nitroglycerine explosive package. In the middle of the twentieth century, leading recording companies, including Decca, were desperately in need of a noise-reduction system for their audio recordings on magnetic media. Following a number of disappointing experiments, the recording industry started to believe that the hissing noise was an inherent part of the microphone, electronics, and the magnetic media, and that it could not be eliminated. Keenly aware of the problem and having failed in his previous efforts, Dolby engaged in deep contemplation. One day, while walking along the roads of New Delhi, while serving as a scientific adviser to the newly created government of India, the solution fell into Dolby's lap. The source of the hissing noise was the magnetic media; to eliminate it, he would first amplify by a factor F the strength of the incoming signal and then record it onto the media. During playback, the output signal strength would be attenuated by F, causing the output audio to be virtually free of the hiss.

For insights into the debate whether the creative solutions are true inspirations and not logically deduced from contemporary knowledge, consider the following evidence. Careful analysis now reveals that many of the leading scientists with significant discoveries were initially unable to prove them, using their own knowledge of mathematics and science. In particular, close examination of Einstein's derivation of the general theory of gravitation reveals numerous mathematical errors and mistakes. Ramanujan, an unprecedented mathematical genius, was famous for stating highly original and unconventional mathematical results in number theory, modular function theory, and infinite theory, that defied formal proofs and for which he could not provide any proofs. Ramanujan even went so far as to openly insist that none of the formulas or equations were his own creation but that they had been handed down to him by Namakkal (the goddess of learning) in his dreams [236]. Thus, it may be logically inferred that these scientists, including Einstein and Ramanujan, must have possessed an incredibly strong belief in their own understanding of the phenomenon and held greater faith in their intuition than in contemporary mathematics and science. Today, most of the errors and mistakes have been corrected, mathematical results have been formally proved, and the research findings can be explained consistently, implying that somehow these scientists were able to bridge the gap from here to there without the help of contemporary knowledge. It is therefore not surprising when Einstein observed, "Imagination is more important than knowledge."

When Fourier theorized that any complex wave function, including a square wave, could be synthesized from an infinite number of pure sinusoidal waves with frequencies related to the highest frequency contained in the original signal, his contemporary and leading senior scientist, Lagrange, put forward a very strong opposition, arguing that the idea lacked a physical basis. At that time, neither Fourier nor Lagrange knew about the concept of energy of a signal and Fourier's theory was not approved for publication for more than a decade. Today, we understand that the exact number of Fourier components is dictated by an error function of the difference in the cumulative energy content of the individual component sinusoidal waves and the energy content of the complex wave function that the application is willing to tolerate.

In 1894, confronted by the problem of detecting and measuring very high-frequency electromagnetic radiation, as high as 60 Ghz, J. C. Bose was guided by a creative inspiration to use different types of junctions [237], connected to a highly sensitive galvanometer, as detectors. Although semiconductors would not be invented for another 60 years, Bose must have anticipated the existence of P-type and N-type semiconductors [238]; otherwise, he would not have left a wealth of systematic measurements of the nonlinear, voltage-current characteristics of the different junctions. Nobel laureate Neville Mott writes, "In fact, he [Bose] had anticipated the existence of P-type and N-type semiconductors."

This section submits the first hypothesis in that the occurrence of a creative inspiration in a scientist or engineer is preceded by the individual explicitly engaged in intense reflection on the basic and fundamental nature of the underlying problem and its constituent subprocesses. *Webster's Third International Dictionary* [239] defines *reflection* as introspective contemplation or meditation on a thought or idea, quietly or calmly, with a view to understanding it in its right relation to all other concepts. Here, the term *reflection* refers to Kant's usage in reflective judgment. That is, reflection is a thought or idea that proceeds from the given particulars up to the discovery of a general concept or universal principle under which the particulars are subsumed. Only after the individual has completed a thorough and deep analysis of all of the fundamental issues, based on all that is known, and exhaustively and meticulously explored every available approach and reasoning technique, does the focus of the reflection converge. At this stage, the individual's mind is concentrated at a single point, and a creative solution literally drops onto the individual, apparently out of nowhere. Thus, reflection serves as a catalyst in triggering the onset of creativity and, as a practical benefit, we may familiarize engineering and scientific trainees to recognize and profitably exploit this phenomenon. Of course, reflection is merely a catalyst; there is no guarantee that it will always lead to a solution. This chapter further submits that the universal knowledge is possibly organized into different levels of depth, with the degree of profoundness increasing with higher levels or increasing depth. Using the state-of-the-art knowledge and reasoning at a lower level, say L_1, one may not reach the knowledge at any of the subsequent higher levels, say L_2 or L_3. The reason may lie in the vastly different laws of physics, energy manipulation, and causality, at the different levels. Through intense reflection, the individual researcher's mind becomes highly focused, generating tremendous power and creating a temporary conduit through which the human mind transcends into level L_2. Then the element of knowledge in question, K, literally flows from L_2 to L_1 as a manifestation of the creative process. Item K is initially viewed as creative knowledge but, in time, it is assimilated into level L_1, thereby raising the degree of profoundness of level L_1.

A well-known example of the explicit employment of reflection in creativity is Descartes' famous philosophical experiment—an effort to determine whether his existence is independent and real or his life experience simply the result of a dream imposed by a powerful controlling monster. He starts to introspect the very thought that he is dreaming, gradually diving into deeper issues, and eventually arrives at the following realization. He argues that, if indeed a monster had been controlling his dream all along, surely it would not have permitted him to invoke within himself the fundamental and disturbing question that someone else may be in control. Descartes finally concludes that since he is able to question his own existence, he must exist.

9.2.2.2 Creative Flashes in Ordinary Activities

Manifestations of creativity are not limited to science and engineering; they can and do occur in many ordinary everyday activities. Recently, the U.S. Army conducted a thorough investigation [240], with the aim of learning about the nature of intuitive decision making under stress. The researchers selected professional firefighters and set out to analyze the decision-making process wherein the decisions are documented as spontaneous yet are uncanny in their precision. The findings that followed were unexpected. Careful analysis revealed that in the middle of severe, fast-moving, and life-threatening fires, experienced and seasoned firefighters, not necessarily senior ranking officers, did not engage in conscious decision making but merely acted on their immediate instincts, their gut feeling. Yet, their actions were precisely accurate and correct decisions, as later revealed by the outcomes. After further analysis, the Army researchers concluded that, first, the seasoned firefighters had accumulated the knowledge of a vast and comprehensive database of different types of fires and their highly dynamic behaviors. Second, from this database, they had synthesized, through an indescribable process, a composite feature that constitutes a highly condensed yet accurate representation of the fire behavior. Third, using the composite feature, they had organized in their minds different types of fire behaviors, and for each of them, they synthesized a mental picture. In an actual firefighting scenario, these individuals would analyze the fire, map it onto one of the mental images, and infer a course of action at lightning-fast speed, one that would eventually be assessed as the absolute correct course of action. The second hypothesis is submitted in that, here, reflection is also at play, though implicitly. Unconsciously, the seasoned firefighters are engaged in deep contemplation while they analyze the different fires, and the intense reflection triggers the mental images to drop from the higher plane into their minds, for later use.

Careful observations and analysis also reveal that pediatric nurses with the most experience with premature babies and their struggle for survival can predict, with uncanny accuracy, which prematurely born babies will survive, long before doctors, highly trained through years of formal medical training and relying on sophisticated medical tests, are able to come up with any kind of prognosis. Like the case of the seasoned firefighters, it is submitted that the highly experienced nurses have unconsciously reflected deeply on their accumulated knowledge of babies' struggling behaviors, with the result that highly condensed mental images of survivor and nonsurvivor babies have literally dropped into their minds, for later use.

9.2.2.3 Nature's Use of Reflection

Evolutionists have long believed that Nature is responsible for evolving creative traits in animals, through trial and error. Nature tries out different possibilities, at random, and the one that succeeds or survives, She allows to continue. The study of genetic algorithms [241] in computer science and engineering relies on an evaluation function that determines which new solution or mutation wins in comparison to other solutions. This, in turn, determines the survivors. In essence, Darwin's concept of survival of the fittest implies that Nature is impersonal, takes a "stand back" attitude following the completion of the design process, and does not care who wins. This chapter argues that while the evolutionist theory may explain a limited number of cases, it is not universal. It submits an alternative theory in the form of the third hypothesis, which offers a logically sound explanation across a wide range of experimental observations. Contrary to the popular evolutionist thinking, this hypothesis submits that, in most cases, Nature's approach is not an accident. It is methodical and deliberate, and Her creative solutions reveal the undeniable influence of reflection. This chapter postulates that Nature starts with a specific goal, purpose, or intent, and then looks at how the current processes function and fail, if applicable, and reflects on the overall process itself. Then, following introspection on the characteristics of the constituent subprocesses and a comprehensive examination of the nature, scope, and range of every conceivable interaction between the subprocesses, Nature generates a solution in the form of (1) an overall meta-level control and coordinating algorithm and (2) specific traits for the individual lower-level subprocesses. Nature validates Her meta-level algorithm in the crucible of the real world, and the testing often spans very long durations and assumes a gigantic scope, extending well beyond our ability to comprehend. In distributing traits to different species, Nature is incessantly trying to achieve a balance among all interacting life forms and is engaged constantly in redesigning to rectify errors that arise in Her design from time to time. In essence, Nature is trying to approach perfection, it is not yet perfect. Equally important, Nature is an active and dynamic participant in the evolution process, not a bystander. To examine this postulate, this section critically reviews two real-world biological behaviors and an analysis of the human immune system design.

Consider shoaling, the synchronized motion of a school of fish consisting of hundreds of thousands of individual fish. Nature achieves this harmonious motion by imparting a simple rule to every constituent member. Every fish maintains a fixed distance from each of its six neighbors—front, back, up, down, left, and right—at all times, under normal conditions. Thus, when the lead fish for a given direction alters its course to match the temperature gradient, water current, or underwater obstacle, its immediate neighbors adjust their distances appropriately, which is followed by their neighbors, and so on, resulting in a spectacular synchronized motion. To provide protection to the school from predators, Nature has imparted another characteristic to the fish. When a predator swoops into the school with the intent of grabbing a meal, the one or more individual fish that sense the foreign invader immediately take evasive actions and maneuver as far away from the invader as possible. Their neighbors sense the sudden maneuver and attempt to match it, in terms of distance and direction. As a result, the space immediately surrounding the point of attack quickly becomes a void, leaving the predator confused. The fish resume their normal behavior when the threat disappears. It is argued that these traits, from the perspective of the fish, are creative, extra-logical. The fish could not have evolved these traits completely on their own, through logical thinking. It is postulated that these traits are Nature's synthetic design, stemming from Her reflection on the intent to foil predatorial attacks on fish schools and Her use of the tremendous resources and knowledge of the world at Her disposal. These unique and spontaneous behaviors received from nature by the life forms are referred to as Nature's creativity. Once imparted by Nature, these characteristics become creative traits for the fish.

This highly successful defense mechanism, however, turns into a fatal vulnerability when a school of fish is attacked in an innovative manner by a pod of humpback whales. For these large predators, intercepting one fish at a time is inefficient; they must scoop up the fish in tens to hundreds in each gulp. The attack strategy is distributed. When they spot a school of herring, first a few whales give chase and the fish school flees by diving deeper into the water. They run into a trap in that several whales, already waiting at that depth, now start to circle the entire fish school, waving their huge fins from all sides, churning the waters, and slowly constricting their space. Instead of fleeing individually in different directions, which would foil the whales' attack with certainty, the frightened fish cling to each other for safety through their tried-and-tested shoaling technique, desperately swimming closer and closer to their neighbors in an ever-tightening formation. When the grip is tight, the whale immediately beneath the school emits a tremendous sound, upwards of 180 dB, and drives the herring to the surface of the water. Finally, with their huge jaws open, the giant whales take gigantic gulps from the densely packed school, each gulp consisting of hundreds of fish [74]. Similar to the reasons presented earlier, it is argued that by reflecting on the overarching objective of balancing all life forms, Nature must have synthesized these behaviors and imparted them to the whales in the form of creative traits, over hundreds of thousands of years.

Biologists have reported [74] [242] on an European bee colony that exhibits the following defense mechanism against predators. When threatened, the guard bees engage a single intruder, one at a time. With multiple intruders, a group of guard bees take on a specific intruder but still limit their attack strategy to one at a time. When one such colony was transplanted to Japan and confronted by a much larger, Japanese killer wasp, biologists observe that the guard bees line up in a single file only to be mercilessly decapitated by the much larger wasp. The entire European bee colony of 30,000 bees is decimated in less than 30 minutes. Thus, Nature's meta-level algorithm design for the specific European bee colony reveals a catastrophic failure. Clearly, Nature designed the overall meta-level algorithm and imparted the specific behaviors to the individual bees, probably over a period of thousands of years, for a different environment, namely Europe, where, perhaps, the predatorial wasps are slightly larger but otherwise similar to the bees in many respects. To prevent fratricide in battle, Nature's algorithm design deliberately avoided the strategy of multiple guard bees attacking a single intruder.

In contrast, a native Japanese bee colony exhibits a dramatically different approach to self defense. When threatened by one or more scouts from the much larger killer wasp colony, the guard bees immediately mobilize and groups of large numbers of them jump onto each intruder as they are about to mark the colony with a scent to return with their peers for battle. While the individual smaller bee is in no position to kill the intruder, each group blankets the corresponding intruder with their bodies and begin to flap their wings furiously. The intruder, now forcibly confined to a limited space, starts to feel the rise in temperature. Eventually, the cumulative heat becomes intense and the temperature reaches 113° F, at which point the wasp dies of oxygen deprivation. The temperature threshold for the bees' survival is only 5° degrees higher, 118° F. Similar to previous arguments, it is inconceivable that the bees know of the temperature thresholds or that they are capable of developing, on their own, such a delicately balanced strategy. We submit that, through reflection on the problem of survival of the bees against the more powerful enemy and under the broad objective of balancing all life forms, Nature must have used her enormous resources and knowledge to design an effective meta-level algorithm and imparted the appropriate behaviors to the individual bees, also perhaps over thousands of years. The Nature-imparted behaviors take on the role of creative traits for the bees.

In protecting the complex body from simple microscopic microbes, the human immune system's front line of defense consists of the skin, which is virtually impenetrable by most microbes, while the hairs and mucus guard the nose, mouth, and other openings, killing most of the invading microbes on contact. For microbes that slip the outer defenses and attack the body from within, the immune system maintains an arsenal of antibodies, T-cells, and memory cells. While the antibodies and T-cells constantly search out and destroy foreign matter, the immune system monitors the result of T-cell battles and creates long-term memory cells that circulate in the blood stream, ready to create new T-cells should the body be attacked by an identical or similar microbe in the future. Clearly, Nature's deliberate design enables the immune system to learn from its present battles with microbes and evolve to meet future challenges. In contrast, Nature has designed microbes to mutate, through which they create different strains that encapsulate slightly different genetic compositions and attempt to fool the human immune system. The result of serious battles with microbes, such as the black plague, yellow fever, and malaria are well recorded in history. Immunologists including Falkow [75] accurately observe that the immune system design reflects Nature's attempt to balance all life forms: Without the complex human host, the microbes cannot survive while unchecked attacks by microbes may result in the ultimate destruction of the complex host.

Based on the quality, thoroughness, and effectiveness of the meta-level algorithms in the two scenarios, it is logical to infer that the probability with which Nature employs reflection in Her synthetic design of the algorithms is high. Given Her access to enormous resources and knowledge, Nature is able to transcend the different planes. Using reflection, She is capable of bringing down knowledge from higher planes and incorporating them as creative traits onto lower-level life forms. In contrast, using knowledge and reasoning at our level, we are unable to directly reach the higher planes. Thus, we cannot synthesize creative solutions completely on our own. The observation that Nature is more than likely to employ reflection, in turn, adds strength to this chapter's key position, as follows. By engaging the vehicle of reflection at will, one can hope to trigger the onset of creativity in science and engineering and catalyze the descendance of creative solutions from the higher plane onto us.

9.2.3 Using Reflection to Trigger Creativity at Will

The recognition that reflection constitutes a key component of creativity raises the possibility that, with appropriately trained individuals and by synthesizing a suitable environment, one may attempt to trigger scientific and engineering creativity at will. The potential benefits are real and significant. First, we can achieve quantum advancement in our scientific and engineering knowledge. Second, just as Nature imparts creative traits and sets into motion biological evolution, scientists and engineers can similarly assume a Nature-like role, designing synthetic creative traits and imparting them to individual robots before sending colonies of them off on unmanned planetary and stellar exploration. Similarly, geneticists can impart creative traits to antibody molecules, chemically synthesized in the laboratory, before launching them into animal and human bloodstreams to fight invading viruses and diseases. Under harsh and abnormal conditions, the creative traits may be the only thing standing between survival and destruction. While Nature uses the crucible of the real world as a testbed to validate Her meta algorithms, behavior modeling and asynchronous distributed simulation [229] [14] can help emulate and test the creative solutions, thoroughly and quickly, before initiating wide-scale deployment. Third, ABET's [243] goal of instilling creativity and design in engineering students may be practically realized through the practice of reflection. Fourth, an individual trained to invoke creative thinking when solving problems may generate dynamic, radically new, and totally unanticipated solutions that may be extremely hard to beat.

In the remainder of this section, five experiments are presented, the first and second occur in academic and industrial research environments, with the remaining three conducted in pedagogical settings in academic institutions. Experiments 3 and 4 may be characterized under explicit reflection, while both explicit and implicit reflection occur in Experiments 1, 2, and 5. Thus, by carefully choosing the problem and available resources, and with the proper encouragement, the subjects are motivated to resort to deep introspection. Experiment 1 depicts an analysis of the author's experience, leading to a proof from physics of the odd parity rule in the disciplines of computer graphics and computational geometry. Experiment 2 represents the experience that serendipitously led the author and his colleagues at Bell Labs to the synthesis of the YADDES [101] algorithm. In Experiments 3 and 4, the instructor provides the subjects—students—with all the necessary and correct knowledge and tools—a deep analysis of the fundamentals of the underlying problem—and encourages them to reflect and introspect. In Experiment 5, the subjects—students—are exposed to a diverse number of projects to help build a database of diverse experiences, knowledge, and principles, from which they can draw in the event of a new unprecedented problem. The results observed are highly encouraging, as reported later.

The origin of Experiment 1 [6] dates back to 1993 when the author, then at Brown University, learned of the odd parity rule for the point location problem in 2-space in the field of computer graphics. After closer examination, two issues emerged. First, while Sutherland and Hodgman [244] had proposed the odd parity rule as early as 1974, they had neglected to provide any proof of correctness of the algorithm. Second, despite highly complex mathematical derivations by a number of leading researchers from computational geometry, the odd parity rule could not be successfully generalized to any arbitrary closed surface in 3-space. Driven by the need to find an explanation of the rule, the author meticulously explored fundamental principles from a number of relevant areas in physics and mathematics, especially the laws governing electromagnetic force, electromagnetic induction, Faraday's law, and Maxwell's equations, but failed. In the process, however, the author gained an intuitive belief that Gauss's law might hold the key. Nevertheless, a connection between the two topics could not be successfully established. Mathematically, Gauss's law [245] states that the surface integral of the electric field along any closed hypothetical surface in 3-space is proportional to the net charge enclosed by the surface. In simple terms, the next flux emanating out of a surface is zero, where no charge is enclosed, and nonzero otherwise. An effort to understand the real meaning underlying Gauss's law led the author to a number of handwritten sketches in [13], where, through constructing a number of small truncated cones and generalizing them to infinitesimal manifestations to resemble the lines of electric flux, Feynman explains why Gauss's law works. In a flash of intuition, the author was able to successfully connect Gauss's law to the point location problem, realizing that to determine whether a point lies within or without any given arbitrary closed surface, one only needs to place a point charge at that location. If the point is located within the surface, any ray emanating from the point, resembling a flux line, must intersect the surface an odd number of times so that the net flux out of the surface is nonzero. Similarly, for a point located outside, any line from the point must intersect the surface an even number of times, yielding a net zero flux, relative to the surface. The benefits of developing the proof are twofold. First, the odd parity rule may now be extended to any arbitrary region in 3-space with complete confidence. Second, mathematical techniques from vector calculus and analytic geometry may be exploited to yield fast and efficient solutions to point location problems in 3-space.

The venue for Experiment 2 was Bell Labs Research in 1988, where the author and his colleagues were closely involved in the design of the Yet Another Distributed Discrete-Event Simulation (YADDES) algorithm [101], the first and only algorithm in the literature to achieve deadlock-free execution of distributed discrete-event simulation on distributed processors. The effort was motivated by an editorial in a leading journal that presented a coherent, logical argument on why such a deadlock-free algorithm could never be developed. The three coauthors first meticulously explored every known approach, principle, and technique to design a suitable algorithm and failed. Then, quite by accident, coauthor DeBenedictis, whose expertise in hardware and operating systems led to his successful design of the 16-node and 64-node Bell Labs hypercube processors, stumbled on the D-algorithm for sequential digital circuits, also known as the iterative test generator [246] in the literature on test generation and fault simulation of digital circuits. Given the difficulty of generating test vectors for sequential digital circuits with feedback loops, and armed with the technique of the D algorithm for combinatorial digital circuits, the iterative test generator adopts the following strategy. The feedback lines in a given sequential circuit, say C_s, are identified and cut and multiple, say p, copies of the resulting combinatorial circuit, say C_c, are generated. At the points where the feedback lines are cut, pseudo inputs and pseudo outputs are introduced in C_c. Thus C_c consists of pseudo inputs, pseudo outputs, and the original primary inputs and outputs. The p copies of C_c are combined into a new circuit, say C_p, where the pseudo outputs of the ith copy are identified with the corresponding pseudo inputs of the $(i + 1)$th copy. Now the D algorithm is applied to C_p, i.e., for a selected fault in the jth copy, the algorithm attempts to synthesize a test vector for the fault. Thus, from the jth copy, the test generator tries to propagate a D or a $\overline{D}$ forward until, in some copy within the p copies, the D or a $\overline{D}$ reaches a primary output. If in the process, one encounters the last copy without reaching a primary output, the test generator gives up and declares failure. DeBenedictis's reflection led him to generate a circuit, similar to C_p in every respect, except that it included only two copies of C_c. He termed this a data-flow network, labeled the first copy, on the left, as primed and the second copy, on the right, as unprimed. The coauthors had earlier identified that the principal difficulty with distributed event-driven simulation of sequential circuits was that, under certain conditions, signal values associated with output ports of specific components would incur no change. As a result, no new events would be propagated to the input ports of subsequent components. Although the signal value, in essence, remains unchanged, the lack of this information precludes the components from any further execution. Thus, despite the presence of outstanding events, all activities would come to a premature and abrupt halt, resulting in a deadlock. DeBenedictis reasoned intuitively that if he could relax the strict event-driven characteristics during the simulation of the primed copy of the data-flow network, it would not succumb to deadlock. The simulation results generated from the execution of the primed copy, however, may be in error. For accuracy, he required that these intermediate results be forced through to the unprimed copy of the data-flow network, which executes under strict event-driven principles and yields precise simulation results. Despite his unusually strong belief, DeBenedictis could neither explain how the data-flow network, a key component of YADDES, followed from contemporary knowledge nor mathematically justify that the approach could be generalized to every possible variation of any applicable problem and always guarantee a solution. The mathematical proof was developed by coauthor Ghosh, and, subsequently, extensive peer reviews coupled with an actual implementation confirmed the soundness of the YADDES algorithm.

Under Experiment 3, in a class on modeling and distributed simulation, the discussion focused on the intricacies of executing an asynchronous distributed algorithm on a loosely coupled parallel processor system, the potential races that may result from timing errors, the problem of isolating races, especially their propensity toward intermittence, and the great difficulty associated with determining the true source of the errors. The instructor started by describing an actual problem that had occurred while executing behavior-level models [27] on the Bell Labs hypercube. Behavior models for the different components of a digital system were developed, and each model was allocated to a unique processor of the 64-node hypercube loosely coupled parallel processor system. The connectivity between the components of the digital system were represented through software connections between the corresponding processors. The overall execution was under the control of an asynchronous, distributed, discrete-event simulation algorithm. As a result, there was no notion of global simulation time, and each model executed independently and concurrently. Upon receiving an external signal transition, a model, say M1, was initiated for execution, following which it would either generate or not generate an output response. When an output transition was generated, it was propagated to all other models that were connected to the output of M1. The communication primitives were nonblocking, implying that when a recipient model was busy but had adequate buffer space available, M1 would succeed in leaving the output transition in its buffer and then continue with its own execution. However, where the buffer of a recipient model, say M2, was full, for whatever reason, M1 would fail in transferring the output signal transition to M2. Under these circumstances, M1 would continue with its execution, but first it would store the output transition and then reattempt to propagate it to M2 at the next opportunity when presumably M2's buffer was no longer full. During execution, erroneous outputs were generated that were ultimately traced to a model, say M3. An initial examination of the behavior description of M3 yielded no errors. Next, a very limited number of print statements were included in the behavior description of M3 to provide a peek into its dynamic behavior. The error disappeared and correct results were obtained. However, as soon as the print statements were removed, the error reappeared. Thus, the error was clearly dependent on the timing, and the addition of the print statements was causing the relative timing to be altered sufficiently to prevent the error from manifesting itself. The scenario bears strong similarity to the classic Heisenberg uncertainty principle in that the use of a probe to observe the source of the error was affecting the very error itself. Every attempt to uncover the source of the error through the execution of the code and the observation of the execution results ended in failure. A few years ago, it had taken the instructor and another researcher at Bell Labs a great deal of time and careful analysis to uncover the cause of the error. As the instructor was about to explain it to the class, one of the students quickly reasoned from the fundamental principles of asynchronism and concurrency and made the following observation which, indeed, constitutes the correct explanation of the source of the error. The intense reflection of the student had successfully triggered the creative solution to drop onto the student. Assume that the execution of M2 is slower than that of M1 and, as a result, one or more of M1's messages are not successfully delivered to M2. That is, these messages are stored within M1 and, thereafter, M1 continues with its execution. During its subsequent execution, M1 generates another output transition, which it immediately sends to M2, successfully. However, because the previously generated output transitions for M2 are still stored within M1, M2 ends up receiving transitions from M1 in incorrect order. To correct the error, therefore, the behavior of the model must be modified as follows. When a new transition is generated, it must first be stored in local storage in the correct order, and then the model must attempt to propagate the entries to their correct destinations.

Under Experiment 4, in a class on data structures and algorithms, the discussion was centered on developing a string search algorithm to determine whether and how many times the sequence of characters in a given substring, SUB, occurs exactly in a master string, MS, of characters, where MS is much longer than SUB. Figure 9.2 presents a picture of the master string, MS, consisting of the characters $\{a, b, c, d, a, z, h, k, \ldots\}$ while the substring SUB consists of the sequence $\{a, b, m, r\}$. In the simple method [247], first the left-most boundary of SUB is aligned with the left-most boundary of MS and then the individual characters of SUB, starting at the left, are compared with that of MS. The comparison is continued as long as the corresponding characters match, up to four characters, the length of SUB. If the result of a comparison

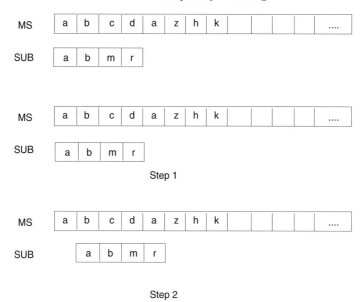

Fig. 9.2. A Simple String Search Algorithm

is negative, the examination is discontinued and, for the subsequent step, SUB must be realigned relative to MS. Step 1 in Figure 9.2 represents the process wherein a match occurs between MS and SUB in the first two characters, a and b, but then a mismatch occurs in the third character. Under realignment, SUB is shifted to the right by one position, as shown in Step 2 in Figure 9.2, and the corresponding characters of SUB and MS are again reexamined, starting at the left-most boundary of SUB. Here, a mismatch occurs in the first character, a. Thus, for every character of SUB, a comparison is performed against every character of MS. Therefore, the complexity of the algorithm, given by the total number of comparisons, is equal to the length of MS multiplied by the length of SUB, and is high. Pothering and Naps [247] present an improvement, labeled Knuth-Morris-Pratt or the KMP algorithm [248]. After analysis of the C++ code, presented in [247], it is noted that the KMP algorithm is founded on two key improvements, described later.

In the string search problem, as the search progresses, the characters of the master string MS are read progressively from an external file. Thus, MS is not known in its entirety to the algorithm during execution, until MS has been examined completely. In contrast, the characters in SUB become available to the algorithm quickly during execution. The KMP algorithm recognizes that analysis of SUB may benefit the search process because the characters of SUB are few in number and are repeatedly examined and compared against the individual characters of MS.

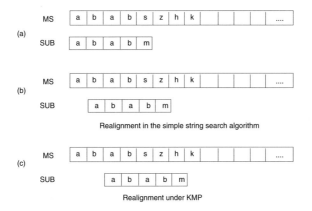

Fig. 9.3. First Improvement of the KMP Algorithm

For the first improvement, the primary focus is on the realignment. Assume that an examination of the substring SUB reveals two repeated patterns of unique characters. After SUB is aligned initially with MS, assume that either a complete match occurs between SUB and the corresponding characters of MS or that both patterns of SUB match with the corresponding characters of MS but that the match eventually fails at a subsequent position. Under both of these circumstances, for the subsequent realignment, SUB is shifted right by as many spaces as the length of the pattern. For a mismatch where even the first pattern does not match, under realignment, SUB may be shifted right only by one place. In Figure 9.3, the sequence ab constitutes the repeated pattern in SUB. The characters in the pattern are unique. Under the simple string search approach, realignment would consist of shifting SUB right by one space, as shown in Figure 9.3(b). Because both patterns—ab and ab—of SUB match with the corresponding characters of MS, as noted in Figure 9.3(a), and as the mismatch occurs in the fifth character of SUB, for the subsequent realignment of SUB, there is no need to shift SUB by a single space and perform the comparison because no match will occur. The first character of SUB will fall directly under the character b of MS, and being unique, they will differ. KMP recognizes this fact, shifts SUB by two spaces, the length of the pattern, ab, as shown in Figure 9.3(c), and initiates a comparison starting at the third position of SUB.

For the second improvement, the KMP algorithm focuses on the starting position of the character-by-character comparison, following a realignment. Assume that SUB consists of a number of contiguous repeated characters, as is likely to be the case with binary strings. Where a match occurs between a few of these repeated characters of SUB, say j, and the corresponding characters of MS, and is followed by a mismatch, SUB is first realigned by shifting it to the right by one space. The subsequent comparison phase skips the first $(j-1)$ characters from the beginning of SUB and starts at the jth position.

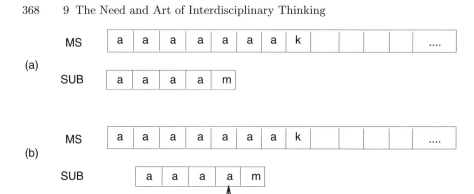

Fig. 9.4. Second Improvement of the KMP Algorithm

KMP recognizes that the result of the comparison of the $(j-1)$ characters is already known to be affirmative from the previous step. In contrast, in the simple string search technique, the comparison phase would commence with the first character of SUB. In Figure 9.4(a), the first four characters of SUB are identical, and a mismatch is observed to occur in the fifth position of SUB. Following a realignment, the comparison phase under KMP, as shown in Figure 9.4(b), skips the first three characters of SUB because they have already been successfully compared against the corresponding characters of MS.

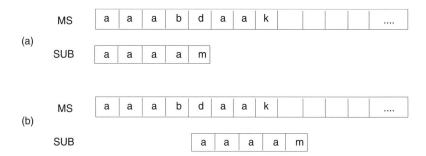

Fig. 9.5. Discovering a Third Improvement over the Simple String Search Technique

At the conclusion of the class presentation of the two key improvements underlying KMP, a student suddenly discovered a new, third key improvement over the simple string search technique. Intense reflection had again successfully triggered a creative solution, never before known, to literally drop onto the student. This mechanism focuses on an improved realignment, where SUB contains a number of contiguous repeated characters. Consider the MS and SUB, shown in Figure 9.5(a), where SUB contains a sequence, *aaaa*. Following initial alignment and examination, SUB appears to differ from MS in the fourth place. Because the first four characters are identical, clearly, the fourth character of MS cannot be a. If, as a part of the realignment, SUB were to be shifted right by one, two, or three places, the subsequent comparisons would fail at the fourth character of MS. The corresponding characters of SUB and MS would be a and b, respectively. Therefore, SUB may be shifted right by four places as a part of the realignment, constituting a genuine improvement.

Under Experiment 5, the innovative thinking process underlying an unusual problem is first explained, very carefully, to the subjects. They are then asked to solve another very different challenging real-world problem [249] [250]. In the mid-1990s in California, State highway 71 needed repair. Traffic would have to be diverted from highway 71 onto another highway, State Route 83, for the duration of the repair. The U.S. Fish and Wildlife Service voiced their concern that an endangered songbird species, least Bell's vireo, that lives along Route 83 would be adversely affected by the increase in the ambient noise level. The adult birds would probably be scared away, leaving the eggs and young chicks vulnerable, eventually jeopardizing the entire population. The U.S. Fish and Wildlife Service and the California Department of Transportation were deadlocked when some brilliant person reflected deeply on the problem and came up with a creative plan. First, the current ambient noise level along Route 83 would be measured and recorded, as say, N1. Clearly, the bird species had learned to tolerate noise N1. Next, the highway department would erect sound barriers along Route 83 and monitor the sound level on the other side of the barrier, as traffic is diverted away from State highway 71, making certain that it never exceeds N1. The plan worked beautifully.

The subjects are then given a challenging problem. The Kansai Airport [251], built by Japan, is an artificial island in Osaka Bay, deliberately located far away from the Japanese mainland so that the airport could be kept operational 24 hours, 365 days a year, without driving the citizens deaf or to insomnia. The decision to locate the airport so far away from the mainland implied that underwater construction would have to confront both alluvial and diluvial soil. While the properties of alluvial soil were well known, especially when subject to heavy loads, those of the diluvial layer were unknown. As construction proceeded, significant problems surfaced. The entire island was sinking faster and deeper than expected and, more critically, the sinking was uneven across the island. The net result was a cost overrun of several billion dollars, a delay of a year in opening the airport, and the precipitous fact that the island was continuing to sink into the bay. The subjects were asked to examine every available document on the topic, which in itself was a challenge because the Japanese government had been attempting to systematically erase all available records to avoid public panic. The subjects were then to study the problem of sinking, reflect deeply on the fundamental issues, and present recommendations for both corrective actions and design guidelines for building future island airports. The subjects returned with a simple yet highly creative solution. Only their recommendation for future island airport design is presented here.

The literature reveals that, from the beginning, complete noise elimination was a fundamental nonnegotiable, criterion of the Kansai project. This dictated the choice of the site far out in the sea, resulting in the problems of absolute and differential sinking, delay, cost overruns, and the undeniable threat that, sometime in the future, the airport may completely disappear into Osaka Bay. As in the example of the endangered bird species along the highway in California, the Kansai project team could have started by first measuring the ambient noise generated by airports for different traffic volumes and its decline as one moves outward from the airport, in a radial direction. Second, the average noise level that is deemed tolerable by people, during the day and at night, could have been determined through a combination of actual measurements, surveys, and computer modeling. As an example, New York State law categorically limits any noise level to 90 db. Armed with these two sets of measurements, the project team could then have calculated how far out into the sea the airport should be located. Under this proposed approach, conceivably, the airport would have been placed closer to the mainland and the problem of confronting the diluvial layer avoided completely. Clearly, the recommendation is original and stems from the subjects resorting to explicit reflection as well as drawing from their rich internal database of a number of creative solutions in diverse scenarios. While the recommendation may appear simple, in hindsight, it is not trivial. The Kansai project team could certainly have used it and avoided the incredible difficulties they encountered.

10

The Future of ADDM Algorithms

Today, human civilization has arrived at a unique crossroad. Standing at this juncture and looking back at the past 3,000+ years of history, it is clear that the essence of the greatest human aspirations and achievements have been material in nature. While abstract thoughts have always been present, the focus had primarily been on matter—large and massive structures of brick, mortar, and steel. As examples, the seven wonders of the ancient world, including the hanging gardens of Babylon and the Taj Mahal, and the modern day achievements including jumbo jets, space rockets, and tall skyscrapers, are all fundamentally material and tangible. In contrast, analysis of the incessant proliferation of computers and networks today clearly points to the following prediction for the future. Humankind's greatest and most noble aspirations, a thousand years from today, will inevitably be focused primarily on the abstract—thoughts, concepts, and ideas of great depth—distinct from the massive material objects of the past. While intangible and possibly transcending the known laws of physics, the abstract notions will be made possible by hardware, software, networks, and simulation. As an example, consider the ongoing transformation of paper-based letter and document correspondence, traditionally handled by the post office and private couriers, into electronic documents that are exchanged via e-mail attachments. Similar paradigm shifts are conceivable in the retail industry in the future where, instead of a store mailing out a physical product, say a wrist watch, the buyer would receive its blueprint through the network from which he or she would then synthesize the watch at home, using a product synthesis machine. Other unprecedented abstract notions may become ubiquitous in the future. For example, the experiences, thoughts, and decision strategies of the great minds and exemplary leaders may be encapsulated in the form of sophisticated programs with which an individual may interact dynamically to seek insights into decision making under intricate contemporary situations. In this projected future era, NIT systems will serve as the underlying infrastructure with ADDM algorithms constituting the founding principle.

The use of NIT systems to meet our current needs and facilitate society's future aspirations is not mere coincidence. Careful analysis reveals that there is an undeniable parallel between the fundamental elements of human civilization and the underlying architecture of NIT systems. The essence of a civilization's progress may be encapsulated as follows. One or more individuals conceive of an idea and then exchange it with other appropriate members. Using feedback and suggestions from others, the idea is refined, and, in the event the modified idea is accepted and endorsed by a significant fraction of the members, it is ultimately adopted and realized. Clearly, the key elements here include intelligent decision making, located within the members, communication between the appropriate members of society, and the overarching purpose or intent behind the exercise. These correspond to the elements of any NIT system architecture, nodes, links, and the underlying control algorithm.

In the author's vision, the evolution of the information age in the future will inevitably witness very large-scale NIT systems, encompassing millions of entities spread over enormous geographical distances. Even if the technology underlying computing undergoes a revolutionary change in the future, embracing chemical, biological, or a purely nonmaterial electromagnetic basis, or if we were to push networking technology higher into the electromagnetic spectrum, exploiting X-ray, gamma-ray, or cosmic-ray frequencies, or discover an entirely new medium of transmission along a different and currently unknown dimension of reality, the nature of computing and networking, and the essence of the interaction between them will remain invariant. As a direct consequence, the foundation of ADDM algorithms will continue to remain in effect well into the future. The support for this vision lies in the observation that NIT systems represent an external manifestation of the innate fundamental nature of human civilization in that each individual human brain processes sensor data and information received from select individuals and computes decisions, which are then used as either control or are shared with other appropriate human beings, subject to a defined purpose. Because every individual, X, will inevitably encounter unique situations in life, and as no one else can walk the path on behalf of X, the more experienced ones can only hope to help guide X by sharing their own decisions, experiences, and insights. A few of the challenges and opportunities associated with ADDM algorithms include the following:

- To help realize large-scale NIT systems and exploit their tremendous potential in innovative ways, society in general and NIT engineers in particular must be educated from the perspectives of concurrent thinking and precise decentralized control, transcending traditional sequential thinking.
- The requirement of creative thinking, subject to the principles outlined in this book, is inherent in the design of ADDM algorithms and intrinsically promises two outcomes. First, it may lead to innovative NIT products and services. Second, and more important, it is likely to foster an environment where new discoveries will feed onto the cycle of innovation, leading to an

unprecedented exponential increase in creativity. The onset of ADDM algorithms can potentially lead to genuine and scientific revolution in transportation; secure and timely access to medical records; military command, control, and communication at tactical speeds and with strategic prowess; fast domestic and international banking; and efficient and rapid inventory management. No longer will a sporting goods store, located in Mesa, Arizona, have to ship a specific pair of sports shoes, on request from a sister store 10 miles away in Tempe, Arizona, first to the central warehouse 450 miles away in California, where it is routed back to Tempe, requiring a total of four business days.

A number of leading researchers in the distributed algorithms community have expressed a desire to have the steps leading to an ADDM algorithm design, defined exactly, in the form of a simple standard. They argue that for a given problem, any engineer should be able to quickly deduce a suitable ADDM algorithm. There are two difficulties with this thinking. First, by their very nature, NIT systems preclude enumeration of ADDM algorithms in the form of a cookbook. An ADDM algorithm must be original and, while difficult to synthesize, the rewards are immense. In this sense, the nature of ADDM algorithms differ fundamentally from centralized algorithms, and their extension, synchronous distributed algorithms. Second, it must be remembered that standards constitute a double-edged sword. While they facilitate the development of products by industry—an undeniable necessity—excessive reliance on standards will invariably lead to lack of progress and stagnation.

- Today's incremental improvements in computing power and the gradual increase in available communication bandwidths, coupled with quantum leaps in networking and computing technologies that we may witness tomorrow, will invariably enable novel and highly useful NIT systems. Building on the shoulders of robust and reliable first-generation NIT systems, newer, more ambitious, and supercomplex NIT systems, beyond our present comprehension, may become realizable. The anticipated progress will herald a true leap into the future, advancing the public's confidence in NIT systems from the quantitative to the qualitative level.
- The design of an ADDM algorithm must be systematic, per the principles outlined in the book, and accompanied by precision thinking and judicious choice of important parameters. The nature of the constituent components must be simple, even when there may be many, and their interactions must be as simple as possible. The underlying simplicity yields reliability. A well-designed algorithm for a highly useful NIT system may last a very long time, providing us with a stable platform from which one may focus on more complex objectives. The focus of the design must be long term, keeping in mind that civilization will last a very long time. In contrast, a quick and poorly designed algorithm may lead to failures, possibly causing human suffering and eroding public confidence.

- Although the synthesis of any ADDM algorithm is a creative exercise that cannot be bound by a predetermined process, the scientific representation, validation, testing, and performance analysis of an ADDM algorithm, following its synthesis, may be greatly facilitated by availability of a suitable language, similar to VHDL in the field of computer design. Along with leading international researchers, the author's research group is currently engaged in developing a secure network-centric system design (SNCSD) language. The required attributes of the language are many; only the most important one is discussed here. In any language design, the semantics of the language constructs must encapsulate, by definition, the complete knowledge of the characteristics of the fundamental constituent components and every conceivable interaction between the components as they are combined together to form high-level complex systems. In this spirit, the SNCSD language must encapsulate the fundamental properties of the basic building blocks of NIT systems and be cognizant of every possible interaction between them. In addition, the language must be amenable to representing ADDM algorithms as the underlying control of NIT systems, naturally, consistently, and accurately. Though challenging, without this ability, the SNCSD language may lead to failures and inconsistent designs.
- In 1990, following the conclusion of his presentation at Bellcore, now Telcordia, of an important ADDM algorithm, YADDES, a senior Bellcore researcher asked the author: Beyond its application to network modeling and simulation, what role, in your opinion, can YADDES play in society? The question struck a chord deep within the author, and a subsequent lengthy introspection on the nature of ADDM algorithms led to an intuitive leap, culminating in the following inspirations. First, conceptually, society must be amenable to an order, an organization where each constituent individual is represented by his or her unique and innate talent set. Also, the talents interact uniformly to constitute the total behavior of the society. Second, as with the entities in an ADDM algorithm, every individual must occupy the same status, and there should be neither centralized control nor any hierarchy of control. Control must be distributed equitably among all of the constituent individuals. Third, society must respect every individual and recognize that they may play a unique role. Furthermore, the manner in which an individual chooses to contribute to society is determined by one's own self, never dictated by another individual. Fourth, clearly, to achieve these goals, a new form of individualized education must be invented that attempts to bring forth the intrinsic ability in each individual, in its best form. Also, all available resources must be distributed equitably among the individuals. Fifth, the direct consequences of achieving these goals would imply (1) a societywide reduction, possibly total elimination, of hopelessness, despair, apprehension, and fear; (2) increase in meaningfulness, purpose, and harmony of individual efforts; and (3) the realization of freedom of individual work, effort, and function in society, beyond the traditional political freedom, i.e., self-governance.

In essence, the practical realization of ADDM algorithms not only inspires us but provides a powerful motivating force that a society with perfect equality and no hierarchy may be practically realizable in a distant future.

References

1. John McLaughlin. Face It, E-ZPass Is Just One Big Multimillion-Dollar Jinx. *Sunday Star Ledger*, New Jersey, 21 July 2002.
2. Lawrence Lessig. *The Future of Ideas: The Fate of the Commons in a Connected World*. Random House Inc., New York, 2001.
3. Harold W. Lawson. Rebirth of the Computer Industry. *Communications of the ACM*, 45(6):25–29, June 2002.
4. Private communications with Dr. Al Aho, Vice President of Research, Bell Labs, Lucent Technologies. Stevens Institute of Technology, Hoboken, New Jersey 07030, December 2001.
5. Private communication with Prof. Gottfried Luderer, Emeritus ISS Chaired Professor and formerly Department Head at Bell Laboratories. Electrical Engineering Department, Arizona State University, Tempe, Arizona 85287, January 2002 and 15 August 2002.
6. Sumit Ghosh. *Hardware Description Languages: Concepts and Principles*. IEEE Press, Piscataway, New Jersey, 1999.
7. Franklin M. Harold. *The Way of the Cell: Molecules, Organisms, and the Order of Life*. Oxford University Press, New York, 2001.
8. Private communications with Dr. Frank Fernandez, Former Director of Defense Advanced Research Projects Agency, Arlington, Virginia. Stevens Institute of Technology, Hoboken, New Jersey, February 2001.
9. Private communications with Raj Ghaman, U.S. Department of Transportation, Washington, D.C. Arizona State University, Tempe, August 2000.
10. Sumit Ghosh and Tony Lee. *Intelligent Transportation Systems: New Principles and Architectures*. CRC Press, Boca Raton, FL, 2000.
11. Noppanunt Utamaphethai and Sumit Ghosh. DICAF, A High Performance, Distributed, Scalable Architecture for IVHS Utilizing a Continuous Function—"Congestion Measure." *IEEE Computer*, 31(3):78–84, March 1998.
12. William Morris (Ed.). *The American Heritage Dictionary of the English Language*. Houghton Mifflin Company, Boston, 1981.
13. R.P. Feynman, R.B. Leighton, and M. Sands. *The Feynman Lectures on Physics Vol I*. Addison-Wesley Publishing Company, Reading, Massachusetts, 1964.
14. Sumit Ghosh and Tony Lee. *Modeling and Asynchronous Distributed Simulation: Analyzing Complex Systems*. IEEE Press, Piscataway, New Jersey, June 2000.

15. R.P. Feynman. *The Character of Physical Law*. The Messenger Lectures. MIT Press, Cambridge, MA, 1990.

16. *Sworn to Secrecy*, aired 18 April 2000. History Channel, Cable television, http://www.historychannel.com.

17. *Suicide Missions*, aired 12 June 2000. History Channel, Cable television, http://www.historychannel.com.

18. *Extreme Machines*, aired 4 June 2000. The Learning Channel, Cable television, http://www.tlc.com.

19. Lt. Col. Robert Hartel. C^4I for the Warrior. In *Symposium on Command and Control Research*, National Defense University, Washington, D.C., 28-29 June 1993.

20. T. Lee and S. Ghosh. A Novel Approach to Asynchronous, Decentralized Decision-Making in Military Command and Control. *IEEE Computational Science and Engineering*, 3(4):69–79, Winter 1996.

21. D.C. Coll, A.U. Sheikh, R.G. Ayers, and J.H. Bailey. The Communications System Architecture of the North American Advanced Train Control System. *IEEE Transactions on Vehicular Technology*, 39(3):244–55, August 1990.

22. D. Gross. Centralized Inventory Control in Multi-Location Supply System. In H. Scarf, D. Gilford, and M. Shelley (Eds.) *Multi-stage Inventory Models and Techniques*, Stanford University Press, Stanford, California, 1963.

23. H.D. Goldstein, Vice President of Strategy and Planning. *Field Test Report*. NYNEX Assurance Services, Elmsford, New York, May 1994.

24. C. Linn and B. Howarth. A Proposed Globally Distributed Federated Database: A Practical Performance Evaluation. In *Proceedings of the Third International Conference on Parallel and Distributed Information Systems*, pages 203–12, Austin, TX, September 1994.

25. T. Markas, M. Royals, and N. Kanopoulos. On Distributed Fault Simulation. *IEEE Computer*, 23(1):40–52, January 1990.

26. Gerard Tel. *Topics in Distributed Algorithms*, chapter 1, page 1. Cambridge International Series on Parallel Computation. Cambridge University Press, 1991.

27. S. Ghosh and M-L. Yu. An Asynchronous Distributed Approach for the Simulation and Verification of Behavior-Level Models on Parallel Processors. *IEEE Transactions on Parallel and Distributed Systems*, 6(6):639–52, June 1995.

28. C. Tron, Y. Arrouye, J.C. de Kergommeaux, J.P. Kitajima, E. Maillet, B. Plateau, and J.-M. Vincent. Performance Evaluation of Parallel Systems: ALPES Environment. In *Proceedings of the International Conference on Parallel Computing: Trends and Applications*, pages 715–18, Grenoble, France, September 1993.

29. R. Ronngren, L. Barriga, and R. Ayani. An Incremental Benchmark Suite for Performance Tuning of Parallel Discrete Event Simulation. In *Proceedings of the Twenty-Ninth Hawaii International Conference on System Sciences*, pages 373–82, Wailea, HI, January 1996.

30. A. Gupta and V. Kumar. Analyzing Performance of Large Scale Parallel Systems: In *Proceedings of the Twenty-Sixth Hawaii International Conference on System Sciences*, pages 144–53, Wailea, HI, January 1993.

31. A. Gupta and V. Kumar. Performance Properties of Large Scale Parallel Systems. *Journal of Parallel and Distributed Computing*, 19(3):234–44, November 1993.

32. J. Brehm, M. Madhukar, E. Smirni, and L. Dowdy. PerPreT—A Performance Prediction Tool for Massively Parallel Systems. In *8th International Conference on Modelling Techniques and Tools for Computer Performance Evaluation*, pages 284–98, Heidelberg, Germany, September 1995.

33. R. Kushwaha. Methodology for Predicting Performance of Distributed and Parallel Systems. *Performance Evaluation*, 18(3):189–204, November 1993.

34. R.L. Braddock, M.R. Claunch, J.W. Rainbolt, and B.N. Corwin. Operational Performance Metrics in a Distributed System, Metrics and Interpretation. In *Proceedings of the ACM/SIGAPP Symposium on Applied Computing*, pages 873–82, Kansas City, Missouri, March 1992.

35. J. Lecuivre and Y.-Q. Song. A Framework for Validating Distributed Real Time Applications by Performance Evaluation of Communication Profiles. In *Proceedings of the 1995 IEEE International Workshop on Factory Communication Systems*, pages 37–46, Leysin, Switzerland, October 1995.

36. A. Kumar, S. Ramakrishnan, C. Deshpande, and L. Dunning. Performance Comparison of Two Algorithms for Task Assignment. In *Proceedings of the 1994 IEEE International Conference on Parallel Processing*, pages 83–87, Raleigh, North Carolina, August 1994.

37. Y. Arrouye. Scope: An Extensible Interactive Environment for the Performance Evaluation of Parallel Systems. *Microprocessing and Microprogramming*, 41(8–9):609–23, April 1996.

38. M.J. Clement and M.J. Quinn. Architectural Scaling and Analytical Performance Prediction. In *Seventh International Conference on Parallel and Distributed Computing Systems*, pages 16–21, Las Vegas, October 1994.

39. O. Kremien. Scalability in Distributed Systems, Parallel Systems and Supercomputers. In *Proceedings of the International Conference on High-Performance Computing and Networking*, pages 532–41, Milan, Italy, May 1995.

40. M. Manwaring, M. Chowdhury, and V. Malbasa. An Architecture for Parallel Interpretation: Performance Measurements. In *Proceedings of the 20th EUROMICRO Conference*, pages 531–37, Liverpool, U.K., September 1994.

41. M. Celenk and W. Yang. Performance Evaluation of the Networks of Workstations for Parallel Processing Applications. In *Proceedings of the 26th Southeastern Symposium on System Theory*, pages 540–44, Athens, Ohio, March 1994.

42. H. Westphal and D. Popovic. Performance Evaluation of Distributed, Intelligent Real-Time Control Systems. In *Proceedings of the 1994 American Control Conference*, pages 2662–2666, Baltimore, June 1994.

43. W. Ertel. On the Definition of Speedup (Parallel Algorithms). In *6th International PARLE Conference Proceedings*, pages 289–300, Athens, Greece, July 1994.

44. R.S. Barr and B.L. Hickman. On Reporting the Speedup of Parallel Algorithms: A Survey of Issues and Experts. In *Computer Science and Operations Research. New Developments in Their Interfaces*, pages 279–93, Williamsburg, Virginia, January 1992.

45. F. Wieland, D. Jefferson, and P. Reiher. Experiences in Parallel Performance Measurement: The Speedup Bias. In *Symposium on Experiences with Distributed and Multiprocessor Systems*, pages 205–15, Newport Beach, California, March 1992.

46. J.C. Yan and S. Listgarten. Intrusion Compensation for Performance Evaluation of Parallel Programs on a Multicomputer. In *Sixth International Conference on Parallel and Distributed Computing Systems*, pages 427–31, Louisville, Kentucky, October 1993.

47. K.N. Lalgudi, D. Bhattacharya, and P. Agrawal. On the Performance Prediction of Parallel Algorithms. In *Seventh International Conference on Parallel and Distributed Computing Systems*, pages 330–35, Las Vegas, October 1994.

48. P.C. Capon. Understanding the Behaviour of Parallel Systems. In *Proceedings of the Workshop on Performance Measurement and Visualization of Parallel Systems*, pages 201–23, Moravany, Czechoslovakia, October 1992.

49. D.E. Culler, R.M. Karp, D. Patterson, A. Sahay, E.E. Santos, K.E. Schauser, R. Subramonian, and T. von Eicken. LogP: A Practical Model of Parallel Computation. *Communications of the ACM*, 39(11):78–85, November 1996.

50. G. Bilardi, K. Herley, A. Pietracaprina, G. Pucci, and P. Spirakis. BSP vs. LogP. In *Proceedings of the 1996 8th ACM Symposium on Parallel Algorithms and Architectures*, pages 25–32, Padua, Italy, June 24-26 1996.

51. H.G. Rotithor. Enhanced Bayesian Decision Model for Decentralized Decision Making in a Dynamic Environment. In *Proceedings of the IEEE International Conference on Systems, Man, and Cybernetics Vol 3*, pages 2091–2096, Charlottesville, Virginia, June 1991.

52. J.N. Tsitsiklis and M. Athans. Convergence and Asymptotic Agreement in Distributed Decision Problems. *IEEE Transactions on Automatic Control*, 29(1):42–50, January 1984.

53. J.N. Tsitsiklis and M. Athans. On the Complexity of Decentralized Decision Making and Detection Problems. *IEEE Transactions on Automatic Control*, 30(5):440–46, May 1985.

54. D.P. Bertsekas and J.N. Tsitsiklis. Distributed Asynchronous Algorithms. In *Proceedings of the 1988 IEEE International Conference on Systems, Man, and Cybernetics*, pages 591–93, 1988.

55. John Tsitsiklis and George Stamoulis. On the Average Communication Complexity of Asynchronous Distributed Algorithms. *Journal of the ACM*, 42(2):382–400, March 1995.

56. H. Ihara and K. Mori. Autonomous Decentralized Computer Control Systems. *IEEE Computer*, 17(8):57–66, August 1984.

57. Yoshiteru Ishida. The Immune System as a Prototype of Autonomous Decentralized Systems: An Overview. In *Proceedings of the Third IEEE International Symposium on Autonomous Decentralized Systems*, pages 85–92, Berlin, Germany, April 9-11 1997.

58. O. Kremien, J. Kramer, and J. Magee. Rapid Assessment of Decentralized Algorithms. In *Proceedings of the IEEE International Conference on Computer Systems and Software Engineering (COMPSAC)*, pages 329–35, 1990.

59. G.F. Coulouris and J. Dollimore. *Distributed Systems: Concepts and Design*. Addison Wesley Publishing, Reading, Massachusetts, 1988.

60. T.H. Cormen, C.E. Leiserson, and R.L. Rivest. *Introduction to Algorithms*. MIT Press, Cambridge, Massachusetts, 1990.

61. F.T. Leighton. *Introduction to Parallel Algorithms and Architectures*. Morgan Kaufmann Publishers, San Mateo, California, 1992.

62. N. Lynch. *Distributed Algorithms*. Morgan Kaufmann Publishers, San Mateo, California, 1996.

63. F. Christian and C. Fetzer. The Timed Asynchronous Distributed Model. *IEEE Transactions on Parallel and Distributed Systems*, 10(6):642–57, June 1999.

64. Z. Kohavi. *Switching and Finite Automata Theory*. McGraw Hill Book Company, New York, 1978.

65. S. Muroga. *Logic Design and Switching Theory*. John Wiley & Sons, New York, 1979.

66. Swami Venkatasananda. *The Concise Yoga Vasistha*. State University of New York Press, Albany, New York, 1984.

67. M.J. Flynn. Parallel Processors Were the Future … and May Yet Be. *IEEE Computer*, 29(12):152, December 1996.

68. J.K. Peacock, J.W. Wong, and E.G. Manning. Distributed Simulation Using a Network of Processors. *Computer Networks*, 3(1):44–56, 1979.

69. K.M. Chandy and J. Misra. Asynchronous Distributed Simulation via a Sequence of Parallel Computations. *Communications of the ACM*, 24(4):198–206, April 1981.

70. K.M. Chandy, L.M. Haas, and J. Misra. Distributed Deadlock Detection. *ACM Transactions on Computer Systems*, 1(2):144–56, May 1983.

71. D.A. Reed and A. Malony. Parallel Discrete Event Simulation: The Chandy-Misra Approach. In *Proceedings of the SCS Multiconference on Distributed Simulation*, pages 8–13, San Diego, California, February 1988.

72. R.V. Iyer and S. Ghosh. DARYN, A Distributed Decision-Making Algorithm for Railway Networks: Modeling and Simulation. *IEEE Transactions on Vehicular Technology*, 44(1):180–91, February 1995.

73. Swiss National Tourist Office. *Switzerland through the Eyes of Others*. Coordinating Committee for the Presence of Switzerland Abroad, Documentation Group, Swiss National Tourist Office, 1992.

74. *Predators: How They Hunt*, aired 2 March 2002. Discovery Channel, Cable television, http://www.discovery.com.

75. *Dangerous Friends, Friendly Enemies*, In *Intimate Strangers: Unseen Life on Earth*, aired 26 February 2000. Public Broadcasting Service, KNME-TV, Albuquerque, New Mexico, http://www.pbs.org/opb/intimatestrangers/.

76. Department of the U.S. Air Force. Draft Request for Proposal F33615-83-R-1003, VHSIC Hardware Description Language (VHDL). *Sources Sought Synopsis PMRE 82-116*, September 1982.

77. The Institute of Electrical and Electronic Engineers. *IEEE Standard VHDL Language Reference Manual*. ANSI/IEEE Std 1076-1993, IEEE, Piscataway, New Jersey, April 14, 1994.

78. N. Ishiura, H. Yasuura, and S. Yajima. Time First Evaluation Algorithm for High-Speed Logic Simulation. In *Proceedings of the ICCAD*, pages 197–99, Santa Clara, California, 1984.

79. R.M. Fujimoto. Parallel Discrete Event Simulation. *Communications of the ACM*, 33(10):30–53, October 1990.

80. J. Misra. Distributed Discrete-Event Simulation. *Computing Surveys*, 18(1): 39–65, March 1986.

81. R.D. Chamberlain and M.A. Franklin. Hierarchical Discrete-Event Simulation on Hypercube Architectures. *IEEE Micro*, 10(4):10–20, 1990.

82. L. Soule and T. Blank. Parallel Logic Simulation on General Purpose Machines. In *Proceedings of the 25th Design Automation Conference*, Atlantic City, N.J., June 1988.

83. D. Jefferson. Virtual Time. *ACM Transactions on Programming Languages*, 7(3):404–25, July 1985.

84. P.J. Ashenden, H. Detmold, and W.S. McKeen. Parallel Execution of VHDL Models. *Technical Report 93-01*, Department of Computer Science, University of Adelaide, Australia, 1993.

85. J.V. Briner, J.L. Ellis, and G. Kedem. Breaking the Barrier of Parallel Simulation of Digital Systems. In *Proceedings of the 28th Design Automation Conference*, San Francisco, June 1991.

86. J. Sissler. Assessing the Potential of Multithreaded VHDL simulatiom. In *VHDL Boot Camp Proceedings, Fall '93 Conference*, pages 131–36, Red Lion Inn, San Jose, California, 10-13 October 1993.

87. P. Chawla, H. Carter, D. Barker, and S. Bilik. Preliminary Design and Analysis of a Hardware Accelerator for VHDL Simulation. In *Proceedings of the VHDL Boot Camp Conference*, pages 267–79, Red Lion Inn, San Jose, California, 10-13 October 1993.

88. F. Mattern. Efficient Algorithms for Distributed Snapshots and Global Virtual Time Approximation. *Journal of Parallel and Distributed Computing*, 18(4):423–34, 1993.

89. I.F. Akyildiz, L. Chen, S.R. Das, R. Fujimoto, and R. Serfozo. The Effect of Memory Capacity on Time Warp Performance. *Journal of Parallel and Distributed Computing*, 18(4):411–22, 1993.

90. D.M. Nicol and P. Heidelberger. Optimistic Parallel Simulation of Continuous Time Markov Chains Using Uniformization. *Journal of Parallel and Distributed Computing*, 18(4):395–410, 1993.

91. T.K. Som and R.G. Sargent. A New Process to Processor Assignment Criterion for Reducing Rollbacks in Optimistic Simulation. *Journal of Parallel and Distributed Computing*, 18(4):509–15, 1993.

92. C.P. Wen and K.A. Yelick. Parallel Timing Simulation on a Distributed Memory Multiprocessor. In *Proceedings of the ICCAD*, pages 131–36, Santa Clara, California, November 1993.

93. J.S. Steinman. SPEEDES: Synchronous Parallel Environment for Emulation and Discrete Event Simulation. In *Fifth Workshop on Parallel and Distributed Simulation (PADS91)*, pages 95–103, San Diego, California, 1991. The Society for Computer Simulation.

94. D. West. Lazy Rollback and Lazy Reevaluation. Master's thesis, University of Calgary, January 1988.

95. V. Krishnaswamy and P. Banerjee. Actor Based Parallel VHDL Simulation Using Time Warp. In *Proceedings of the Tenth Workshop on Parallel and Distributed Simulation (PADS96)*, Philadelphia, pages 135–42, 22-24 May 1996.

96. M.L. Bailey. A Time-Based Model for Investigating Parallel Logic-Level Simulation. *IEEE Transactions on CAD of Integrated Circuits and Systems*, 11(7):816–24, 1992.

97. K.M. Chandy and J. Misra. Asynchronous Distributed Simulation via a Sequence of Parallel Computations. *Communications of the ACM*, 24(4):198–206, April 1981.

98. Ronald DeVries. Reducing Null Messages in Misra's Distributed Discrete Event Simulation Method. *IEEE Transaction on Software Engineering*, 16(1):82–91, January 1990.

99. L. Soule and A. Gupta. Characterization of Parallelism and Deadlocks in Distributed Digital Logic Simulation. In *Proceedings of the 26th Design Automation Conference*, Las Vegas, June 1989.

100. K.M. Chandy and R. Sherman. The Conditional Event Approach to Distributed Simulation. In *SCS Multiconference on Distributed Simulation*, pages 93–99, Tampa, FL, March 1989.

101. Eric Debenedictis, Sumit Ghosh, and Meng-Lin Yu. An Asynchronous Distributed Discrete Event Simulation Algorithm for Cyclic Circuits Using Data-Flow Network. *IEEE Computer*, 24(6):21–33, June 1991.

102. Sumit Ghosh and Meng-Lin Yu. A Preemptive Scheduling Mechanism for Accurate Behavioral Simulation of Digital Designs. *IEEE Computer*, 38(11):1595–1600, November 1989.

103. Narsingh Deo. *Graph Theory with Applications to Engineering and Computer Science*. Prentice Hall Inc., Englewood Cliffs, New Jersey, 1974.

104. Sumit Ghosh. Behavioral-Level Fault Simulation. *IEEE Design and Test of Computers*, pages 31–42, June 1988.

105. S. Ghosh, D. Luckham, Y. Huh, and A. Stanculescu. The Semantics of Non Anticipatory Timing Constructs in Behavior-Level Hardware Description Languages. *Technical report 11354-860321-02tm*, Bell Laboratories Research, Holmdel, New Jersey, March 1986.

106. Steven Levitan. *VHDL Compiler (Vcomp) and VHDL Simulator (Vsim)*. *Technical report*, University of Pittsburgh Department of Electrical Engineering, June 1993.

107. John L. Hennessy and David A. Patterson. *Computer Architecture: A Quantitative Approach*. Morgan Kaufmann Publishers Inc., Palo Alto, 1990.

108. Interstate Commerce Commission. Ninety-Ninth Annual Report Transport Statistics in the United States. December 1987.

109. Private communication with Mr. Ryuji Sakamoto, General Manager, International Division, East Japan Railway Company. 1-6-5 Marunouchi, Chiyoda-ku, Tokyo 100, Japan, 1993.

110. P.H. Bernard. ASTREE: A Global Command, Control, and Communication System. *Transportation Research Record*, Transportation Research Board, Washington, D.C., pages 133–39, 1991.

111. R.J. Hill, S.L. Yu, and N.J. Dunn. Rail Transit Chopper Traction Interference Modeling Using the Spice Circuit Simulation Package. *IEEE Transactions on Vehicular Technology*, 38(4):237–46, 1989.

112. R.G. Ayers. Selection of a Forward Error Correcting Code for the Data Communication Radio Link of the Advanced Train Control-System. *IEEE Transactions on Vehicular Technology*, 38(4):247–54, 1989.

113. A.U.H. Sheikh, D.C. Coll, R.G. Ayers, and J.H. Bailey. Atcs—Advanced Train Control-System Radio Data Link Design Considerations. *IEEE Transactions On Vehicular Technology*, 39(3):256–62, 1990.

114. R.J. Hill. Optimal Construction of Synchronizable Coding for Railway Track Circuit Data-Transmission. *IEEE Transactions on Vehicular Technology*, 39(4):390–99, 1990.

115. Y.R. Shayan, L.N. Tho, and V.K. Bhargava. Design of Reed-Solomon (16,12) Codec for North-American Advanced Train Control-System. *IEEE Transactions on Vehicular Technology*, 39(4):400–09, 1990.

116. Private communication with Mr. George H. Way Jr., Vice President, Association of American Railroads, Research and Test Department, Washington D.C., February 1992.

117. W.R. Stevens. *Unix Network Programming*. Prentice Hall Inc., Engelwood Cliffs, New Jersey, 1993.

118. Sumit Ghosh, Erik Debenedictis, and Meng-Lin Yu. YADDES: A Novel Algorithm for Deadlock-Free Distributed Discrete-Event Simulation. *International Journal in Computer Simulation*, 5(1):43–83, 1995.

119. Bruce J. Summers. Clearing and Payment Systems: The Role of the Central Bank. *Federal Reserve Bulletin*, pages 81–90, February 1991.

120. David B. Humphrey. Payments System, Risk, Market Failure, and Public Policy. In *Electronic Funds Transfers and Payments: The Public Policy Issues*, Ed. by Elinor H. Solomon, pages 83–110, Kluwer Publishers, Boston, 1987.

121. Christian Vital and David Mengle. SIC: Switzerland's New Electronic Interbank Payment System. *Economic Review*, 74(6):12–27, November/December 1988.

122. Jane Kingman-Brundage and Susan A. Schulz. *The Fundamentals of Trade Finance*. John Wiley and Sons Inc., New York, 1986.

123. Bank for International Settlements. Survey of Foreign Exchange Market Activity. *Technical report*, Bank for International Settlements, Basle, February 1990.

124. George J. Juncker, Bruce J. Summers, and Florence M. Young. A Primer on the Settlement of Payments in the United States. *Federal Reserve Bulletin*, pages 847–58, November 1991.

125. Sumit Ghosh. NOVADIB: A Novel Architecture for Asynchronous Distributed Real-Time Banking Modeled on Loosely-Coupled Parallel Processors. *IEEE Transactions on Systems, Man, and Cybernetics*, 23(3):917–27, May/June 1993.

126. Noshir R. Dhondy, Richard J. Schmalz, Ronald M. Smith, Julian Thomas, and Phil Yeh. Coordination of Time-of-Day Clocks among Multiple Systems. *IBM Journal of Research and Development*, 36(4):655–65, July 1992.

127. Lt. Gen. John H. Cushman. *Handbook for Joint Commanders*. United States Naval Institute, Annapolis, Maryland, 1993.

128. U.S. Department of the Army. *Field Manual 100-5 Operations*. Technical Report, U.S. Government Printing Office, Washington, D.C., 1986.

129. Erwin Rommel. *The Rommel Papers*. Harcourt Brace, New York, 1953.

130. Ronald Lewin. *Rommel as Military Commander*. Van Nostrand Reinhold Company, New York, 1968.

131. Lt. Col. S.E. Dietrich. From Valhalla with Pride. *U.S. Naval Institute Proceedings*, pages 59–60, August 1993.

132. H. Essame. *Patton: A Study in Command*. Charles Scribner's Sons, New York, 1974.

133. Martin Blumenson. *The Patton Papers*. Houghton Mifflin, Boston, 1972-1974.

134. Col. R.M. Swain. Compounding the Error. *U.S. Naval Institute Proceedings*, pages 61–62, August 1993.

135. 1st Lt. Gary A. Vincent. In the Loop: Superiority in Command and Control. *Airpower Journal*, VI(2):15–25, Summer 1992.

136. Lt. Col. John G. Humphries. Operations Law and the Rules of Engagement in Operation Desert Shield and Desert Storm. *Airpower Journal*, AFRP-50-2:25–41, Fall 1992.

137. Col. Thomas Cardwell. Wizard Warriors of the Desert Storm. *Military Review*, LXXII(9):55–65.

138. Lt. Col. Price T. Bingham. The Airforce's New Doctrine. *Military Review*, pages 13–19, November 1991.

139. Maj. William O. Odon. The Rudder in the Storm—George Washington as Senior Leader. *Military Review*, LXXIII(6):54–66, June 1992.

140. Maj. Victor M. Roselle. Operation Just Cause: The Divisional M1 Battalion, the Nonlinear Battlefield, and Airland Operations—Future. *Military Intelligence*, 17(3):28–31, July/September 1991.

141. Lt. Col. James M. Dubik. Decentralized Command: Translating Theory into Practice. *Military Review*, pages 27–38, June 1992.

142. U.S. Army Training and Doctrine Command. Airland Operations. *Technical Report TRADOC PAM 525-5*, U.S. Government Printing Office, Fort Monroe, Virginia, August 1991.

143. Col. James G. Burton. Pushing Them Out the Back Door. *U.S. Naval Institute Proceedings*, pages 37–42, June 1993.

144. M.J. Shapiro. *Tank Command, General George S. Patton's 4th Armored Division*. David McKay Company, Inc., New York, 1979.

145. Gen. Gordon Sullivan. Delivering Decisive Victory: Improving Synchronization. *Military Review*, LXXII(9):2–11.

146. Lt. Gen. Michael A. Nelson. Combat Requirements for C2. In *Symposium on Command and Control Research*, National Defense University, Washington, D.C., 28-29 June 1993.

147. T.W. Mastaglio and R. Callahan. A Large-Scale Complex Virtual Environment for Team Training. *IEEE Computer*, 28(7):49–56, July 1995.

148. M.A. Breuer and A.D. Friedman. *Diagnosis and Reliable Design of Digital Systems*. Computer Science Press, Rockville, MD, 1984.

149. S. Seshu. On an Improved Diagnostic Program. *IEEE Transactions on Electronic Computers*, EC-14:76–79, February 1965.

150. D.B. Armstrong. A Deductive Method of Simulating Faults in Logic Circuits. *IEEE Transactions on Computers*, C-22:464–77, May 1972.

151. E.G. Ulrich and T. Baker. Concurrent Simulation of Nearly Identical Digital Networks. *IEEE Computer*, 7:39–44, April 1974.

152. S. Davidson. Fault Simulation at the Architectural Level. In *Proceedings of the International Test Conference*, pages 669–79, Washington, D.C., September 1984.

153. M.M. Denneau. The Yorktown Simulation Engine. In *Proceedings of the 19th ACM/IEEE Design Automation Conference*, pages 55–59, 1982.

154. J.K. Howard et al. Introduction to the IBM Los Gatos Logic Simulation Engine. In *Proceedings of the International Conference on Computer Design*, pages 580–83, Rye Town Hilton, White Plains, New York, October 1983.

155. T. Sasaki, N. Koike, K. Ohomori, and K. Tomita. HAL: Block Level Hardware Logic Simulator. In *Proceedings of the 20th ACM/IEEE Design Automation Conference*, pages 150–56, Miami Beach, FL., June 1983.

156. ZYCAD Corporation. The ZYCAD Logic Evaluator: Product Description. *Technical report*, ZYCAD Corporation, N. Roseville, Minnesota, 1983.

157. S. Patil and P. Banerjee. Fault Partitioning Issues in an Integrated Parallel Test Generation/Fault Simulation Environment. In *Proceedings of the International Test Conference*, Washington, D.C., September 1989.

158. J.F. Nelson. Deductive Fault Simulation of Digital Circuits on a Hypercube Multiprocessor. In *Proceedings of the 9th AT&T Conference on Electronic Testing*, Ramada Inn, Princeton, New Jersey, October 1987.

159. R. Daoud and F. Ozguner. Highly Vectorizable Fault Simulation on the Cray X-MP Supercomputer. *IEEE Transactions on Computer-Aided Design of ICs*, 8(12):1362–1365, 1989.

160. J.T. Rayfield and H.F. Silverman. Operating System and Applications of the Armstrong Multiprocessor. *IEEE Computer*, 21(6):38–52, 1988.

161. S. Ghosh and T.J. Chakraborty. On Behavior-Level Fault Modeling of Digital Designs. *International Journal of Electronic Testing*, 2(2):135–51, June 1991.

162. S. Ghosh and T. J. Chakraborty. On Behavioral Fault Modeling of Digital Combinational Designs. In *Proceedings of the International Test Conference*, Washington, D.C., October 1988.

163. S. Ghosh. Behavior-Level Fault Simulation. *IEEE Design and Test*, pages 31–42, June 1988.

164. H-C. Shih, P.G. Kovijanic, and R. Razdan. A Global Feedback Detection Algorithm for VLSI Circuits. In *Proceedings of the International Conference on Computer Design*, pages 37–40, Boston, September 1990.

165. Anish Bhimani and Sumit Ghosh. Input FIle GENerator for the Implementation of Asynchronous Distributed Decision-Making Algorithms on Parallel Processors. *Technical report, No. 74*, LEMS, Division of Engineering, Brown University, Providence, Rhode Island 02912, 1990.

166. S. Davidson and J. Lewandowski. ESIM/AFS—A Concurrent Architectural Level Fault Simulator. In *Proceedings of the International Test Conference*, pages 375–83, Washington, D.C., October 1986.

167. Dave Richards and Earl Vogt. The Value of ISDN for Banking Applications. *IEEE Communications Magazine*, pages 32–33, April 1990.

168. Collin Canright. Will Real-Time Systems Spell the End for Batch Processing? *Bank Administration*, 64(9):42–46, September 1988.

169. William M. Randle. Banks. In *Proceedings of the Conference on Payments in the Financial Services Industry of the 1980s*, pages 61–68, Quorom Books Publishers, Westport, Connecticut, 1984.

170. Anna Hac and Hasan B. Mutlu. Synchronous Optical Network and Broadband ISDN Protocols. *IEEE Computer*, 22(11):26–34, November 1989.

171. M. Schwartz and T.E. Stern. Routing Techniques Used in Computer Communications Networks. *IEEE Transactions on Communications*, COM-28(4):539–52, April 1980.

172. R. Sedgewick. *Algorithms*. Addison-Wesley Publishing Company, Reading, Massachusetts, 1988.

173. R.E. Warfield. Model of Traffic and Networks for Distributed Simulation of Congestion in B-ISDN. *Technical Report*, Bellcore Internal Memorandum, Red Bank, New Jersey, 1990.

174. H. Mendelson, J. Pliskin, and U. Yechiali. A Stochastic Allocation Problem. *Operations Research*, 28(3):687–93, 1980.

175. K. Simpson. A Theory of Allocation of Stocks to Warehouses. *Operations Research*, 7:797–805, 1959.

176. Y.S. Zheng and P. Zipkin. A Queuing Model to Analyze the Value of Centralized Inventory Information. *Operations Research*, 38(2):296–307, 1990.

177. G. Eppen and L. Shrage. Centralized Ordering Policies in a Multi-warehouse System with Lead Times and Random Demand. In L. Schwarz (ed.) *Multilevel Production/Inventory Control System*, pages 51–68, Amsterdam, North Holland, 1981.

178. G. Eppen. Effects of Centralization on Expected Costs in a Multi-Location Newsboy Problem. *Management Science*, 25(5):498–501, 1979.

179. H.M. Wagner. *Principles of Operations Research*. Prentice Hall, Englewood Cliffs, New Jersey, 1975.

180. R. Roundy. 98%-Effective Integer-Ratio Lot-Sizing One-Warehouse Multiretailer Systems. *Management Science*, 31:1416–1429, 1985.

181. Jing-Sheng Song and Paul Zipkin. Inventory Control in a Fluctuating Demand Environment. *Operations Research*, 41(2):351–70, March/April 1993.

182. Robin O. Roundy. Efficient, Effective Lot Sizing for Multistage Production Systems. *Operations Research*, 41(2):371–85, March/April 1993.

183. Soren S. Nielsen and Stavros A. Zenios. A Massively Parallel Algorithm for Nonlinear Stochastic Network Problems. *Operations Research*, 41(2):319–37, March/April 1993.

184. S. Axsater. Exact and Approximate Evaluation of Batch-Ordering Policies for Two-Level Inventory Systems. *Operations Research*, 41(4):777–85, July/August 1993.

185. D. Anderson, D. Sweeney and T. Williams. *Management Science—Qualitative Approach to Decision Making*. West Publishing Company, St. Paul 1994.

186. L. Robinson. Optimal and Approximate Policies in Multiperiod, Multilocation Inventory Models with Transhipments. *Operations Research*, 38(2):278–95, March/April 1990.

187. K.S. Trivedi, B.R. Haverkort, A. Rindos, and V. Manikar. Techniques and Tools for Reliability and Performance Evaluation: Problems and Perspectives. In Proceedings of the 7th International Conference on Computer Performance evaluation: Modelling Techniques and Tools, Springer-Verlag, pages 1–24, Vienna, Austria, May 1994.

188. Richard J. Tersine. *Principles of Inventory and Materials Management*. Prentice Hall, Englewood Cliffs, New Jersey, 1994.

189. John E. Freund. *Statistics: A First Course*. Prentice Hall, Englewood Cliffs, New Jersey, 1970.

190. Erwin Kreyszig. *Advanced Engineering Mathematics*. John Wiley and Sons, New York, 1971.

191. Sumit Ghosh and Norbert Giambiasi. Breakthrough in Modeling and Simulation of Mixed-Signal Electronic Designs in nVHDL. *Modeling and Simulation Magazine*, pages 279–81, July 2001.

192. Gregory M. Nielson. Visualization in Scientific and Engineering Computation. *IEEE Computer*, pages 58–66, September 1991.

193. Arthur Chai and Sumit Ghosh. Modeling and Distributed Simulation of Broadband-ISDNetwork on a Network of Sun Workstations Configured as a Loosely Coupled Parallel Processor System. *IEEE Computer*, 26(9):37–51, September 1993.

194. Aaron Marcus and Andries van Dam. User-Interface Developments in the Nineties. *IEEE Computer*, pages 49–57, September 1991.

195. D.J. Thomas. A False-Color Look-up Table for Images of Large Dynamic Range. *Journal of Applied Crystallography*, 22:498–99, 1989.

196. William B. Barnett. User Interface Design for Analytical Instruments: Art or Science? *Analytical Chemistry*, 60(20):1169–1175, October 1988.

197. Private communications with Andy van Dam, Computer Science Department, Brown University, Providence, Rhode Island 02912, November 1991.

198. Sumit Ghosh. On the Proof of Correctness of Yet Another Asynchronous Distributed Discrete Event Simulation Algorithm (YADDES). *IEEE Transactions on Systems, Man, and Cybernetics*, 26(1):68–74, January 1996.

199. W. Kohn and A. Nerode. Multiple Agent Hybrid Control Architecture in Hybrid Systems. In *Lecture Notes in Computer Science*, Eds. R.L. Grossman, A. Nerode, A. Ravn, and H. Rischel, LNCS-736. Springer-Verlag, Berlin, 1993.

200. W. Kohn and A. Nerode. Logical Methods. In A Hybrid Systems Architecture. Eds. J.L. Crossley, J.B. Remmel, R.A. Shore, and Moss E. Sweedler. Birkhauser, Boston, 1993.

201. G.B. Thomas and R.L. Finney. *Calculus and Analytic Geometry.* Addison-Wesley Publishing Company, New York, 1985.

202. L.C. Young. *Lectures on the Calculus of Variations and Optimal Control Theory.* Saunders Publishing, Philadelphia, 1969.

203. W. Kohn, A. Nerode, and J.B. Remmel. Hybrid Systems as Finsler Manifolds: Finite State Control as Approximations to Connections. *Technical Report 95-22*, Mathematical Sciences Institute, Cornell University, Ithaca, New York, 1995.

204. D. Ferrari. *Computer Systems Performance Evaluation.* Prentice-Hall Inc., Englewood Cliffs, New Jersey, 1978.

205. Sumit Ghosh. A Distributed Algorithm for Fault Simulation of Combinatorial and Asynchronous Sequential Digital Designs, Utilizing Circuit Partitioning, on Loosely Coupled Parallel Processors. *Microelectronics and Reliability—An International Journal*, 35(6):947–67, 1995.

206. Sumit Ghosh. NODIFS—Simulating Faults Fast: Asynchronous, Distributed, Circuit-Partitioning Based Algorithm Enables Fast Fault Simulation of Digital Designs on Parallel Processors. *IEEE Circuits and Devices*, 10(5):26–38, September 1994.

207. C.R. Mechoso, J.D. Farrara, and J.A. Spahr. Achieving Superlinear Speedup on a Heterogeneous, Distributed System. *IEEE Parallel and Distributed Technology: Systems Applications*, 2(2):57–61, Summer 1994.

208. U. Gropengiesser. Superlinear Speedup for Parallel Implementation of Biologically Motivated Spin Glass Optimization Algorithm. *International Journal of Modern Physics C*, 6(2):307–15, April 1995.

209. Junhwa Kim and Jongho Nang. Implementation of Parallel Genetic Algorithm on AP1000 and its Performance Evaluation. *Korea Information Sciences Society*, 23(2):127–41, Feb 1996.

210. C.E. Chow, J.D. Bicknell, S. McCaughey, and S. Syed. Performance Analysis of Fast Distributed Link Restoration Algorithms. *International Journal of Communication Systems*, 8(5):325–45, September 1995.

211. A.M. Lyapunov. *The General Problem of the Stability of Motion.* Translated by Editor A.T. Fuller. Taylor & Francis, 1992.

212. Chi-Tsong Chen. *Analog and Digital Control System Design: Transfer-Function, State-Space, and Algebraic Methods.* Saunders College Publishing, Philadelphia, 1993.

213. Alexander M. Letov. *Stability in Nonlinear Control Systems.* Princeton University Press, Princeton, New Jersey, 1961.

214. Thomas L. Casavant and John G. Kuhl. Effects of Response and Stability on Scheduling in Distributed Computing Systems. *IEEE Transactions on Software Engineering*, 14(11):1578–1588, November 1988.

215. Edsger W. Dijkstra. *Self-Stabilization in Spite of Distributed Control*, pages 41–46. Texts and Monographs in Computer Science. Springer-Verlag New York Inc., 1982.

216. Edsger W. Dijkstra. Self-Stabilizing Systems in Spite of Distributed Control. *Communications of the ACM*, 17(11):643–44, November 1974.

217. Debra Hoover and Joseph Poole. Distributed Self-Stabilizing Solution to the Dining Philosophers Problem. *Information Processing Letters*, 41(4):209–13, March 1992.

218. Albert Mo Kim Cheng. Self-Stabilizing Real-Time Rule-Based Systems. In *Proceedings of the 11th IEEE Symposium on Reliable Distributed Systems*, Houston, Texas, October 1992.

219. Shing-Tsaan Huang, Lih-Chyau Wuu, and Ming-Shin Tsai. Distributed Execution Model for Self-Stabilizing Systems. In *Proceedings of the 1994 IEEE 14th International Conference on Distributed Computing Systems*, pages 432–39, Piscataway, New Jersey, 1994.

220. Ernest J.H. Chang. On the Costs of Self-Stabilization. *Information Processing Letters*, 24(5):311–16, March 1987.

221. Baruch Awerbuch and George Varghese. Distributed Program Checking: A Paradigm for Building Self-Stabilizing Distributed Protocols. In *Proceedings of the 32nd IEEE Annual Symposium on Foundations of Computer Science*, pages 258–67, Los Alamitos, California, 1991.

222. K. Mani Chandy and Leslie Lamport. Distributed Snapshots: Determining Global States of Distributed Systems. *ACM Transactions on Computer Systems*, 3(1):63–75, February 1985.

223. S. Venkatesan and Brahma Dathan. Testing and Debugging Distributed Programs Using Global Predicates. *IEEE Transactions on Software Engineering*, 21(2):163–77, February 1995.

224. Vijay K. Garg and Brian Waldecker. Detection of Strong Unstable Predicates in Distributed Programs. Department of Electrical and Computer Engineering, University of Texas, Austin, 1995.

225. Fabio A. Schreiber. Notes on Real-Time Distributed Database Systems Stability. In *Proceedings of the 5th Jerusalem Conference on Information Technology*, pages 560–64, Los Alamitos, California, 1990.

226. John A. Stankovic. Stability and Distributed Scheduling Algorithms. *IEEE Transactions on Software Engineering*, SE-11(10):1141–1152, October 1985.

227. J.F. Meyer. Performability Modeling of Distributed Real-Time Systems. In G. Iazeolla, P.J. Courtois, and A. Hordijk, eds, *Mathematical Computer Performance and Reliability*, pages 361–69. Elsevier Science Publishers B.V., North-Holland, 1984.

228. Pankaj Garg, Svend Frolund, Allan Shepherd, and Nalini Venkatasubramanian. Towards Distributed Applications Stability Engineering. In *Proceedings of the 5th California Software Symposium*, pages 528–29, Irvine, California, March 1995.

229. Peter Heck and Sumit Ghosh. A Study of Synthetic Creativity through Behavior Modeling and Simulation of an Ant Colony. *IEEE Intelligent Systems*, 15(6):58–66, November/December 2000.

230. M. Bloom. *Configurations of Human Behavior*. Macmillan, New York, 1984.

231. M.W. Eysenck. *Simply Psychology*. Psychology Press, East Sussex, U.K., 1996.

232. T.L. Engle and L. Snellgrove. *Psychology: Its Principles and Applications*. Harcourt, Brace, & Jovanavich, New York, 1969.

233. F. Cox. *Psychology*. Brown, Dubuque, Iowa, 1970.

234. Richard Hamming. You and Your Research. In *Transcription of the Bell Communications Research Colloquium Seminar*, Bell Communications Research, Morristown, New Jersey, 7 March 1986.

235. Jacques Hadamard. *The Psychology of Invention in the Mathematical Field*. Dover Publications, Inc., New York, 1954.

236. Godfrey H. Hardy. Ramanujan: 12 Lectures on Subjects Suggested by His Life and Work. http://www.uz.ac.zw/science/maths/zimath/ramanhdy.htm, 1940. Cambridge University, England.

237. G.L. Pearson, and W.H. Brattain. History of Semiconductor Research. *Proceedings of IRE*, 43:1794–1806, 1955.

238. B. Mitra. Early Microwave Engineering: J. C. Bose's Physical Researches during 1895-1900. *Science and Culture*, 50:147–54, 1984.

239. Philip Babcock Grove (Editor in Chief). *Webster's Third International Dictionary, Unabridged*. G & C Merriam Company, Springfield, Massachusetts, 1968.

240. *6th Sense*, aired 1 October 2000. The Learning Channel, Cable television, http://www.tlc.com.

241. Menalie Mitchell. *An Introduction to Genetic Algorithms*. MIT Press, Cambridge, Massachusetts, 1996.

242. *ESP in Animals*, aired 19 September 2000. Discovery Channel, Cable television, http://www.discovery.com.

243. A.J. Dutson, R.H. Todd, S.P. Magleby, and C.D. Sorensen. A Review of Literature on Teaching Engineering Design through Project-Oriented Capstone Courses. *ASEE Journal of Engineering Education*, 86(1):17–28, January 1997.

244. I.E. Sutherland and G.W. Hodgman. Reentrant Polygon Clipping. *Communications of the ACM*, 17(1):32–42, January 1974.

245. D. Halliday and R. Resnick. *Physics, Part II*. John Wiley and Sons, New York, 1962.

246. Alex Miczo. *Digital Logic Testing & Simulation*. Harper & Row, New York, 1986.

247. George J. Pothering and Thomas L. Naps. *Introduction to Data Structures and Algorithm Analysis with C++*. West Publishing Company, Minneapolis/St. Paul, Minnesota, 1995.

248. Thomas H. Cormen, Charles E. Leiserson, and Ronald L. Rivest. *Introduction to Algorithms*. MIT Press, Cambridge, Massachusetts, 1992.

249. D.E. Barrett. Traffic-Noise Impact Study for Least Bell's Vireo Habitat Along California State Route 83. *Transportation Research Record*, (1559):3–7, 1996.

250. D.E. Barrett. California Study Addresses Issues of Roadway Noise Control for the Benefit of Endangered Songbirds. *Road Management and Engineering Journal, TranSafety, Inc.*, http://www.usroads.com/journals, pages 1–6, October 1997.

251. *Kansai International Airport*, aired 26 November 2000. The Learning Channel, Cable television, http://www.tlc.com.

Index

abstraction levels, xv, 6, 17, 18, 19
  architectural level, 17
  control, 17
  exceptions, 17
  gate level, 17
  logic, 17
  register-transfer level, 17
  timing, 17, 18, 19
accuracy of simulation results, 41, 299
  spatial resolution, 134, 144, 299
  temporal resolution, 134, 299
activity, 3, 20, 21, 29, 34
acyclic graphs, 38, 42, 173, 175
ADDM algorithms, xi, 2, 3, 4, 9, 15, 16, 23, 276
  accuracy, 23, 33, 36, 40, 80, 102, 106, 144, 165
  canonical principles, 16
  case studies, 28, 33
  characteristics, 2, 16
  complex timing relationships between events, 275, 276
  conceptual understanding, 8, 261
  correctness, 13, 16, 23, 275
  enormous potential, 16
  flaws, 261
  fundamental characteristics, 16
  highest-level architecture, 8, 15
  inconsistencies, 19, 24, 33, 33, 36
  large-scale systems, 7, 9, 61, 257, 314
  maximize local computations, 9, 140
  meta intelligence, 8, 15, 27
  minimize communication, 9, 140

  monitoring execution of, 261
  nature of, 15
  performance, 9, 15, 16
  performance parameters, 99, 311
  progressing toward its objective, 24
  proof of correctness, 13, 16, 23, 275
  reduce human intervention, 25
  resolution of time, 18, 19, 23, 101, 134
  robustness, 9, 15, 16, 25
  resilient to natural and artificial disasters, 25
  safety, 23, 70, 71, 137
  stability, 9, 15, 27, 127, 327
  survival, 8, 136
  synthesis of, 16, 27, 28, 33
  formal methodology, 289
  termination, 13, 24, 91
  underlying intent, xvi, 3
  universal time, 18, 19, 115
algorithm, 1
  behavior, 3, 15, 16
  control, 1, 4
  coordinating, 4
  data-parallel, 11, 15, 312
  meta-level, 4, 27, 31, 352, 358
  scalable, 9, 13, 15, 25, 26, 106, 255
  synchronous-iterative, 15, 312
  synthesis, 16, 27
analytical, xv, 134, 225, 233
  manipulation tools, xv, 238
  models, 35
approaches, 4
  bottom-up, 3, 4, 28

About the Author

Sumit Ghosh is the Thomas E. Hattrick '42 Endowed Chair Professor of Information Systems Engineering in the Department of Electrical and Computer Engineering at Stevens Institute of Technology in Hoboken, New Jersey. He founded the Secure Network Systems Design Laboratory (SENDLAB) at Stevens, and is the architect of the Graduate Certificate Program in Secure Network Systems Design. Prior to his appointment at Stevens, he had served as the associate chair for research and graduate programs in the Computer Science and Engineering Department at Arizona State University(ASU). At ASU, he also chaired the faculty search committee for three consecutive years and was responsible for assessing the quality and content of graduate courses. Before ASU, Sumit had been on the faculty of Computer Engineering at Brown University, Rhode Island, and prior to that he had been a member of the technical staff (principal investigator) of VLSI Systems Research Department at Bell Laboratories Research (Area 11) in Holmdel, New Jersey. He earned his B. Tech. degree from the Indian Institute of Technology at Kanpur, India, and his M.S. and Ph.D. degrees from Stanford University, California. Sumit completed his B.Tech. project under the supervision of Prof. V. Rajaraman, and his Ph.D. advisors were Prof. Willem van Cleemput (primary) and Prof. Robert Dutton (associate advisor). Sumit's additional industrial experience includes Silvar-Lisco in Menlo Park, California, Fairchild Advanced Research and Development, and Schlumberger Palo Alto Research Center.

Sumit was appointed the first vice president for education in the Society for Modeling and Simulation International (SCS) in July 2003. He has been asked to architect undergraduate and graduate programs in modeling and simulation and also to establish the accreditation procedures. Sumit organized a National Science Foundation-sponsored workshop titled Secure Ultra Large Networks: Capturing User Requirements with Advanced Modeling and Simulation Tools (ULN'03) (with Prof. Bernard Zeigler of University of Arizona and Prof. Hessam Sarjoughian of ASU) at Stevens Institute of Technology, May 29–30, 2003. Sumit is on the Advisory Board of the Executive Leadership Institute (ELI) and the "Management of Technologies" (MOT) Annual Symposium Series. He is the primary author of five authoritative books: *Hardware Description Languages: Concepts and Principles* (IEEE Press, 2000); *Modeling and Asynchronous Distributed Simulation of Complex Systems* (IEEE Press, 2000); *Intelligent Transportation Systems: New Principles and Architectures* (CRC Press, 2000; first reprint 2002); *Principles of Secure Network Systems Design* (Springer-Verlag, 2002; translated into Simplified Chinese by Chongqing University Press, China, 2003-2004); and *Algorithm Design for Networked Information Technology Systems: Principles and Applications* (Springer-Verlag, November 2003). He has written five invited book chapters and edited (with Profs. Ted Stohr and Manu Malek) a book, *Guarding Your Business: An Organizational Approach to Security* (Kluwer Academic Publishers, January 2004). Sumit has written more than 95 transactions/journal papers and 90 refereed conference papers.

He is a senior member of IEEE, serves as associate editor for the *Transactions of the Society for Computer Simulation International* and *IEEE Transactions on Systems, Man, and Cybernetics*, and is on the editorial board of the *IEEE Press Book Series on Microelectronic Systems Principles and Practice*. In focusing on fundamental and challenging yet practical problems, his research offers potential benefit to society. Current research pursuits include long-term issues in networked systems security for the financial services industry; architecture (control and coordination algorithm) for homeland security to enable the first responders to continue their mission in the event of terrorism by highly sophisticated terrorists; network-centric systems design language (NCSDL) and execution environment to facilitate the modeling, testing, and performance analysis of any networked information technology system; next generation secure ATM network design; determining network operating point for operational networks; novel network architecture to resist lightning-fast intrusions; identifying requirements of future network design from the perspective of law enforcement; new forms of cyberattacks that may be enabled by advances in networking in the future; next generation nVHDL; and analyzing phenomena in biology and conceptualizing and adapting the underlying principles into engineering problems. His education-related interests include developing a new program in networked information systems engineering (NISE) at the undergraduate and graduate levels; issues in the Ph.D. process; a new approach to instilling critical thinking and creativity in engineering design; and humbleness as a practical vehicle for engineering ethics education. His research is the result of support from the IEEE Foundation, U.S. Air Force Office of Scientific Research, U.S. Army Research Office, DARPA, Telcordia (formerly Bellcore), Nynex, National Library of Medicine, NSF, Intel Corp., U.S. Army Research Lab, U.S. Ballistic Missile Defense Organization, National Security Agency, U.S. Air Force Research Labs (Rome, New York) through Motorola Corp., Sandia National Labs (Albuquerque, New Mexico), Electronics and Telecommunications Research Institute (ETRI), FIPSE-US Department of Education, and U.S. Army CECOM (Ft. Monmouth, New Jersey) through Mitre Corporation. He has also served as a consultant to the

U.S. Army Research Lab, Raytheon Corporation, U.S. Air Force Rome Labs, and Scientific Systems Company Inc. Sumit also founded (1995) the Networking and Distributed Algorithms Laboratory at ASU and is a U.S. citizen. He has held visiting professor positions at Federal University of Rio de Janeiro (Brazil), University of Marseilles (France), and Kuwait University (Kuwait).

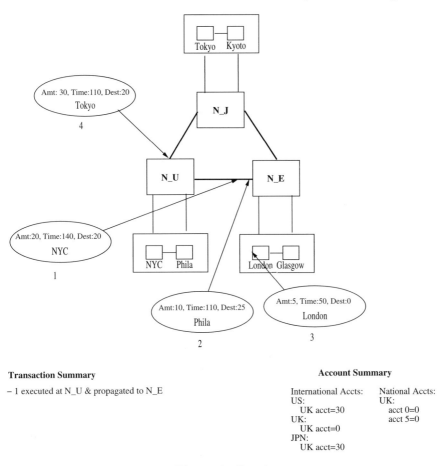

Fig. 3.57. Step 3

of as the 2.3 model with an additional group-network. However, the addition of a group-node to the group-networks, as in the 3.3 model relative to the 2.3 model, does not appear to require appreciably larger CPU time. Thus, in NOVAHID, the addition of a group-network has greater impact on the performance than the size of the individual group-networks.

3.3.4.2 Total Time Required for International Transactions

This section details the performance analysis of the international transactions through the following experiments. In these, only international transactions are asserted at the group-nodes. A total of 20 transactions are marked for use in the measurements. These transactions originate from a specific node A of a group-network X and are destined for a specific node B of a different group-network Y. Note that in all three representative networks, there are at least

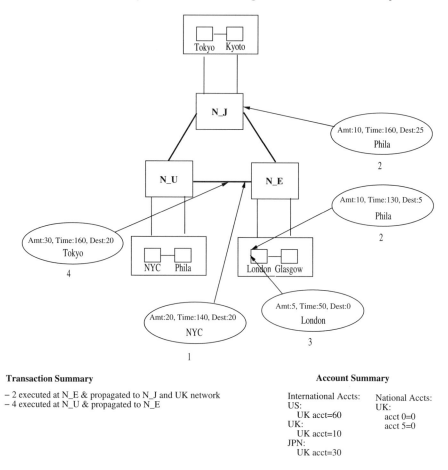

Fig. 3.58. Step 4

three group-networks and X and Y are so chosen that the Int-Node for Y is one Int-Node distance away from the Int-Node for X. This imposes signifi- cant activity at the top-level network for each of the marked transactions. The average number of unmarked international transactions between two consecu- tive marked transactions is modeled by the symbol load_var, whose value also reflects the volume of transactions. Consider two marked international trans- actions with assertion times of t_a and t_g, where $t_g > t_a$. A load_var value of 5 implies an average of 5 unmarked international transactions with assertion times ranging between $t = t_a$ and $t = t_g$.

Figure 3.65 presents the total simulation time required for the process- ing of the 20 marked international transactions in the 3_3 model. Figure 3.65 reveals that transactions with higher numbers, i.e., those that are asserted later, require successively larger processing times. The observation is true for all values of load_var ranging from 1 (minimal volume) to 20 (high volume).